LOLLAPALOOZA

ALSO BY RICHARD BIENSTOCK AND TOM BEAUJOUR

*Nöthin' But a Good Time: The Uncensored History
of the '80s Hard Rock Explosion*

LOLLAPALOOZA

THE
UNCENSORED
STORY OF
ALTERNATIVE ROCK'S
WILDEST FESTIVAL

RICHARD BIENSTOCK
AND TOM BEAUJOUR

ST. MARTIN'S
PRESS
NEW YORK

First published in the United States by St. Martin's Press, an imprint of
St. Martin's Publishing Group

Foreword by Kim Thayil of Soundgarden

www.stmartins.com

Designed by Steven Seighman

Endpaper: crowd © Boston Globe/Getty Images

The Library of Congress Cataloging-in-Publication Data is available upon request.

ISBN 978-1-250-28370-2 (hardcover)
ISBN 978-1-250-28371-9 (ebook)

Our books may be purchased in bulk for promotional, educational, or business use.
Please contact your local bookseller or the Macmillan Corporate and Premium Sales
Department at 1-800-221-7945, extension 5442, or by email at
MacmillanSpecialMarkets@macmillan.com.

First Edition: 2025

10 9 8 7 6 5 4 3 2 1

To Carla. And to Levi, who continues to make seeing
Jane's Addiction an unforgettable experience.
—Richard Bienstock

To my wife, Maria, and in loving memory of my awesome sister-in-law,
June, whose light and laugh were extinguished much too soon.
And, of course, to Elvis aka "Monsieur Papa" the puggle, who made
it to the grand old age of twenty before leaving the building.
—Tom Beaujour

CONTENTS

Foreword by Kim Thayil of Soundgarden ix
Cast of Characters xiii

INTRODUCTION

1. "The best band in the world" 5
2. "Lolla *what*?" 14
3. "I still think it's odd that it worked" 25

1991

1. Day One 35
2. "The most intense thing I've ever seen done on a stage" 49
3. "Body Count's in the house" 58
4. "Job number one was to be as punk as fuck" 68
5. "Perry was standing naked like Jesus" 83

1992

1. "This car is like punk rock!" 99
2. "Eddie was a monkey" 109
3. "This is s'pposed to be rock 'n' roll, not Moat-*zart*!" 124
4. "A lean, mean freak machine" 133
5. A Brief History of the Second Stage 148

1993

1. "Are we selling out by doing this thing?" 163
2. "The most nakedest band on Lollapalooza" 172
3. "A party on wheels" 182
4. A Brief History of the Village 193

1994

1. "Oh shit—now we have to do it!" 207
2. "Boxing the snowman" 217
3. "Where are you going to find tofu in the middle of a field?" 225
4. "A scene where a lot of the people use really pure heroin is
   probably not a scene meant to last" 230
5. "Have you guys seen a Titleist?" 236

1995

1. "You can't be cool if nobody cares" 245
2. "I don't think anyone expects that kind of violence" 254
3. "Nerds on Lollapalooza" 261
4. "Courtney was the spectacle" 264
5. "Spiñal Tap playing at the theme park" 270
6. "Sinéad ended up just walking off the tour" 274
7. "It was probably a very brief bit of nudity" 280
8. "Fuck you, frat boy!" 286
9. "Fantastic Voyage" 292
10. "It was a beautiful afternoon" 295
11. "It felt like we were winning for a few years" 302

1996

1. "It looked like a scene from *Island of Lost Souls*" 313
2. "Welcome to the Lollapalooza that has a big cock!" 323

1997

1. "I begged Perry to shut the fucking thing down" 343
2. "To some alternative kids, 'nu metal' was a dirty word" 347
3. "I have tits, put me on your shoulders" 353
4. "Allegedly, they drew guns on him" 357
5. "We were still always going to be these outcasts" 361
6. "I was never one of these cool drug addicts" 366
7. "He was doubled up in pain" 370
8. "A tepid success" 374

EPILOGUE

1. "Amazing illegal cheese" 381
2. "A full-on bloodbath" 389
3. "I don't know how much you know about Lollapalooza . . ." 393

Acknowledgments 401
Notes 403

FOREWORD

by Kim Thayil of Soundgarden

I don't recall the context the first time I heard about Lollapalooza, but the idea of a festival that toured, rather than having it be anchored geographically and having to draw its audience to that location, seemed like a great concept. In contrast to the underground, indie, post-punk, collegiate circuits that Soundgarden had been participating in, Lollapalooza would be a great opportunity for us and up-and-coming bands to perform in front of larger audiences and play new markets. The first times we played places like Nebraska or Oklahoma, it was opening for major hard rock bands like Guns N' Roses and Skid Row. There weren't many big touring bands in our indie-rock world that would have been able to do that.

Yet, when Soundgarden was asked to perform on Lollapalooza '92, I was a little cynical about the idea of a big summer tour with a shared collective vibe. I was also critical of Lollapalooza being called "alternative." I remember saying in an interview something to the effect that, "This is just targeting a subspecies of suburban white kid." Even the fact that they billed hip-hop acts on those early tours didn't convince me otherwise, because commercial success with many rap artists, as with rock and pop acts, required, for the most part, addressing a suburban, white, MTV-familiar audience. If they wanted to be truly "alternative," I thought, Lollapalooza might include music from distinctly different genres, with culturally distinct youth audiences that represented diverse nationalities, socioeconomic classes, languages, and even faiths. Perhaps they could book roots reggae, folk, country, contemporary jazz (free, cool, or fusion), Asian, Hispanic, or Native American music groups . . . you know, bands from other cultures, but that wasn't happening. They were primarily booking newer and fresher genres of hard rock.

But while I was going into the tour stiff-arming the experience—a traveling "We Are the World" for college and "alternative" culture—there was part of me that loved the aspect of sharing these events with our peers and contemporaries, while also meeting other bands and reaching new fans. An added bonus of a touring festival is the duration of contact with, and proximity to, many other performers and artists. Over a period of two months, I built and solidified lifelong friendships—with the Jim Rose Circus Sideshow, Pearl Jam, Ministry, and many road-crew folks who ultimately ended up working for us and with us. When all was said and done, a lot of great experiences came from touring with Lollapalooza. The tour successfully promoted and marketed "alternative" culture by introducing and sharing it with a larger audience in various pockets of America. It was defining the genre, and it was great for the bands. We all expanded our audiences.

In 1996, when Metallica asked if we would join them on the festival, Soundgarden had become a different band with a much larger audience. We had had what I like to refer to as our "'Black Hole Sun' moment." There aren't many books out there to tell you what to do when you find yourself playing for fifty thousand people and selling millions of records. There are only a few people who can write that book, or read it and have an understanding of it. With our success came a sense of responsibility and duty to our peers who hadn't yet had that success. So it was great when Lollapalooza specifically asked who we would like to have on the tour. We answered with "the Ramones!" We thought, They're influential; everyone seems to know and love them, so how come they haven't had a gold record yet? We also suggested our Pacific Northwest brethren, the Screaming Trees, who were well deserving of playing for larger audiences. The opportunity to support friendly colleagues, well . . . there was something kind of *kumbaya* about that, and Lollapalooza provided that platform and audience—for music, for culture, for ideas.

Thirty years after the fact, the impact of Lollapalooza's inception is definitely still felt. The influence of Lollapalooza as something alternative, and integrating, has borne its fruit and its benefit. We're at a place now in American popular culture and youth culture that is far more integrated and tolerant in terms of racial, ethnic, sexual, and gender identity issues. When I look at my peers, what they believed about themselves is actually more visible and manifest in the kids they raised.

Those are the sons and daughters of Lollapalooza, and right on! Let the baby boomers all go and yell at spiders to "get off their lawn" back in their retirement communities. . . . These kids will do just fine.

CAST OF CHARACTERS

For easy reference, individuals are ID'd, with applicable titles, at first mention in each chapter.

AD-ROCK MC, guitarist, Beastie Boys

NATE ALBERT guitarist, the Mighty Mighty Bosstones

THE AMAZING MR. LIFTO performer, Jim Rose Circus Sideshow

BRETT ANDERSON singer, the Donnas

KIMBA ANDERSON performer, Sharkbait

KEN ANDREWS singer, guitarist, Failure

BILLIE JOE ARMSTRONG singer, guitarist, Green Day

GINA ARNOLD journalist, author

MELISSA AUF DER MAUR bassist, Hole

ERIC AVERY bassist, Jane's Addiction

MICHAEL AZERRAD journalist, author

LORI BARBERO drummer, Babes in Toyland

LOU BARLOW singer, multi-instrumentalist, Sebadoh

MUD BARON organizer, MC, Rev. Samuel Mudd's Revival Tent, Lollapalooza 1994

BECK artist

MIKI BERENYI singer, guitarist, Lush

KEN BETHEA guitarist, Old 97's

GARY BONGIOVANNI editor, *Pollstar* magazine

TIM BOOTH singer, James

STEVE "CHOPPER" BORGES production manager, Lollapalooza 1993–97

BRANDON BOYD singer, Incubus

CARRIE BRADLEY violinist, the Breeders

TOM BUNCH manager, Butthole Surfers

PHIL BURKE head rigger, Lollapalooza

GIZZ BUTT guitarist, the Prodigy

ERNIE C guitarist, Body Count

JERRY CANTRELL guitarist, singer, Alice in Chains

GERALD CASALE singer, bassist, Devo

NICK CAVE singer, Nick Cave and the Bad Seeds

JIMMY CHAMBERLIN drummer, Smashing Pumpkins

DAN CHOI front-of-house coordinator, Lollapalooza 1994–97, 2003

ANDY CIRZAN promoter, Jam Productions

LES CLAYPOOL bassist, singer, Primus

KING COFFEY drummer, Butthole Surfers

TIM COMMERFORD bassist, Rage Against the Machine, Audioslave

GARY LEE CONNER guitarist, Screaming Trees

VAN CONNER (1967–2023) bassist, Screaming Trees

T. C. CONROY front-of-house coordinator, Lollapalooza 1991

BILLY CORGAN singer, guitarist, Smashing Pumpkins

WAYNE COYNE singer, guitarist, Flaming Lips

MATT "THE TUBE" CROWLEY performer, Jim Rose Circus Sideshow

CHRIS CUFFARO photographer

ROBERT "NITE BOB" CZAYKOWSKI front-of-house sound engineer, Psychotica

MIKE D MC, drummer, Beastie Boys

PAUL D'AMOUR bassist, Tool

JAY DEE DAUGHERTY drummer, Patti Smith Group

SAUL DAVIES guitarist, violinist, James

JONATHAN DAVIS singer, Korn

KELLEY DEAL guitarist, singer, the Breeders

DEAN DeLEO guitarist, Stone Temple Pilots

GREG DEMOS bassist, Guided by Voices

DUANE DENISON guitarist, the Jesus Lizard

DENNIS DENNEHY publicist, Geffen Records

JIM DeROGATIS pop music critic, *Chicago Sun-Times*

VINNIE DOMBROSKI singer, Sponge

CHRIS DOWD keyboardist, trombonist, Fishbone

STEVEN DROZD drummer, multi-instrumentalist, Flaming Lips

E singer, guitarist, keyboardist, Eels

GREG EDWARDS guitarist, bassist, Failure

MIKE EINZINGER guitarist, Incubus

ERIC ERLANDSON guitarist, Hole

MONTSHO ESHE dancer, background vocalist, Arrested Development

NATE FARLEY roadie, Guided by Voices

PERRY FARRELL singer, Psi Com, Jane's Addiction, Porno for Pyros; cofounder, Lollapalooza

JOSEPH "AMP" FIDDLER keyboardist, George Clinton and the P-Funk Allstars

JENNIFER FINCH bassist, singer, L7

NORWOOD FISHER bassist, Fishbone

DANNY FLAIM roadie, projectionist, Butthole Surfers

JIMMY FLEMION singer, guitarist, the Frogs

TIM FOLJAHN guitarist, Mosquito

LONN FRIEND editor in chief, *RIP* magazine

JUSTINE FRISCHMANN singer, guitarist, Elastica

NIKKI GARDNER assistant to Ted Gardner; special groups coordinator, Lollapalooza

TED GARDNER (1947–2021) manager, Jane's Addiction, Tool; cofounder, Lollapalooza

MARC GEIGER agent; cofounder, Lollapalooza

JOE GITTLEMAN bassist, the Mighty Mighty Bosstones

GABBY GLASER singer, guitarist, Luscious Jackson

COREY GLOVER singer, Living Colour

DANNY GOLDBERG chairman, Warner Bros. Records; former manager, Nirvana, Hole

KIM GORDON bassist, guitarist, singer, Sonic Youth

STONE GOSSARD guitarist, Pearl Jam

GARY GRAFF music writer, *Detroit Free Press*

JIM GREER senior editor, *SPIN* magazine

JAN T. GREGOR road manager, Jim Rose Circus Sideshow

BRIAN GROSS intern, William Morris Agency

KORY GROW senior writer, *Rolling Stone* magazine

BOB GUCCIONE JR. editor, publisher, *SPIN* magazine

ROBIN GUTHRIE guitarist, Cocteau Twins

KIRK HAMMETT guitarist, Metallica

KATHLEEN HANNA singer, Bikini Kill

MICK HARVEY guitarist, Nick Cave and the Bad Seeds

CHRIS HASKETT guitarist, Rollins Band

GIBBY HAYNES singer, Butthole Surfers

LYNN HAZAN front-of-house tour accountant, Lollapalooza

BILLY HOWERDEL guitar tech, Fishbone, 1991, 1993; guitar tech, Smashing Pumpkins, 1994; guitarist, A Perfect Circle

LIAM HOWLETT producer, keyboardist, programmer, the Prodigy

LYLE HYSEN manager, Cell

ICE-T MC; singer, Body Count

MIKE INEZ bassist, Alice in Chains

JERRY JAFFE manager, the Jesus and Mary Chain

MICHAEL "CURLY" JOBSON stage manager, Lollapalooza 1991–92; tour manager, Hole, 1995

CHARLIE JONES founding partner, C3 Presents

AL JOURGENSEN singer, multi-instrumentalist, producer, Ministry

SCOTT KANNBERG guitarist, Pavement

MARK KATES A&R representative, Geffen Records

PETER KATSIS partner, the Firm

LENNY KAYE guitarist, Patti Smith Group

MAYNARD JAMES KEENAN singer, Tool, A Perfect Circle

DAVE KENDALL creator, host, MTV's *120 Minutes*

KENNEDY DJ, KROQ; VJ, MTV

ANTHONY KIEDIS singer, Red Hot Chili Peppers

JON KLEIN guitarist, Siouxsie and the Banshees; touring guitarist, Sinéad O'Connor

STEVE KNOPPER editor at large, *Billboard* magazine

GREG KOT music critic, *Chicago Tribune*

RICK KRIM executive, MTV

BEN KWELLER singer, guitarist, Radish

ANDY LANGER Austin, Texas–based journalist and radio host

BOB LAWTON agent, Sonic Youth

PAUL LEARY guitarist, Butthole Surfers

ELLIOTT LEFKO promoter, MCA Concerts Canada

JO LENARDI vice president of alternative marketing, Warner Bros. and Reprise Records

MARISKA LEYSSIUS cofounder, keyboardist, Psi Com; organizer, Desolation Center

JEFF LILLES performer, Cottonmouth, Texas

BEN LURIE guitarist, the Jesus and Mary Chain

KEVIN LYMAN stage manager, Lollapalooza 1991–92; artist liaison, main stage, Lollapalooza 1994

CRAIG MARKS editor in chief, *SPIN* magazine; author

ROSE MARSHACK bassist, Poster Children

STEVE MARTIN owner, Nasty Little Man publicity

J MASCIS singer, guitarist, Dinosaur Jr.

JOEY MAZZOLA guitarist, Sponge

MIKE McCREADY guitarist, Pearl Jam

STEVEN McDONALD bassist, singer, Redd Kross

MAC McNEILLY drummer, the Jesus Lizard

JAMES McNEW bassist, Yo La Tengo

MONTE A. MELNICK tour manager, Ramones

MAURICE MENARES touring staff, Sonic Youth

JIM MERLIS publicist, Geffen Records

FRITZ MICHAUD monitor engineer, Nine Inch Nails, 1991; stage manager, Ministry, 1992

RHETT MILLER singer, guitarist, Old 97's

MOBY artist

ANGELO MOORE singer, saxophonist, Fishbone

THURSTON MOORE singer, guitarist, Sonic Youth

TOM MORELLO guitarist, Rage Against the Machine, Audioslave

TRACIE MORRIS poet, Lollapalooza 1994

DON MULLER agent; cofounder, Lollapalooza

MURPH drummer, Dinosaur Jr.

AARON NAPARSTEK editor, SPINonline

BOB NASTANOVICH percussionist, background singer, Pavement

DAVE NAVARRO guitarist, Jane's Addiction

KEITH NEALY drummer, Cell

BUZZ OSBORNE singer, guitarist, Melvins

MARK O'SHEA tour manager, Nine Inch Nails

JULIE PANEBIANCO A&R representative, Capitol Records

DEB PASTOR roadie, the Jesus Lizard

RICHARD PATRICK guitarist, Nine Inch Nails

TERRY PEARSON front-of-house sound engineer, Sonic Youth

STEPHEN PERKINS drummer, Jane's Addiction, Porno for Pyros

ROBERT POLLARD singer, Guided by Voices

RIKI RACHTMAN co-owner, Cathouse; host, MTV's *Headbangers Ball*

C. J. RAMONE bassist, Ramones

LEE RANALDO guitarist, Sonic Youth

RASA DON drummer, Arrested Development

MARKY RAY guitar tech, Nine Inch Nails, 1991; roadie, Ministry, 1992

JIM REID singer, guitarist, the Jesus and Mary Chain

WILLIAM REID singer, guitarist, the Jesus and Mary Chain

TRENT REZNOR singer, multi-instrumentalist, producer, Nine Inch Nails

RICHARD 23 percussionist, vocalist, Front 242

HEIDI MARGOT RICHMAN L.A. scenester

HEIDI ELLEN ROBINSON-FITZGERALD publicist, Lollapalooza

HENRY ROLLINS singer, Rollins Band

JIM ROSE founder, performer, MC, Jim Rose Circus Sideshow

STUART ROSS tour accountant, Jane's Addiction; tour director, Lollapalooza

JOHN RUBELI second-stage manager, Lollapalooza 1993–95

CARLTON SANDERCOCK owner, Easy Action Records; Jane's Addiction superfan

JOEY SANTIAGO guitarist, Pixies

SUSANNE SASIC production designer, Sonic Youth

KATE SCHELLENBACH drummer, Luscious Jackson

PATTY SCHEMEL drummer, Hole

ADAM SCHNEIDER former manager, Jane's Addiction, Porno for Pyros, Perry Farrell; producer, Bill Graham Presents, 1991–92; concourse creative director, Lollapalooza 1997; producer, Lollapalooza 2003

SEAN E SEAN onstage performer, security, Body Count

MONICA SEIDE-EVENSON publicist, Warner Bros. Records

SEN DOG MC, Cypress Hill

STEVEN SEVERIN bassist, Siouxsie and the Banshees

JAMES "MUNKY" SHAFFER guitarist, Korn

TONY SHANAHAN bassist, Patti Smith Group

STEVE SHELLEY drummer, Sonic Youth, Mosquito

CLAUDETTE SILVER political-tent organizer, Lollapalooza 2003

DAVID WM. SIMS bassist, the Jesus Lizard

SLUG THE SWORD SWALLOWER performer, Jim Rose Circus Sideshow

CHAD SMITH drummer, Red Hot Chili Peppers

PATTI SMITH singer, Patti Smith Group

ELLYN SOLIS publicist, Epic Records

DONITA SPARKS singer, guitarist, L7

SPEECH MC, producer, Arrested Development

TOBIN SPROUT guitarist, singer, Guided by Voices

STEVE-O performer

STEVE STEWART manager, Stone Temple Pilots

PETER STONE organizer, Cyber Pit, Lollapalooza 1993

STUART SWEZEY founder, Desolation Center

ROB TANNENBAUM journalist, author

MISCHA TEMPLE lighting director, the Prodigy

KIM THAYIL guitarist, Soundgarden

MARY TIMONY singer, guitarist, Helium

BRAD TOLINSKI editor in chief, *Guitar World* magazine; author

THE TORTURE KING performer, Jim Rose Circus Sideshow

JEFF TREMAINE cocreator, director, *Jackass*

KATHERINE TURMAN journalist, author

LARS ULRICH drummer, Metallica

PAUL V. national director of alternative radio promotion, Warner Bros. Records

RICK VALENTIN guitarist, singer, Poster Children

EDDIE VEDDER singer, Pearl Jam

DAVID "BOCHE" VIECELLI agent, the Jesus Lizard, Pavement, Jon Spencer Blues Explosion

JOAN WASSER violinist, singer, the Dambuilders

MIKE WATT bassist, singer, Mike Watt and the Crew of the Flying Saucer

CRAIG WEDREN singer, guitarist, Shudder to Think

ANDREW WEISS bassist, Rollins Band

KELLY WEISS box office manager, Lollapalooza

JUSTIN WELCH drummer, Elastica

JOSEPHINE WIGGS bassist, the Breeders

JAMES WILBUR guitarist, Superchunk

KRISTEN WORDEN-HARRIS artist liaison, second stage, Lollapalooza 1995–97

MISSY WORTH marketing consultant, Lollapalooza 1991

JON WURSTER drummer, Superchunk

DAVID YOW singer, the Jesus Lizard

JON ZAZULA (1952–2022) manager, Ministry

DANNY ZELISKO promoter, Evening Star Productions

INTRODUCTION

On September 24, 1991, Nirvana released their second album, *Nevermind*, and, as the story goes, instantaneously rearranged the popular music landscape. Seemingly overnight, big hair, bright hooks, and blatant hedonism were out; raw, urgent sounds, thrift-shop DIY style, and social consciousness (with a healthy dose of cynicism) were in. A generation of music fans discarded the out-moded sounds and ethos of their older brothers and sisters, and the underground music scene, long operating and surviving via a network of college radio stations, sweaty dive bars, fanzines, and indie record labels, squinted its eyes and stepped out into the main-stream sun. The alternative nation was born.

It's the widely accepted narrative, but it's also—all apologies to Nirvana—inaccurate. By the time *Nevermind* hit store shelves and "Smells Like Teen Spirit" became an inescapable anthem perched at the upper reaches of the *Billboard* Hot 100, the Lollapalooza festival—a modern-day medicine show featuring "seven raucous bands and a circus tent full of political and social-action groups," as *The New York Times* put it in an early review—had just, mere weeks earlier, wrapped its inaugural run. The brainchild of Perry

Farrell, the shamanistic front man of psychedelic L.A. hard rockers Jane's Addiction, Lollapalooza's two-month expedition across the US in the summer of 1991 had helped to coalesce an ideology and aesthetic that would not only wash over popular music but seep into fashion, film, television, literature, food, politics . . . essentially, the culture at large.

Throughout the 1990s—specifically, the years 1991 to 1997, when the festival closed its first chapter—Lollapalooza functioned as the nerve center and proving ground for the alternative music revolution. The list of bands that graced its stage reads like a who's who of nineties superstars (Jane's Addiction, Pearl Jam, Red Hot Chili Peppers, Beastie Boys, Nine Inch Nails, Sonic Youth, Green Day, Beck, Smashing Pumpkins, Soundgarden, Alice in Chains, Snoop Dogg, Tool, Rage Against the Machine, Ice-T, Hole, Pavement), with a healthy smattering of outsiders (Jim Rose Circus Sideshow, Shaolin Monks, Waylon Jennings . . . *Metallica*?) thrown in for good measure.

Year in and year out, the festival garnered wall-to-wall coverage on MTV, in music mags like *Rolling Stone* and *SPIN*, and across mainstream media. The ascent and influence of Lollapalooza are inextricably linked to the rise of alternative music through the decade (did the bands fuel the fest, or did the fest fuel the careers of the bands?). And the cultural and societal concerns—women's rights, gun control, racial inclusiveness, progressive politics—that were given tent space, both figuratively and literally, at Lollapalooza (the then-new Rock the Vote organization registered twenty-five thousand new voters on the first Lollapalooza tour, fueling a wave that would be credited with helping to put Bill Clinton in the White House), likewise became tied to the scene itself. Lollapalooza was a traveling "Woodstock for the Lost Generation," a *New York Times* headline screamed, a gathering as much about people, philosophies, and shared values as it was about the bands performing onstage. It set the template for the modern American music festival and paved the way for touring concerns like Warped, Lilith Fair, Ozzfest, and, later, Bonnaroo, Coachella, and the scores of other contemporary destination fests that are now an integral part of how audiences experience live music.

Which was not necessarily Farrell's initial intention. "I'm often asked, did I think Lollapalooza was going to be what it became?" he says. "I mean, that's ridiculous. Of course not! How could I? I was just in it for kicks, period."

Back in 1991, Farrell, along with a brain trust that included then–Jane's Addiction manager Ted Gardner and agents Marc Geiger and Don Muller, conceived of a music extravaganza in the vein of England's long-running Reading Festival, but with an unprecedented and logistically daunting itinerary of roughly two dozen stops in various US cities. Needless to say, it was a risky undertaking.

Against all odds, Lollapalooza did finish its inaugural run in the black and launched a franchise that would only grow with the explosion of alt rock. But the festival's most significant achievement was far from financial: If Lollapalooza didn't single-handedly inaugurate what came to be known as "alternative nation," it went a long way toward codifying its ideals for a generation of teens and twentysomethings via a diverse mix of boundary-pushing musical acts, outsider fashion and art, political activism, and straight-up performative weirdness.

"The music was the root of it, but you're making culture as well as making music," Farrell says of his original intention. "And who knows? It could be shitty culture—you could be into something dumb and then it'll go away after a little while. Or . . . you can shoot for eternity."

Or, at least, for the late nineties, which was when Lollapalooza initially ceased operations. By that point, the alternative nation, once a bastion for outsiders of all ilks, had been almost completely assimilated by the mainstream. Flannel, combat boots, tattoos, and piercings were ubiquitous on fashion runways, and every major label had a roster of bands that, at first glance, were as freaky looking and sonically riotous as anything that might have been found in the deepest, darkest trenches of the underground a decade earlier. Alternative was big business, and Lollapalooza, which had been fending off accusations of corporatization as early as its second go-round, took a big hit in 1996 when it put Metallica at the top of the bill. Farrell quit the tour in protest of what he deemed a bow to big money, as well as the "macho-ization" of his initial, in his words, "include everything" utopian ideal, and instead turned his attention to a new project, the electronic-music-celebrating Enit Festival. Observed Living Colour guitarist Vernon Reid, an alumnus of the 1991 lineup, "What happened with Lollapalooza, and this is Perry Farrell's genius, is it commodified 'alternative,' simultaneously carving out a new market and ending it."

Of course, 1997 was hardly the end of Lollapalooza. The festival reemerged in 2003 with Farrell back on board and a reunited Jane's Addiction once again installed as headliners. These days, it takes a page from successors like Coachella and Bonnaroo and exists as a multiday destination event staged in a single US location, Chicago's Grant Park (in a novel and very Lolla-like move toward inclusivity, there are also global offshoots). It may not be as unique, or alternative, a happening (2023 headliners included Billie Eilish, Kendrick Lamar, and the Red Hot Chili Peppers, acts that are all mainstays at the tops of contemporary festival bills), but it still makes headlines— in 2021, for instance, for being the first major festival to brave the new pandemic world, bringing together more than 150 bands and close to 350,000 fans with (mostly) safe results, or in 2024, for having a main stage fully powered on a hybrid battery system.

To be sure, the world in which Lollapalooza today exists is very different from the one in which it was spawned. But what Lollapalooza helped to create was a moment—perhaps the last of this sort—where people believed that music might just have the ability to change the world. Through hundreds of new interviews with headliners, main-stage acts, second- and third-stage hopefuls, tour founders, festival organizers, promoters, publicists, sideshow freaks, stage crews, record label execs, reporters, roadies, and more, this book looks back on that moment to chronicle Lollapalooza's pioneering 1991–97 run, and, in the process, alternative rock's rise, as well as the reverberations that led to a massive shift in the music industry and the culture at large. This is the story of Lollapalooza and the 1990s alternative-rock revolution.

1 "THE BEST BAND IN THE WORLD"

ROB TANNENBAUM (journalist, author) Certainly, in the early eighties, say, 1983, the thought that alternative would take over the mainstream seemed impossible.

MICHAEL AZERRAD (journalist, author) The whole idea of the American indie underground in the eighties was to make exactly the music you wanted to make and then figure out how you could do that sustainably. So you had very different bands, such as the Butthole Surfers, R.E.M., They Might Be Giants, Minor Threat, et al., all very much doing their own idiosyncratic thing—that was the point.

PAUL LEARY (guitarist, Butthole Surfers) The early days of the Butthole Surfers felt like a slow suicide.

KING COFFEY (drummer, Butthole Surfers) It was like joining a cult, in a way. You had to be a true believer to actually want to choose to not have a home, to leave behind your girlfriends or whatever, to just be stuck in a van with four miserable people and a dog, playing shows and sleeping on strangers' floors.

CHRIS HASKETT (guitarist, Rollins Band) It's not a healthy lifestyle.

MICHAEL AZERRAD The major labels were never going to sign the new breed of indie rock bands, so a community formed and created a kind of shadow music industry, an infrastructure that could support this music: underground venues, music stores, fanzines, radio stations, record labels, and distributors.

ROB TANNENBAUM Record companies by and large didn't want to mess around with alternative music because the seventies weren't over yet. MTV comes around in 1981, and that's the start of the end of the seventies. But it's not the real end of the seventies, because record companies were still looking for the next Journey or REO Speedwagon or Boston.

DAVE KENDALL (creator, host, MTV's *120 Minutes*) I came to MTV in '86 and started *120 Minutes*. And the reason it was called *120 Minutes* is that no one knew what format it was going to be—they just knew it was going to be two hours long. So I was the guy that said, "Well, actually, there's this new type of music . . ." It didn't have the name "alternative" back then. But I was a print journalist and I'd just recently come over from England, so I was aware that there were various scenes, like post-punk and New Romantic. And then in the US there was stuff like R.E.M. and Let's Active and a whole bunch of guitar-rock bands. So there was a genre, and radio stations like WDRE in New York were playing it. But it wasn't really recognized by the mainstream or by MTV.

MARC GEIGER (agent; cofounder, Lollapalooza) There were thousands of bands banging on the door at that time. And not just in America. There was the Cure and Depeche Mode and the Smiths and Cocteau Twins and Echo & the Bunnymen and Siouxsie and the Banshees. The Clash before them. They were all instrumental in this.

JON KLEIN (guitarist, Siouxsie and the Banshees) From that period in the early eighties up to '90, '91, it was really cool to be a Brit! At least until Seattle happened.

KATHERINE TURMAN (journalist, author) How does Perry Farrell fit into it? He was definitely a ringleader in bringing alternative to the world. That said, he was an unlikely candidate for being any sort of spokesman. He was way too out-there. He's probably *still* way too out-there.

ANGELO MOORE (singer, saxophonist, Fishbone) The first time I saw Perry was '83, maybe '84. He was with his band Psi Com, who were kind of goth-y. Goth and rock. I remember them in a parking lot over on Wilcox and Hollywood Boulevard.

NORWOOD FISHER (bassist, Fishbone) They were playing at a hot dog stand. And Angelo came running up: "You guys gotta come see this band!"

CHRIS DOWD (keyboardist, trombonist, Fishbone) He has a praying mantis tattoo on his arm, and nobody was tatted up then. And he was sort of wide-eyed—like Perry is, you know? Dude was all types of ahead of his fucking time.

LEE RANALDO (guitarist, Sonic Youth) We were friendly to some degree with Perry. His band Psi Com opened this famous show we did in the L.A. desert for the Desolation Center.

STUART SWEZEY (founder, Desolation Center) Desolation Center was basically a nomadic venue. We used rehearsal spaces, loft spaces, anything cool that was unconventional. In '83 we started doing shows in the Mojave Desert, busing people out to what was basically a dry lake bed. Perry was at all of 'em. And he played at the last one, which we called the Gila Monster Jamboree, in January of '85. It was Psi Com, the Meat Puppets, Sonic Youth, who were doing their first-ever L.A. show, and Redd Kross.

STEVEN McDONALD (bassist, singer, Redd Kross) It was, like, a hundred weirdos in school buses going out to this undisclosed location, really as an excuse to take acid, trip out, and listen to some weird art rock under the moon. Even back then Perry was known for his strobe light and his Space Echo delay.

STUART SWEZEY With Desolation Center, there was this idea of curation and putting together groups that were different enough, but at the same time had some kind of a vibe and a sensibility. Gary Tovar, who started Goldenvoice, which now produces Coachella, came to one of the desert shows. And it seemed like it had a big impact on what Perry would do later.

MARISKA LEYSSIUS (cofounder, keyboardist, Psi Com; organizer, Desolation Center) He kept that vision of doing something carnivalesque, less corporate.

MARC GEIGER I made contact with Perry because he was reaching out to me about Psi Com. He wanted me to represent him because he liked all the bands Don Muller and I worked with at Triad [Artists]. I don't want to go through which ones—I had eighty clients, including all the 4AD stuff, which he was into. In L.A., especially if you want to be successful, you find out who reps what bands and who you want to be in business with, you don't just sit back and wait for it to come to you. Perry knew, "I wanna get people in my corner." But I thought it was early. Psi Com were not ready for prime time. I think they got signed by the guys at Triple X.

PETER HEUR (cofounder, Triple X Records) We came across Perry just after the Psi Com days, when Jane's Addiction were doing shows around town with Fishbone. It was hard rock, classic rock, post-punk. We thought, My god, this is something we haven't seen before . . . It really was a mixture of these four individuals coming together that produced something that hadn't been heard at the time.

STUART SWEZEY I think he wanted to do something that rocked more than Psi Com.

STEVEN McDONALD They had this badass drummer, and this pretty kid that shredded on guitar. It was like, "Oh, this weirdo dude from the Melrose scene went fishing in the metal scene, and is co-opting some wannabe arena rockers, and what's going to happen now?"

GREG KOT (music critic, *Chicago Tribune*) Jane's definitely had bigger ambitions than being an underground band. They wanted to be huge.

PERRY FARRELL (singer, Psi Com, Jane's Addiction; cofounder, Lollapalooza) I wanted to be in a great group that would alter the history of music. A band that would change the rotation of the earth.

NORWOOD FISHER When he had the musicians that would become Jane's Addiction, Perry asked if they could rehearse at my mom's place, which is where Fishbone rehearsed. So the first two Jane's Addiction rehearsals were in my mom's living room—a little two-bedroom apartment in the 'hood.

CHRIS DOWD This is basically Norwood's junior high school bedroom. Everybody in Fishbone is there. We had just got done rehearsing and Perry calls up: "I want you guys to check out my new band." So Perry comes by. Eric Avery comes by. Stephen Perkins shows up with Dave Navarro. And they fucking go into "Comin' down the moun-*taaiinnn*!" And they just *rip*. They leave and we're like, "Clearly our friend's band is going to be the next Led Zeppelin."

TOM MORELLO (guitarist, Rage Against the Machine) The first time I heard Jane's Addiction was on a bootleg tape of a live show, and they instantly became my favorite band in L.A. Then one day someone called the squat I was living in and said, "Jane's is rehearsing on this little street off of Melrose." I went over and just walked in, sat down on the floor next to a few people, probably some girlfriends, and watched Jane's Addiction rehearse for a couple hours. Just in awe of my favorite band rocking me on a dirty carpet.

PETER HEUR We did a live record at the Roxy with the intention of securing a deal that could provide the band the resources to do what they needed to do. Perry had a vision and he needed the financing and the promotion in order to make it work. And having a record was also a vehicle to get them on college radio. KXLU, out of Loyola Marymount University in L.A., played the hell out of it.

MARC GEIGER We had reach-outs from Triple X about Jane's.

PETER HEUR We were looking for an agent, somebody that could take the band and get them booked throughout the country and throughout the world. At the time, Triad was a smaller company—still big, but they had that indie vibe. And Marc and Don really understood the band.

DON MULLER (agent; cofounder, Lollapalooza) They sent over a video, and I think it was "Mountain Song," one of the early ones the guys did up in the backyard of a house somewhere in the Hollywood Hills. Perry was like Medusa. He had the dreads with the metal tips, the lights were flashing, he's doing this whole dance with his head. It looked like snakes were coming alive and what have you. I was mesmerized by it.

PERRY FARRELL Our whole thing is pageantry and explosiveness and drama and art.

DON MULLER I hadn't been at Triad very long, and I didn't have a god-damn clue what I was doing. But I knew that Jane's was important. The minute I saw the video and heard some of the stuff, I was in. They were the first band I signed as an agent.

MARC GEIGER Don loved them. I fell in love with them afterward. But everybody thought there was something super special with Perry—the vibe, the vision, the ambition. And the ambition wasn't just about career. It was about the shows and what they could become and how he wanted to be perceived. People wanted to be around him. He had a real aura.

TOM MORELLO It had all of the heavy metal fury that checked my boxes, but it was also intelligent and poetic and had this kind of softer, vulnerable side.

ERIC AVERY (bassist, Jane's Addiction) I had a lot of friends tell me about being into bands like Mötley Crüe and all that stuff, and that we were sort of the gateway into being heavy but being interesting. Just doing something more unusual with heavy music.

PETER HEUR It brought together all these different groups of people in L.A.—rock, punk, post-punk, goth, hair metal. Riki Rachtman, who was big in that Sunset Strip world and ran the Cathouse, was a huge supporter of the band.

RIKI RACHTMAN (co-owner, Cathouse; host, MTV's *Headbangers Ball*) The people that were part of our scene loved Jane's Addiction. We never looked at it like, "Oh, this is a different type of band." We felt like they were still part of the Cathouse scene, just like Guns N' Roses.

MARC GEIGER In L.A. in the late eighties, Guns N' Roses and Jane's Addiction *were* the scene.

KATHERINE TURMAN Both bands played the same clubs, and they both had the same kind of rabid followers. Obviously, Axl Rose and Perry are very different, but I think they're both equally charismatic.

TOM MORELLO A big part of Jane's Addiction wasn't just the music, it wasn't just the shows—it was a citywide vibe that they created. Like, there'd be flyers in coffee shops and record stores and head shops for some event that Jane's Addiction was putting on, but it wasn't a gig at the Roxy, it was in downtown L.A. . . . in a train yard . . . with an S&M performance. Or it was thirty miles south of Big Bear, and they're gonna have a bohemian butterfly picnic . . . and Jane's Addiction's gonna play! This was a band that was much more than just music—they had ideas about how life should be *lived*.

PETER HEUR Everybody was talking about Jane's and their live performances, and the major labels became interested. The reason why Warner Bros. was chosen was because they were very artist-friendly. Perry and the guys felt that they were going to be able to do the things that they wanted to do, everything from the music to the artwork, the way they wanted to do it.

HEIDI MARGOT RICHMAN (L.A. scenester) Perry was only going to leave Triple X and his indie world if he had control over the artistic output. He fought for creative control of mixes, of videos, of everything. It was a really big deal when he negotiated for that—and got it.

STUART ROSS (tour accountant, Jane's Addiction; tour director, Lollapalooza) Around that time, I was going to this weekly gathering at a pub in Tarzana, and I would talk to a guy named Ted Gardner, who was an Australian who had managed bands like Men at Work. He told me that he was going to work for this band, Jane's Addiction, who I knew nothing about. He said, "They're getting bigger and bigger and bigger, and I can't handle it. These guys are out of control. I need a tour accountant." I had worked with Tom Waits, George Benson, Jean-Luc Ponty—all kinds of acts. I remember I went to see Jane's at a club in San Francisco and it was just total chaos. It was fantastic. And so, I took the job. As the tour progressed, it seemed to get bigger and bigger every day.

PETER HEUR Ted was the road manager initially. And then he was the manager.

MARC GEIGER Ted was big and tough and gruff. He was smart and no-nonsense and he had a really good sense of credibility and what was bullshit. And he was very effective with Jane's.

PERRY FARRELL He definitely had that fighting spirit. But he was so good-natured, too.

TED GARDNER (manager, Jane's Addiction; cofounder, Lollapalooza) I got introduced to the band; Warner Bros. rang me up and asked me to fly to Dallas to meet with them to take over their tour. It was their first date. So I flew down, met them, you know, big lovefest. And I rang Warner Bros. two days later and I said, "Do you know that a couple of these guys are junkies?" And they went, "No . . . are they?"

MARC GEIGER Jane's Addiction was a heroin band. As well as other things.

DAVE NAVARRO (guitarist, Jane's Addiction) I mean, we always had high drama.

KATHERINE TURMAN There was what seemed to be a lot of mystical, magical, scary stuff going on with Jane's that perpetuated this mythology around them. They seemed dangerous and on the edge. But they managed to keep it together and, you know, make "alternative" a household word.

MICHAEL AZERRAD What Jane's Addiction signaled to the music biz establishment was that there was an organic musical movement happening, not a manufactured one, and the time was ripe to capitalize on it.

JIM DeROGATIS (pop music critic, *Chicago Sun-Times*) As Dante had Virgil, every music lover needs somebody to introduce them to the subculture, right?

MARC GEIGER Music happens on a timeline. And at the time, Jane's Addiction was the best band in the world. Then they broke up. Who knows what would've happened if they hadn't? But launching Lollapalooza, and their breakup also being the impetus for it, is part of their legend now.

STUART ROSS You might ask, would Perry be the guy who would envision a touring festival? I don't think anybody was the guy who could envision a touring festival, because it really didn't exist. The concept was like the concept of cell phones. But Perry was a musical visionary, and he picked up on the fact that the demand for this genre was much higher than what the industry would allow at the time. So Lollapalooza was a confluence of a lot of factors. And Lollapalooza combined with a confluence of other factors switched the mainstream onto a whole different train track.

PERRY FARRELL It's called "culture." That's what I'm always trying to create. And one guy doesn't create culture—we all do together, and it's beautiful.

2 "LOLLA *WHAT?*"

TED GARDNER (manager, Jane's Addiction; cofounder, Lollapalooza) The genesis of it all was that Perry decided that Jane's Addiction was gonna break up.

GREG KOT (music critic, *Chicago Tribune*) It was well known that they were not loving each other as a band at that point.

STUART ROSS (tour director, Lollapalooza) I don't believe that Perry felt that the trajectory of the band versus the extracurricular activities of the band were sustainable. And when Perry decided to break the band up, he was very specific that he wanted them to go out on a high note, rather than fade into obscurity.

NIKKI GARDNER (assistant to Ted Gardner; special groups coordinator, Lollapalooza) Lollapalooza would be their big farewell, with a bunch of bands getting together to celebrate the end of Jane's Addiction.

STEVE KNOPPER (editor at large, *Billboard* magazine) It's actually a canceled appearance at the 1990 Reading Festival that sparks the whole thing. Which is kind of funny to think about—that a show that doesn't even happen leads to something so much bigger.

MARC GEIGER (agent; cofounder, Lollapalooza) Jane's is playing the Reading Festival, and they have a warm-up club show. It's a tiny club. Can't remember the name of it. It was about 180 degrees inside. The walls were sweating. Simon Le Bon's in the club. Everybody who's somebody made it to that show for Jane's Addiction. It was an amazing show.

CARLTON SANDERCOCK (owner, Easy Action Records; Jane's Addiction superfan) It was a club called Subterania, underneath a flyover in West London. Jane's Addiction, prior to that point, were cult in the UK, but by summer of 1990 they were a big band, and for our small group of people who were crazy about them, to see them in a club like Subterania was a fucking big deal.

DAVE NAVARRO (guitarist, Jane's Addiction) I totally remember that show at Subterania, and I'll tell you why. I was a big heroin user back then, and the day before, I had hooked up with a bunch of street kids that knew where to cop. We got ahold of a bunch of dope and ended up going to a squatters' flat in an abandoned building.

So me and a couple of these street kids were getting high, and somewhere along the line, I overdosed. And then all the kids that were living there, except my one friend, split, because they didn't want to have a body on their hands. They all ran away, and my friend called an ambulance and dragged me down a flight of stairs to put me on the street corner to hopefully have an ambulance come and pick me up. And he said that when he pulled my body up to lean against a street sign, I started coughing. I had come back. So he had to pull me back up the flight of stairs and watch through the window as the paramedics were looking for whatever it is they were looking for. And they never found it and they went away.

I remember coming to the next day, somewhere in the afternoon. And my friend was perched over me, saying, "Dave! Dave! You were dead! You were dead last night!" I was completely confused. And the first thing I said to him was, "Is there any more dope left?" So my next move was to get high again, which is insane.

Then I realized that the Subterania show was that night. I looked at the clock, it was at four or five in the afternoon, and I think I had missed sound check. And this was before cell phones and computers. So I had to somehow find the venue, and I think I made my way there maybe twenty minutes before we were supposed to go on. Just before the show I was completely asleep, and someone had to tap me on the shoulder and say, "It's time." So I went from an immediate drug-induced sleep to being onstage. And then we played, the show went great, and everybody had a good time.

STEPHEN PERKINS (drummer, Jane's Addiction) I tell you, man, nothing is better than playing to a roomful of people that want your music. They know the lyrics, they're there for you. There's a union. And Perry, he's a shaman when he's up there. You can go into the room and let him take you somewhere.

CARLTON SANDERCOCK I just remember the fucking heat.

MARC GEIGER It was cool outside, hot in the club. Perry went outside after the show, caught a cold, lost his voice. Perry wakes up in the morning, the band cancels because he can't sing.

PERRY FARRELL I got too fucked up. So I didn't make it to Reading. My voice was just shot.

DAVE NAVARRO I felt bad for Perry, of course, because no one wants to get injured like that. But I remember a sigh of relief coming over me that I could just go back to my hotel room instead of to Reading.

MARC GEIGER Stephen and I go, "Fuck it. We're going down to the festival anyway. We're going to have a good time." We went all three days. There's a thousand bands: The Pixies, who were friends and my client, and were ruling the UK at the time. Inspiral Carpets were my client. The Fall was a client. And we had such a good time hanging with all of them. Stephen and I said, "This is what we should do in America." A camaraderie of all these cool alternative bands.

STEPHEN PERKINS We knew the music was growing. We knew X and Black Flag and the Minutemen, all the bands that inspired us, they had hit the ceiling. But when we saw what was happening at Reading, there was the sense that there's something about this music that's not being shown or heard yet. And we knew the audience was there and ready for it. To have that eclectic day, eclectic night, that experience where the genres kind of just melt together and the fans are there.

MARC GEIGER They didn't have this in America. So we went back to the hotel, and we described our day at Reading. With Jane's, Perry had said, "We're breaking up the band. We want to do something magical for our last tour." So at that point, I described what I thought a format should be, and I said, "I think we should bring seven bands. Everybody should pick a band." I literally just threw it out there, and everybody started picking bands. I was like a waiter taking orders, including my own. I think Dave picked Siouxsie and the Banshees, and Eric picked the Butthole Surfers . . .

ERIC AVERY (bassist, Jane's Addiction) I was a huge Butthole Surfers fan.

MARC GEIGER . . . and Perry picked Ice-T, and I picked the Pixies and Nine Inch Nails, and Stephen picked Rollins, I want to say.

DON MULLER (agent; cofounder, Lollapalooza) They came back from the UK and said, "What do you think? Can we do this?"

MARC GEIGER When I went to contact the bands, everyone said yes. Except the Pixies.

JOEY SANTIAGO (guitarist, Pixies) That probably sounds like something stupid that we would do. I mean, we should have done it. Because we worked with one of the founders—he was our agent. So it's like, "Fuck, why *didn't* we do it?"

MARC GEIGER So then the Pixies choice eventually evolved into Living Colour. Great rock band. And they had the only hit record out of the whole bunch.

DAVE NAVARRO My first memory of hearing about the festival was in our rehearsal space. I wasn't very coherent for the days prior, but that conversation didn't happen until we were well back in Los Angeles. We were in this dingy little studio, and we kind of threw names around of who would be good to be on it. I just thought it was going to be another festival gig. I had no idea what it would become.

DON MULLER I'll be brutally honest with you, we didn't have a clue about what the hell we were doing. Zero. If anybody says differently, they're lying. Because it was like, Okay, we're going to put all these bands together, and we think we can move it around the country . . . but what do we do with it?

RICK KRIM (executive, MTV) This was 1990, 1991, way before festivals were really a thing over here. These days you have three festivals every weekend. There's nothing unique about it. But at that time, and in this musical lane, no one had done it on that kind of scale.

GINA ARNOLD (journalist, author) Marc Geiger told me, "Oh, we have this great idea. We're gonna do these festivals, just like in England . . ." And I was like, "That's never gonna work." I mean, think about the difference between those festivals and America. The size of America . . . it's just too big. Also, I told him, "There's no market for those bands."

MARC GEIGER But the key point was it wasn't about creating an alternative tour to represent the time. Jane's was looking for ideas to go out with a bang, something different, okay? This is true. They'll tell you they were splitting up. They were fighting, *da, da, da, da, da.* I think Eric was trying to be straight and the other guys were not. That was causing some frictions.

Now, it turned out that the right thing *was* reflecting alternative culture in a package that could get to a lot of people and be presented with force. But it wasn't the front burner. Reading and England was the front burner. The back burner was the hair-band sleeve. MTV in England wasn't showing Faster Pussycat and Winger videos every thirty seconds. England was Inspiral Carpets. Madchester. The BBC and Pete

Tong and John Peel and Nick Cave. America was still scared of that. At Reading, the Pixies were headlining an eighty-five-thousand-person festival. Here, they were a club act. You're trying to get that culture and that mindset over in America, which is still promoting Winger videos.

DAVE NAVARRO I wasn't really aware of it being a farewell tour, just because we were on the verge of every show being a farewell show. I think that's what Perry had in mind, but I don't know that he shared that with us. Although it was pretty obvious to me that we weren't going to be doing much after that.

PERRY FARRELL I told Marc, "I'm out of here after the tour, so let's do something good." And he looked at me and said, "Perry, you can do whatever the fuck you want." And I said, "I'm going to hold you to that."

STUART ROSS Perry called us all in for a meeting and told us what was going to happen and what his concept was. I remember it as being Ted Gardner, Marc Geiger, Don Muller, and Peter Grosslight, who was one of the partners at Triad. Tom Atencio, one of Jane's Addiction's managers. Bill Vuylsteke, also known as Bill V., who was the business manager. I think it was at Bill's office. And Perry sat us all down and said, "Guys, I'm breaking the band up. I want to go out on a high, good note. And for the last tour, we'll get six other bands. We'll get the promoters to provide crazy food like giant burritos, and we'll do politics. We'll get the NRA to set up a booth next to PETA. And we'll get crazy art. And I've got a name for it, we're going to call it Lollapalooza."

PERRY FARRELL I do remember coming up with the name. Because everybody always wants you to title a tour. In all truth, it was a very humble moment. I was on a dirty carpet in an apartment in Venice. It was a shag carpet, I think it was green, it was kind of ugly, and there were crusty things on the carpet. I had books, like old secondhand books, and I picked up a dictionary. It's kind of a rarity to have a real dictionary, but we all had them in those days. I used to like to use the dictionary for words when I would write songs, because you might run across a word that's so amazing that it sparks something. And then sometimes I would read the dictionary just for fun. But I came across "lollapalooza," because I was up to *L*.

TED GARDNER No one could pronounce it. No one could spell it.

STUART ROSS Nothing like this had been done before. There were a few festivals like WOMAD, which was the Peter Gabriel event that started in Europe that traveled a bit. And I believe there was one other smaller festival . . .

DON MULLER I don't want to throw water on our fire, but there was a show down at the Pacific Amphitheatre in Costa Mesa called A Gathering of the Tribes, I think that was 1990. And that pretty much was a model, even though nobody wants to talk about it, of how to put something like this together. It was the vision of Ian Astbury from the Cult. I was a huge Cult fan, and I went and saw the show and I thought, Fuck, this is amazing. But then again, living in Southern California, it works, right? But not in Cleveland.

STUART ROSS But none of us ever said, "How are we gonna get these bands on and off the stage? We should reach out to the Gathering of the Tribes people." I don't think we even called those things traveling festivals at the time. They were kind of "multi-act packages." None of them were considered operations where we could just use their playbook. This was a much larger scope.

MARC GEIGER This was a presentation of this music and culture in a format that could get to everybody. Because it wasn't England. It wasn't a small country. You already had some culture in pockets, right? You had KXLU and KCRW and 91X and KROQ in Southern California. So those people benefited compared to others. You had to take this around.

This is where Stuart Ross and the whole team need their credit. Those guys made it work. They were killers. They figured out how to mobilize an army. That's a little different than setting up base camp, which is today's festival model, right? "I'm going to build a big village, and we're not going to move for three days, and then I'll tear it down." That's a very different product, massively. There were tons of logistical challenges.

STUART ROSS We were creating something that literally had to be redone every day. None of us had experience in putting together a seven-act traveling concert package with a ton of extra activities going on. And so we leaned on the promoters. We said, "Okay, you're going to book Jane's Addiction, and you're going to book six other opening acts, and here's who the acts are, and here's what you're gonna pay them." They weren't offered separately, but they were contracted separately. The promoters were told who the bands were going to be and what their guarantees were going to be. But there was no, "Oh, I don't wanna pay that much for this band." That was not an option.

And then we said, "And we need you to find alternative food"—not just the hot dogs and hamburgers and pretzels that were kind of prevalent as venue food in those days—"and if you can invite any political groups that want a table, that would be great." And we got, obviously, varying results.

T. C. CONROY (front-of-house coordinator, Lollapalooza 1991) It was my job to make that field turn into Perry's dream. And he was ethereal about it because he's an ethereal guy. He was probably really high, too. But what they did was they gave me an office at Triad: "Here's your desk, here's your telephone, here's your legal pad, here's your Yellow Pages." And I would go into Triad every day and work on organizing that front of house. And it was not easy because nobody knew what Lollapalooza was. I mean, it was a cold call . . . the coldest of cold calls. Because if you think about it in context, even the word "Lollapalooza" was weird. "Lolla *what*? Can you spell that?"

MISSY WORTH (marketing consultant, Lollapalooza 1991) Perry was very insistent on making sure that we represented the alternative world, both onstage and off. For instance, I remember having a big discussion with him, and I'm just using examples, I'm not saying they were on the tour, but it was, "If you're gonna have the ACLU, do you also have the

NRA?" Like, "You have to represent the world, not just our point of view."

PERRY FARRELL I wanted to have a debate booth where the Republican and the Democrat and the Independent each gets up there and says their thing. Because doesn't that seem, like, fair?

T. C. CONROY He asked me to get pro-lifers and then get the abortion clinics, and to get the military and then get Greenpeace. He had this concept of, "It all goes on the field." The liberal side was more open to the concept. On the other side, I just remember them all saying no.

GARY GRAFF (music writer, *Detroit Free Press*) In the US we didn't have the culture of the midway with all the booths, whether it was merchants or social causes or whatever else. It was an unusual thing.

STUART ROSS When we talked to promoters and said that we needed art, they pretty much all passed on that. Because they couldn't figure out how to do it. So Perry found an art gallery owner in West Hollywood. Didn't really work out well, but he curated it for us.

DON MULLER Stuart and I did most of the work putting the actual deals together, and it was literally going out and talking to people and saying, "Hey, do you believe in this?" "Can we work this?" "Do you need backing?" Because a lot of the promoters just didn't have the wherewithal or the resources to do a show of this magnitude. But we needed them on the ground. We needed them marketing. We needed to hit all the clubs. We needed to work radio. There needed to be cohesiveness in getting the message out. Also, the idea was to be able to play a GA [general admission] place, so the kids could come and go as they wished.

STUART ROSS We're talking about 1990, going into 1991, and amphitheaters were the new cool thing. They're not the shopping centers that they are now. And everybody wanted to play them. They were brand-new buildings and they held eighteen thousand people, and there was a big general admission component. So that's where we wanted to play.

DON MULLER It was one of those situations where we were, in a weird way, creating promoters in different cities as we went along. Seth Hurwitz is one that comes to mind. He had the 9:30 Club in D.C., and he grew his business off alternative music and things like Lollapalooza. We go to Toronto and there's a guy named Elliott Lefko who gets it, breathes it, understands it, and likes it. Great Woods in Boston, same thing. But then we had people like Belkin Productions in Cleveland, which, for all intents and purposes, didn't know what this was at all. I'm not certain if I sold that show or Geiger did, but we sold the show.

STUART ROSS Danny Zelisko, who had Compton Terrace in Phoenix, an alternative venue, was one who got it. As did Andy Cirzan with Jam Productions, who had the World Music Theatre in Chicago and Harriet Island in St. Paul, another unusual venue.

DANNY ZELISKO (promoter, Evening Star Productions) Festivals at that time were kind of passé—Woodstock happened twenty years earlier, and it just wasn't something that was going on. Lollapalooza was a brand-new thing that we had to explain to the market and to rock audiences everywhere.

ANDY CIRZAN (promoter, Jam Productions) I'd already been working with Don and Marc, because I had relationships with a number of their bands, like the Beastie Boys. When they started talking about this, all I was saying was, "I wanna be involved. Okay? Please let me be involved!" It wasn't a question of, "What are you guys doing?"

STEPHEN PERKINS I think promoters and everyone realized that this music is bigger than we thought it was.

DON MULLER We were also smart about our ticket prices. We knew we needed to be realistic about what we were doing.

STUART ROSS Our tickets were $27.50 the first year. And these were the days before Ticketmaster charges cost more than the ticket, so there might be $2.75, $3.00 on top of it. That was it. In 1991, that was a moderate price.

DON MULLER Some of these promoter guys we had to browbeat, but we were going, regardless. If you wanted to be a part of it, great. If you didn't, you didn't. But we were gonna make this thing happen.

BOB GUCCIONE JR. (editor, publisher, *SPIN* magazine) Lollapalooza came along and was a natural organic invention. I look at so many of the music festivals today, and they're such total shit because they're trying to re-create a blueprint from other times. You know, there's no point in replicating Woodstock. You can't re-create that spontaneity or authenticity. But Lollapalooza was purely a product of the imagination of the people of its time.

GARY GRAFF It was Brave New World in a lot of different directions, because festival culture in the United States really didn't exist in '91.

PERRY FARRELL It was early years. Do you know that 1991, that was the year Michael Jordan won the NBA title? Also, the World Wide Web was formed that year. And for mystics—if you speak to the sages—the rebbe, his greatest writings came in 1991, when he was talking about Mashiach and the era of redemption, ushering it in. It was all in 1991. So I look at that period as all the strong things that happened at that time. And that made Lollapalooza possible.

3 "I STILL THINK IT'S ODD THAT IT WORKED"

GINA ARNOLD (journalist, author) What was interesting about Lollapalooza was that it took a gamble on assuming that enough people were interested in what, at the time, was music that didn't get played on mainstream radio.

GARY GRAFF (music writer, *Detroit Free Press*) Touring packages, we had . . . what? The *Dirty Dancing* tour? The Turtles' "Happy Together" show? So a package like this was not something that was very familiar to people. And then put on top of that a lineup of bands that you were like, "Okay, they're playing the shed? They're playing the big amphitheater? Is this really gonna fly?" So I remember being very surprised when I got the announcement. I thought, Wow, this is intriguing . . .

GIBBY HAYNES (singer, Butthole Surfers) All of us had already been exposed to these big festivals in Europe for alternative-style bands, but that just didn't exist in the United States. But the idea of an alt-rock traveling festival, we knew it would work.

ERIC AVERY (bassist, Jane's Addiction) The perception was that none of the bands on that first Lollapalooza were supposed to be able to play to the size of crowds that we would be playing to in the sometimes-tertiary places that we were going to. At the time, Jane's had played Madison Square Garden. But outside of New York and L.A. it was a different thing.

HENRY ROLLINS (singer, Rollins Band) It was my impression that if Perry thought he could pull it off, he would do it. He's one of those guys.

GINA ARNOLD Perry had a vision about inclusivity and making the sort of, quote unquote, musical palate of Middle America wider. And more adventurous. And I think that he succeeded, in a very narrow way, at doing that.

ROB TANNENBAUM (journalist, author) I'm trying not to use the word "lifestyle," but I guess I have to. This was a lifestyle, and if you went to Lollapalooza what you realized was that the lifestyle was bigger than just, "I'm going to see a band." It made you feel not just that you were part of the Jane's Addiction Fan Club, but you were part of the world that embraced, you know, tattoos.

GARY GRAFF "Oh, I can see bands . . . and also buy tie-dye, get something pierced, and get some sort of unique drink?" All of those elements were very new to the concert-going experience back then.

STUART ROSS (tour director, Lollapalooza) All of it was based on an idea that Perry had in his head that this was going to be all day. And it wasn't just seeing an act, waiting twenty minutes to change equipment, and seeing another act. From the very beginning, from day one, it was, "Let's provide interesting or provocative activities at places other than the main stage." So the entire venue is an entertainment area, not just one stage.

PERRY FARRELL I do love to be a party planner, but I plan the party around the music. The music is the taproot of it. And when I know that it's all built and wonderful, the doors will open.

GINA ARNOLD I still think it's odd that it worked.

JIM GREER (senior editor, *SPIN* magazine) I was definitely . . . what's the word? Skeptical. Like, maybe in the big cities you'll get a crowd . . .

BOB GUCCIONE JR. (editor, publisher, *SPIN* magazine) I knew it was going to work. I thought, Damn, why didn't I do that? We could've had the *SPIN* tour!

GIBBY HAYNES I wish I had come up with the idea.

GARY GRAFF There was definitely an anxiousness about it. And I'm sure in some quarters even a nervousness. As a journalist, I remember the organizers and producers, Marc Geiger and so on, being very available to the press. Wanting to talk about it and wanting to explain where the idea came from and what it was they were doing and what they were hoping to achieve. Basically, just trying to generate as much attention as they possibly could.

HEIDI ELLEN ROBINSON-FITZGERALD (publicist, Lollapalooza) The press was massive the first year, even though people didn't really understand what it was and what it could be. Some people got it—*SPIN*, obviously, was a very important audience for Lollapalooza, not only because of its readers, but because the two entities were really made for each other.

MICHAEL AZERRAD (journalist, author) *SPIN*, as the avowed antidote to the boomer-yuppie *Rolling Stone*, was in the right demographic place at the right demographic time.

BOB GUCCIONE JR. The generation that we were editing for had come into prominence, just as the boomers had back in the late sixties, early seventies. I always point out, Italians don't call it "Italian food"—they call it "food." For *SPIN*, alternative culture was just culture.

HEIDI ELLEN ROBINSON-FITZGERALD But in general, Lollapalooza was such a new idea in rock 'n' roll that it was sometimes a little difficult to get across—whether it was the daily newspapers, the weekly stuff—just how cool it was. Which is why MTV became such a valuable tool. Because people could see it.

DAVE KENDALL (creator, host, MTV's *120 Minutes*) By that point, the folks at MTV had accepted that there really was a thing called alternative, and they were relatively supportive of it. There were also some big record labels behind it as well. And MTV was always very, very sensitive to what the record companies wanted. So they were very happy to send me out to the shows that first year.

PAUL LEARY (guitarist, Butthole Surfers) We could definitely feel that people were coming around to alternative music, even though I hated that term "alternative." I've always liked to think of myself as punk rock. But we were able to sell out shows by that point, and our venues were getting bigger . . . although we still weren't making a whole lot of money. We were sleeping on people's floors.

KING COFFEY (drummer, Butthole Surfers) I mean, we were called the Butthole Surfers. Come on! We understood the limitations of what we were trying to do.

CHRIS HASKETT (guitarist, Rollins Band) It was a funny bill dynamically to make work because you try and think about, okay, Nine Inch Nails and the Banshees, that kind of meshes, right? But Nine Inch Nails and Living Colour? Like, *what*? Or Living Colour and the Banshees, you know what I mean?

COREY GLOVER (singer, Living Colour) Our whole thing was that we were always a fish out of water. We have loud guitars and it's bombastic and all that stuff, but we weren't Whitesnake, that's for sure.

JIM DeROGATIS (pop music critic, *Chicago Sun-Times*) Perry, who has many faults, has good taste, and I think he was sincere in wanting to celebrate this diverse music. Enough women? No, but some women. And including hip-hop as part of it. I thought it was absolutely brilliant to have such a diverse bill traveling the country at this peak moment of alternative rock exploding.

DAVE KENDALL The fact that the name didn't really mean anything also helped, because it meant that the festival itself was quite undefined.

STEPHEN PERKINS It was a camp. And there was a great team of freaks and artists that went out together to do it. And that, to me, was the union—all those people that made it work.

KEVIN LYMAN (stage manager, Lollapalooza 1991–92) In the late eighties, early nineties, I was running about 320 shows a year in Southern California. I had my own production company, Kevin Lyman Production Services, but my biggest thing was running all the shows for Goldenvoice. We were doing a lot with Perry—Jane's Addiction shows when I remember them opening for Dramarama at Fender's Ballroom. Ted Gardner was with them and I started to get along with Ted a lot, just because we were always figuring out these crazy things that bands wanted to do. Like, they approached us about doing a special show to film parts of the "Stop" video.

Then, sometime in the fall of 1990, I was asked to go on the road with them and stage-manage. I'd never been on the road at that point. But I said yes, and I wound up stage-managing the first year of Lollapalooza with a guy named Curly Jobson.

MICHAEL "CURLY" JOBSON (stage manager, Lollapalooza 1991–92) I'm from Fife, Scotland, and my first break in my career was when I got a job working with Echo & the Bunnymen. And through that period our tour manager was Ted Gardner. Ted was my mentor, my pal. He reminded me so much of my dad, actually. Tough guy, didn't pull any punches, super intelligent and very good at everything he did. Through the period of the Bunnymen, we became very close.

At the time, Ted was also tour-managing Jane's Addiction. He went on to manage Jane's Addiction, and when the Bunnymen broke up Ted offered me a European tour with them. I did settlements and production work. I got along incredibly well with all the guys, particularly Perry, and when they were going to do Lollapalooza they invited me to America. They had a production guy that was a bit too old-school for the new wave of new wave, if you like, which was the Lollapalooza type of acts that were going on. I fit the mold a lot more. I had the shaven head and the turnip hairdo on top, and I was a Scottish guy who didn't mind a fight in the loading dock with anybody who cared to have a go with me.

KEVIN LYMAN I think there were probably old, seasoned touring veterans that were really skeptical if it could work. Me, I just charged in, like, "Yeah, this is great. Let's go!"

MICHAEL "CURLY" JOBSON It was a magical idea that Perry brought forward. And Lollapalooza 1991 was a groundbreaking set of dates for everybody out there that was learning how to do it. It was the mold, the cast, for every festival that came after it.

LOLLAPALOOZA 1991

DATES: JULY 18–AUGUST 28

MAIN STAGE: Jane's Addiction, Siouxsie and the Banshees, Living Colour, Nine Inch Nails, Ice-T (with Body Count, unbilled), Butthole Surfers (occasionally billed as "BH Surfers"), Rollins Band (occasionally billed as "Henry Rollins Band"), Fishbone (select shows), Violent Femmes (select shows)

The first Lollapalooza, which launched on July 18, 1991, at Compton Terrace in Chandler, Arizona, was hardly intended as a moon shot. Rather, it was envisaged as a finale: a massive sendoff for Jane's Addiction, who, even while riding high on the breakout success of their second studio album, 1990's *Ritual de lo Habitual*, were imploding due to personality conflicts and substance abuse issues. The group disbanded—for the first time—almost immediately following the tour. But Farrell's desire to throw a colossal and euphoric bon voyage party, one that transcended mere music, was foundational to what Lollapalooza would become.

"Young people like to have their minds blown," Farrell says. "They're so bored. I'm so bored, you know? So I figured, unless we could blow their minds, we weren't really doing our job."

Farrell did his job, and he did it with a lineup that in 1991, and even now, is impressive in its embrace of musical extremes: The tour, which helped to launch the career of low-on-the-bill Nine Inch Nails, also included Henry Rollins leading his post–Black Flag aggro-fusion-punk act Rollins Band, a shotgun-wielding Gibby Haynes fronting Texas art-rock weirdos the Butthole Surfers, and hardcore rapper Ice-T, dedicating half his set time to premiering his controversial new metal project, Body Count. After Nine Inch Nails came New York rockers Living Colour, British goth icons Siouxsie and the Banshees, and, finally, a combustible-even-by-their-standards Jane's Addiction.

The largely left-of-the-dial lineup functioned as its own statement of purpose. But from the very beginning there was also a coalescing cultural point of view, one that would be adopted by alternative rock at large in the early nineties. In Lollapalooza's first year, a yellow-striped circus tent set up at each stop housed local artists and advocacy groups like National Abortion Rights Action League, Refuse and Resist, and Handgun Control Inc., which handed out literature, buttons, and other items to get their progressive messages across. Between sets, *The New York Times* reported, "a display above the stage flashed statistics in the style of the *Harper's* Index, on topics from textbook censorship to the Persian Gulf war."

There was also an embrace of hot-button issues onstage. Just months after Rodney King, a twenty-five-year-old Black man, was pulled from his car and beaten by four Los Angeles police officers, Ice-T and Body Count debuted their controversial song "Cop Killer" to throngs of moshing, mostly white teenagers and twentysomethings. Later in the day, Ice-T would also join Jane's Addiction onstage to duet with Farrell on Sly and the Family Stone's "Don't Call Me N****r, Whitey," with the two vocalists squaring off and sneering the titular epithets at one another, before ultimately embracing and dancing arm in arm across the stage. "That's a serious song," Ice-T says. "But Perry's edgy, you know? He knows how to push buttons. So I trusted him and followed his lead."

Of course, as much as Lollapalooza was confronting weighty topics, it was also an assembly of rockers on the road. Which meant plenty of sex and drugs, and also everything from tour-bus mishaps and gear malfunctions to onstage brawls and firearm misadventures.

Ultimately, all of 1991's performers survived the arduous cross-country trek, and so did the fledging Lollapalooza. Which wasn't guaranteed: Festivals were far from a sure bet, or even much of a thing at all, in the US in 1991—Woodstock remained the touchstone, Altamont the cautionary tale, while Monterey Pop and the Newport Folk Festival were viewed as relics of a bygone era, even if the latter was still in operation. Even comparatively recent ones—the Texxas and California Jams, San Francisco's recurring Day on the Green, Steve Wozniak's two mammoth US Festivals—were stationary, at most once-a-year events. Ditto European traditions like Reading, Glastonbury, Pinkpop, Roskilde, and Isle of Wight.

And yet, Lollapalooza, a unique, traveling festival dominated by outside-the-mainstream acts and augmented with lifestyle attractions, proved to be a shining light in a summer concert season that, due to a combination of factors—among them a faltering economy and rising production costs—the *Los Angeles Times* reported as "the worst summer concert season in more than a decade" for live rock and pop performances, with artists like Whitney Houston and Huey Lewis, Diana Ross and David Lee Roth tanking at the box office. But similar to the Grateful Dead, '91's top-grossing live act and one of the year's few success stories, "the advantage of Lollapalooza is that they're trying to do more than provide a musical experience. It's something of a cultural event," Gary Bongiovanni, the editor of concert and music industry trade publication *Pollstar*, told *The New York Times*.

A new model had been established. "For a lot of people," says festival cofounder Don Muller, "their eyes got opened big time to the fact that this was a real force that they had to pay attention to."

Indeed they did. But it all could have gone bust, as soon as day one . . .

1 DAY ONE

KING COFFEY (drummer, Butthole Surfers) The first show was brutal. It was 120 degrees, I think, maybe only 110. Either way, you're in Arizona in the full sun in the daytime playing a show. And it's the first show, too, so you're still getting your bearings.

PAUL LEARY (guitarist, Butthole Surfers) It's weird what a guitar feels like in your hands when it's that hot. It feels like you're playing a sponge or something.

KEVIN LYMAN (stage manager, Lollapalooza 1991–92) We started at a place called Compton Terrace. The hottest place.

SEAN E SEAN (onstage performer, security, Body Count) Hot as *fish grease*.

ICE-T (MC; singer, Body Count) Too fucking hot for humans on the face of the fucking earth that day.

KEVIN LYMAN Our promoter there was Danny Zelisko, and he was still kind of young, he was alternative. I don't think he'd ever promoted anything that big at that point. I don't think anyone expected Lollapalooza to be that big.

STUART ROSS (tour director, Lollapalooza) Compton Terrace was Danny's venue, and it was an unusual venue. Because there was no real amphitheater in Phoenix at the time.

DANNY ZELISKO (promoter, Evening Star Productions) Compton Terrace was originally opened by Jess and Gene Nicks. Jess is Stevie Nicks's dad, and Gene is Jess's brother. And Stevie was the third owner. So Stevie Nicks was involved in the very first Lollapalooza. I think they started the tour there in part because I had a hand with Perry in moving the idea forward, and also because they didn't want to start in Los Angeles—they wanted to break it in and do it somewhere away from all the prying eyes of the press and the media.

STUART ROSS We certainly weren't going to start in Los Angeles. Or New York, you know? You want to be really good at what you're doing by the time you get to New York. But mostly, it probably had to do with routing, in trying to find venues that were available in the order we needed them to be available. Because one of the things, make no mistake about this, is that we opened doors at noon every day. And the show ended at 11:00 p.m. Between 11:00 p.m. and noon, we had to move this enormous amount of equipment and people from place to place, unload it, set it up, and get ready to open the doors. And that was a Herculean task. So the routing had to be precise, because this was not normal touring.

DANNY ZELISKO Compton Terrace was a nice venue, but it was in the middle of a desert. The place is southeast of the city and nobody was living there yet. And it did have a reputation for being difficult to get in and out of because the infrastructure just wasn't there. You walked in and there was a couple of pretty archaic refreshment stands and some bathrooms, and that was basically it as far as amenities. Although they did serve beer. But it was perfect for Lollapalooza because the show, it was a circus. They had all these vendors and crazy people selling everything from pipes and hookahs to clothing, tattoo artists, body painting . . .

PHIL BURKE (head rigger, Lollapalooza) We did our main production rehearsals there, so we were there almost a week before opening day. And yeah, it was pretty bad.

KEVIN LYMAN Some of it was still coming together. The production company was a big Australian contingent, Delicate Productions. Because Ted Gardner, being Australian, went with a company he knew and had worked with. They were also the sound company for Supertramp, so the Delicate guys talked about Supertramp a lot. But otherwise, a lot of these artists, their production teams, their crews, we weren't all, let's say, seasoned at that level of touring. It was, like, 117 degrees and we're trying to figure it out, readjust things.

MICHAEL "CURLY" JOBSON (stage manager, Lollapalooza 1991–92) We were dying. We went back to some golf resort; I didn't even make it into my room. I fell asleep in the grass 'cause it was cooler outside. You couldn't touch the steel of the stage; people's equipment was melting.

KEVIN LYMAN We were using technology that had never really been used too much. Moving lights, things like that.

PHIL BURKE We had something that we called the Reader Board that flew right over the stage. It was basically a really, really early-generation LED screen. Two-color. To put it in the context of its time, it would be like something you'd see driving down the freeway: "Accident Ahead," that kind of thing. It ran all day long and would carry social and political messaging as well as regular show messaging. It was definitely the first of its kind and it was purpose-built. I think everybody enjoyed goofing with it.

KEVIN LYMAN I'll never forget when Ice-T's tour bus pulled up during rehearsals and twenty-four people came off. It was like a mass of humanity coming off that bus.

SEAN E SEAN Ice had his rap squad out there, meaning Evil E., a DJ, two hype men. Then the rap crew, which could consist of up to, let's say, seven to eight people. Then you have Body Count, which was like seven people by themselves. Then we had a road manager. So Ice was out there with at least twenty, twenty-one guys, all on that one bus. Which was interesting. Chaotic at times.

KEVIN LYMAN Later that same evening, we were working so hard trying to get everything to work onstage. And I look over and there's this guy sitting on a road case watching us work, and that was Ice-T. I walked over and I introduced myself and I said, "What are you doing here? You're not sound-checking now." And he says, "I'm here to learn everything you guys do. I want to understand what you do." That really stuck with me forever. Everyone was at the hotel or doing whatever they were doing, and there's Ice-T in the middle of the evening, watching us put together a show.

MICHAEL "CURLY" JOBSON When it came to the show itself, the stage was badly designed, we were using forklifts to do changeovers with risers. Everything was super perilous. But we made it work. As you do.

KEVIN LYMAN It was very physical. We used big rolling riser systems; it was like a big dance of equipment onstage. If you flinched, you got run over.

JON KLEIN (guitarist, Siouxsie and the Banshees) I remember seeing almost a forklift accident, where the forklift was across a big ditch between a couple of little hills. I guess that was part of the adventure, wasn't it?

PHIL BURKE I had some experience with trucking a festival around, because I had done a little bit of that with the first Reggae Sunsplash tour here in the States. But that production was significantly smaller, not at the same level and certainly not at the same magnitude as Lollapalooza.

DANNY ZELISKO They were flying by the seat of their pants. And I'll tell you what, for this being in the middle of Phoenix, 110 degrees, the first time this show ever saw the light of day, it was fantastic. Nothing short of a miracle.

DANNY FLAIM (roadie, projectionist, Butthole Surfers) No one really knew each other yet. I remember Siouxsie and the Banshees' dressing room had an adjoining sliding glass door in Phoenix, but me and King were too scared to talk to them because it was like, "That's Siouxsie and the Banshees!" But they turned out to be the nicest people in the world.

COREY GLOVER (singer, Living Colour) I was in awe of Siouxsie Sioux, because her music was something I grew up with. She felt, like, untouchable to me.

JON KLEIN My old roadie, a South London geezer, had turned up, and he was in a dressing room that was right alongside the main stage. And he said, "Oh, come in here." I didn't know at the time it was the Butthole Surfers' dressing room, and he'd been chopping out lines of amphetamines. I don't know what kind of crystal or what kind of speed, but you [*snorts*] and you get that kind of stabbing-in-the-eye sensation and everything kind of goes fast for a while. And then this huge, six-foot-plus man walks in and he goes, "Hey there! How many people you've never seen before in your fucking life in your own dressing room!" And I'm just like, "Oh, hello." I go over and shake his hand, and he grabs my hand and he goes, "Hey, meet my *wart*! I'm seeding at the moment!" That was the first time I met Gibby Haynes.

CHRIS HASKETT (guitarist, Rollins Band) That first show is where I met Vernon Reid. I came offstage and he's sitting on the couch, wanting to say hello. I was like . . . [*gasps*].

PERRY FARRELL I remember running into Ice-T for the first time on the backstage grounds. He looked at me and he said, "Perry, you a playa!" I was all dressed up. I had just come from Miami and I had on a Che Guevara shirt and this, like, cheap gold-plated watch. But it was gigantic. So he thought I had a lot of money or something, I don't know. I mean, he probably knew I didn't, but he just called me a playa. I never forgot that. That was a great compliment to me.

DANNY ZELISKO We did the show pretty much without incident.

STEVEN SEVERIN (bassist, Siouxsie and the Banshees) Well, it kicked off at midday with the spectacularly untalented Henry Rollins and his knuckle-draggers, followed by some lovely hillbilly psych rock from the Surfers, then some shameless faux chaos from Nine Inch Nails, all bar the vocals on tape, fifty-dollar guitars especially bought to be trashed on cue. The Who, they weren't.

HENRY ROLLINS (singer, Rollins Band) By the time Nine Inch Nails were out there, it could get really hot.

JON KLEIN They were running their tape machine on a TEAC four-track cassette-like thing. A rack-mounted Portastudio, effectively. And I guess the rubber bands in that just melted.

SEAN E SEAN Trent Reznor, he was *pissed*. It was like, "Uh-oh, this is how we starting off?"

ICE-T It was a lot of equipment to make that show sound the way it sounded. And shit went bad.

FRITZ MICHAUD (monitor engineer, Nine Inch Nails) I don't think any of us really knew what we were doing. None of us had done any shows that size.

TRENT REZNOR (singer, multi-instrumentalist, producer, Nine Inch Nails) Our equipment was . . . duct tape and homemade cases. It wasn't pro-level gear we were touring with. And I look, and there's Living Colour, and they've got . . . shit that looks like Guitar Center racks, put together properly, professional job, stenciled logos on the side of their . . . they had cases! I thought, Man, we don't have our shit together. We didn't have any money, but we didn't know any better.

RICHARD PATRICK (guitarist, Nine Inch Nails) Nine Inch Nails, there's stuff that you just can't reproduce live. You could bring fifteen guys out and it would sound, you know, *kinda-sorta* like the record. So we had to bring sequencers out that play a good chunk of the music. So Trent would sing and play guitar. I would play guitar and sing backups. We had a keyboard player playing the main keyboard line, we had a drummer, and we had a sequencer. And the sequencer was on the stage, on the drum riser, and it was plugged into a faulty quad box. Every time the riser moved it would short out. And we can't play without it. Period. There's just no way.

MARKY RAY (guitar tech, Nine Inch Nails) What happened was, the drum rack is plugged into some quad box at the back of the stage, AC power 110. And we're two thirds of the way through "Terrible Lie," basically our first song, and then, all of a sudden, everything just goes *woo*. Drum rack dies, drums are dead except for the acoustic drums, and the guitars go dead. It happened instantly. And we're like, "What the fuck?" Trent's looking at us, so we run back to the back of the stage, we see the quad box, it's shorting out. We plug the thing back in, comes back up. We finish "Terrible Lie," go into "Sin." We're like a bar or two into "Sin" and it goes out again. And Trent just goes *berserk*. He fucking trashes the stage, storms off, and he says, "Fire everyone." We're all standing there with our dicks in our hands.

RICHARD PATRICK We were so emotionally pissed off about it that we just trashed everything. Threw our guitars around, destroyed the stage, walked off.

MARC GEIGER (agent; cofounder, Lollapalooza) I ran back and watched the band going onto the bus. I get on the bus with them to go, "Blah, blah, blah," and MTV comes in behind me with cameras. Then they're filming Trent. At that point, I just keep to the background. It's sort of a famous interview. It's online. Trent's fairly calm, cool, and collected, saying what happened.

RICHARD PATRICK Trent handled it perfectly. Actually, he didn't. He said something about an incompetent crew. And so the crews of Lollapalooza were fucking furious with us. We had really pissed everybody off, day one.

TRENT REZNOR (MTV interview, July 18, 1991) *"I guess what happened is a lot of our equipment in the back was sitting in the sun for quite a long time, baking in the desert heat. And since we are an electronic-based kind of band, when the main part of your sound becomes ruined and melted, which I think is what happened, it was cutting out and just becoming a nightmare. And that, complemented with incompetence on the crew part, led to a disastrous embarrassing situation."*

MARKY RAY The Lollapalooza crews took that very harshly. Curly Jobson, Kevin Lyman, they all took that personally.

MICHAEL "CURLY" JOBSON I didn't enjoy reading something like that in the paper when it was something they brought upon themselves. Especially about people who were working in very difficult circumstances. It didn't go down too well, blaming a bunch of guys that were busting their asses to get it done. I don't think anybody in the crew turned their backs on them, but I think there was a little bit of an acrid taste in the mouth for a few days.

DANNY ZELISKO Nine Inch Nails were getting ten grand for the show, and somebody came to get paid. I said, "You didn't play! Why am I paying you?" And remember—Nine Inch Nails was not *NINE INCH NAILS* at that time. They were nobodies. But it wasn't me being rude to them. It was like, "Why would you ask to get paid when you didn't play?" I went through this whole litany of things: "You knew it was gonna be hot . . ."

Finally, Ted Gardner comes to me and he goes, "Look, Danny, you're paying them." He goes, "Don't look at it like you're paying them money and they didn't play. Their name was on the bill, right? We used them to promote the show, right? They came here to play, right?" I go, "Yeah . . . but they didn't!" Ted says, "Doesn't matter. Pay them."

There comes a point where you stop being stubborn, and I was hoping Ted Gardner would reach that point before me. He didn't. I paid.

RICHARD PATRICK This is also just the kind of chaos that could erupt onstage. I mean, there was a lot of turmoil between the members of Jane's

Addiction. This was supposed to be their last tour. Dave and Perry actually got into a fight onstage that first night.

CHRIS CUFFARO (photographer) I was shooting Jane's Addiction at that first show, and I sat backstage in the dressing room with the guys before their set. During that time, Dave was struggling with his problems. Perry was doing his shit, and Stephen was as happy as he is today. Eric was never anywhere to be found. But backstage there was just this bad mood. I don't know what anybody else told you, but it was just there. It was very stressful. And then, you know, the heat didn't help.

NIKKI GARDNER (assistant to Ted Gardner; special groups coordinator, Lollapalooza) The band themselves were on two buses. Eric was clean at that point in time, and Stuart was actually on Eric's bus. Ted and I were on the other bus, and David used to switch between the two. When he was managing to get clean, he would go over with Eric because Eric wanted to be clean.

DAVE NAVARRO (guitarist, Jane's Addiction) I was really wanting to get clean, but it was really hard on that tour. So I went back and forth quite a bit.

TED GARDNER (manager, Jane's Addiction; cofounder, Lollapalooza) Dave was really like the child within a divorce. Do I go with Eric and get sober? Do I stay with Perry and, you know, continue doing what we're doing? Dave was desperate to get clean. Perry was not desperate to get clean. So that caused a great deal of friction within the band.

T. C. CONROY (front-of-house coordinator, Lollapalooza 1991) So here we are in Arizona, and Dave Navarro shows up, and as far as I can tell, he doesn't want to go onstage because he doesn't have the right guitar. I mean, this is the vibe, right? And, you know, this is Perry's day. So Perry's pissed, everyone's pissed. It's tense and it's 120 degrees and people are acting like assholes. Now, my boyfriend at the time was Dave Gahan from Depeche Mode, and we lived together, and it was my birthday. So I was in Arizona, and he was coming from L.A. to join me at the show.

And Dave's guitar that he wanted was at a pawnshop in Hollywood. It was still early in the day, so I said, "Hey, can you go pick up Dave Navarro's guitar on your way?" So he goes and gets the guitar, gets on a plane, and a few hours later he and Depeche Mode's manager, Jonathan Kessler, pull into the backstage area in Arizona in a long black stretch limo. Dave Gahan saves the day.

DAVE NAVARRO God, that's very nice. I don't remember that. But Dave Gahan had always been very supportive and kind to us, and obviously we love him, so if that happened, I will take the opportunity right now to say, "Thanks."

T. C. CONROY The guitar gets there, but, I mean, the tone was set. It didn't fix anything. It just took away one excuse.

CHRIS CUFFARO So first night in Arizona, Jane's is performing, and toward the end of the set, Dave's kind of running around, bumping into Perry and just doing his thing. I'm trying to get pictures, and I'm like, "What the fuck is this all about?" I never saw this before. And then Dave trashes his stacks and throws his guitar into the audience. Dave walks off and then Perry walks off and then they start fighting off the side of the stage.

DAVE NAVARRO I had gotten too high on heroin and I couldn't really get up. So then I was given cocaine by an unnamed source that got me too speedy. Then I had to come down from that, so I took a handful of pills and drank a bunch. By the time I got onstage, I didn't know which way was up. And Perry and I got into it.

MISSY WORTH (marketing consultant, Lollapalooza 1991) I was at the soundboard, watching all of it. It's been super hot. It *is* super hot. Tensions were high and they weren't getting along. And they went at it, in front of everyone, onstage.

PERRY FARRELL I thought we were *off* the stage. I didn't know that we were on the stage. Were we? No, I don't think so. Not on the stage. I waited until we were off the stage. The problem was, we got off the stage and Dave didn't want to go back out. That's what that was. And I don't feel good about that at all. That was a stupid thing to do and I really regret it.

MICHAEL "CURLY" JOBSON I think it was about Dave not wanting to play an encore. And look, Perry, spindly little dude. But one of the toughest men you're ever gonna meet. You wouldn't wanna get into it with him.

MISSY WORTH No, no. Because he goes *crazy*.

MICHAEL "CURLY" JOBSON And he just knocked Dave around, you know? I'm pretty sure that Perry would've knocked me around if he had chosen to. So Dave didn't have a hope.

PAUL V. (national director of alternative radio promotion, Warner Bros. Records) I've heard that Ted Gardner was ready to punch Dave in the face.

NIKKI GARDNER Okay, this is a picture—it's from the nineties, so it's not very clear. But Ted is kneeling beside David on the floor backstage in Arizona . . . and punching the shit out of him. Perry is lying beside them, trying to calm the situation down.

PERRY FARRELL Ted reminded me a lot of a wrestler. I'm not sure that he *wasn't* an amateur wrestler in Australia. And not, like, "amateur collegiate." I think he might've messed around with pro wrestling. I don't know if I can really get too deep into detail on how he would get Dave back out on a stage, but just know that it was very aggressive and it was very hard to say no when Ted wanted you back out there.

NIKKI GARDNER This was literally backstage while the fans were cheering for an encore. And I believe they did go back on and do one.

CHRIS CUFFARO So they come out for the encore. And what I remember is that Dave is running around, body-checking Perry and trying to knock him over. Perry's trying to sing and it was . . . weird. And instead of taking pictures, I'm just in shock about what is going on. I would've been a lousy press photographer. At the crash of the zeppelin I would've been standing there going, "This thing's up in flames!" With a camera in my hand, you know?

DON MULLER (agent; cofounder, Lollapalooza) We were all kinda looking at each other going, "Shit, we probably won't make it to the next show." We were free-falling at that point.

DAVE NAVARRO I take responsibility for that. I was the one that was fucked up, and I was the one who made it difficult for everybody.

KEVIN LYMAN The tour could have collapsed right there.

DAVE NAVARRO I didn't have any questions as to whether it was going to go on. I knew it was. We're not going to put together this tour and then not do it.

DANNY ZELISKO We drew twelve thousand people at twenty-five dollars a head. Thirty bucks day-of. Compton Terrace held a lot more people than that, but twelve thousand people in any space, that's a lot of people. And they all had a blast.

CHRIS HASKETT I remember at the end of the gig, me and our soundman, Theo, who was a full band member, we see the crew from Delicate Productions, which was the PA company, and they're putting these boxes in the trucks. Now, I'm a CBGB, 9:30 Club guy, right? You see something that needs to go in a truck, you pick it up, you carry it into the truck. So we grabbed some gear and starting moving it. And somebody in charge, it wasn't Kevin Lyman, but somebody, was like, "Get out!" And the crew goes, "Why are you throwing them out? What did they do?" The guy points at me, "He's in the opening band." And then he points at Theo. "And he's a soundman!" He's like, "We can't have musicians moving gear!" So we got thrown out of the trucks for helping.

KEVIN LYMAN You weren't supposed to touch the equipment, if that makes sense. A union person was supposed to carry the drum kit or move the risers. But for us the only way to make it work was to be all hands on deck.

KING COFFEY Everybody's equipment got shoved onto eighteen-wheelers. So everything had to be on wheels and in hard-core cases. Which was daunting for us, because up to that point everything the Butthole Surfers had just fit in a van. We didn't have, like, big industrial rolling cases for the drums. We had to spend a couple thousand dollars to get the cases up to spec.

JON KLEIN I should have counted the buses—it looked like fifty forty-foot buses, at least. That kind of number. I don't know what were the increments of time management for getting the whole thing struck, shipped across the state lines, set up, and ready to start another show, how tight that was, but the logistics were impressive.

KEVIN LYMAN I'll just never forget that first load-out. The promotor, Danny, was well known for having tons of strippers hanging around backstage.

DANNY ZELISKO I'm sure there were! Back in the day, strippers came to a lot of the good rock shows. That was something that was always a fun sight.

KEVIN LYMAN I was yelling at Danny because we didn't have enough crew for load-out. And I look at him and I look at the strippers and I go, "Maybe they could help me load the trucks."

DANNY ZELISKO I don't recall having any sort of ownership rights or any ability to direct anybody to do anything, but, you know, dumber things have happened. I'm just going to trust that Kevin's memory is better than mine. He was the one that was running the load-out after that insane day.

NIKKI GARDNER Nobody really knew what we were doing. It was just mayhem.

MICHAEL "CURLY" JOBSON We were still ragamuffin. We were kind of gypsy. Nowadays it's hi-vis vests and we're driven by health and safety. But we were driving forklifts into the middle of the audience to go fix a barricade. My way of allocating stagehands to a load-out was to write the names down on Post-its, like sticky white things, and put them on their shirts.

KEVIN LYMAN It took us a long time to load out. And then we headed to San Diego. I was struggling, to be honest. I think I got heatstroke or some sort of heat thing. The next show, we were down in San Diego at the school, in the stadium [Devore Stadium, at Southwestern College in Chula Vista]. We worked really hard all day long, we get through it. And I walked into the production office and collapsed into a pile of towels. I passed out.

2 "THE MOST INTENSE THING I'VE EVER SEEN DONE ON A STAGE"

CHRIS HASKETT (guitarist, Rollins Band) How the Rollins Band got on Lollapalooza, it's a fluke where I think when they first put the bill together, their kind of really left-field-indie opening band was the Butthole Surfers. There were originally six bands on the bill. But we did two weeks opening for Jane's Addiction in the spring of 1991 . . .

HENRY ROLLINS (singer, Rollins Band) We were touring with them, our little van following their bus. And on one of the days I was told to fall in to the Jane's bus because Perry wanted to talk to me. I had never been on a tour bus before. I sat in the back lounge with him and he explained this thing he was going to call Lollapalooza. He gave me the particulars and asked me what I thought. I said it sounded like it would be great.

CHRIS HASKETT I don't think Rollins Band ever said no to a gig. So the Butthole Surfers got moved from the bottom slot.

ANDREW WEISS (bassist, Rollins Band) We were playing at, like, noon or twelve thirty or something. You roll out of bed, drink some coffee, and then go play. And it was kinda weird—most of the gigs on that tour were sheds. And usually the inside of the shed was all reserved seats and then the lawn was general admission. So a lot of times when we went onstage, it was surreal—maybe 10 percent of the seats in the shed would be filled, and then you'd look and, like, a quarter mile away up on the hill, in the grass area, there'd be a swirling mosh pit going on.

MISSY WORTH (marketing consultant, Lollapalooza 1991) I tried to get people to want to come earlier. But they had seats—they didn't have to. To this day, I still have people complaining about this. Not about Lollapalooza, but in general. It's the problem of an amphitheater.

CHRIS HASKETT If you got your binoculars and looked up to the far part of the grass at the back of the hill, those were the tickets our fans could afford. But I think we thrived on that. We were coming out of a scene where you had no expectation that you were ever going to be playing to crowds this big. So there's no reason not to do exactly what you want and do it in a way that you're really proud of. So it was like, "We gotta go on first in the daytime to a bunch of Siouxsie and the Banshees fans? Fuck it, turn it up!" That was very much the ethic. Which, I think, is a very "Henry" ethic.

ICE-T (MC; singer, Body Count) I was not aware of how devastating a lead singer Henry Rollins was. I knew him from Black Flag, but Rollins Band is a whole 'nother groovy, dark, hard-core shit. I stole a lot of my stage presence from Henry Rollins, just watching him on that tour. How he would get into that vibe and stuff.

DAVE KENDALL (creator, host, MTV's *120 Minutes*) Henry Rollins, his way of dealing with the heat was to do pull-ups on the doorframe of the rooms in the compound somewhere. That's how I met him; walking up and he was just doing pull-ups. I'm like, okay . . .

PERRY FARRELL He looked like a pro wrestler, like one of those figures you can get at Target today.

ICE-T I used to see him on the side of the stage, listening to "Welcome to the Terrordome" by Public Enemy, hopping around barefoot with his shirt off, getting ready to go onstage. I'm thinking, This is a bad motherfucker right here!

HENRY ROLLINS For me, it was just playing. Took some getting used to. Oh-nine-hundred hours. Get up, brush your teeth, stick your head in the sink, change up, and start stretching because you're on in twenty minutes. We played in front of a fraction of what all the other bands played in front of but we felt lucky to be on the tour at all.

CHRIS HASKETT I remember one time we came offstage, drenched as we always were. And Gibby Haynes is there, and he's holding a glass. And he hands the glass to Henry and he goes [*in a serious voice*], "Water?" And . . . it was straight vodka. Henry only smelled it at the last moment, so he didn't drink it. I think he was annoyed . . . and also amused. Because how mad can you get at Gibby? Unless you're actually in a band with him.

KING COFFEY (drummer, Butthole Surfers) The Rollins Band and Butthole Surfers were probably the two closest in style as far as our backgrounds and our approach.

JIM GREER (senior editor, *SPIN* magazine) Rollins is definitely an acquired taste. But, I mean, Rollins and Butthole Surfers, one after the other . . .

CHRIS HASKETT We were on first, they were on second. And the coolest thing we did—I'm pretty sure it was me and [Butthole Surfers bassist Jeff] Pinkus that came up with this—was, "What if we did the transition between the two bands via jam?" So there were four occasions where we had both bands' gear set up onstage at the same time, and we wrote a very simple, kind of dirge-ish riff, with a verse and a chorus and lots of notes. It was really easy. We got together, everybody learned it. And then at the end of our set, they would come out onstage and we'd play the last four or five minutes of our set doing this jam with them, into the first four or five minutes of their set. I know there are two extant recordings of it. It's just called "Jam with the Butthole Surfers."

HENRY ROLLINS Those jams were so cool. Suddenly, it's Gibby and I and all those guitars. It drove Kevin Lyman a little nuts logistically, but we had a good time.

CHRIS HASKETT The first jam was great. And the second one was pretty good. And then, I think it was the drummer for Nine Inch Nails who was like, "Hey, can I come out?" Sure! And then it was Mooseman and a couple of the other guys from Body Count. Next thing you know, Eric Avery's been given a guitar. Now Jon Klein from Siouxsie is playing. The last time we did it, there was just an absurd number of people from other bands onstage.

JON KLEIN (guitarist, Siouxsie and the Banshees) As a guitar player, I was a bit jealous 'cause I felt our set was quite subtle, and everyone else was making a right royal racket. Like, "It's cool to be heavy metal in America again! That's not fair!"

ERIC AVERY (bassist, Jane's Addiction) I played regularly with the Rollins Band. I played regularly with the Butthole Surfers. It was a very, very musical experience, which was really great.

ANDREW WEISS The Butthole Surfers, they're one of my favorite bands of all time. There was one show of theirs, at the old Ritz in New York City, 1987, that was hands down the best show I've ever seen in my life. In that period, '86 to '88, their shit was *intense*. It was sensory overload, with the projections and the lights and the strobes and the smoke and the dancing girls and all that. What they were doing on Lollapalooza, although I still enjoyed the shit out of it, was relatively toned down.

JIM GREER They were a fantastic live band . . . but in a dark, smoky club at midnight, where Gibby's setting the cymbals on fire and it actually felt dangerous. But in the middle of the day, in a festival setting?

TOM BUNCH (manager, Butthole Surfers) It was hard for them to replicate what they were known for, but it was a huge opportunity and we did the best we could to adapt to it.

KING COFFEY Lollapalooza was a totally different vibe for us. Plus, outdoors. I think we work best when it's dark and claustrophobic. So us doing our shtick in broad daylight at three in the afternoon, it was, Okay, this isn't about us. This isn't our show. We're just the warm-up act here . . . or one of many warm-up acts.

PAUL LEARY (guitarist, Butthole Surfers) We didn't get to run our projectors or strobe lights or any of that stuff. I think we were down to smoke machines.

KING COFFEY So we tried to do more cheap theatrics. Like the shotgun . . .

HENRY ROLLINS I think that was easily the most intense thing I've ever seen done on a stage. It only lasted a show or two. Kevin had to put an end to it. The band would go out there, and then their road crew guy—his name was Danny Flaim, as I remember—walked out to Gibby dragging a shotgun by the stock. He gives it to Gibby. Gibby racks it so the mic picks it up. "I didn't see any of you dancing to the Rollins Band!" He then shoots the gun into the audience.

GIBBY HAYNES (singer, Butthole Surfers) I bought what they call popper loads. They're dog-training shotgun loads that don't have any buckshot in 'em. But they're louder than a real shotgun shell because they're meant to freak out a dog.

HENRY ROLLINS Of course, there's no shot in the rounds, but the fire and report were enormous. People panicked. It wasn't anything I would have ever done to an audience. How could they possibly have known? It was completely insane.

TOM BUNCH It was . . . *Boooom!* The first two, three thousand people could feel it. Just the wadding and the force of the gunpowder blast, I mean, it would blow your chest open. Gibby would come out and shoot it a few times and get everybody's attention, and everybody went *ooh* and *ahh*. Then a song or two later he would toss a beach ball up in the air and blow it to bits, and that got everybody going again.

KING COFFEY We really tried to impress.

COREY GLOVER (singer, Living Colour) I saw this man with a shotgun as, "This is a representation of who he is and what kind of person he is."

And it wasn't out of violence, which I thought was fascinating. It was like, "This is how I show my joy. I'm having a good time and I'm gonna whoop it up and shoot it up."

KEVIN LYMAN I don't think you could do that now. I don't know if you'd get away with it.

HENRY ROLLINS Your entire family tree would get sued.

ICE-T You know, when we came out, we came out shooting guns, too. But I wanted Gibby's shotgun.

PAUL LEARY Ice-T goes, "Oh, I'm up here with my little peashooter, and you've got that twelve-gauge pump."

GIBBY HAYNES Those guys were totally in love with it. They were like, "Holy shit, man!" We totally bonded over that.

CHRIS HASKETT We played one date in Canada [at CNE Grandstand in Toronto], and I just remember that the Canadian customs officials confiscated the Buttholes' shotgun. Even though it didn't have a functioning firing pin . . . at least, I don't think it did. In any case, they confiscated it. But then the Body Count bus had, like, guns! Real ones. And they got through. I don't know how that happened.

ERNIE C The guns just stayed under the bus, and you don't say nothin'. Don't ask, don't tell, you know? We mixed 'em in with our road equipment. Kevin Lyman did that—he just didn't know it!

KEVIN LYMAN I don't know if they had any guns. But if they did, customs didn't find them. But I know those guys did get in trouble because they had porn on the bus. They got fined or something. But they made the show.

JON KLEIN I remember when we got to Toronto I went and watched the Surfers, and it was a more football-stadium-y type space. It was quite empty in the front half of the venue except around the stage, where there was maybe a thousand kids that had come to check out the band. And Gibby, he walks onstage and smashes a Jack Daniel's bottle across his head—he'd got these fake wax bottles made up, but I didn't know. I said, "Wow! This geezer's for real!"

TOM BUNCH The breakaway bottles, well, you can order 'em online now, but back then we had to find prop shops and places like that. Before each one of the shows, we had to show the fire officials and the police the guns and the breakaway bottles and all that stuff. We didn't want them rushing onstage thinking people were killing each other with these things. We had to get approval.

CHRIS HASKETT Toward the end of the tour that year, Gibby went around collecting as much women's clothing as he could fit into, grabbed his shotgun and a beer, and walked out onstage in the middle of the Banshees' set. It was hilarious.

JON KLEIN That was in Denver, at Fiddler's Green [Amphitheatre]. Sioux had met Gibby and it was, "All right, Gibby's coming on tonight to do 'Helter Skelter'!" Now, the Banshees had covered that one on a really early album, but we hadn't rehearsed it. It was like the rule of "Helter Skelter": We're just going to do it one night, but you're not allowed to rehearse it. So you better know it! So it was decided Gibby was coming on to do it, and I said, "Well, can we get his guitar player on, too? He's great." "Yeah, all right, but you can't practice it." I grabbed Paul and we kind of learned it up a little bit anyway.

PAUL LEARY We were all hanging out, playing on each other's sets. What else were you going to do?

JON KLEIN So that night in Denver we had an extra little guitar and amp out, and we built this song into the end of the set. Paul turns up at the side of the stage, we plug him in and we let the guitar start feeding back to get things going. Now we're doing "Helter Skelter," and there's no sign of Gibby anywhere. Then about halfway through, I look over at the side of the stage and . . . it looked like one of the Golden Girls, you know, the tall one in the *Golden Girls* sitcom? I see this large human in a big floral dress and a huge wig. And of course, it's Gibby. He just walks out onstage, without a microphone, and starts stripping. I may be wrong, but in my memory, I seem to recall he had a Dr Pepper can gaffered to his knob.

STEVEN SEVERIN (bassist, Siouxsie and the Banshees) We did know Gibby would be joining us. We didn't know he'd come as Norman Bates's mother brandishing a firearm.

JON KLEIN It was all a bit *Silence of the Lambs* last scene.

CHRIS HASKETT He stripped off his clothes and fired the gun. Then Siouxsie sees him and she's like, "What the fuck is this?" She's just trying to carry on. Maybe she tackled him, I don't remember.

PAUL LEARY I had my eyes closed and was just jamming out. I opened my eyes and looked down and there's Gibby and Siouxsie and they're wrestling over the shotgun, with two sets of hands grasping at the trigger . . . and the thing's pointed right at my head. I jumped like ten feet in the air. It was like seeing a rattlesnake.

JON KLEIN Then Sioux suddenly stops and goes, "Right! Everyone—get him!" And we all just kind of piled on Gibby. It ended up this pile of bodies in the middle of the stage, with a few guitar necks sticking out of it. A sonic sculpture kind of moment.

GIBBY HAYNES It wasn't the last time Siouxsie tackled me. And it might not have been the first.

PAUL LEARY There was real terror out there. That shotgun could've blown my head off!

STEVEN SEVERIN After a slightly awkward beginning, the Butthole Surfers were the band Siouxsie and the Banshees bonded with the most. I hung out with Gibby a lot. We shared a similar sense of humor and a certain cynicism about this new "alternative" music tag. Great band, great people. It's probably a Texan thing. My wife is from Beaumont.

GIBBY HAYNES We used to go into the Banshees' dressing room and take the Gouda off their deli tray so that we could say we stole Siouxsie and the band's cheese. It's a pun—the highest form of humor.

PAUL LEARY I was pretty surprised to see how many people were showing up night after night after night at Lollapalooza. It was like, "Holy cow!" It was like going to the moon—none of it seemed real. Because for a long time before that, radio wouldn't even say our name.

JIM GREER The Butthole Surfers probably won over some fans. Because they did end up getting signed to a major label, and they did end up getting produced by John Paul Jones, and they did end up with a minor hit . . . which was a direct rip-off of Beck's "Loser." But that's beside the point.

TOM BUNCH We actually signed to Capitol right before Lollapalooza. So the tour helped, but it was one of maybe ten or twelve things that were happening at the time that raised the band's profile substantially. I like to say the mainstream moved more toward us than we did toward them.

KING COFFEY At that point the name was still pretty taboo. Sometimes it was B Surfers or BH Surfers. But then family newspapers were saying "Butthole Surfers." So that was one thing.

PAUL LEARY I think Lollapalooza helped soften people up to the word "butthole." Next thing you know, they're saying it as much as they can, because it's fun to say!

3 "BODY COUNT'S IN THE HOUSE"

DAVE KENDALL (creator, host, MTV's *120 Minutes*) That first Lollapalooza lineup is actually fantastic because it was so broad-ranged. Going from the sort of guitar rock of Jane's Addiction to Siouxsie and the Banshees, stalwarts of the British goth and post-punk scenes, and then Living Colour, Nine Inch Nails on the industrial tip, the Butthole Surfers, the Rollins Band . . .

And then you had Ice-T. This was not the first crossover between rock and hip-hop, but it was certainly an early crossover between alternative and hip-hop. It was significant.

ROB TANNENBAUM (journalist, author) You had three Black rock bands that first year—Living Colour, Ice-T with Body Count, and, on a few dates, Fishbone. I don't think that Perry Farrell did this in any sort of manipulative way. I think he just liked the music.

ERNIE C (guitarist, Body Count) Body Count was out there and so was Living Colour. But there was nothing similar about us. Only thing similar is we're Black!

NORWOOD FISHER (bassist, Fishbone) Perry came to us asking us to do Lollapalooza, the first one, and I was down with it. We should be riding with the homie, you know? And on some level it was a natural environment. We were a Black band, but our audience was largely white.

ANGELO MOORE (singer, saxophonist, Fishbone) Flies in the buttermilk. But I just thought to myself, It's shitloads of people coming out to Lollapalooza, and we gotta make 'em believers, man! We gotta *transform* them so that when they leave out of the gate they'll be talking about us for years to come.

CHRIS DOWD (keyboardist, trombonist, Fishbone) Us and Ice-T, we had already known each other, too, from back when L.A. had its first hip-hop club, the Radio. Because people didn't know what to do with us, ever, as a band, we ended up getting put on these crazy shows, and some of 'em were, like, Fishbone with Run-D.M.C. and Ice-T. So when Body Count and all that stuff happened, I always felt like that was because maybe Ice would see us play and see the reaction and be like, "I wanna do some rock shit like that!"

ICE-T (MC; singer, Body Count) There's a big misconception with Ice-T and Body Count that my rap followers have a problem with me doing something else. Not really. It's always people that aren't really your fans that are always trying to wave a flag and say, "Oh, you shouldn't like him because he's doing *this*." But your real fans rock with you. So my fans are like, "Yo, if Ice wants to rock, he wants to rock." I've had other people that aren't real fans say, "You're going to lose your hip-hop cred." I'm like, "Shut the fuck up."

ERNIE C When it came time to do Lollapalooza, Perry put Ice on for forty-five, sixty minutes. Then Ice turned around and said to me, "Let's also put the band on."

ICE-T I knew Perry, because I worked with him on his movie, *Gift*. Perry was trying to do the song "N****r/Whitey" with Sly Stone for that, but I think Sly was not easy to get connected with. Ernie knew Perry, and Ernie suggested that I do it instead.

ERNIE C I was playing with Ice, but back in the day I also used to be a messenger in L.A. One day I was delivering packages to this management company, and I see Perry Farrell. He was talking to someone, and he said he was going to do this song, "Don't Call Me N****r, Whitey," by Sly Stone. He wanted to do it for a movie he was working on. This is around 1990. So he and I start talking and I say, "I know Sly Stone." And everyone's like, "Who are you?" "I'm the messenger." "Can you get Sly Stone?" "Yes, I can get Sly Stone."

But Sly was in a rehab. He couldn't make it. So I said to Perry, "You know this guy Ice-T?" He said, "Yeah, I know Ice-T." I said, "Can we get him instead? Because Sly can't make it." He said, "Yes, I'd love that." Ice was over at Record One working with Quincy Jones, and I called him up and said, "Can you get here?" He drove over after he was finished.

PERRY FARRELL We sang that Sly Stone song together and it played over the rolling credits at the very end of the film. That was the first time we met each other. I remember I had a switchblade in my back pocket and I whipped it out. But Ice-T, he's used to being in dangerous situations, so he kinda liked me. We had a good laugh about it and then we just decided to be friends.

ICE-T That's how it started. Then later, Perry says, "I got a tour coming along. It's very eclectic. Why don't you come out as the rapper?" Of course I said, "Hell, yeah." There was never any intention to have Body Count out there, but as time developed, Perry told me I had a sixty-minute set. I'm like, "Wow, I got sixty minutes?" And I asked him, "I can do whatever I want within that sixty minutes?" He said, "Whatever you want." And that's when I decided to split the set and bring the band.

CHRIS HASKETT (guitarist, Rollins Band) Ice-T was doing, I think, two-thirds his own rap show and one-third Body Count.

ICE-T Was it the first time we were performing for all-white audiences? As a rock band, yes. Not as a rap band. Because you gotta remember, the eclectic rock tour or rap tour was only new to the United States. The festivals in Europe had been going on for years. What people don't understand is that rap, it was all Black when it was in the 'hood. But Black kids can't afford those big concert tickets. The white kids economically could afford to pay two hundred, three hundred dollars to go to a concert. A Black kid's like, "I'll wait till I see you in the 'hood!"

ERNIE C Body Count only played for fifteen minutes on that tour because we didn't have a lot of music. We didn't have an album. We only knew, like, five songs, but we knew those five songs really good.

SEAN E SEAN (onstage performer, security, Body Count) That was our first big tour like that. Before that we had just done some local shows, which were good, but nothing on the magnitude of Lollapalooza. That was new for us.

CHRIS HASKETT They were groundbreaking. I mean, the music itself was not that different from a lot of the stuff like Anthrax and things like that. But to have it done back then by people of color, and by an artist who is predominantly known from hip-hop and rap, that was great. That was punk, right?

MARC GEIGER (agent; cofounder, Lollapalooza) We were very conscious of where music was, of being in touch with kids and street culture, and that hip-hop was street culture. And this was West Coast, which was scarier than East Coast—more guns, more gangs. So with Lollapalooza we were putting things out there that would challenge society. The good news was we were putting them in a safe box for people to open and look at.

PERRY FARRELL Body Count were fucking amazing, but in those days it wasn't very common—it still isn't very common—for a bunch of Black kids to get together and blaze on metal.

ICE-T I always said Living Colour was the Black band on Lollapalooza. We were the n****rs.

COREY GLOVER (singer, Living Colour) I got the sense that they thought we were a little more, um, seasoned than they were. But nothing could be further from the truth. At that point we were all out there trying to make a living and we were all out there doing interesting things.

ICE-T The thing of it is that I got nothing but respect for Living Colour. Living Colour is a phenomenal rock band who we really admire, and who were already on the top of the charts. But of course us coming in from hip-hop, our whole image, it was kinda like, "Okay, these are gonna be the rowdy Black cats." And you know, that's who we were. That's how we let it go.

ERNIE C Some of the songs we started just playing for the first time in front of people. I know we played "There Goes the Neighborhood." We did "Body Count's in the House." Might have played "KKK Bitch." We played "Cop Killer" for the first time onstage at Lollapalooza. And we did it every night.

SEAN E SEAN That was the Rodney King era. And at that time we in the band were still having a lot of drama with the police. But you know, we had people that identified with what we were going through. People were conscious of law overreaching. And it was the perfect setting for us at the time because Ice got a chance to explain himself. He would start by saying "Not *all* cops." Okay? "It's the ones who use their badge to take advantage of their position. Police brutality is a real thing." He would explain himself as far as what he was against. "Cop Killer," it's just a protest record.

RICHARD PATRICK (guitarist, Nine Inch Nails) Ice-T brought that to the forefront and talked about it. And you could kind of understand it a little bit more through what he was saying. He was pressing the buttons on that tour.

SEAN E SEAN His number-one enemy was racism. "KKK Bitch," that's a sing-along song! But at some point you have to be paying attention to what these lyrics are actually saying. And the more we went along on that tour, the more the audience knew the songs.

ERNIE C I never even looked at the audience as a white audience. I just looked at it as, "This is the music I play and this is who's coming to see it." As far as racism, I didn't see it at all. And we played Kansas. We played Montana. I mean, we played some obscure places.

JO LENARDI (vice president of alternative marketing, Warner Bros. and Reprise Records) I remember watching Body Count and I was like, "This is so fucking cool. All these white kids are getting introduced to this." I mean, it wasn't the greatest music there is, but most of these venues were probably thirty miles outside of the cities, so it was a lot of different kids from all over the place seeing this. And I thought that was really great.

ICE-T Everyone was loving it, man. There was no negative reaction. You gotta remember, before that you had Millions of Dead Cops, you had Henry Rollins and Black Flag coming out, talking shit and doing "Police Story." The police had always been a target of rock. And it was accepted. So we never really dealt with any knuckleheads.

ERNIE C After Rollins heard "Cop Killer" he started coming out and singing it with us. So that was a lovefest. You could've bottled that and taken it around the world. It was a great thing.

HENRY ROLLINS (singer, Rollins Band) I ended up doing a lot of time onstage with Body Count on that tour. I'd sing a few songs with them almost every day. I still have the lyric sheet they gave me for "There Goes the Neighborhood." People loved Ice. He had them as soon as he walked out there. It was an interesting show, half rap, half band. It totally worked.

ERNIE C We played "Cop Killer" every night on that tour, and everyone had a great time. It was only the next year when the record came out and it was a political year that everything hit the wall.

ANDREW WEISS (bassist, Rollins Band) That kind of kicked up right in the middle of the tour, actually. There were some cities, especially in the

Midwest, where I remember there was a heavy police presence because of that song. But yeah, it was Bush who eventually spoke out against that record, right? Bush or Quayle . . .

THE NEW YORK TIMES (June 20, 1992) *Vice President Dan Quayle today accused Time-Warner Inc. of shirking its responsibility by selling an "obscene record" called "Cop Killer" by the rap performer Ice-T. "They are making money off a record that is suggesting it's O.K. to kill cops, and that is wrong," Mr. Quayle told a luncheon meeting of the National Association of Radio Talk Show Hosts.*

SEAN E SEAN We had to pull the "Cop Killer" song off the record [1992's *Body Count*]. It was a lot of drama. Everybody was like, "Ahhh, treason!" "He's saying 'Kill cops!'" Which he totally wasn't.

JO LENARDI That was our only rap act. We got out of that business after Body Count because of the death threats. We had to evacuate the building, I don't know, maybe six times that I remember. "Evacuate the building. There's a bomb in the building." So, we'd all stand out in the parking lot.

ICE-T I think the twist was once the verdict came out and the riot popped off, people turned around and tried to say we were promoting the riot, and we were trying to ride off the juice of what had happened. But the song came out *after* the riot. And it was written *before* Rodney King. That's the crazy part. The song was written about injustices that were happening prior to all that. It was just a true song about real things that, once again, America wasn't aware of, and that we tried to make America aware of.

HENRY ROLLINS I found Ice-T to be one of the most fascinating people I've ever met. He takes big ideas and crystallizes them into an essential truth. He's seen a lot of heavy stuff go down. He's alive and a lot of his friends aren't. I think we had a mutual respect of two people going for it with all they had.

KING COFFEY (drummer, Butthole Surfers) Part of the personal thrill for me on Lollapalooza was seeing Body Count and Ice-T every day, and becoming friends with them. If it was us touring on our own, we'd always be playing with "like" bands. We would have never played with Body Count on our own. It took the vision of Lollapalooza to bring it all together. It was super fun and it was super cool.

PAUL LEARY (guitarist, Butthole Surfers) Those guys, they were like kids. They were real fun to hang out with, especially [late Body Count bassist] Mooseman.

KING COFFEY I recall by the time we got to Denver, where we had to drive from, I think, probably Texas, I was with Mooseman and he was saying, "Man, we're in the *country*! There's squirrels and shit!" I was like, "Squirrels is your idea of country?" I guess if you grew up in L.A., you'd be like, "Wow, squirrel! Wildlife!"

SEAN E SEAN That first tour, we was just wildin'. Tryin' not to catch any cases out there, which we didn't.

ICE-T They say those who say don't know, and those who know don't say. A lot of those stories I'm taking to my grave.

JON KLEIN (guitarist, Siouxsie and the Banshees) The most visible orgies would have been the Ice-T, Body Count bus parties. Basically all these kind of huge dudes in L.A. Raiders gear would be going out into the gig with handfuls of laminates and bringing all these girls backstage. They seemed to have quite a penchant for blondes . . . or that's how my memory seems to serve that particular story. From a distance occasionally you'd see the Ice-T tour bus actually bouncing.

PAUL LEARY There was a show in New Jersey where it rained a lot, and it turned the whole area into a mud pit. I remember after the show, seeing the Body Count tour bus trying to get out of the parking lot, and it was just spinning its tires and grinding itself into the mud and got really stuck. And I looked to see who was driving it . . . and it's freaking Ice-T driving the bus! I think he got pissed off at their driver and fired him, and was going to drive it himself. And then he got it stuck in the mud.

KEVIN LYMAN (stage manager, Lollapalooza 1991–92) Their equipment was in cardboard boxes to start. It was all brand-new and they brought a lot of it. So throughout the first couple weeks of that tour, we were just trying to make everything more road-ready for them. Then they had some cases show up, but we had to help them label their cases.

ERNIE C We were just making it up as we went. We didn't really have a crew. We didn't hire professional people. We had so many people that wanted to come along that we had them come along and move equipment. So they really didn't know what they were doing. I basically knew my setup and I knew what needed to be done, but if anything would have gone wrong, it would have gone *really* wrong. 'Cause we had no one to fix it.

KEVIN LYMAN At the Shoreline Amphitheatre [in the San Francisco Bay Area] they had a run-in with Bill Graham. Not so much the band members, just a lot of people around Ice that were his crew. They got in a lot of trouble because they were selling passes. And they went down and kicked people out of their seats because they wanted to sit closer to the stage. And Bill Graham, I'll never forget him down there. The legendary Bill Graham, just before he passed away, just in these guys' faces: "You're not going to kick these people out of their seats!"

ERNIE C We had a bunch of people that didn't know what it was to be on the road, didn't know what proper etiquette was. So yeah, they probably were selling laminates!

ANDREW WEISS There was a certain naïve charm to their thing, you know? It was dudes playing metal, but it was unschooled in a way. They were just kind of out there. And the drummer, Beatmaster Vic, he was kinda like the guy from Flipper in a lot of ways, where he had this really huge drum set and he would do these fills and solos that would go on for, like, one beat too long. And then the whole band would have to catch up to him and stuff. It was very endearing.

SEAN E SEAN That solo was insane! And it's funny because when Body Count first started, we had some people in real bands critiquing us, like, "Ahh, Body Count. I see what you're doing, Ice. But you might want to think about a new drummer." Oh! When Vic heard that? He was livid! But what it did was, it put a fire up under him. And the weakest link became the strongest link.

CHRIS HASKETT Vic also had a hat roadie, which was awesome. There was a guy whose main job was to put Vic's hat back on his head when it fell off while he was playing. At least, that's what it looked like.

PAUL LEARY But the Body Count guys, they didn't ask for pointers and they didn't need pointers. In fact, we probably learned more from them than they learned from us. That's part of why I love them, is that they had a really distinct vision as to what they wanted to do. They wanted to rock, but they also wanted to be true to their rap fans. And they did it so well. They were there to kill and they knew it.

ICE-T With Body Count, it was, "We're gonna do whatever the fuck we wanna do." You don't let the culture tell you what to do if you're a real artist. You go out there and you jam that shit down their fucking throat. If they don't like it? Fuck 'em.

4 "JOB NUMBER ONE WAS TO BE AS PUNK AS FUCK"

TOM MORELLO (guitarist, Rage Against the Machine) That first Lollapalooza? Let's not mince words: Nine Inch Nails kicked *everybody's* ass. I had never heard of that band. Would unreservedly *never* buy a cassette that had keyboards on it other than Pink Floyd. And let me say, I went to the L.A. show, and I ran out the next day to buy *Pretty Hate Machine*. They did the thing that concerts are supposed to do—create converts. And I was one.

DAVE NAVARRO (guitarist, Jane's Addiction) Watching them on Lollapalooza was one of the most exciting things that I'd ever seen, probably up until this day.

CHRIS HASKETT (guitarist, Rollins Band) Lollapalooza as a festival was very of-the-moment, but in a way the bands on that first one were sort of the ethos of what had just been. Look at that year: Rollins Band—Henry had been in Black Flag. And the rest of us, it was very much a group of journeyman musicians working our craft. And then the Buttholes, Siouxsie, Ice-T . . . we were all from the eighties. Then you had Jane's, who were newer, but were also about to break up. Whereas Nine Inch Nails, they were up-and-coming. They were going to be the next big thing. They really captured the ethos of "What's next?"

MARC GEIGER (agent; cofounder, Lollapalooza) Every show, it was Jane's against Nine Inch Nails, like a prizefight. Those were the two bands that brought the whole audience running down to the stage. It was exciting.

PERRY FARRELL They were the only group that was messing with electronica to that degree.

DANNY ZELISKO (promoter, Evening Star Productions) They were truly there at the birth stage of bringing electronics into rock music. Or at least using the electronics to make harder music and different-sounding music.

DAVE NAVARRO Here you've got this brand-new band, this brand-new sound, and they went on at four in the afternoon, in broad daylight. And I'm not one to hang out at venues. I like to get there an hour before, and I like to warm up and get onstage and get on with it and get out of there. But Nine Inch Nails went on at four, so every day I was at the venue at four.

JON KLEIN (guitarist, Siouxsie and the Banshees) Having Nine Inch Nails in the middle of the bill was absolutely bonkers.

RICHARD PATRICK (guitarist, Nine Inch Nails) I referred to us as the "king of the shit bands." Because we were the last band to go on that didn't have lights. Living Colour were right after us, and that's when it would be starting to get dark. So it was like, "Oooh, you guys get lights!"

MARKY RAY (guitar tech, Nine Inch Nails) We had some UV lighting, and the band would come out in UV paint, but that was about it. And then they spent a fortune on this dry-ice fogger that never worked. Jeff Pinkus from Butthole Surfers said it looked like a barbecue out of control, or something to that effect.

RICHARD PATRICK It was the first time we were ever on a stage bigger than, like, twenty foot by twenty foot. We were very happy with playing in theaters and clubs, very comfortable with our lights and all our creature comforts of being the headlining thing on our own tour. And then the next thing we know, we're on in daylight at Lollapalooza, like, "Ewww!" The little goth kids that we were, we were not happy about being in the sun.

MARK O'SHEA (tour manager, Nine Inch Nails) We were playing at, I think, four to four-fifty each day, you know? And Trent was like, "What the fuck am I gonna do?"

RICHARD PATRICK Trent was only, like, twenty-four, twenty-five. I was twenty-two, twenty-three. We felt like we were creating something new. And we were from *Cleveland*.

MARK O'SHEA I started working with the band as their road manager in the fall of '89. I was their first official crew person. I knew Trent from the Cleveland scene. I knew Richard from the scene. I knew their manager, John Malm, from the Cleveland scene. I knew Marky, too, who I brought on as a backline technician.

MARKY RAY This is beginning of 1990, and the first thing I did for them was to go shoot the video for "Head Like a Hole" up in Chicago, at Exit Lounge. And you know, when Trent's strung up and writhing there at the end of the video, that's a real reel-to-reel tape that he took of one of the mixes he didn't like that they strung all over this Thunderdome thing. He was dangling and thrashing upside down from the top of it. I would have to lower Trent down and clean him up in between shots. It was a crazy thing.

MARK O'SHEA I knew the band was onto something when we were in Miami in early 1990, opening for the Jesus and Mary Chain. There was a lot of chaos going on onstage, but we had no pyro, we had no smoke, we had no light show. The intensity of the show, or the entertainment factor of the show, was based on their delivery. And afterward Trent simply said to me, "I need to feel each night when I walk off the stage that we as a band have given our best shot to entertain the audience." That was the come-to-Jesus moment where I was like, "Okay, I get it."

The chaos and the destruction—we used to nickname it "violence"—really drew the audience in, like, "Wow!"

JERRY JAFFE (manager, the Jesus and Mary Chain) I remember watching the stage, and Trent was kicking over the wedge monitors. He wasn't careful about anything. And I went into their dressing room after and I said to him, "Listen, you guys can do whatever the fuck you want for forty-five minutes. I don't give a *shit*. Piss on the stage, do whatever you wanna do. But please don't fuck with those monitors!"

MARKY RAY In the summer of 1990 Nine Inch Nails had toured with Die Warzau. They toured with Meat Beat Manifesto. And, my god, they just beat the shit out of their gear. That's when Trent started breaking guitars, and then started breaking Richard's guitars, like shit through a goose.

TRENT REZNOR (singer, multi-instrumentalist, producer, Nine Inch Nails) I am not going to be pretentious enough to say I never realized that if I break things it gets reactions. It is entertainment, right? That's the bottom line.

MARKY RAY By the time we got to Lollapalooza, we had the same gear that we'd had on all those fucking club tours, okay? And Trent was suing to get off of TVT Records and all the money was locked up in legal fees. They didn't have any money to put into the production. We were told with Lollapalooza, "Oh, it's a forty-five-minute set." Based on the Reading Festival sort of lineup rotation, with gear stacked sequentially, each band would play, they'd put the rolling risers forward, they'd finish, they'd reel them off the stage, set up the next band, et cetera, et cetera.

MARK O'SHEA At some point in the spring of '91, John Malm called me and said, "You're gonna fly out to L.A. for this meeting for this music festival that we're gonna be a part of." He goes, "Here's the bands who are gonna be on it." I was like, "Wow, that's a pretty cool lineup." So

John and Trent and I had a meeting and I put together a whole list of questions that they wanted answers for. And then I went to this meeting in L.A.

MARC GEIGER The meetings were at the Triad office, and most of the meetings were just the Lollapalooza organization team—Ted, Don, myself, Perry, maybe Stuart or Heidi or whoever else from the core group. They were planning and organizational and otherwise. There was maybe one or two where everyone else attended.

STUART ROSS (tour director, Lollapalooza) In those cases, it was a very limited, narrow subject that was discussed, usually dealing with artist participation.

MARK O'SHEA During this particular meeting, Ice-T is there, Gibby Haynes is there, Perry is there. Marc Geiger. Don Muller. A couple other VIPs. And here's this kid from Cleveland, kind of like a little bit of a deer-in-the-headlights thing, but also kind of understanding why I'm there. Eventually they introduce Kevin Lyman and Curly Jobson as the stage managers, and they're talking about fifteen-minute set changes, they're talking about rolling risers. Lots of stagehands. Rotation. Okay. I get it.

Then they say, "Does anybody have any questions?" And of course, I had a list of questions that John Malm and Trent wanted answered. I have my yellow legal pad out, I ask seven or eight questions, and I'm writing down all the answers. After the meeting, Marc Geiger comes looking for me and he goes, "Who are you?" I say, "I'm Mark O'Shea, and I'm here representing Nine Inch Nails." He goes, "I expect a lot of great things from you and the band." I go, "Why's that?" He says, "You're the only guy that asked questions."

TRENT REZNOR I look back at that as a real turning point of Nine Inch Nails breaking through to some degree. The level of audience increased significantly after those shows. It was a homemade, low-budget operation, and we got up to Lollapalooza, now we're playing real, professional venues.

ERIC AVERY (bassist, Jane's Addiction) With Nine Inch Nails playing at four in the afternoon, and everyone's talking about this new band with their "Head Like a Hole" single and stuff, that was a real coming-out moment for them.

RICHARD PATRICK MTV started playing "Head Like a Hole," but then because of Lollapalooza, they started playing it in the daytime.

HENRY ROLLINS (singer, Rollins Band) Every day, people went nuts when they played. They were completely different than any of the other bands in that lineup.

JIM GREER (senior editor, *SPIN* magazine) I thought they would just stand there behind their keyboards, sort of like Kraftwerk or something. But it was very kinetic.

DAVE NAVARRO The band would start playing and Trent would come out, and I'm telling you, man, it was like Elvis or the Beatles. Trent would creep out all tangled up in his mic cord, kind of almost like defeated and broken, and he would break into their opening song, which I don't think was ever recorded, and you could hear the girls losing their minds. It was like old Beatles footage where you hear the screams and you're expecting girls to faint out there.

RICHARD PATRICK Job number one on Lollapalooza was to be as punk as fuck. We were absolutely dedicated to total mayhem and anarchy. Trent would tackle me several times during the show, I would throw beers at him, I would throw beers at the audience. It was the most decadent, crazy, do-not-give-a-fuck thing.

FRITZ MICHAUD (monitor engineer, Nine Inch Nails) I had to cover every single monitor wedge with Visqueen plastic wrap and duct-tape it on there every show, because Trent would throw beer and water in the crowd all day long, and he would immediately throw it right into the monitors if I didn't cover them. Then the horns would stop working and the monitors would sound like there was a blanket over them.

JON KLEIN They'd be filling the keyboards up with beer and smashing them, busting the guitars up . . .

MARK O'SHEA Trent was throwing Richard around onstage, yelling at the crowd, "Come on, you fuckers! Let's go!" Just working the audience up.

TRENT REZNOR The show developed as we got more angry at the audience and they liked it. And then it got more abusive and dangerous and they seemed to like us more.

RICHARD PATRICK My knees are still fucked up from that tour. I actually had to have back surgery because I walked with a limp for, like, ten years. Because my whole right leg was just whaled on. Chiropractors and doctors were like, "How long did you play college football?" I'd go, "It wasn't college football. It was Trent Reznor."

FRITZ MICHAUD And then the band was coming out covered in, like, cornstarch or whatever.

KENNEDY (DJ, KROQ; VJ, MTV) They looked . . . not dirty, but not touchable. They were so edgy and angry and the whole thing was super, super hot. It was great.

FRITZ MICHAUD We made a mess everywhere we went.

RICHARD PATRICK We were just in trouble all the time on the tour. We'd be driving down the highway and throwing shit out the sides of the bus onto people that were in convertibles. Spewing water, beer, plates of food out the windows at cars passing by. And then inevitably, a guy would get in front of the bus and slam on his brakes and be like, "You motherfuckers got my brand-new car dirty!" It was just insane shit that only, like, teenage boys would do.

CHRIS HASKETT Rollins Band actually shared a bus with the Nine Inch Nails crew—an old Eagle 01.

FRITZ MICHAUD Nine Inch Nails wanted to have a bus for the band and for the crew, but they couldn't afford it. And Rollins Band wanted a bus, but *they* couldn't afford it. So they put the Nine Inch Nails crew with the Rollins Band, which was actually really fun.

AL JOURGENSEN (singer, multi-instrumentalist, producer, Ministry) I went to Lollapalooza when it came through Chicago that year, just to see Trent. Because Trent had been a roadie for my band the Revolting Cocks. I wanted to tell him, "Just a couple of years ago, you were teching for us. You did good, kid!" So I went backstage and got on the bus that the crew was sharing with Rollins. Henry didn't know me, and he's like, "Get off my bus." I told him, "Well, I'm waiting for Trent . . ." It got a bit chippy.

MARK O'SHEA I heard that Al was coming that day and, I'll be honest with you, at the time Al had a crew of people that would follow him around that we called the Cretins. So I'm thinking the worst thoughts. And then I remember that the buses were parked at a loading dock, and I believe that Rollins . . . you know, Henry used to work out with his weight bench, like, out in public. Every day. It was intense. But Al shows up with the Cretins, and what I do remember is that there was shouting at each other.

HENRY ROLLINS I was walking through the lounge and Al is there. Someone introduces me and I said, "The world's greatest scumbag," and kept walking. This was completely out of line. I don't know him, have nothing against him, and shouldn't have said it. Why did I? Youthful stupidity? I don't know, but the long and short of it is that I had no reason to say that.

MARKY RAY Henry was irascible at times.

AL JOURGENSEN I just thought he was being a dick. So I took a swing at him, and he took a swing at me, too. I think I missed my punch and he missed his, and then everyone got involved in holding us back.

MARK O'SHEA I believe at one point in time Al was maybe a semipro baseball player. He had a hell of an arm. He threw a Budweiser long-neck at Henry and nearly hit him. But I don't remember fists, and I don't remember anybody hitting anybody.

HENRY ROLLINS There was no physical interaction whatsoever. What's that, like thirty-odd years ago? We're so old now.

AL JOURGENSEN We both kind of pissed in the sand and established our territories, you know what I'm saying? It wasn't Ali–Frazier.

HENRY ROLLINS Nine Inch Nails were great that day. Of all the bands on that tour, even more than Jane's, you knew that Nine Inch Nails were going to be massive. It was so obvious.

JON KLEIN They had this thing where every time they'd turn up in town, the crew would go out and buy cheap secondhand guitars and keyboards.

MARKY RAY So what happened was, on a day off, Mark O'Shea would give me a couple grand in cash. And we're in the middle of America. Lollapalooza was the stay-forty-five-minutes-outside-of-every-major-city-in-America-tour, okay? So we're at the Great Woods in Mansfield [Massachusetts]. We're at Waterloo Village in New Jersey. We're at Blossom Music Center outside of Cleveland, where I live. They'd give me money and I would have to call up a pawnshop, a music store, find whatever was open. And remember, this is pre-internet. No cell phones, no anything. I'm calling on a landline using the Yellow Pages in a hotel room. I'd be like, "Do you have any . . ." We always needed to have a Kramer, a Schecter, a Jackson, a Charvel Charvette, some cheap student-line guitar.

MARK O'SHEA As long as we could get something with great pickups in it, which most of those guitars at the time had, we were good to go.

MARKY RAY So I'd be at a hotel in the middle of nowhere, I'd have to get to an airport, rent a car, drive into the city with my two thousand dollars in cash, find a pawnshop, and go, "How much you want for these five Charvels and a Schecter?" "Two grand? Here you go." Then I'd take all the guitars—no cases, not even strung—throw them in the trunk, drive back to the venue, and set them up. And we had one song in the set, "Ringfinger," that Trent would smash the guitar.

CHRIS HASKETT I'd be on the bus with poor Marky Ray, who was having to rebuild guitars that Richie Patrick and Trent had smashed that day, getting them ready and working for the next day.

MARKY RAY The other thing I'd do is I'd go out there like the guy cleaning up shit after the elephants and take all the broken parts and literally put them in a trash can that Kevin Lyman and I would throw on the back of the semis at the end of the night. And yes, we learned how to fix guitar necks so they could use them the next day. And that consisted of, you take a broken neck and you throw as much wood glue as you can in there, and then you C-clamp it, and then you run drywall screws countersunk on either side of the truss rod, and then you break off the ends on the back of the neck and sand them down, and then you sit 'em overnight, and you can restring 'em just enough that they'll hold for maybe a song. *Maybe.* And those would be some of the guitars I would hand to Trent to smash.

RICHARD PATRICK Trent always wanted to raise the bar higher. He would be hyper-focused on trying to figure out different ways to elevate the show. We still had the punk ethic of "Fuck you, we've got a lot to prove." It wasn't the fully realized thing that Nine Inch Nails became. We were paying our dues, but at the same time, we were very, very, very confident as to what was going on. We knew we were the shit.

MARK O'SHEA They definitely exploded. And I think that fatalistic, chaotic moment at the first show in Phoenix, when the gear melted down, helped us out. Because it gave us a little bit of a story. So then there's the follow-up: What's gonna happen on day two? What's gonna happen on day three? And by day three, it came out that our two merchandise items, the two T-shirts we had, were outselling the Lollapalooza event shirt. That's when we knew.

JON KLEIN The story I heard is that Nine Inch Nails' T-shirt outsold every other band's T-shirts added together, as well as the official Lollapalooza shirt. That one design with the "nin" in tiny little letters. That probably needs some kind of verification, but I can believe it because walking out into the crowd, it was the one that everyone was wearing.

STUART ROSS They were a very popular band, make no mistake. But judging how merch sales equate to artist popularity may be a flawed formula. Sometimes merch sales explode because it's an act that hasn't been in the marketplace selling merch previously. There isn't always a straight cause and effect.

MISSY WORTH (marketing consultant, Lollapalooza 1991) I was the promoter at the venue in Ohio [the Blossom Music Center], and Nine Inch Nails is from Cleveland and had not played Cleveland in forever. We all kept telling the venue, "You need more security than you've got." But also, "The security has to be really cool. They can't just go crazy." So Nine Inch Nails starts playing . . . and the place goes fucking wild. Everyone from the lawn is now in the seats. Everyone is *everywhere.*

MARK O'SHEA Basically they came down en masse, and you could see all the ushers literally turn sideways, like a turnstile gate. They just let everybody run down.

MISSY WORTH This is mayhem that you're not gonna fix. You lost the venue. Like, "Holy fuck!" Now all you can do is pray and hope that no one's getting hurt. And thankfully no one did. It was probably the most fun I've ever had at a show. And it was my own show.

MARK O'SHEA The Cleveland show is where Eric Avery and Dave Navarro were encouraged to come out and play guitar on "Head Like a Hole."

DAVE NAVARRO We smashed guitars, we did a lot of stage diving and banging into each other and just the whole thing that was going on with them at the time.

MARK O'SHEA There was this mass of people up front, so Eric and Dave smashed their guitars and then dove into the audience. Then Trent stage dives. Then Richard stage dives. Next thing you know, I'm in the audience and I'm trying to grab Richard and throw him back up onstage. When I finally pulled him out, he had nothing left but his combat boots and his tighty-whities.

MARKY RAY The "Head Like a Hole" thing, during the course of the shows, Fritz and I started playing on that song. I think the first time we did it was at Sandstone Amphitheater, near Kansas City. We came up onstage, and all the crews and bands lost their shit. They were like, "Oh my god, that's so cool! You guys played live auxiliary guitar on 'Head Like a Hole'!" After that, it was open season. Everybody wanted to do it. The next thing you know, Eric and Dave were playing. Ernie C from Body Count. The Butthole Surfers. Ice-T would come up to me and he'd be like, "Marky Ray, I want to smash a guitar." And I'd go, "But Ice, man, it's the last one I got." Then John Malm would say, "Marky Ray, give Ice-T a guitar." I'd hand him a guitar, and he'd go out onstage and wouldn't even plug it in. He just acted like he was playing, like *blinka . . .* smash!

MICHAEL "CURLY" JOBSON (stage manager, Lollapalooza 1991–92) I even went on and played one day in New Jersey. And Richard Patrick took it upon himself to spit beer in my face, which . . . yeah, I remembered that. But there was nothing coming out of the guitars. As much respect as I've got for Nine Inch Nails as songwriters and pioneers of a type of music, well, you know, you don't get any safer than miming, do you?

MARK O'SHEA That's not true. We would plug in all the guitars. Whether Curly was plugged in, you know, that could have been somebody just not plugging him in.

JON KLEIN The last Lollapalooza show Nine Inch Nails did, Dave Navarro gave me his video camera and said, "A load of us are going to jam, 'cause they've invited us to smash guitars up." And I sat on the side of the stage filming it for Dave. And what I remember is all the usual suspects come out and grab a guitar. And then one of the big Body Count geezers comes out. And it's like, "Oh, this looks interesting . . ." Zoom in on him. He wasn't the kind of guy that you'd normally see picking up a guitar. And he walks up, walks straight past the rack of cheap guitars, grabs one of Trent's really expensive ones and turns it into matchwood. I seem to remember it was a Gibson Explorer that he smashed up that night.

MARKY RAY Henry [Rollins] would sit there on our bus, incensed, going, "How can a guy break a fifteen-hundred-dollar Explorer? What kid wouldn't give his right nut for something like that?"

RICHARD PATRICK We just *did not give a fuck.* We were just out to satisfy our animal instincts onstage. I think we spent forty thousand dollars on gear that we smashed on Lollapalooza.

MARKY RAY The last show we did on Lollapalooza '91 was in Orlando. There were four dates after that, but we weren't there. We flew to Mannheim, Germany, to play with Guns N' Roses.

TRENT REZNOR I'd kind of gone into it, like, "Well, we did Lollapalooza and that worked out okay and in the big picture it benefited us and, well, what's the difference?" Well, it was a big difference. It was the worst of situations. It was us, Skid Row, Guns N' Roses.

JIM GREER It didn't go well for them at all.

RICHARD PATRICK Now we weren't playing in front of alternative Lollapalooza kids that were looking for something new. We're playing in front of fucking hair band people from Europe that could give a fuck about Nine Inch Nails. It was like, "Who the fuck is this band up there playing fucking industrial synth shit?"

TRENT REZNOR So we open up. First song, people are, like, "Yeah, there's a band onstage," and they're slowly realizing we're not Skid Row. Second song, "Okay, these guys are not Skid Row and I think I hear a synthesizer." Third song, "We definitely hear a synthesizer—this is bullshit. These guys suck, they're faggots, let's kick their ass." There is something about the feeling of standing in front of sixty-five thousand people giving you the finger . . . An intense terror took over. In a word, it sucks.

MARKY RAY Those were tough shows, because nobody knew who we were. They were throwing shit at us.

TRENT REZNOR The point when it actually became humorous was when I saw a sausage flying up onstage at the show in Germany. A link sausage.

MARK O'SHEA It literally arched about forty-five, fifty feet in the air, going end over end. And Trent is playing guitar at the time and he's singing, and you could see that all of a sudden he sees it, and you see his head go up, and then it goes behind him as he watches it hit the backline. And he turns around and he's giggling, and he has to collect himself before he can go back to singing.

RICHARD PATRICK That was very . . . anticlimactic.

FRITZ MICHAUD But those Lollapalooza shows, the crowds were just insane. It was mayhem every day.

TRENT REZNOR Musically, it felt like, hey, here's a new home for people that couldn't do something like this before, 'cause it didn't exist.

JIM GREER In terms of the story of Lollapalooza, I don't think that Nine Inch Nails had a particular effect on how successful Lollapalooza was or not. But I think Lollapalooza probably enormously helped them reach another level. A great band is a great band, and Nine Inch Nails proved themselves to be a great band on that tour.

RICHARD PATRICK All the hair bands had pretty much clogged up MTV and we were sitting there watching all that. And the hair bands picked on us back in Cleveland. If you didn't have a Marshall amplifier you were a pussy. Trent and I had these little GK [Gallien-Krueger] amplifiers, and we're like, "Whatever, it's got a fuckin' line out! Same thing!"

But with Lollapalooza it was, "This is a movement. This fucking shit has legs and this is happening." It was amazing to see it, because it was just insanely overwhelming. It felt like . . . justice. It felt like, "See? Told ya!"

5 "PERRY WAS STANDING NAKED LIKE JESUS"

STUART ROSS (tour director, Lollapalooza) The first Lollapalooza was nothing more than a Jane's Addiction farewell tour that was branded. It was designed, but not necessarily promoted, that way.

MICHAEL "CURLY" JOBSON (stage manager, Lollapalooza 1991–92) Things were tense with Jane's on that tour. And the biggest tension was that Dave lived in a silo. He had his issues that were going on with him and his girlfriend. They traveled separately and did their own thing. They were more kind of attuned to the Siouxsie and the Banshees goth world, you know?

STEVEN SEVERIN (bassist, Siouxsie and the Banshees) Both Dave and Perry said they were fans. Truth be told, none of us had ever heard of Jane's Addiction.

CHRIS CUFFARO (photographer) Dave's girlfriend, Tania, was a good friend of mine. But they were the Sid and Nancy of the tour, basically. And there was just this really negative, stressful energy.

CHRIS HASKETT (guitarist, Rollins Band) I'd become friends with Dave Navarro when Rollins Band was out opening for Jane's before Lollapalooza. We used to hang out a lot. But it was almost like psychically there was this other place he would go to, which was heroin world. And he kept that very closed off. I mean, it was visibly obvious, it wasn't a secret, but it also wasn't like, "Hey, come up to my room, I'm gonna shoot up and then we can go out!" So I was very aware he was having his issues on Lollapalooza.

DAVE NAVARRO (guitarist, Jane's Addiction) I was struggling with addiction, so there would be weeks where I was clean, and then there would be weeks where I wasn't. I was dealing with my own inner demons, and it was definitely a tumultuous tour, for sure.

MICHAEL "CURLY" JOBSON Eric and Perry, they didn't even talk. We would put carpets out for them onstage, and we used to call it "The Bridge on the River Kwai." Those two would never cross into each other's territory. If you look back at some of the video footage, you'll see. Perry might go out front, but he wouldn't get into the area near Eric's monitor or into his playing zone. And much the same for Eric.

DAVE NAVARRO There's ways to maintain distance from people until you hit the stage, and then you either interact or you don't. And some nights, Perry and I got along great and interacted a lot, and some nights we didn't, and I think the same holds true for him and Eric.

CHRIS CUFFARO Eric was trying to get sober and be sober and stay sober. And he couldn't be around guys like Dave and Perry that weren't. I mean, Dave especially was a fucking mess. Eric would show up, like, five minutes before the show and leave five minutes after the show. He just didn't wanna be around it.

ERIC AVERY (bassist, Jane's Addiction) It was really personally alienating for me. I was like, "Okay, I'm leaving the band because I don't feel a part of this thing anymore."

STEPHEN PERKINS (drummer, Jane's Addiction) Maybe some great advice for us would've been to take some time off. A career is many, many years. It doesn't have to be consecutive work, record after record. But we were coming off *Ritual [de lo Habitual]* and feeling it was time to make the third Jane's record. And no one was in the headspace to move even an inch in that direction.

PERRY FARRELL Well, it's very interesting. We're gonna look at life now as very *plastique*, right? If Jane's wouldn't have broken up after Lollapalooza, things might have looked very different. And sometimes people say, to me anyway, why would I break a band up pretty much at their height? Why would I do that? The answer is, I was immature. I was just living through instinct and emotion at that time. And as an artist, I just wanted to have a brand-new canvas.

STEPHEN PERKINS Me and Perry were already talking about the existence of another band, about Porno for Pyros. Just thinking, What's next?

NIKKI GARDNER (assistant to Ted Gardner; special groups coordinator, Lollapalooza) Those were trying times. But we had great crew and people, and everybody was enthusiastic. Really, the band just had to turn up and play, which was great because that's what they were great at.

STEPHEN PERKINS Even if there was trouble inside the camp, the shows were on fire on Lollapalooza. The audience got a real Jane's Addiction. The emotion was there because we cared. So even though it was painful to know we were finishing and it makes no sense to break the band up, I was in the moment and still loving it.

ERIC AVERY The shows themselves, those were great. With the exception of, you know, Perry and Dave tumbling off in a tussle that first night.

DAVE NAVARRO It never got physical between anybody prior to that. But I've gotta tell you, I think that in some ways, the frenetic nature of all of our relationships made those shows much more intense. If we were all taking days off together and going to museums, they wouldn't have been as ferocious. You could feel the aggression in our souls coming off the stage.

RICHARD PATRICK (guitarist, Nine Inch Nails) One of my favorite things to do on Lollapalooza, and I did this starting two or three days in, was to get a pack of cigarettes and some beers from backstage and go out to the front of the stage and use that to pay the security guards. I would say, "Please don't let anyone land on my head." And then I would sit in the little moat area between the audience and the stage, a little drunk, a little stoned, and watch Jane's Addiction. And they were incredible, every night.

TOM BUNCH (manager, Butthole Surfers) Fricking *everybody* watched Jane's Addiction. All the bands, all the managers, all the crew. Anybody that wasn't working was there to see it.

MICHAEL "CURLY" JOBSON Perry coming down the mountain was a bit to me like white light, you know?

RICHARD PATRICK Perry would come out, and he's absolutely immaculate. He's got zero fat on his body. He's so fucking cool looking, and he's wearing the best clothes. And Dave and Eric and Stephen, their performances were just incredible. They would wave to me from the stage. Perry would go, "Richie, I see you . . ."

PERRY FARRELL It's kind of like riding a wave. You're on the wave, but you can never be too certain. You always have to concentrate your muscle. There was a certain tensity that you had to have at all times with Lollapalooza.

MARC GEIGER (agent; cofounder, Lollapalooza) After the first night in Arizona we went to San Diego. The next two shows were Irvine Meadows in L.A. Then two at Shoreline Amphitheatre. Those were historic shows. That's when the *NME* wrote about it. It was after all that shit happened the first night, and the place just went berserk for Jane's.

CHRIS CUFFARO By the time we got to Irvine, it was a blast. I met up with the band and the mood was completely different from Arizona. Everybody was happy. It was like, Huh?

MICHAEL "CURLY" JOBSON I remember a show in the countryside in New Jersey . . . Waterloo Village, I believe it was. Jane's Addiction on that night was, for me, like the first time I heard "(White Man) in Hammersmith Palais" by the Clash. The first time I witnessed that kind of power from an artist. Perry's power. Eric's bass playing. I was not a great fan of Dave Navarro's style of guitar, but I was a big fan of his performance. And Steve Perkins, look, there is no better team player. What a great drummer, but what a *band person,* you know? The guy that just never stops smiling, never stops representing the guys that he is up there playing with.

PERRY FARRELL I had found out that my mother was buried in New Jersey, not far from the venue. That night, I ate a tab of acid or so—I can't remember how much. I felt that my mother's spirit had to be close by. I never really told anybody that. I was singing for her and her friends.

PHIL BURKE (head rigger, Lollapalooza) We played a place called Harriet Island, in St. Paul. And Jane's came out and played "Been Caught Stealing," and the crowd was shaking the stage hard enough to swing the PA and bang it into the towers. And that stage is a big steel thing—a hundred feet wide, sixty feet deep, it travels in six trucks. I'd never seen that level of enthusiasm before.

JIM GREER (senior editor, *SPIN* magazine) They went on at prime time, with all the lights and all the staging and all the theatrics, and the sound was great. So it was very effective. Jane's was so L.A.–centric and I was so New York–centric at the time that I don't think I realized how big they were. But at Lollapalooza I was like, "Okay, I see why people like this band."

ICE-T (MC; singer, Body Count) I knew that Jane's Addiction was dope. I didn't know *how* dope they were till I actually went on tour with them. And I didn't know how dope a person Perry Farrell really is. He's just one of those few special people in rock 'n' roll that's like a visionary. A real artist and a really cool person.

CHRIS CUFFARO Ice-T would come out and perform with Perry during their set. They would do the Sly Stone song "Don't Call Me N****r, Whitey."

ICE-T Someone came to me: "Ice, Perry wants to perform this song." Now, remember, we were the third band on the show. It was Rollins Band, Butthole Surfers, Body Count. Right? And then it was Nine Inch Nails, Living Colour, Siouxsie and the Banshees, and Jane's Addiction. By the time Jane's came on, the crowd was at full fucking power. Like, this is *it*. So to ask me to go onstage with Jane's Addiction? Hell, yeah, I wanna go on in front of that audience.

DAVE NAVARRO Obviously, the content of what they were talking about was pretty intense, but the performance of that song was just a lot of fun, and it was something where no one would ever imagine Jane's Addiction and Ice-T performing a song together.

ERNIE C (guitarist, Body Count) Me and Ice, we'd go out and play "N****r/ Whitey" with Jane's almost every night. I'd play some leads with Dave, and Ice and Perry would do their thing. It was a blast.

ICE-T When I went out there, I just followed Perry's lead. They would start playing the bass line and he'd start talking that shit. And then I'd come out behind him. I knew he wanted me to be badass, like we were going to fight.

RICHARD PATRICK I just remember being like, *Damn* . . . It was so enlightening, you know? Like, here's racism, right here on the stage. But it was a beautiful, positive, teachable moment for everybody, to just stand there and see what it looks like. Perry, he was saying shit.

CHRIS DOWD (keyboardist, trombonist, Fishbone) Perry was trying to confront fear and prejudice in real time. And he was trying to create this environment of acceptance and tolerance.

ICE-T I knew that Perry knew what he was doing. And I knew right out the gate, from the minute I met him, that he wasn't on no racist bullshit. So I just rocked out with him and we had a great time.

ERNIE C They'd dance together, they'd spin around. But Ice would always try to lead . . .

RICHARD PATRICK At one show, I think it was North Carolina [at Walnut Creek Amphitheatre in Raleigh], Ice-T and Perry were doing their thing and there was this moshing kid and he was like, "Fuck you two!" Perry, he throws the mic out to this kid and he says, "Go ahead, man, say your piece. Tell us what you think." The kid eventually shut up, but Perry kept at it: "No, I'm Jewish. If you want to say what you want to say about me, go ahead. Here's the mic." And this kid was, like, a skinhead punk-rock Nazi.

PERRY FARRELL This guy didn't understand that these are my friends, man. I've been butt naked with these dudes. He went on and on, and I thought, This is great, I want to hear what this man's got to say.

CHRIS DOWD At that point we were all so punk rock that we were like, "Fuck you if you're intolerant! Go fuck yourselves!" You know? It's like, "I have my Black friends and my Jewish friends and my Asian friends, and we're all gonna have a great time and you're gonna be jealous that you weren't a part of it. We're not gonna sugarcoat this shit. And we don't have to kiss your ass because now the freaks are in power!"

ERNIE C Perry would drink Moët every night, and since Ice and I had to stick around to play with Jane's at the end of the show, I would drink Moët with him. And I wasn't really a champagne drinker. But it was just a bunch of love.

SEAN E SEAN (onstage performer, security, Body Count) Perry had some guy that would go up ahead of the tour, go get the best dancers he could find. And then Perry would have the stage turn into a strip club. I was like, "Is this a bordello? What is this?" Every town, new strippers.

PAUL LEARY (guitarist, Butthole Surfers) Jane's Addiction would have Oriental carpets and chandeliers and candelabras and things, and chicks hanging out. Backstage, it seemed like a movie. It seemed like it wasn't real.

SEAN E SEAN It was a wild scene backstage. Only thing I ever seen wilder than that is once we were out with Guns N' Roses, and they had hot tubs in the backstage. But Perry had some wild shit going on. I didn't see orgies, but I saw the backdrop on where all that could easily take place.

PERRY FARRELL Yeah, there were [orgies]. But I can't elaborate on that. I mean, I wish I could . . .

CHRIS HASKETT There was a complex interaction between Dave and Tania and Siouxsie and [Siouxsie and the Banshees drummer] Budgie. Um . . . I'll just leave it at that.

JON KLEIN (guitarist, Siouxsie and the Banshees) I guess everyone kind of knows that something was going down. But no one really knows exactly what, outside of those two couples.

DAVE NAVARRO The behavior that took place offstage with other artists, it's not my place to out them. But we all became very close.

MICHAEL "CURLY" JOBSON Whatever floats your boat, is what I say.

CHRIS DOWD That whole summer was a fucking free-for-all. Rock excess at its finest.

JON KLEIN So at some point close to the end of the tour there was a big party. It all went off in the hotel one night and it was utter carnage and debauchery. And I remember I got a phone call by mistake, I think it was Perry or one of his gang, but it was an invitation to a "hard party." Like a heroin party. It sounded like Perry and it sounded like he sort of called me without meaning to call me. Because I definitely wouldn't have been on the hard party list. So I did not go to that party.

But I *did* go to a crack party. It seemed like there were lots of different parties going on all over this hotel, and I remember banging on a door, like, "What's going on in there?" "Oh, we're having a crack party! Do you wanna come in?" "Yeah, I'll come have a look!" It was just a part of the surreal nature of that tour. I'm kind of thinking that was in a hotel somewhere heading down to Florida. After that we went to Dallas and Colorado and wrapped things up in Seattle.

DON MULLER (agent; cofounder, Lollapalooza) We played the final show at King County Fairgrounds, which was right outside the Twin Peaks town, near Mount Rainier. A crazy, crazy weekend.

GIBBY HAYNES (singer, Butthole Surfers) In Seattle me and Perry put on these wigs and mustaches that I had and went to the Pike Place Market in disguise. He ran around shoplifting things and then I would run behind him and throw down, like, forty bucks before he got arrested in front of me. It's not clear whether or not he knew I was paying for that which he stole.

NORWOOD FISHER (bassist, Fishbone) Seattle was *insane*. It was, like, mythical in scope, because of this fog that sat over the whole thing. I remember watching a bunch of the festival and then being backstage because I wanted to talk to Perry, and actually having a moment of feeling intimidated to go in the Jane's Addiction dressing room. Like, Oh, man, I don't wanna bother 'em. But I opened the door, and Perry's in the center of the room in a chair, and he's being tended to on some level—I don't remember exactly how—and there's dancers running around half-dressed and people smoking weed and maybe other shit. I don't know. I was like, "This shit look like a scene outta *Caligula*! And Perry *is* Caligula!"

CHRIS CUFFARO That final show, I went to document Jane's, and by this time I had gotten to be good friends with Eddie Vedder and Pearl Jam, who were brand-new and who I had been shooting. So I'm up in Seattle and I ask Eddie, who was with his girlfriend Beth, "You guys want to come to Lollapalooza? I'll get you laminates." And Eddie worshipped Jane's Addiction. So we drive to the venue, Ted Gardner hooks us up with laminates, and I'm taking Eddie around and introducing him to everybody. And Pearl Jam was not really known at that point. Everybody's like, "Pearl what?" "Eddie who?" And then a year later, you know, Pearl Jam's playing Lollapalooza.

STEPHEN PERKINS We were planning on breaking up in Seattle, but Ted Gardner, our manager at the time, was an Australian, and he said, "I'd love to take you back home and show everybody what I've got." So we decided not to break up in Seattle in front of twenty thousand people, and instead go out to Australia and play clubs. And then we broke up in Hawaii on the way home.

CHRIS CUFFARO They finished Lollapalooza, and I think a week or so later they're in Australia, and then they go to Honolulu for two shows. I just know by hearsay, I wasn't in any meetings, I don't know facts, but my impression was after those two Hawaii shows, that was the end of the touring for *Ritual* and Eric was done. I asked Eddie if he wanted to go with me, but he couldn't make it. So I flew out with Beth to come and be a witness with me.

KEVIN LYMAN (stage manager, Lollapalooza 1991–92) Those shows were promoted by Goldenvoice, and I worked as the production manager. We were using a new venue, the Aloha Tower, which was basically where all the customs and shipping came through in Honolulu.

CHRIS CUFFARO This venue, it wasn't even a venue. It was like a warehouse. And it was hotter than fuck.

PAUL V. (national director of alternative radio promotion, Warner Bros. Records) It was about 110 degrees and it was packed to the gills. Everybody was sweating puddles.

DON MULLER I'm looking around, and everything around the walls and the ceiling looked to me like asbestos. And I'm thinking, Fuck, this is gonna go off. So it was one of those kind of things where you're like, Should I stay or should I go?

CHRIS CUFFARO But the first show, it was great. Perry had a bunch of his friends there, you know, *woo-hoo*. And then the second night, they come out and they're playing the show, and about halfway through Perry goes offstage, pulls his pants off and comes back out onstage.

KEVIN LYMAN Perry was standing naked like Jesus in the middle of the venue.

STUART ROSS It wasn't just Perry. It was all of them.

CHRIS CUFFARO I'm shooting, but I'm also waiting for security, like, Is somebody gonna stop this? And then eventually it's just like, Never mind. Nobody's gonna stop this.

STUART ROSS It was basically chaos. It was crowd-surfing and mosh pits and no real sense of security. Kind of the worst scenario for a general admission show. That's how I remember it.

DON MULLER In Hawaii moshing was probably a new thing, but it was just a swirling dervish of people.

PAUL V. Jane's, you know, were unpredictable. That was part of their charm and allure, to my mind.

CHRIS CUFFARO They finish the set, they leave the stage, they come back out for the encore, and they do "Chip Away." And then at the end of the set Perry dives into the audience. The lights are on, and the managers, the crew, everyone, they're pulling him out of the audience. I have this picture from the stage of them pulling him out. And by the time they do, Eric was already gone. I think he walked off the stage, got into a taxi, and was gone.

KEVIN LYMAN I think his girlfriend was there, or his wife at that point. I can't remember. And they just drove off.

CHRIS CUFFARO To this day, I always tell people that for me, that was the last moment of Jane's Addiction.

STUART ROSS I had been with them through their career build—from nightclubs to theaters, college gyms, the whole thing. And to think that this was the end . . . personally, I was really sad.

DAVE NAVARRO God, man, we were just so young. We didn't know any better. We just didn't know the gift that we had or what we had created.

KEVIN LYMAN I watched everyone's faces that worked around the band at that point, and their faces were blank. Because it was over. I turned on the house lights and that was the end of it.

LOLLAPALOOZA 1992

DATES: JUNE 18–SEPTEMBER 13

MAIN STAGE: Red Hot Chili Peppers, Ministry, Ice Cube, Soundgarden, the Jesus and Mary Chain, Pearl Jam, Lush

SECOND STAGE: Jim Rose Circus Sideshow, Sharkbait, Archie Bell Dancers, Boo-Yaa T.R.I.B.E., Rage Against the Machine, Stone Temple Pilots, Cypress Hill, Vulgar Boatmen, Truly, Porno for Pyros, various

Lollapalooza's inaugural outing was only a few months in the rearview mirror when plans got underway for the follow-up. And in the short time since the festival had been completed, the music world had changed drastically. Just weeks after Lollapalooza '91's final date, Geffen Records released Nirvana's major-label debut, *Nevermind*. The same day, Warner Bros. issued the Red Hot Chili Peppers' *Blood Sugar Sex Magik*. Two weeks later, Soundgarden's *Badmotorfinger* came out on A&M. By that time, Pearl Jam's Epic debut, *Ten*, had been on record-store shelves several months, lying in wait for the massive commercial embrace soon to come.

That these albums were all products of the major-label universe speaks to the fact that the industry was already betting on, and heavily investing in, a new sound to supplant glossy eighties rock and hair metal. Even so, how quickly and fully alternative and grunge penetrated radio and MTV, as well as mass-market media and fashion, was remarkable.

And so Lollapalooza '91 could be viewed as something of a

bellwether for the ascendency of alternative rock as not only a musical but also a cultural force. It was as if a switch had been flipped: If in '91 Rollins Band and Butthole Surfers came off as acquired-taste outsider art, and listening to Jane's Addiction felt akin to opening a portal into a mysterious alternate reality, by 1992 it seemed like every other kid in the high school cafeteria or suburban shopping mall was a proudly pierced-and-tatted freak.

Whether Lollapalooza initiated this shift or merely anticipated it is up for debate. "I don't know if we were following it or they were following us," tour director Stuart Ross admits. "But when we did the first one, and we ended up with seven bands that drew eighteen thousand people a night, everybody paid attention." What's more, Lollapalooza's out-of-the-box success came at a particularly dismal moment for the touring industry in general. Gross US ticket sales in 1991 had declined close to 25 percent from the previous year, with the dependably lucrative summer season particularly depressed. But with a reported half-million tickets sold, Lollapalooza '91 bucked the trend (not to mention created a template for touring packages like the Blues Traveler–curated jam-fest H.O.R.D.E., which debuted in '92).

Combined with the potency of the musical moment, in which the multiplatinum *Nevermind* supplanted Michael Jackson's *Dangerous* at the top of the *Billboard* album chart, an abrasive alt-metal act like Helmet signed a million-dollar contract with Interscope Records, and Marc Jacobs was preparing his "grunge" collection for designer fashion brand Perry Ellis, Lollapalooza organizers had every reason to feel confident going into '92. And so their move was to go bigger in every way. Lollapalooza '92 was routed through twenty-seven cities, for thirty-six shows across almost two months, including a two-day stint at Shoreline Amphitheatre in the Bay Area to kick things off, and three consecutive dates at Irvine Meadows in Southern California to wrap it all up. The midway, or Concourse Oddities and Curiosities, as it was officially labeled, which was home to political and social-action groups, local artists, and craft and food vendors, was expanded significantly (charity gambling, a cyber bar with smart drinks, an audience-participation sound sculpture called the Rhythm Beast) and placed under the guiding hand of industry-leading concert production company Bill Graham Presents. And a second stage, arguably the first of its kind, was introduced as a showcase for new and local acts, presenting some of the earliest performances by Stone Temple Pilots, Rage Against the Machine, and Perry Farrell's post-Jane's band, Porno for Pyros, as well as serving as home base for the not-to-be-missed troupe of pain-threshold-testing, gross-out eccentrics, the Jim Rose Circus Sideshow.

The main stage, meanwhile, gave top billing to the Red Hot Chili Peppers, who, like Jane's Addiction the year prior, had emerged from the L.A. underground. In the Chili Peppers' case, they were also riding high on a bona fide smash single, "Under the Bridge." Further mirroring the '91 blueprint, the lineup featured a musically and visually extreme industrial-metal juggernaut (Ministry) and a West Coast gangsta rapper (Ice Cube). Rounding out the bill were grunge powerhouse Soundgarden, Scottish post-punk legends the Jesus and Mary Chain, drone-y British dream pop unit Lush, and, way down on the ticket, a new Seattle act named Pearl Jam, who exploded into the mainstream after the Lollapalooza lineup was finalized but before the tour officially launched. This meant that the band, becoming more famous by the day, took the stage early at each show, right after openers Lush.

"It changed the whole dynamic of Lollapalooza," says festival co-founder Don Muller, who was also Pearl Jam's agent. "People had to get there early to see them, and then they stayed all the way through the Chili Peppers. They didn't leave. So all of a sudden, now we've got a beast, right? We've got our hands on this mountain of an event going around and just dominating and selling out everywhere."

Heidi Ellen Robinson-Fitzgerald, Lollapalooza's longtime press agent, concurs. "The success of the second year . . . I still have the records someplace, so I could double-check, but I think that that entire tour sold out. And the press on the second tour was absolutely through the roof. Just outta sight. The '91 tour and how it contributed to music and culture had seeped into the environment, and it all contributed to year two being an even greater success."

Going forward, Lollapalooza would continue to get bigger. But it was arguably never better.

1 "THIS CAR IS LIKE PUNK ROCK!"

DON MULLER (agent; cofounder, Lollapalooza) After those Jane's Addiction Hawaii shows I went back to my hotel, and Beth, Eddie Vedder's girlfriend, who later became his wife, she and I just hung out. And I said to her, "You know, the board's changing." Because Jane's, they just had to go down as a cultural changer of the world. I mean, obviously you would have Kurt and Nirvana and Eddie and Pearl Jam. But Perry opened the door.

PERRY FARRELL You go back to '91, *Nevermind* came out, sure. But *Nothing's Shocking* and *Ritual [de lo Habitual]* came before that.

DON MULLER And now Jane's was done. So it was like, "Is the world gonna collapse and, I hate to say it, go back to the world of Bon Jovi?" I hoped not.

PAUL V. (national director of alternative radio promotion, Warner Bros. Records) Perry unlocked that door and Kurt Cobain basically kicked it open. With my job, I saw it firsthand. This music was always the bastard child of the record label, like, "College radio, alternative . . . that's that *weird* music. Some people like it, so of course we're gonna give it to them, but that's not the big-selling or important music." But Lollapalooza changed the approach of record companies—not only what kind of bands they were gonna sign, but what bands could be their priority and what bands could sell records and be heard on the radio and have their videos on

MTV. Lollapalooza did that. It brought all this incredible music from the underground to the mainstream.

GARY GRAFF (music writer, *Detroit Free Press*) Would the mainstream explosion that happened with alternative rock have happened without the first Lollapalooza? Probably. But it was one more thing that could be pointed to. And I think even radio promotion guys will tell you that they felt that with Lollapalooza having been such a hot tour in '91, when they started taking records like the Red Hot Chili Peppers' *Blood Sugar Sex Magik* and Pearl Jam's *Ten* and Soundgarden's *Badmotorfinger* to radio, they felt like they were now speaking to the converted, rather than having to have to sell these stations on a genre.

KIM THAYIL (guitarist, Soundgarden) We weren't trying to befriend MTV or radio, but it happened. I don't think it was because we were addressing a particular marketplace as much as everything in the marketplace bent toward what was happening. There was a movement, culturally, which incorporated the audience and the bands and the kind of music they played, the way they dressed, how they behaved at rock shows, the language of how people talked to each other about anything—political issues, gender issues, music issues, movies they liked, whatever. It was a general addressing of a generational and cultural change. And eventually it got big enough that industries and institutions turned and looked and said, "Hey, how do we get our percentage off of this?"

MICHAEL AZERRAD (journalist, author) To the rest of the world, the real impact of alternative rock wasn't musical, it was commercial: It announced that a new generation of consumers had arrived. These consumers had their own culture and their own historical context, and they needed to be marketed to accordingly. And that's when we got that infamous Subaru ad in 1992 with the quasi-grungy kid who excitedly proclaimed, "This car is like punk rock!"

ROB TANNENBAUM (journalist, author) The Brown student in me is fascinated by the idea of Lollapalooza being both inclusive and exclusive at the same time. It was this idea of "We're all in the subculture, let's see how big we can make the subculture." You know, "How many freaks can we find? And how do we let them know they're not alone, and give them a good time that draws them deeper into this culture?"

PERRY FARRELL In this case, you're talking about creating a new scene. When that happens, people are looking at it, they're studying it, they might be a little afraid of it. That's why, in that last Jane's run in 1991, I didn't think to make it all about myself. It would've been cool. But I felt like it all would've just evaporated. I thought, No, I'm going to bring the community out of their homes.

JIM GREER (senior editor, *SPIN* magazine) I remember for *SPIN*'s year-end issue, I interviewed Perry after the first Lollapalooza. It must have been in October, for the January issue. And I said to him something like, "Okay. So we've got Lollapalooza. We've got this movie *Slacker* by Richard Linklater. We've got Douglas Coupland's book *Generation X.*" I was like, "Do you think this represents some sort of boom?" And of course Perry hadn't heard of the movie or the book, but he wrote them down. I asked him, "Does it feel like something's happening here?" This was sort of a ham-fisted way of trying, in a journalistic sense, to capture a trend—this sort of mainstreaming of a kind of culture that had previously been underground, I guess. But he agreed.

CHRIS HASKETT (guitarist, Rollins Band) You've got this indie mindset with alternative ways of thinking about anything from society to politics to vegetarianism to music to the music industry . . . all these things are getting mixed in with each other. But you have to make them palatable. And Lollapalooza, it kind of defanged some of the really rough indie aspects of it, and then presented it to a much, much larger audience.

KEVIN LYMAN (stage manager, Lollapalooza 1991–92) At the end of the '91 tour, I flew home from the last show in Seattle and two days later I worked a show at the Hollywood Palladium—it was Sepultura, Napalm Death, and someone else that I can't remember. I went back to my roots right away. Then at some point I got a call, I'm sure it was Ted Gardner, saying, "Hey, would you like to come back out as stage manager for '92?" When something is that successful, people immediately start looking at doing it again.

MICHAEL "CURLY" JOBSON (stage manager, Lollapalooza 1991–92) I mean, it was obvious to them after year one that it was a cash cow, right?

STUART ROSS (tour director, Lollapalooza) As far as I know, in '91 we didn't know that this was going to continue on. We were just trying to put together a big farewell package for Jane's Addiction. But maybe Geiger or Muller had ideas going forward that I didn't hear about.

MARC GEIGER (agent; cofounder, Lollapalooza) It was actually prior to the first tour that it was clear this thing could continue. I approached Perry Farrell in February of '91, in the backstage greenroom bathroom at the Universal Amphitheatre. He was in the shower before or after Jane's went onstage, I can't remember which. And I said, "This is an ongoing touring vehicle." We got into a discussion about it, I made a financial proposal, I told him what I thought, and he said, "Okay." End of story.

STUART ROSS I was not aware of that conversation. But I will say that Marc Geiger's a visionary, and he's always been a visionary. He always knew what was going to happen in the industry before anybody else did.

TED GARDNER (manager, Jane's Addiction; cofounder, Lollapalooza) In '91, there was an element of risk. It was like, God, what if this is a dismal failure? In '92 . . . there was a promoter that said, "Play my venue, and I'll get you all Corvettes."

GREG KOT (music critic, *Chicago Tribune*) I was already calling it a corporate event by year two. You could see the money start to roll in.

ROLLING STONE (September 17, 1992) *Lollapalooza '91 was the underdog tour that could, charmed by the homespun hippie idealism and*

I'm-a-freak-touch-me eccentricity that were Jane's Addiction's stock in trade. That it turned out to be big business seemed little more than a side effect, a happy bonus. This year, everyone wants to be alternative, and Lollapalooza '92 was viewed as a golden egg from the git-go.

STUART ROSS Once we had some road behind us, we all sat down and said, "Okay, this is now a viable entity." And the promoters, after the tour, I think the first year was twenty-eight shows, wanted us back. At that point we started a company to actually produce it and we structured it completely differently, both financially and production-wise. So it was Lollapalooza LLC. And the difference is, in 1991, the promoters bought Jane's Addiction for a guarantee plus a percentage, and then Nine Inch Nails for a guarantee, Siouxsie and the Banshees for a guarantee, Rollins Band for a guarantee, et cetera. Right? The acts got contracted through the promoter, and the show we worked on was the contract for Jane's Addiction, because Jane's Addiction were the profit participants. But starting in 1992, Lollapalooza LLC contracted all of the bands. We made a deal with each act, the promoters paid us, and then we paid the bands.

PAUL V. The first one, there were so many what-ifs, you know? It was more of an adventure. Whereas by the time '92 happened, Marc Geiger and everyone had been able to fine-tune it and make sure that it ran correctly. I wouldn't say that it was some drastic underground-versus-mainstream transition, but everything did get bigger.

MARC GEIGER It was bigger, there's no question. It felt like a machine. We're taking more gear, more people, more front-of-house, more art, more politics, more of a village. Second stage. It was significant.

STUART ROSS There really was nothing called a second stage until we invented it, as far as I know.

ROB TANNENBAUM I think of Lollapalooza as an idea Bill Graham would've wished he'd had. There was a period of time where you heard a concert ad on the radio and they told you who the promoter was, because the promoter was building that brand. And you would hear, "Bill Graham Presents the Fillmore East, the Fillmore West . . ." And then you would go on any Friday or Saturday night, not even necessarily knowing who was going to play, trusting that the bands that Graham booked were going to be good.

With Lollapalooza, the success created a brand, and it was a brand with not only a big following and a lot of media attention, but great specificity. I have no doubt that there were kids that went to Lollapalooza every summer the same way stoners in 1968 went to the Fillmore East. You could reliably assume that if you liked Jane's Addiction or Soundgarden, you were going to like the other bands. Maybe Body Count wasn't exactly your band, but it wasn't like going to see the Monkees and having Jimi Hendrix open up.

DON MULLER Marc and Ted and I, and what Stuart did as kind of being the field general, and Kevin in his position, we all knew a lot more in '92 than we did in '91, that's for damn sure.

KEVIN LYMAN The whole energy was completely different in '92. But by then it was like, the team had done one tour together, we were working with Delicate Productions, the same sound and lighting company, again, so it was like we picked up where we left off. We knew how everything was gonna work. If anything, we had to figure out a lot once we got to rehearsals, because the bands themselves had much more equipment, because everyone was trying to one-up each other a little bit, production-wise.

MIKE McCREADY (guitarist, Pearl Jam) The Chili Peppers had this giant psychedelic wheel that they'd turn during their set. And they had these fire hats, which were crazy. I think sometimes they worked and sometimes they didn't work, and if it was too windy there was an issue with that, obviously. It just seemed intense and scary.

CHAD SMITH (drummer, Red Hot Chili Peppers) I remember flames shooting up and looking over at [guitarist] Arik [Marshall], he was like the new guy in the Chili Peppers, first show, Lollapalooza, windy, playing with fire on his head. And the wind blew and it went all down his back and he got all freaked out. The next night, he stood there still as he could, with all this salve all over him, just playing.

MARC GEIGER Don, myself, Ted Gardner, and Perry would discuss picking the bands for '92 on a regular basis. Mostly Don and I would propose what we thought to those two, and then we'd debate and go around and around. It was like a band in a studio at that point, deciding on the songs. We'd mock up lineups, we'd talk about it, lobby for bands, do all that kind of stuff.

If you wanna know who lobbied for who? Don and I and Perry felt incredibly strongly about the Chili Peppers. I was working for Rick Rubin, I knew *Blood Sugar Sex Magik* was coming out, Perry had grown up with the Peppers, so we were all close. Ministry was something we thought was the right thing to follow up Nine Inch Nails. Everyone agreed. Don Muller felt very strongly about Pearl Jam and Soundgarden, and he obviously has great ears and vision.

DON MULLER Soundgarden was the third band I ever signed as an agent. It was Jane's, the Beastie Boys, and then them. I bought in the minute I heard their music. I was like, "I gotta be involved with these guys."

MARC GEIGER Then I think we all agreed, and Perry was very adamant, rightly so, about Ice Cube, who was making incredibly dangerous records at the time, with *Kill at Will* and *AmeriKKKa's Most Wanted*. And I pushed pretty hard for the Jesus and Mary Chain, and also Lush, who were the opener.

MIKI BERENYI (singer, guitarist, Lush) Marc was our agent in America, and we had played two or three shows with Jane's Addiction on the *Ritual de lo Habitual* tour on the West Coast, in some ridiculously huge hockey stadiums. That was a completely terrifying experience, but Perry would come by and hang out with us, which was really sweet. I think he quite liked a lot of the 4AD stuff and he seemed genuinely into Lush. I thought all these sort of American rock bands would just run a mile from a band like us, but they were quite into the idea of having us on Lollapalooza.

Also, I think that possibly we had a bit of a bump because it was a very "male" bill. So they probably needed someone with a vagina on-stage at some point who wasn't just, you know, a go-go dancer for the Chili Peppers.

KIM THAYIL Soundgarden had just come off of tours opening for Guns N' Roses, opening for Skid Row, where we were branching out and expanding our audience to the more mainstream and more metal audience. It was a different culture—more conservative, less oriented toward subversive youth culture, with different ideas about the understanding of gender roles at a rock show. So I think we saw Lollapalooza as beneficial in that we would be back with an audience we'd been building for a number of years previously.

DON MULLER With Soundgarden, there was that kind of mentality for me, like, "Okay, we did some stupid shit, now let's rip 'em back into where they belong."

KIM THAYIL Then the bonus was that Pearl Jam was doing it, Ministry was doing it. There were women onstage in a band like Lush. The audience was well integrated and, it seemed, more considerate of each other, regardless of gender.

MIKI BERENYI There were loads of women on the tour that year, and loads of women in the crew and who were part of the organization, which I wasn't expecting. Although I remember thinking it was quite funny to turn up at some place with these huge tour buses with, like, Roger Dean paintings on the side, and see a woman with a Bon Jovi backstage pass tattooed on her arse, wearing a thong and a kind of crop top. It didn't feel like the festivals in the UK. It felt very "Huge American Rock."

MIKE McCREADY We had the most ostentatious bus, with the *Hotel California* cover painted on the side of it. It was our first bus. Apparently it was Gene Simmons's or something at one time. We got a lot of shit for it.

LONN FRIEND (editor in chief, *RIP* magazine) In 1992 Bon Jovi were making *Keep the Faith* at Little Mountain Sound Studios in Vancouver, and Lollapalooza came through town. And I said to Jon [Bon Jovi] and Richie [Sambora], "C'mon, we're going to a concert. We're gonna go see Pearl Jam and Soundgarden." Richie says, "Cool," and Jon says, "I don't really wanna go." But I dragged them. We get there, it's a rainy day, and the vibe is awesome. The mud, twenty thousand fans . . . Richie says, "This shit's incredible. This is the next thing." When he saw Eddie Vedder hanging from the scaffolding twenty feet in the air and singing "Alive," he knew. He got it.

Jon, not so much. I don't think he felt in any way threatened, it just wasn't his kind of music.

GARY GRAFF It was definitely for a generation of fans that had little or no interest in hair spray or spandex or, you know, boy-girl fucking songs. This was a generation that was going through its own angst, and was looking for bands that expressed that. And they found it in Nirvana and Pearl Jam and Soundgarden.

AL JOURGENSEN (singer, multi-instrumentalist, producer, Ministry) The Pearl Jams and the Soundgardens were exploding. It seemed like the Seattle bands were getting all the love at that time. Then when they started rooting around for other bands they called us, and I had the feeling of just like, "Is this, like, some kind of corporate sellout?" And what does it mean for my career? I actually wasn't really fond of doing it. But I said, "Okay, I'll check into it."

KIM THAYIL And then there was the Jim Rose Circus, and those guys all lived in and around Seattle, or most of them did, and we had known of them, too.

MARC GEIGER I think Perry or Ted brought up the Jim Rose Circus Sideshow, who played on the side stage, which was new that year. And Jim Rose defined the side stage, to be honest with you.

DON MULLER It was like, "Jesus Christ, I've never seen anything like this before." And Jim was a character.

ROB TANNENBAUM With Jim Rose, what Perry Farrell understood was that alternative wasn't just a type of music, it was an ethos.

JIM ROSE (founder, performer, MC, Jim Rose Circus Sideshow) People always say, "Jim Rose, what's the line that you won't cross?" Fuckin' blood, man.

STUART ROSS Because '91 was such an explosive year and it came out of nowhere, we didn't have any trouble selling it in '92. We had more opportunities to play than we had time to do it, because everybody wanted it and they wanted as many shows as they could possibly get. So selling was not an issue. It was a matter of routing it and making the deals.

MIKE McCREADY There was this feeling that you were part of something that was special and different. And it was just like this cool honor to be there, because you had, like, Ice Cube and Ministry and Soundgarden and Lush . . . all these different types of bands together when that didn't necessarily happen that much, especially in America. It was unique.

DON MULLER As far as I'm concerned, that year will always go down for me as being the best touring festival.

MIKI BERENYI It was a bit silly and a bit American and a bit of a fucking circus. But so what? It was really good fun. I was really grateful to do it, 'cause I had a fucking blast.

2 "EDDIE WAS A MONKEY"

KEVIN LYMAN (stage manager, Lollapalooza 1991–92) Lollapalooza, the name, caught on very quickly within the alternative music scene. And I think there were a lot of people who were like, "Oh, I missed out the first year, I gotta go this year." Combine that with the fact that, by the time we hit the road in '92, the grunge movement was taking such a grip on the scene. So the shows were crazy. Every day Pearl Jam would come on and basically the whole venue would blow up.

MIKI BERENYI (singer, guitarist, Lush) Lush were the opening band, but we had an extra kind of bump because Pearl Jam had been booked to go on in the second slot. And in the interim between being booked onto the tour and the tour actually happening, they became one of the biggest fucking bands on the planet. So because of that, there was a healthy number of people there when we played. I mean, none of them gave a fucking shit about us, but it's slightly more rewarding than having the place completely empty. And to Pearl Jam's credit, I think they were offered to go way up the bill and they were like, "No, no, no, it's fine. We're happy where we are."

STUART ROSS (tour director, Lollapalooza) Don Muller represented Pearl Jam before their album came out, and he booked them.

STONE GOSSARD (guitarist, Pearl Jam) Jeff [Ament, bass] and I had been playing music together at that point for ten years. We were in Green

River together and then Mother Love Bone, and had gone through a lot in both of those situations. And then Andy Wood, the singer of Mother Love Bone, died [Wood passed away on March 19, 1990, at the age of twenty-four, following a heroin overdose], and we were at that point where we decided to start all over again and to kind of go, "Okay, well, what's next? How do we do it and how do we find a singer?"

DON MULLER (agent; cofounder, Lollapalooza) I was close to signing Mother Love Bone when Andy died. So Stone and Jeff and I had a relationship. And what happened after that was Jeff called me one day, he was in L.A., he's like, "Hey, man, I've got this tape. You wanna listen to it?" It was the Mookie Blaylock [Pearl Jam's original band name] demo. I listened to it and just fell in love right away. As soon as Eddie [Vedder] opened his mouth, I was like, "Yeah, this is gonna be big . . ."

STUART ROSS I think we paid them eighty-five hundred dollars a night and they were on second from the start.

DON MULLER We're all in a conference room at William Morris, and Perry comes in and, you know, Perry's Perry. I don't know if he was of right mind, I'll leave it at that, but all he wanted to talk about was, like, these giant communal burritos, where you could sit down at picnic tables and everybody could eat as much as they wanted and then they would leave it for other people. It was, "I wanna do this *thing,* man . . ." And it's like, we were already dealing with health department issues all the way around the first Lollapalooza. But I loved the freedom of how he was thinking.

So then I said, "Perry, we're gonna put this band on called Pearl Jam." He's like, "No way. I don't fucking like them, blah, blah." I said, "First off, you don't even fucking know them." They were out at the time opening for the Chili Peppers and Smashing Pumpkins on a theater run, and I said, "We're doing it." And I went head-to-head with him. It was nasty. We were across the table from each other. It almost came to blows in a weird way.

STUART ROSS Obviously we didn't know—maybe Don did—that they were going to be enormous. And so their position on the bill was, um, complicated.

KIM THAYIL (guitarist, Soundgarden) I believe Pearl Jam went through the roof when the "Jeremy" video came out that summer.

RICK KRIM (executive, MTV) A great song made greater by a great video, which then became a big hit.

MIKE McCREADY (guitarist, Pearl Jam) There was this sort of feeling of something's happening and it's bigger than all of us in the band, so we've gotta embrace it. Because now it's out of our control, you know?

KIM THAYIL That was their "Black Hole Sun" moment. Which was a moment, by the way, that we had not yet had at that point. Even though we were playing more in the early evening and they were playing in the afternoon.

STUART ROSS If you think of it logistically, you have eighteen thousand people coming to the show. They didn't scan tickets back then. We did not have the same entrance efficiency levels that we have now, because they were paper tickets and had to be examined. Somebody had to look at your ticket, tear off the stub, maybe there was a pat down to make sure you wouldn't bring in stuff you shouldn't have brought in, and then you came in. But so many people wanted to see Pearl Jam that it was not people coming in over the course of the day, hoping to be there in time for the nighttime acts. They wanted to come in early. And we had a really hard time in some cities trying to get people in that early. If we didn't get people in efficiently, and the kids heard Pearl Jam starting to play while they were still in line, there were times they tore our fences down.

NIKKI GARDNER (assistant to Ted Gardner; special groups coordinator, Lollapalooza) When Pearl Jam was playing, I have a vivid memory of standing on the stage and just watching this mass of kids running toward us. Like a riot.

ELLYN SOLIS (publicist, Epic Records) It was this feeling of, like, riding a tiger at that time. And we couldn't keep up with it.

STONE GOSSARD Having gone through everything we'd gone through, and then to get to the point where we had made a record and now people are actually starting to come to see us—and this is after watching a lot of Seattle bands have some real success and not knowing if we even fit into that world—it was a thrill. It was also nerve-racking. On a lot of levels, I was out there just fucking shaking, in terms of wanting to be confident enough to live up to that excitement and also not always knowing whether it was justified by what we were doing.

MIKE McCREADY It was very bizarre and exciting, like, "What the *fuck* is going on?" And we didn't have a ton of music back then, just the first record and one cover—the Beatles' "I've Got a Feeling," I think. But it was mind-blowing, because you'd see these kids just rush the stage at, like, four o'clock sharp, in a frenzy and jumping over seats. They were just so passionate about seeing us.

KEVIN LYMAN It was right on that teetering brink of complete chaos. The crowd, without any instigation or anything, had to be close to that stage. So they would almost invariably overrun security and it was just a sea of people coming forward.

MICHAEL "CURLY" JOBSON (stage manager, Lollapalooza 1991–92) I've got a photograph of me onstage somewhere, I think it might have been in Virginia, with Eddie Vedder above my head. I'm bare-chested, I've got these neck and shoulder muscles . . . it's from jumping down into the barricade, having young kids put their arms around my neck, and I would use my back and neck and shoulder strength to pick them up out of the barricade and get them over. Stage managers wouldn't be doing this these days.

LYNN HAZAN (front-of-house tour accountant, Lollapalooza) All the crew guys would go and try to prevent the riots and the mosh pits from really coming in. I would be on the side of the stage when Pearl Jam performed, and one of my jobs was that everybody would take off their rings and give them to me. So I would stand there with everybody's rings on my fingers, because nobody wanted to hurt any of the fans.

MICHAEL "CURLY" JOBSON We had twenty thousand kids all crushing into one another and we were pulling them out like lemmings, *boom!* Just outta control. I was putting more chemicals in my system during those three months than I think I'd done in the previous fifteen years. Just to get through it.

JIM ROSE (founder, performer, MC, Jim Rose Circus Sideshow) You can watch the Jim Rose Circus all you want, but the greatest circus performer on that tour was Eddie.

KEVIN LYMAN Eddie, he was climbing up in the ceilings of those amphitheaters . . .

NIKKI GARDNER Eddie was a monkey. He would climb anything and everything. That in itself was a bit challenging just because we obviously didn't want anything to happen to him.

PERRY FARRELL I remember Eddie did a second-story dive off the speaker stacks into the crowd. I thought, For sure this guy broke something.

KIM THAYIL Chris [Cornell] and Eddie, they bonded on that tour over riding bikes and climbing pipes, I guess. Back in our club days, Chris would regularly climb the ductwork and piping work of the venues and treat it all as his personal monkey bars and swing out over the crowd. And then Eddie started doing that on Lollapalooza.

STONE GOSSARD It kind of became part of the show in the sense where, if he felt he needed to or was willing to take it over the top by doing something extreme like that, he would take that chance, and just let the music sort of carry him into some other place.

PHIL BURKE (head rigger, Lollapalooza) There were a couple times when he actually got up on top of the roof. And you're not dropping down from there—that's, like, fifty feet in the air. But most of the time it was just kind of climbing up the side scaffolding, by the PA. And those outdoor stages, they're scaffold-based. So it's kind of like a big jungle gym, anyway.

MIKE McCREADY We'd play "Porch" and he would just take off and start cruising up. And it was like, "Oh, here he goes again." It was exciting and I was also terrified that Ed was going to kill himself. Then he'd jump into the crowd and come back onstage and he'd have all these fingernail markings on him.

EDDIE VEDDER (singer, Pearl Jam) We'd get to the hotel after the shows and I'd feel pretty good physically. And then I'd take a shower and realize that I had, like, a thousand deep scratches on my back.

ANDY LANGER (Austin, Texas–based journalist and radio host) Each time he climbed I remember watching Jeff and Stone and the guys, and they would sort of watch their fingers—because they weren't a jam band but they were forced to improv, improv, improv and stretch out the song—but they were also just as curious and just as wrapped up in the situation unfolding above their heads as we were. Because there was a better-than-likely chance that we all were about to watch a guy fall and die. And no question, death would've been the result.

PHIL BURKE I was tasked with getting his wireless microphone back when he went on his climbing adventures. So we would go up together. He would start climbing, I would follow him, and then he would give me his really expensive wireless mic and I would get it back down and give it to the monitor engineer. But it wasn't discussed or rehearsed. It was all spontaneous.

EDDIE VEDDER Over the gigs it got higher and higher. You'd do one, and then you'd notch it up because you survived the last one, so . . . We're gonna take this to some level that people aren't gonna forget. And if that means risking your life, we're gonna do it.

PHIL BURKE Would I have preferred he *not* do it? Yeah. But that was not my thing. My thing was, "Get the microphone before he drops it." Because even today, those mics are really expensive. And you know, it's a lot easier to climb up with it than climb down. You kinda need both hands on the way back.

STONE GOSSARD I think when he stopped doing it, we were all relieved. Because as fun and exciting as it was, it was gonna end badly at some point.

AL JOURGENSEN (singer, multi-instrumentalist, producer, Ministry) Eddie was a gas on that tour. At one point we had three days off, so he flew with me from Atlanta to Chicago, just to stay at my loft for a few days and party. He was game for anything back then. Of course, now he's very serious and an erudite citizen. But back in the day? Yeah . . .

MIKE McCREADY I remember being at a hotel somewhere down South, and Chris Cornell and Ed throwing a TV out a window. They were doing it to mock *actually* doing it or something. I don't know. But I think they freaked out a little bit, because it was still kind of dangerous.

JIM ROSE I was walking past the hotel and a fuckin' television comes hurtling down and splats right next to me. They didn't know I was walking by.

KEVIN LYMAN The craziest thing was when we did Jones Beach in New York. Right when Pearl Jam was coming on, a giant storm swept up through the bay there. And I'm onstage and I see our village getting blown up. Tents flying up in the air, we're trying to evacuate the crowd under the bleachers . . .

MICHAEL "CURLY" JOBSON Jones Beach in those days was a pretty old place. It was built into a bay, and the water's all around you. They had these arches left and right of the stage where the PA would go, and these kind of wooden walkways to get from place to place.

PHIL BURKE You're on Long Island, and when you're out there you can actually see the weather coming. But it's not like you get a lot of warning. And this was '92, so Doppler radar didn't really exist then. You couldn't take out your smartphone and look online and see where those weather cells are. So it was really seat-of-the-pants. And, boy, I remember the staging guy coming and grabbing me and saying, "Look at this." And we looked out over the water and it was black.

MIKI BERENYI What I remember is that everyone all day was going on about it, the weather report, and blah, blah, blah. I'm not really used to American weather. So I was like, "Yeah, whatever." I thought, All right, it might rain a bit . . . And basically the very last song we played, I remember saying, "Okay, this might be the last song before the rain comes." Within half an hour it was just complete insanity.

MIKE McCREADY A fucking hurricane came in. I remember all my Marshalls went [*makes exploding noise*].

LYNN HAZAN Somebody said, "It's a tornado." And I was like, "It's not a tornado. We don't have tornadoes on Long Island." But I think it kind of was a tornado.

PHIL BURKE We got Pearl Jam off the stage, and then we immediately lowered everything. I think we had maybe ten minutes before that first cell hit, and the first one was really, really violent. It was picking up the roof probably five or six feet. This thing's still hanging on twelve three-ton motors, and it was getting lifted up, unweighting everything, and then dropping again. So you've got sixty thousand pounds getting lifted five feet and then free-falling five feet. I'd never seen anything like it.

MIKI BERENYI I think two people got blown into the fucking sea.

PHIL BURKE I know Curly went for a swim.

MICHAEL "CURLY" JOBSON I was on top of the stage-right PA stack, strapping down tarpaulins to weatherproof it. Was I silly for being up there? Probably. I was *really* stupid for being up there trying to save this equipment. Anyway, it hit us, and I got blown clean off the top. Just picked me up and threw me in the air. I didn't have a hope. Then I was in the water, underneath one of the walkways, trying to crab-crawl my way out of the situation. If you know anything about what happens to water in that kind of turbulence, it's a pretty intense experience. And at that stage in my life, I couldn't swim.

ANDY LANGER The bathrooms were big concrete structures, and I ducked into a bathroom-slash-locker room. And the Pearl Jam guys were in there. The Soundgarden guys were in there. I want to say I remember seeing Ice Cube coming and going. At one point Vedder and Cornell started leading everyone—basically their bandmates and roadies and people like me who dove into whatever cover they could find—in a mini-Sinatra set. I think it was just sort of nervous coping. We were safe, but we were also scared.

KEVIN LYMAN We canceled the show. Our lighting rig was kind of destroyed, and we had to send it down to Georgetown University so they could fix it and put it back together. But my friends in the Ramones' crew came to visit us that day, and the Ramones always had their own lighting system. And we're like, "Oh my gosh, we have to go to Waterloo Village," in Jersey, which was our next show. So I hired the Ramones' crew with their lighting rig to come to Waterloo Village and do our show. It was just a front/back truss, but it worked out fine. All these bands played without their normal lights, their special effects, still conveying all the emotion that was in their music. We just did a straight-up punk-rock show.

And there was another date, I think it was Chicago or St. Louis, that Eddie actually got left at a truck stop.

MIKE McCREADY It was a gas station, at, like, four in the morning. He got out and then the bus took off. This was before cell phones or anything. But we show up to Lollapalooza the next day and . . . Ed's not there. At a couple of the other shows, he and Chris would go to the second stage and do a Temple of the Dog song, so we talked to Cornell and Matt [Cameron] to see if we could do some Temple stuff with them, because we didn't have a singer. I think we did "Hunger Strike" and one other song. And we're starting "Hunger Strike" . . .

KEVIN LYMAN . . . and all of a sudden, you see this truck pull up, and Eddie's coming! He had hitched a ride in a semi to the show.

MIKE McCREADY I look up as we're playing, and I see a guy running through the crowd. I'm like, "What the hell?" And it's Ed! He's fucking running from the back of the stadium to get to the stage. There's some security running with him, and the crowd's kind of parting a little bit as they come through. And we played right when he got onstage. I'm pretty sure I'm remembering this correctly. We had ten, twenty minutes left, and I think we did four songs and we were off.

KEVIN LYMAN Basically my whole life revolved around maintaining the venue to get through Pearl Jam, knowing that Jesus and Mary Chain were the most boring band in the world and we could then get the venue back under control.

MIKI BERENYI At that point, after Eddie's fucking leapt from the scaffolding and everyone's gone completely crazy, and then they all fuck off to the merch stall and to get some beers. And then the Mary Chain are playing in front of a vanishing number of people.

LYNN HAZAN There's a quote not to be attributed to me because I didn't say it, but with Jesus and Mary Chain I remember someone saying, "Oh, the live intermission is on."

JERRY JAFFE (manager, the Jesus and Mary Chain) We always had a few hundred of our fans there in the front. But when you look out at ten, fifteen, twenty thousand people, it was really sparse. The band was used to playing indoors, with smoke and lights, where kids would gather around the stage and it would be kind of an intimate thing. Now they're playing and looking out and seeing vast spaces of just, you know, greenery.

JIM REID (singer, guitarist, the Jesus and Mary Chain) Lollapalooza was a ten-week tour and in the first few days, we realized it wasn't for us. We realized we weren't really going to have a good time.

MIKI BERENYI The Mary Chain, it's quite introverted music, to be fair. And the vibe on that tour was very much Pearl Jam, Soundgarden, Ministry, Chili Peppers . . . a certain kind of blokey, very "male" music.

JERRY JAFFE The Jesus and Mary Chain looked at them all as metal bands. It was something that they just didn't cotton to whatsoever.

WILLIAM REID (singer, guitarist, the Jesus and Mary Chain) That was the worst experience of our lives. We had to play something like forty dates over two months or something. By the second gig, we realized we'd made a mistake, and we had another thirty-something gigs to play to thousands of Beavises and Butt-Heads.

BEN LURIE (guitarist, the Jesus and Mary Chain) We were a bunch of little introverts, and suddenly we're on this big tour that's kind of like school camp or whatever, and we're expected to hang out with everybody. It just wasn't our nature.

JIM REID We tried to get off the tour. We asked if we could just leave the tour. They were basically saying we couldn't or they'd sue us. We were stuck with it. The only way we could get through it was to get absolutely fucked up. We were on at two o'clock in the afternoon, which was partly the problem. We are kind of a nighttime band. It was really bad for your health, too, because I'd get incredibly drunk for the show and afterward I'd collapse in my bunk, then wake up at eight in the evening and get drunk all over again. There was a drug aspect to it, as well. It got pretty mental on that tour.

ANTHONY KIEDIS (singer, Red Hot Chili Peppers) The whole show was a lovefest except for the Jesus and Mary Chain . . . who were just bitter. They'd polish off a giant bottle of booze by two in the afternoon and curse and put everyone down.

JO LENARDI (vice president of alternative marketing, Warner Bros. and Reprise Records) They were all miserable men. And I always thought, Is this a show or is this real? Bicker, fight, bicker, fight, break up every night. That's what they were always like.

ANTHONY KIEDIS One time they went too far with the guys from Ice Cube's band, and they got themselves a beating.

JERRY JAFFE What happened was, there was a communal eating area for lunch. And Ice Cube had a fairly large entourage, to say the least. There was one day where the guys were eating, and somebody from Ice Cube's camp made some derogatory remark to William and then pushed his plate. So William, he picked up something off the table and threw it at the guy. And a fight ensued.

MICHAEL "CURLY" JOBSON It was alcohol fueled, culturally fueled . . . you know, Scottish guy and guy from Compton. Not quite sure how well that mixes.

JERRY JAFFE There were a couple of punches thrown. If memory serves, William had a black eye or something. He didn't need medical attention, but he was hurt.

MICHAEL "CURLY" JOBSON I mean, look, there was a bottle involved in the whole process. Nobody likes to see that sort of thing. I made no bones about it, being a Scottish guy myself, and also someone who wasn't much troubled about throwing down. The violence wasn't nice. It was unseemly. It left a bit of tension around the place for a while.

MIKI BERENYI There was another bit of a tussle because Ice Cube had these huge bodyguards, and I can't remember if there was one or two of them, but they would stand onstage with these sort of Super Soaker water guns. It was a bit fucking ridiculous, if I'm honest. But some fight kicked off when William from the Mary Chain was walking around backstage with his girlfriend, and one of these guys sort of soaked her top in a kind of targeted, wet T-shirt kind of way. And William, in his red mist, went up to basically have a fight with someone who was about three times his size. He did score points for having the balls to challenge someone that big.

JERRY JAFFE The size of the guy would never make a difference to William. He reacts first and would say later, "Well, that guy was huge . . ."

BEN LURIE We were all children. Running around with a Super Soaker and then getting annoyed about it? Ridiculous.

AL JOURGENSEN It must've seemed to Ice Cube like being behind enemy lines. Like, this was an experiment—let's put hip-hop culture in the middle of this rock culture and see how it works. I'm sure he felt under siege.

KEVIN LYMAN Ice Cube's crew, legitimately, were a little bit worried. Because they're going to go out on a tour with a predominantly white crew and, like, how's this going to work? And the Nation of Islam came out for the first few shows, too. So there was a little bit of an edge there. But that edge kind of wore down and everybody understood we were there to cooperate. But man, when you had to go out and mingle or deal with police and stuff, I mean, there was some problems.

MICHAEL "CURLY" JOBSON He and his people had their battles. There was racism pointed at them by dipshit skinhead, right-wing clowns. And I would stand shoulder to shoulder with those guys and fight the skinheads any day of the week over those kinds of issues. I had fights in the crowd. I had fights backstage. I had run-ins with dudes with big Doc Martens. I'm not scared of them. Never been scared of them.

KEVIN LYMAN There was something in North Carolina, I don't recall exactly what. But there were some issues.

AL JOURGENSEN We did a show and there was a bunch of rednecks, like typical MAGA-type people today, that were all pissed that there was a rap band on a rock festival. And they were there for violence.

MICHAEL "CURLY" JOBSON The Carolinas were tough. The skinhead inclusion. And it wasn't really just directed at Ice Cube. It was directed at, you know, "lefty lovies," like we all were to them. And it wasn't just Carolina. We'd have it happen in Atlanta. We'd have it happen in Texas, we'd have it happen in Florida. In the heartlands of racist America, it was going on.

FRITZ MICHAUD (stage manager, Ministry) The fight in North Carolina actually happened at the hotel where we were all staying.

AL JOURGENSEN I remember I was sitting on the balcony of the hotel, watching my crew fight a bunch of rednecks. And I had no idea, but Ice Cube was in the room next to me, so he was out on his balcony with his guys, seeing what all the kerfuffle was about. He looked over at me on my balcony as we're watching and he goes, "Damn, man, I never seen so many white people fight at one time in my life!"

FRITZ MICHAUD What was told to me later was that one of Ice Cube's guys said, "Homeboy jumped out the tree like Wolfman!" And I was homeboy. I came out from behind a bush, basically, because this guy was swinging a spiked belt around. So I just came up behind him and jumped him. And I broke my hand on the guy's face. Then everybody beat on them for a minute and they ran off and that was the end of it. We went back inside the hotel and had a drink. Well, I went to the hospital. But everybody else had a drink.

AL JOURGENSEN When Ice Cube found out what the fight was about in North Carolina, he came up to me and he goes, "You guys are cool." So we had a good relationship from there on out. But it didn't start out that way. I remember at the beginning of the tour, he and his crew were in our dressing room taking our beer. And I was like, "Well, fuck that." I'd just gotten out of the shower after getting offstage, and I had a towel wrapped around me and I basically chased him down the hall with my fucking dick in my hand, going "Here! You want some of *this*?" I know that his bouncers got a big kick out of it. Instead of getting my ass kicked, they were laughing their asses off about the whole thing.

So in the end it all turned out well. You know, people *can* get along.

3 "THIS IS S'PPOSED TO BE ROCK 'N' ROLL, NOT MOAT-*ZART!*"

KEVIN LYMAN (stage manager, Lollapalooza 1991–92) If there was ever a reincarnated pirate on the road, it was Al Jourgensen.

MIKE McCREADY (guitarist, Pearl Jam) There was always a crazy party when Al was around.

MICHAEL "CURLY" JOBSON (stage manager, Lollapalooza 1991–92) Al brought the straight-up comedy, but Ministry, that band was also the absolute best part of the show. They were the power and the humor on that '92 tour.

AL JOURGENSEN (singer, multi-instrumentalist, producer, Ministry) Well, the whole thing about how we wound up on there was super bizarre to start with. I went to the first Lollapalooza, because I knew Gibby from the Buttholes and of course Trent from Nine Inch Nails. And it seemed like kind of a novelty thing. But when it came time to do a second one, they were trying to wrangle bands together and they called us. Then they sent me back the schedule for the day and we were on at, like, two in the afternoon. And I just said, "Ministry is not a picnic band." That's what I told them. "There's no way we're doing this. I can't play during the day."

MARC GEIGER (agent; cofounder, Lollapalooza) So that's Al saying, "I negotiated a better slot," basically? I don't really remember. I think we did feel Ministry was kind of perfect for the "Siouxsie" slot. But he probably did say something. Who knows? He could be right.

AL JOURGENSEN So eventually they switched us to the nighttime slot, sandwiched right between Ice Cube and the Red Hot Chili Peppers. And there's no reason that I should have been in that slot. Soundgarden and even Pearl Jam were much bigger bands than us at the time. But it was the perfect storm for us.

MARKY RAY (roadie, Ministry) I mean, I love the Chili Peppers. I've known them since 1984. They're friends of mine. But we blew them off the stage every night.

KEVIN LYMAN I just remember Ministry showing up for the tour with a giant floor package of lighting, and all these bones and skeletons.

MIKI BERENYI (singer, guitarist, Lush) To me, they looked terrifying. Like a biker gang. Tattoos everywhere, shaved this and pierced that and fucking god-knows-what.

MARKY RAY The Ministry entourage was huge—twenty-two people, band and crew. And we were a motley crew. It's like if you took a pirate ship, took the worst characters off of it, and put them on a rock 'n' roll tour bus. I mean, Jesus Christ, we were some serious characters.

KEVIN LYMAN They had a guy with tattoos all over his face, their "bone man," who collected roadkill.

MICHAEL "CURLY" JOBSON Turner Van Blarcum, from Dallas. One of the finest guys out there.

JON ZAZULA (manager, Ministry) His job was to collect roadkill, cut it down, put it in acid, dry the bones out from all the skin, and make statues for the stage set. Al was into the whole thing. I remember going out to Al's apartment in Chicago once, and we're hanging out and I told him I needed some air. I go through this vestibule to his roof, and there's nothing but carcasses everywhere, covered with maggots. It was insane, man.

AL JOURGENSEN We were the first to use Turner's bone sculptures as mic stands and stuff like that. But after us, I think Metallica hired him and Aerosmith hired him. So he did well.

FRITZ MICHAUD (stage manager, Ministry) These sculptures, Turner was constantly having to remake them, because Al would break them onstage. He would smash them up, or he would tear bones off and throw them in the crowd.

AL JOURGENSEN With Ministry, the visuals were important. And the volume. Basically I made no money on Lollapalooza because we exceeded the sound limits in every venue. So I had to pay fines every single show. But it was worth it to differentiate us from the other bands. As long as we could be loud and have our visuals and our lights, we were happy playing for free.

MARKY RAY We were 126 dB in the side fill. A complete audio assault on the crowd. We pummeled them into submission.

STONE GOSSARD (guitarist, Pearl Jam) I remember really enjoying just the complete, like, sonic concussion of Ministry, and just how crazily pumped and loud that band was.

TOM BUNCH (manager, Butthole Surfers) It was fucking brutal. The loudest thing I think I've ever been to. I had known Al for a while, but not back in his super-disco-poppy time. I probably met him in '88-ish, '89, when the industrial thing started happening in Chicago. Over those few years Ministry definitely got really fucking heavy and really hard.

JON ZAZULA Ministry came from the industrial, alternative world. I was a metal guy. But what Al was doing at that time, with the *Psalm 69* album, it was metal, for sure. When he did "Just One Fix," I had Chuck Billy from Testament in my office and I said, "Chuck, you wanna get your ass blown away?" I put on "Just One Fix" and he said, "Fuck! That's heavy, man!" And it was. Al had crossed that line. His shit was heavy.

MARKY RAY When we played those Lollapalooza shows, the fans would tear the lawns up at these outdoor venues. There were sod fights, there were bottle fights, there were mud fights . . .

LYNN HAZAN (front-of-house tour accountant, Lollapalooza) I'm sure you heard about the flying sod in Boston . . .

FRITZ MICHAUD We were at Great Woods in Mansfield, out in the suburbs of Massachusetts. The crowd ripped up the entire lawn and were just throwing these huge clumps of grass. They tore down the back fence and made a gigantic bonfire that I would say was easily fifty feet high.

PHIL BURKE (head rigger, Lollapalooza) The amphitheaters all have that upper lawn, and a lot of them have an upper fence. So, during Ministry it became like this pagan ritual—tear up the lawn, throw the sod down on the stage, rip the fence apart, light it on fire, and dance around the fire. It was like a scene out of Dante's *Inferno*.

AL JOURGENSEN That was a very difficult situation for us. I was up there saying, "Really, people, you've got to stop." Because it was starting to get dangerous. They were literally ripping up benches and barricades and sod and throwing them at the stage. We got, like, three lawsuits out of that particular show. There must've been a million bucks' worth of damages to the place.

FRITZ MICHAUD Apparently they had a Boston Pops thing happening either the next day or a couple days later, and they had to do some kind of emergency delivery for a bunch of grass. But it wasn't Ministry's fault. It just got crazy.

JAN T. GREGOR (road manager, Jim Rose Circus Sideshow) In general, everything on that tour that was drama or that cost money was usually caused by someone with Ministry.

AL JOURGENSEN Well, I was a full-blown junkie back then. The time I met up with my dealer was more important than the time I had to be onstage, if you know what I mean. I lived on Dealer Standard Time throughout that whole tour, and that's just the way it was.

MIKI BERENYI There was somewhere in Atlanta where I seem to recall Al spiking everybody's drinks with chocolate mescaline, which I'd never heard of. He had half the hotel running around all night, and there was one guy going, "Where's Al? I'm gonna fucking kill him!"

MIKE McCREADY Al had two holsters full of Bushmills. I remember that. Actual holsters that he would walk around with.

KEVIN LYMAN Once in a while right before he went onstage he would pour a capful for the crew, and we'd have a little toast. We really didn't drink when we were working, but a capful of Bushmills wasn't going to ruin your life.

AL JOURGENSEN I always used to put a few drops of this very pure liquid LSD in the Bushmills, because Timothy Leary was part of our little crew back then. Him and William Burroughs would intermittently come to some of our shows on that tour.

PAUL D'AMOUR (bassist, Tool) Back in '92, Tool's manager was Ted Gardner, and we were just kind of coming up and we got invited to go hang out at Lollapalooza and got to meet some of the bands. I was a huge Ministry fan, and we wound up partying with them backstage. Then somebody comes in and says, "All right, you guys gotta get toward the stage." Al's walking out the door and he hands me his bottle of Bushmills. He goes, "Here you go, kid, knock it back!"

AL JOURGENSEN You remember that Coca-Cola commercial with "Mean" Joe Greene of the Pittsburgh Steelers, where he gives the kid his jersey as he's walking down the tunnel to the locker room after the game? That's what it was like with my bottle of Bushmills.

PAUL D'AMOUR There was a good inch or two left in the bottom, and I just slugged the whole thing down. Little did I know he had it laced with his Tim Leary–grade LSD.

MAYNARD JAMES KEENAN (singer, Tool) I didn't get dosed. You don't walk into a room with a person like Al Jourgensen and put your glass down. He might have dosed Paul, but he definitely didn't get me.

AL JOURGENSEN There was a couple of times where I would do a shot and go into a nod. And it's like, "Come on, Al, five minutes! You gotta be up there!" I remember the Chili Peppers' roadies, one of them had dreads and he would just borrow my cowboy hat and he would go up and sing the first song for me if I was late. This is true. He did it a couple of times where I couldn't make it onstage 'cause I was just so wasted. By the third song, I would come out there and I think maybe only half the people even noticed the difference.

JON ZAZULA Al Jourgensen was quite the guy. The only one who seemed to be on par with Al was Perry Farrell, who played the second stage with Porno for Pyros on occasion. Perry and Al related very heavily to the point of, I think, Perry having to be excused from the Ministry dressing room once.

AL JOURGENSEN I think it was a California show where the bus had just dropped us off, and we went back to our little dressing room and there was this guy shooting up in the dressing room. I just thought, That's fucking rude. So I go, "Dude, you gotta leave." Then after he left, somebody says to me, "That's Perry Farrell." I wish I would've known because I would've asked him if he had any extra.

KEVIN LYMAN Then there was an instance one time with Gibby and Ministry, they took a bunch of fireworks and blew up their tour bus.

MIKI BERENYI Gibby Haynes came along for some of the Ministry shows. And look, I get it. He's a fucking wild man. But you know, after a while that whole kind of tongue-lolling shtick . . . I just find it a bit irritating.

You don't have to sit there going, "Hey, I bet you're a *tiger* in the sack," and all of that. It's like, "You can stop all that. It's fine. We can just have a normal conversation." But some people are just completely unable to do that.

JON ZAZULA Gibby would come on the tour to do an occasional "Jesus Built My Hotrod" with the band.

TOM BUNCH No. Gibby did show up, but he did not do "Jesus Built My Hotrod." They *asked* him to do it, but Gibby decided he wasn't going to rehearse, he wasn't going to sing, it was too hard for him. But he *was* gonna go to the shows and just get high and do dope and chase women or men or whatever the fuck.

GIBBY HAYNES (singer, Butthole Surfers) The way those guys played, there was no way I could do it with them. You have to sit there and count: 1, 2, 3, 4, 1, 2, 3, 4. *"Every time you tell me, baby, when I settle down . . ."* That would be really hard.

MICHAEL "CURLY" JOBSON Hijinks was a big part of Gibby's life, and Al loved it, of course.

GIBBY HAYNES In Houston me and Al hijacked a golf cart, which is kind of de rigueur for what a singer in a rock band does at such events. And we got stopped by the cops pulling onto I-10. But the cool thing was, we weren't on the entrance ramp. We were on the *exit* ramp.

AL JOURGENSEN One day we wound up buying all these bootleg pyrotechnic fireworks at a gas station in the South. And we decided, not so smartly, to light them all up on the bus, and the bus caught on fire. It was an incredible fire, though, because it was multicolored, just like the fireworks would have been.

GIBBY HAYNES What do you call 'em? Mortar shells? It's a tube, and then you get a ball with a fuse on it, you light the fuse, it falls down the tube, and *bam*!

MICHAEL "CURLY" JOBSON They went to the front of the bus and fired it from where the driver was, all the way through the bunks into the back lounge. Setting the back lounge on fire.

GIBBY HAYNES The bus immediately filled with deathly smoke. And then the bus driver slammed on the brakes. And if you've ever been on a tour bus, when the driver slams on the brakes, it's not like a smooth thing. It's like *bopbopbopbopbopbopbop* . . .

AL JOURGENSEN He pulled over and threw a fit. "Get off my bus! Get off my bus! You ruined my bus!" He called the police on us, and the state troopers came out. By that point, somebody had gone back into the flames and gotten our keg of beer off the bus. So we were just sitting there on the side of the road drinking beer, and this guy's screaming at the cops saying, you know, we're Satan incarnate, we're evil and this and that. And then these fucking cops, I'll never forget, just went, "Well, boy, what'd ya expect? This is s'pposed to be rock 'n' roll, not Moat-*zart*!" And that was it. We got back on the bus, the driver took us to the next show, dropped us off, and quit. And then we got a new bus.

JON ZAZULA I have to be honest with you, there were times where I had had enough. I had to take a break from it. And Al included me in maybe 60 percent of what went on, and 40 percent he knew I didn't wanna be included, or he didn't want me around. He didn't want any authority figures. I tried to keep it cool and keep things somewhat safe. But there were times when cool and safe were not on the calendar.

AL JOURGENSEN It actually turned out to be a really dysfunctional functional tour.

KEVIN LYMAN We finished in Dallas the second year, and I'll never forget, at the end of the last show, the trucks are leaving, and Al's bone man walks up and he's like, "I'd love to give you this, Kevin, as a thank-you." And he handed me a cow head with rat heads, with squirrel heads, with bird heads, with insects, all glued together. I didn't know what to do with it, so I took it with me as a carry-on and flew home with it. Security had to put it through the X-ray machine and they had a lot of questions. Probably the strangest and coolest post-tour gift I was ever given.

AL JOURGENSEN The nineties . . . they were pretty much like the Wild West, you know? By the way, a footnote: I've been clean now for more than twenty years. So that's a good thing. But at the time, yeah, things were very different.

4 "A LEAN, MEAN FREAK MACHINE"

DAVE KENDALL (creator, host, MTV's *120 Minutes*) The Jim Rose Circus Sideshow was a very significant part of creating the vibe of that '92 tour, just because of the visuals, the theatrics . . . it was a talking point for everyone to congregate around, with this sort of early Burning Man feeling.

KIM THAYIL (guitarist, Soundgarden) Those guys were fun to hang out with. You learned different ideas through the things they found interesting.

MIKE McCREADY (guitarist, Pearl Jam) They had such a unique kind of democratic weirdness to them. Jim was a trip, and just all the eccentricities—Mr. Lifto, the fact that they're drinking bile and doing all this weird shit—it was part of the coolness of Lollapalooza that year.

PERRY FARRELL The Jim Rose Circus . . . that really defined the whole alt nation, what we were about and up to.

JIM ROSE (founder, performer, MC, Jim Rose Circus Sideshow) The phrase "alternative nation" had just been coined, and what the hell is that? But Perry did an interview at the time and he said that the Jim Rose Circus is what "alternative" meant. Now, I didn't set out to be an alternative darling. I was on heroin for ten years and I got off heroin just to do Lollapalooza. I never got back on it, though. So that's kinda cool . . .

DAVE KENDALL I think what the Circus Sideshow did was create kind of a visual metaphor for feeling like an outsider.

JIM ROSE I was born cross-eyed, and, man, that doesn't seem very freak-ish, but I stuck out like a sad thumb. I'd go to school and I'd get beaten up, and I'd go home and my dad would beat me, too. Plus, I had severe fucking tinnitus, which I still have today. And sleep apnea. And then I had asthma. So, you know, there was a lot going on there.

MATT "THE TUBE" CROWLEY (performer, Jim Rose Circus Sideshow) I think the nature of sideshows appeals to the general vibe of transgression common in rock music and "youth culture."

THE TORTURE KING (performer, Jim Rose Circus Sideshow) Was it a statement? I guess an awareness of taking down restrictions was part of what it was. The whole idea of the sideshow, whatever era it's set in, is that you're showing things that aren't normal, right? It's like, "Here's some weird things that can happen with the body." It's a lot of body explora-tion and endurance, things like that. Maybe to that degree, this was a revelation to some young people that they had more control over their bodies than perhaps they were told they did. Certainly I think some people got that out of it or thought that was the message, whether it was intended or not.

THE AMAZING MR. LIFTO (performer, Jim Rose Circus Sideshow) I thought we were just out there having fun. We didn't really get much into the whole politics of it. It was like, "Look! I'm going to get naked in front of an audience!" That's my political statement. "Nudity forever!" But, you know, hindsight is twenty-twenty, right?

JIM ROSE My thing was playing on anti-censorship. I always made the show feel like what you're seeing is illegal, even though it wasn't. This was right when political correctness was showing up. So the rules weren't really firm. People were just finding their way and, quite frankly, I pushed the whole anti-censorship thing so heavy that a lot of these people thought they were being PC by supporting that. I don't know if that makes sense to you, but that's what happened.

DAVE KENDALL Jim reminded me of Malcolm McLaren. The ultimate impresario.

THE AMAZING MR. LIFTO A pure sense of will, I want to say.

SLUG THE SWORD SWALLOWER (performer, Jim Rose Circus Sideshow) The complete con man. The complete hype-ster. He's a natural at it.

JIM ROSE Before me, it was guys with wax mustaches barking at carnivals.

SLUG THE SWORD SWALLOWER The first time I met Jim, I said, "I swallow swords." I think he said, "Great, will you swallow a sword in my show?" Next thing you know, I'm the greatest sword swallower that ever lived, there's only one in the world and that's me and blah, blah, blah. I'm just kind of a nerdy, crazy character and I'd never experienced sensationalism like that. Someone that could just boast and make up the truth. Lie, basically.

JIM ROSE When I was a kid I worked next to the Arizona State Fair, and we would jump the fence and get jobs vending soft drinks and stuff. We were just neighborhood hoodlums—we started stealing as much as we were selling, because they weren't really paying us. But anyway, that allowed me access to all kinds of freak shows and, oh my god, I was just so drawn to it. To this day I can still recite the patter: "*Step-right-up-what-you're-about-to-see . . .*" Using that kind of voice and shit. I was hearing it every day, all day long. And I thought, You know what? I'm going to take this off the fairgrounds, and I'm just going to start trying to jam it into different types of venues. And I'm going to use humor to make the atrocities palatable.

THE TORTURE KING The thing about Jim, you've got to realize that he spent a lot of time in Venice Beach doing street performing. A lot of his skills are kind of like a street performer. They've just been changed a little bit for the stage.

JIM ROSE Eventually I went to U of A in Tucson. But just before I left to do that I was jumping motorcycles. I jumped . . . I think it was eighteen cows at one of these little rinky-dink places. And when I landed I must have hit some spent cud because I came down a little wobbly and hurt my back. That's why, as I speak to you today, I've got the posture of a jumbo shrimp.

But anyway, I had all this pain from my back injury and I got on heroin. Eventually, to get *off* heroin, I went to France, because my wife, she's French. But the first few times I went to France I was still *on* heroin, and they had all these people doing these old-time freak-show things in front of the [Centre] Pompidou. And the whole picture became clear to me. I said, "I know what to do with this." I started going every day, watching it, learning to be a street performer, learning to do freak-show performance stuff. And as soon as I learned it all I went straight to Venice Beach. That's where Perry, I'm sure, first saw me. He told me he saw me there, anyway.

PERRY FARRELL You know, if he says I did, then I'm just not thinking. You know what I mean? A piece of my brain is erased. But I'd like to hear that story . . .

JIM ROSE So in Venice Beach, I used to make seventeen thousand dollars a month in fucking quarters, doing face-in-glass, human dartboard, all that stuff. I did chains-and-handcuffs because I was aggressive in collecting the money and the police would keep an eye on me. And I'd always say, "Well, look, how much can I be intimidating these people? I'm in chains and handcuffs!"

By my last year in Venice I noticed the audience had changed. It was all these kids that were super fascinated with what I was doing, but I wasn't connected to pop culture. I was too busy hunting down heroin and just doing these damn shows. And so I got off the beach and I went to Seattle. This is before grunge. I just needed to get to a new town where I didn't know where to get heroin. And I decided, This is where I'm going to make my mark.

THE TORTURE KING I met Jim Rose in Seattle, in like, '90, maybe early '91. He had done one show at the Ali Baba, this place in the Capitol Hill district. And then I went to the second show he did at the Ali Baba. Jim would just yell out people's names in the audience and they would do stuff. I think Lifto was in the audience. He was Joe Jism at that point. Joe Jism! I remember this.

THE AMAZING MR. LIFTO I was doing weird performance-art stuff, like nailing my wiener to a board through my Prince Albert [piercing], which freaked everybody out. I saw some flyers for this crazy show—Jim's first show at the Ali Baba—and I remember it was packed. A lot of people wanted to see what this was all about. I remember looking out and Mark Arm from Mudhoney, his face was pressed against the window. Someone else, too, maybe Jeff Ament.

JIM ROSE I knew the Seattle bands. These guys, before they were famous, they were coming to my shows. I mean, Kurt Cobain was trying to sneak into my show.

THE TORTURE KING After I saw the show at the Ali Baba I went up to Jim Rose and I said, "Hey, nice to meet you. I do *this* . . ." And I showed him a few things.

MATT "THE TUBE" CROWLEY I was the last to join, and that happened at a club in downtown Seattle called Club Sophie. I did a very simple version of my tube act.

JIM ROSE Matt was just one of these people that showed up and said, "Hey, I'd like to join your circus." He was a pharmacist in Montana. I mean, so much of what I would say on that show was bullshit, but that was actually true.

MATT "THE TUBE" CROWLEY Though originally from Montana, I didn't practice pharmacy in Montana. I had a steady job as a pharmacist at Pay 'n Save, a Seattle pharmacy chain that's now defunct.

THE TORTURE KING This shows you how Matt's mind works: He had a friend who had given him this veterinary syringe, and then he thought, Well, maybe I can do this bar bet with it . . . I talked him into doing that as a public performance at this Church of the SubGenius kind of event on Capitol Hill. This wasn't really, let's say, a classic sideshow stunt. It was a very weird thing.

MATT "THE TUBE" CROWLEY A nurse friend of mine in Missoula intercepted a box of gastric lavage units—stomach pumps—on their way to the garbage. He gave me one. I tried putting a tube down one nostril and it wouldn't go there. The other got down to my throat but hit my gag reflex and made me feel like vomiting. I set the thing and the idea aside for some years. In Seattle it occurred to me that I could do a bar bet in which I could consume the contents of a beer without it touching my lips. I thought a cork stopper with a tube on the end would push the beer into my stomach if I shook up the bottle. It didn't quite work, so I returned to the gastric lavage unit, a.k.a. stomach pump.

THE TORTURE KING We moved to a few different venues, and started performing at the Crocodile Café. That place was somewhat of a petri dish of the early grunge scene, and there were people from all kinds of bands who were in the audience. We were doing two nights every two weeks and packing it out consistently. After that, we did this tour of Canada and we went all the way across from the west to the east and then back. And then all of a sudden here we are on Lollapalooza . . .

HEIDI ELLEN ROBINSON-FITZGERALD (publicist, Lollapalooza) The Sideshow was something that was so exciting because, to me, it fit into what my concept of what Perry's concept was of Lollapalooza—something that was just so outrageous and that you'd never seen before. The first time I saw the show, I was appalled. Like, Oh my god, this really nice guy does *this*?

THE TORTURE KING Lollapalooza was a circus theme looking for an alternative circus act. But nobody knew who we were, really.

JIM ROSE By that point I'd done theater shows and sold-out tours across Canada, but I hadn't been thrown into a situation like Lollapalooza before. I was ten years older than anybody that was there, onstage or off. I remember somebody pointing to a crowd and saying, "That's Jane's Addiction." And I said, "I hope she gets treatment!" I didn't have a *clue* who any of them were.

But I realized, Okay, this is a really big opportunity, and I don't think the way I do the theater show is going to work. So I watched, like, twenty minutes of MTV, and that was right when they were doing that real-quick-edit crap. And I read *SPIN* magazine. And I go, "Okay, I gotta use the F-word and talk real fast." So that's what I did. The show you saw on Lollapalooza, you were watching a theater guy that just sped everything up and said "fuck" a lot.

JOHN RUBELI (second-stage manager, Lollapalooza 1993–95) Jim Rose was basically a concourse of oddities that went alongside the music, that was put on the second stage.

JIM ROSE I remember the first day, I could have fired a cannon and not hit anybody. I mentioned it to Chris [Cornell] and he says, "Oh, well, just introduce our band and then I'll take care of it." You have to remember that my show came on the second stage right after Soundgarden's set on the main stage. So I would go introduce Soundgarden and run over to the second stage, and then when they finished their set Chris would say, "All right, everybody—let's go to the other stage with me and watch the Jim Rose Circus!" And man, that's what got us our huge crowds. You needed alligator repellent and a weed whacker to get to that second stage. So Chris solved that for me.

THE TORTURE KING Word of mouth was really strong. And by the time it really began going across, the word of mouth was extending outward into the press and things like that. Perry Farrell himself came out for a photo shoot that ended up in *SPIN*. We got in *People* and all these magazines and newspapers. It was like, even though we were the under-advertised act, everybody was paying attention.

HEIDI ELLEN ROBINSON-FITZGERALD We got more press on Jim Rose than for anybody else on that tour. I wanted to put so much attention on him because, to me, what he did just crystallized what Lollapalooza was and wanted to continue to be. And it had all the elements needed for a really great story in every market, every paper.

JAN T. GREGOR (road manager, Jim Rose Circus Sideshow) I was a really jaded guy and it really did my jaded heart good to see big burly guys in leather jackets faint during our show. We would get three or four paramedics to our stage, and I would talk to them before the show and I would say, "People are going to faint." And you could just tell that they did not believe me. And then when people started fainting, you know, it's like, "Wow . . ." What they were doing at that time, you just couldn't believe people would do that.

THE TORTURE KING We basically revived this art form that had been for-gotten. And especially for the young people of the day, they were com-ing up to us and saying, "How did you guys think of all this stuff?" We were just bringing back these old classic sideshow things, but presenting them in front of a modern-rock audience.

THE AMAZING MR. LIFTO What were we doing? Well, the Torture King, he was doing human pincushion. He had, like, a whole chest full of pins, and then he'd put one through his cheeks, one in his wrist, poke it up so you could see the skin stretching out and stuff.

KIMBA ANDERSON (performer, Sharkbait) Sharkbait were on the second stage, and we shared a tour bus with the Jim Rose Circus. I'd come on the bus and see the Torture King setting himself up, getting the needles put into him. His chest and belly and everything would be just com-pletely riddled with syringes—*hundreds* of them. And then he would take an hour or two, put his robe on over all of it, and head to the stage.

Henry Rollins (foreground)
and Chris Haskett of
Rollins Band, 1991 (*from the
collection of Chris Haskett*)

Perry Farrell and
dancers, onstage with
Jane's Addiction, 1991
(© *Chris Haskett*)

Farrell (left) and
Dave Navarro of
Jane's Addiction, 1991
(© *Chris Haskett*)

Ice-T, 1991 (© *Chris Haskett*)

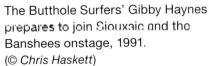

The Butthole Surfers' Gibby Haynes prepares to join Siouxsie and the Banshees onstage, 1991.
(© *Chris Haskett*)

BELOW: Haynes strips down and shoots with Siouxsie, 1991. (From left) Steven Severin (in purple), Sioux, Haynes, Jon Klein (in green), and Paul Leary of the Butthole Surfers. (© *Chris Haskett*)

ABOVE: Lolla crowd surfers, 1991
(© *Chris Haskett*)

Vernon Reid (left) and Corey Glover of
Living Colour, 1991 (© *Chris Haskett*)

BELOW: Ministry's Al Jourgensen (left)
and Soundgarden's Chris Cornell
(center) join Eddie Vedder (right)
and Pearl Jam onstage, 1992.
(© *Matt "The Tube" Crowley*)

The Amazing Mr. Lifto, second stage, 1992 (© *Jan T. Gregor— Circus of the Scars*)

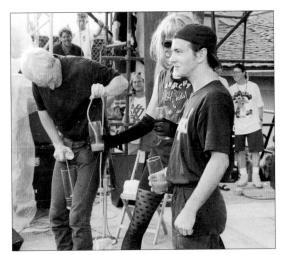

Vedder (right) prepares to drink bile beer with the Jim Rose Circus Sideshow's Matt "The Tube" Crowley (left) and the Amazing Mr. Lifto (in drag), second stage, 1992. (© *Jan T. Gregor— Circus of the Scars*)

Vedder climbs a lighting rig, 1992. (© *Matt "The Tube" Crowley*)

ABOVE: Jim Rose commands the Safe Sex Wheel of Fortune, 1992.
(© *Jan T. Gregor—Circus of the Scars*)

Lou Barlow of Sebadoh, 1993
(© *John Rubeli*)

BELOW: Mosquito, second stage, 1993.
(From left) Steve Shelley, Jad Fair, and Tim Foljahn. (© *John Rubeli*)

Rage Against the Machine, anti-PMRC protest, Philadelphia, July 18, 1993. (From left) Tim Commerford, Zack de la Rocha, Brad Wilk (obscured), and Tom Morello. (© *Sarah P. Weiss*)

Kim Gordon (left) and Julia Cafritz of Free Kitten, 1993 (© *John Rubeli*)

Timothy Leary watches Tool perform on the second stage, 1993. (From left) Leary, Maynard James Keenan, and Paul D'Amour. (© *John Rubeli*)

Ted and Nikki Gardner, backstage, 1993 (© *John Rubeli*)

Nick Cave (left) and Wayne Coyne of the Flaming Lips, second stage, 1994
(© *John Rubeli*)

Guided by Voices, second stage, 1994. (From left) Mitch Mitchell,
Kevin Fennell, Robert Pollard, and Greg Demos. (© *John Rubeli*)

Billie Joe Armstrong
of Green Day, 1994
(© *John Rubeli*)

BELOW: Luscious Jackson
dance routine, second stage.
(From left) Vivian Trimble, Jill
Cunniff, Gabby Glaser, and
Kate Schellenbach, 1994.
(© *Kate Schellenbach*)

ABOVE: The Verve, second stage. (From left) Richard Ashcroft, Nick McCabe, Peter Salisbury, and Simon Jones, 1994. (© *John Rubeli*)

Ad-Rock of the Beastie Boys (left) and Donita Sparks of L7, 1994 (© *John Rubeli*)

Q-Tip of A Tribe Called Quest, 1994
(© *John Rubeli*)

Billy Corgan of Smashing Pumpkins
(left) and Jimmy Flemion of the Frogs,
second stage, 1994 (© *John Rubeli*)

BELOW: The Breeders, backstage.
(From left) Jim MacPherson, Kelley
Deal, Josephine Wiggs, and Kim Deal.
(© *Kate Schellenbach*)

Mike D (left) and MCA of the
Beastie Boys undercover, 1994
(© *John Rubeli*)

Coolio, 1995 (© *John Rubeli*)

Patti Smith, second stage, 1995 (© *Catherine McGann*)

Moby, second stage, 1995
(© *Catherine McGann*)

Cypress Hill and audience, 1995 (© *John Rubeli*)

(From left) Thurston
Moore of Sonic Youth,
John Rubeli, and Beck,
1995
(*courtesy of John Rubeli*)

Ken Andrews of Failure,
second stage, 1997
(© *Sarah P. Weiss*)

BELOW: Porno for Pyros, second
stage. (From left) Stephen
Perkins, Farrell, and Peter
DiStefano, 1997. (© *Sarah P. Weiss*)

Radish and crew member (Ben Kweller at center) with Snoop Dogg, 1997
(© *NoiseCo Archives*)

Eels, second stage. (From left) E, Jonathan "Butch" Norton,
and Tommy Walter, 1997. (© *Sarah P. Weiss*)

Ken Bethea (left) and Rhett Miller of Old 97's, second stage, 1997 (© *Sarah P. Weiss*)

Stuart Ross (center) with Devo. (From left) Josh Freese, Mark Mothersbaugh, Bob Mothersbaugh, Bob Casale, and Gerald Casale. (*courtesy of Stuart Ross*)

THE TORTURE KING Somebody sticking needles in himself in the back of a tour bus on a rock tour, it shouldn't be an outrageous thought. But probably the way I was doing it . . .

THE AMAZING MR. LIFTO Slug the Sword Swallower would play keyboards and then he would come out and swallow a sword and eat worms and bugs.

JAN T. GREGOR The bug eating, it was kind of a variation of a geeky act, but, I mean, it was just gross. Eating crickets, big mealworms, slugs . . .

SLUG THE SWORD SWALLOWER It was shock value. But also, people didn't know you could eat those things back then. Nobody knew what was going to happen to you. When I first ate a slug I was with the Torture King, and I called up the Poison Control Center and said, "Oh, my son ate a slug. Is he going to be okay?" And they said, "Sometimes there's microbacteria that could be harmful, or if it was on a rhododendron it could have poison in it. But otherwise, no, you'll be okay." So I was like, "Great!"

THE TORTURE KING Lifto, I think, was the most quote-unquote modern-primitive performer in the Sideshow.

MATT "THE TUBE" CROWLEY His act in particular appealed to the growing body-piercing movement.

THE AMAZING MR. LIFTO Let's see . . . I put a coat hanger in my nose and I'd hang up my jacket, and then I would lift up steam irons with my ears and swing 'em around. And then the crowd-pleaser was I would put hooks in my nipple rings and lift a cement block.

PERRY FARRELL I had so much fun watching that guy Mr. Lifto lift up big, heavy weights with his balls—it might have been his dick—it showed you how strong a dick can be when it really needs to.

THE AMAZING MR. LIFTO The first month or so I would lift weights with my wiener, through my piercing. I would put shaving cream on it so you could kind of see it, but it was theoretically covered up. Certain places didn't like that. I could look out in the crowd and see the cops sitting there watching and waiting, because you know, it was an all-ages show. So that was, Yeah, I'm not going to jail for that just yet . . .

JAN T. GREGOR The threat was always hanging over the swingin' dick a little bit. There were examples where it really kind of came to a head, so to speak. One was in St. Louis. And that's when we started getting legal threats not to have that act performed. And in fact, the city council set up this little mini stage riser so they could watch the show and monitor it. After that, Jim made the call for the rest of the tour to rarely do the swingin' dick.

JIM ROSE How much weight would he lift with his penis? Oh god, that's a good question. Twenty pounds? Thirty? It won't sound like a lot to you, but when it's through a piercing in the head, it can bring a tear to your eye.

THE AMAZING MR. LIFTO There's a certain amount I can do every day that stretches it out just right, so you get the crowd reaction. It gets longer, but thinner. Like a pencil. But then if I have time off it kind of snaps back, like a turtle.

JIM ROSE I was eating razor blades. I had darts thrown in my back. I put my face in glass, let people step on the back of my head. And BeBe, my wife, she would have a watermelon on the back of her neck and we hit it with a sword. She'd walk up a ladder of swords. What else? Oh—she'd get in a plastic bag and have the air sucked out with a vacuum cleaner. She also did the human cannonball, which by the way, was a different version than what Homer did in the episode of *The Simpsons* later on where Homer joins the Jim Rose Circus. But you know that . . .

SLUG THE SWORD SWALLOWER When you can do something that nobody's ever seen, nobody's even thought of, it's such a magical thing. And what we were doing was real magic—it wasn't an illusion. It was people putting themselves out there. This is before the internet, this is before . . . who are those crazy stunt kids? It's before *Jackass*. Before all of that. We were doing all this crazy stuff and it was real.

JIM ROSE You're seeing what's happening . . . it's just that I know more about what's happening than you do. I'll put it to you this way: I taught Eddie Vedder to put his face in glass, and he let me step on his head for five minutes. Now, it was real glass, and it was the glass I broke. It's just that there's stuff I know about the glass that you don't.

I'll tell you the trick: You break the glass in a bag and then you have people in the audience verify that it's real. Then you say, "Okay, shake it up!" Now, when they're shaking the glass up like that, it knocks off all the sharp edges and gets smooth. Of course, not every one of those shards gets completely smooth, so, you know, I've been cut doing it. It's not *nothing*.

PERRY FARRELL And then the other cat who drank his own vomit, his own bile. I remember watching them with Flea and then the guy said, "I want one person from the audience to come up and drink my bile." Flea volunteered to do it, saying, "Me, me, me!" Then he got sick for three days . . .

MATT "THE TUBE" CROWLEY Chris Cornell was the first rock star to consume the contents of my stomach, though not the first human to have done so. It took place in Detroit, and I didn't know beforehand it was happening. After it happened I trailed off after him, asking him typical fan questions like, "Why did you do that?" But he said nothing and his motive remained a mystery.

KIM THAYIL Jim probably invited me to come up and do it. And I said, "*Nooooo*." And then he invited Chris up to do it. Chris said, "Sure!" And then Chris got Eddie to do it . . .

THE TORTURE KING Eddie Vedder was certainly, I think, the most thirsty. He might've done it the most.

EDDIE VEDDER (singer, Pearl Jam) Just looking for attention, I guess. Every city there'd be some old friend or my wife's parents, and I'd get to gross everyone out.

DON MULLER (agent; cofounder, Lollapalooza) Remember that by that summer Eddie was the biggest star in the world. And him going out in the crowd, walking to the side stage, he had security, whatever, but the swarm of kids . . . I equate it to when Tiger Woods wins the Masters or the British Open, and all those people just run, but they're held back. It was like that kind of shit. And then he gets up there and drinks bile . . . I'm fucking looking for a trash can.

JAN T. GREGOR It kinda became one of those one-upmanship things on that tour, 'cause the sideshow's making everything wilder. And then during the off time in the cafeteria, or backstage playing foosball and all that kind of stuff, Jim's goading everybody: "You're going to come up and drink it, right?" Or, "Chris came up in Detroit. What about you, Eddie?" Jim's amazing at selling stuff, amazing at manipulating people. And that was perhaps his greatest manipulation: getting somebody from every band, except I think Jesus and Mary Chain and Ice Cube, to come up for a drink.

MATT "THE TUBE" CROWLEY Eddie Vedder [did it] four times, Al Jourgensen four times . . .

AL JOURGENSEN (singer, multi-instrumentalist, producer, Ministry) We would drink that shit and just go, "This is nasty!" But at that point you can't back down. You just gotta keep doing it. So it kept going.

MATT "THE TUBE" CROWLEY . . . Flea once. Not Gibby, that I recall. I think Miki from Lush imbibed, as did Matt Cameron from Soundgarden.

MIKI BERENYI (singer and guitarist, Lush) I do remember standing with Jim from the Mary Chain, and he was just looking at me, going, "You're not fucking doing this, are you?" And I was like, "Of *course* I'm doing it—I need the fucking attention!" He just looked at me, absolutely appalled.

JIM ROSE What did it taste like? I don't know. I didn't drink it.

THE AMAZING MR. LIFTO I drank it a couple times. But, you know, that was the nineties . . .

JIM ROSE Realistically, it's pretty much what we put in the pump and pulled right back out. You know how if you drop food on the floor and you pick it up within ten seconds, you can eat it? Well, it was only in his stomach for about ten seconds.

MATT "THE TUBE" CROWLEY Beer, ketchup, Maalox, sometimes an egg, sometimes chocolate syrup. I'd put seven feet of soft tubing into my nose and push it all into my stomach. At the other end was a very large plastic syringe I had built myself using a drill press. We would usually pour in forty ounces of beer. Push it all in, then slowly begin to suck it back out, just like an ordinary syringe.

THE AMAZING MR. LIFTO It came back up warm, which was a little weird. That would make you kind of gag. Like if you left a beer out in the sun overnight, and then added ketchup to it . . . and chocolate sauce. It's odd. It's hard to describe.

JIM ROSE Once Eddie shows up and does it, well, that makes it on MTV. Now, when I offer it to the audience, fucking half the crowd comes up. They all want to drink vomit. And that was becoming a security problem. So I had to stop offering it. I mean, hell, one time they just basically knocked the stage over trying to get to our vomit! We started this whole thing where everybody's trying to outdo each other and be the freakiest they can be. And the next thing I know, all the rock stars, they end up with my phone number. They call me up, "Jim, what are you doing today, *da da da*." Everybody wanted to hang out with me.

THE TORTURE KING Jim Rose, whenever he heard somebody might be remotely famous, he would want to get his photograph taken with them. I wasn't that much into celebrity culture.

MATT "THE TUBE" CROWLEY I got to know Kim Thayil during that tour and we became friends.

KIM THAYIL I became very close with Matt the Tube. As a matter of fact, I ended up being the best man at his wedding.

MIKE McCREADY That's hilarious. Oh my god, I wanna see Kim in a tux!

JIM ROSE They all came toward me. They all wanted a piece of that freak show vibe. As soon as Lollapalooza was over, the Red Hot Chili Peppers put out a video with a freak show in it. I mean, they weren't thinking of that before they saw me.

THE TORTURE KING Toward the end of the tour we had a few days off in New Orleans and they had a Lollapalooza party at, like, a Margaritaville or something, for the bands and crew. And Lifto decided, "Hey, why don't we do a performance?"

JAN T. GREGOR Everybody was basically on mushrooms and hurricanes.

THE TORTURE KING I remember this thing where Lifto was doing his act, and then they put a straw, like a drinking straw, through his Prince Albert urethra piercing, and then put that into a cup that had some alcohol in it. And it's like, "Who wants to drink from the straw?" Next thing you know, there's a big line, and Al Jourgensen is sucking down on this straw, which was going right through Lifto's dick into the thing of booze.

NIKKI GARDNER (assistant to Ted Gardner; special groups coordinator, Lollapalooza) I have a picture of Al Jourgensen wearing a fake pair of breasts, drinking out of a hurricane straw stuck through Mr. Lifto's penis. It was very funny.

AL JOURGENSEN Well, I vaguely remember that night. Although I actually think I did that a couple of times. The amazing part about that whole thing is that they kept trying to talk me into getting a Prince Albert, and somehow I avoided that. Thank god.

JAN T. GREGOR The buzz at the end of Lollapalooza was really high. So from that, we were invited up to the fifteenth floor of Triad, where we sat around a big table. All the agents came in and made offers for Europe and Australia and the US and everything. No one really knows what's going to sell tickets, but there were lots of people willing to gamble on the Sideshow. So at that point we signed to Triad, which was later sold to William Morris.

DON MULLER How could you not be involved with those guys? The whole thing was fucking nuts.

JIM ROSE I was on *The X-Files*. I had a TV show on the Travel Channel, *The Jim Rose Twisted Tour*. I had a bestselling book. And then some kid that watched *Beavis and Butt-Head*, who were always going, "Fire! Fire!," he lit his parents' mobile home on fire. Everything became imitable. That became a big problem. So I had to go carve out another career in Europe. Actually, I'm better known in Europe now. But anyway, by the time I came back to the United States to reclaim some stock, *Jackass* had filled the void.

THE TORTURE KING I always thought it wasn't going to last very long. I thought, like, Oh, geez, we're going to be a faddish thing and it'll be gone. Or somebody else will start doing some similar thing and then it'll lose its novelty.

THE AMAZING MR. LIFTO Like, I have face tattoos, and it used to be you'd see somebody with face tattoos and you'd go, "Okay, you're a biker." Or, "You're a convict." It was kind of a club. Now everybody has words written on their face. Big plugs in their ears. It's like, "Hey, that's cute, kid." You go pat 'em on the head.

JIM ROSE What I did is I created a new tentacle for the punk movement. There's a freak show in every city now!

5 A BRIEF HISTORY OF THE SECOND STAGE

MARC GEIGER (agent; cofounder, Lollapalooza) We decided to do the side stage to have more bands, because seven was not enough.

STUART ROSS (tour director, Lollapalooza) So the side stage was a really interesting dynamic. First thing is, nobody had ever done a second stage before, not that I'm aware of. The other thing is that we set up the side stages in the concourse area of the amphitheater. Now, in those days, amphitheaters didn't really have much in the way of activations. It was basically food and bathrooms—now they look like shopping malls. Often we didn't have the room to put it up, and we used to have to get the amphitheaters to tear out fences and to go into parking lots or wooded areas because we literally could not fit the number of people that would be watching, let's say, Jim Rose, in the space available. We really made promoters jump through hoops to pull this thing off.

So beginning in '92 the side stage existed, and it was controversial. But I'm not really clear on the programming, because I honestly didn't get out there that much. John Rubeli is the world expert on the side stage.

JOHN RUBELI (second-stage manager, Lollapalooza 1993–95) In 1992, the stage was literally plywood on milk crates. There was Jim Rose, but otherwise it was loose and it wasn't publicized and it was kind of here and there. It was sporadic.

KIMBA ANDERSON (performer, Sharkbait) We were one of the few acts that toured as part of the side stage in '92. Us and Jim Rose and, I think, the Archie Bell Dancers.

THE TORTURE KING (performer, Jim Rose Circus Sideshow) Archie Bell was this performance-art type thing. So you'd always have a lot of these beautiful female dancers just hanging around at the second stage.

KIMBA ANDERSON Sharkbait got on there because someone from Bill Graham Presents saw our show. We had a lot of pyrotechnics, full frontal nudity, a lot of fire. I don't know if you've heard of Einstürzende Neubauten? We had a lot of that—true industrial music with contact mics on metal and steel. Someone showed it to Perry and he was like, "These guys are on the tour, right?"

For Lollapalooza we had this thing called the Rhythm Beast, a sculpture that people could bang on and play. We would do these processions, which was basically like a parade, from the stage over to the field where the Rhythm Beast was, and then start people playing it. Then we had a "crush cage," where we would have upward of about fifty broken televisions in there for people to crush. We would get people set up with gloves and goggles and everything, pour denatured alcohol on it, and they would go in and crush these flaming television sets. We called it "total destruction of your reality."

JAN T. GREGOR (road manager, Jim Rose Circus Sideshow) Sharkbait did a lot of the early Burning Man festivals, and I think Burning Man had a lot to do with bringing that sort of subculture out to Lollapalooza, too.

KIMBA ANDERSON We got put on a bus with the Jim Rose Circus, and we were all like, Oh my gosh, we're traveling with the freak show! And that was really thrilling, because Sharkbait was kind of a freak show in itself.

JOHN RUBELI The Jim Rose Circus was an attraction, right? But I think as it was going along that year, Lollapalooza decided here and there to work in other musical acts, but it wasn't something that was put together at the beginning. I know that Stone Temple Pilots, who were really early in their career, did a couple dates in '92. Cypress Hill. And Rage Against the Machine, who were also new, did one.

DEAN DeLEO (guitarist, Stone Temple Pilots) We played the second stage in Phoenix that year—our first real gig ever, outside of, you know, some little club in east L.A. We were way, *way* far away from the main stage. We didn't even see the Chili Peppers and Soundgarden and Pearl Jam, all those cats. I remember it was about 110 degrees, we're loading and unloading our gear out of the truck. We get onstage, and Scott [Weiland, Stone Temple Pilots singer] really didn't know about trying to salvage your voice through an entire show. He came out guns a-blazin' and lost his voice after the second song. We played maybe one more and then we split. We thought our career was over.

STEVE STEWART (manager, Stone Temple Pilots) Atlantic Records came out to that show. It might've been the first live show that a lot of those people had seen. It was middle of the afternoon, and it was 115 degrees. And I don't know if it was production, I don't know if it was in the band. I don't know what it was, but yeah, it was just not happening. And I remember the label executives just looking at me like, How much have we spent on this band?

DEAN DeLEO Then about a week later, we did one more side-stage show, at Irvine Meadows [Amphitheatre] in Orange County. It was us and . . . who was it . . . those Samoan rappers, the Boo-Yaa T.R.I.B.E. Remember them? And Rage Against the Machine was there. We kind of knew those guys, especially Tom Morello, because we used to play, like, the Coconut Teaszer and Club Lingerie in L.A. together, with the band he was in prior to Rage. But this was a whole different vibe.

TOM MORELLO (guitarist, Rage Against the Machine) We opened up for Boo-Yaa T.R.I.B.E. at that show. We had just formed, our first album wasn't even out, and Perry invited us to play the Lollapalooza side stage at the Los Angeles date, one of the last shows of the '92 tour. Which was a huge coup for us.

TIM COMMERFORD (bassist, Rage Against the Machine) That was big for me, because I grew up right near there. My whole musical experience as a kid was sneaking into Irvine Meadows for every show, no matter who was playing. Now it's called TikTok Amphitheatre or some dumb shit.

SEN DOG (MC, Cypress Hill) We did a few dates on that second stage on that tour. When we first got to the venue, I think it was in Northern California, we saw the second stage, it was tiny. There was no one around. We just immediately wanted to say, "Hell with this, let's leave." But I'm a beer head, so I said, "Let me get a beer, and then we'll leave." I go to get the beer and kids are coming up to me, like, "Cypress Hill, three forty-five, yeah!" I went back and told the guys, "Let's not leave. I think it's gonna be good." So three forty-five comes around, and the stage that was empty prior, all of a sudden it's jumping off.

JOHN RUBELI The next year, I was officially brought on to do the second stage. I had met Ted Gardner, who was managing Jane's at the time, and I had known Perry because I was a Jane's Addiction fan and I had roommates that used to play the club Scream in L.A. with them all the time. And so it just became, "Let's give this kid free rein."

STUART ROSS The side stage changed in 1993. And the only reason—or the big reason, at least—that it did is because a company out of Montreal developed a trailer stage that, using hydraulics, basically set itself up. There's hundreds of these things now, but one of our crew discovered it, went up to Montreal to look at it, and we bought the very first one. It was a company called Stageline, and it was the SL100 mobile stage. They still make 'em. The only way we could pull this off was to get something that we could set up and tear down in a very short period of time.

JOHN RUBELI That year I showed up to my office and it was just empty. It was a desk, a chair, a phone, and that was it. I wasn't sure what to do—I was twenty-three years old. But I had booked shows in college, and I had brought everyone from Primus and Nine Inch Nails to Nirvana and the Flaming Lips to campus. And in doing that, I watched people get exposed to something that was unfamiliar to them, and have their whole world kind of turned upside down. You had this festival showing up in these suburban markets, outside of the main handful of alternative markets, and that was wonderful, because people were there to see the talent on the main stage, but they were also there for eight or nine hours. So having another stage meant we were going to have the opportunity and the time to expose them to so much more music.

STUART ROSS John started booking the side stage from our offices. He put out a note in zines saying, "You wanna play the side stage at Lollapalooza? Send a cassette to . . ." With a post office box address. And he would come in with crates of tapes. I remember seeing him two feet deep in cassettes, sitting there with a boom box literally listening to every single one.

JOHN RUBELI Perry kind of just left me to it, which then led to, Okay, what do I do? I started thinking about all the different bands that meant something to me, and bands that would complement and augment the main stage. And the first band I booked was a band called Cell, who Sonic Youth had signed to DGC. I reached out to their manager, Lyle Hysen, who had been in the band Das Damen.

LYLE HYSEN (manager, Cell) I remember Rubeli calling me, and that it seemed like a pretty blank slate. I was like, "Well, what else do you got?" But I was friends with all these bands or friends with the managers, so it was all pretty natural to be like, "Let me help all of these bands possibly make the most money they might ever make." What a great thing to hook your friends up with. "Hey, dude, you wanna do this thing? I'm not sure if it's going to be sick, but you get some cash and you get to play some shows and do some weirdo gigs."

KEITH NEALY (drummer, Cell) We were just like, "Oh my god, what are we doing here?" But I think in general we were psyched, just because it was a pretty new festival.

JOHN RUBELI Lyle became kind of like my ultimate ambassador to the indie rock world. He knew everyone and had the ability to get ahold of everyone. And so that gave way to meeting Kristin Thomson and Jenny Toomey from the band Tsunami and the label Simple Machines. They were really helpful in reaching out to a lot of the Dischord, Teen-Beat kind of indie East Coast rock bands at the time. Then I was friends with Dan Koretzky, who had Drag City and who recommended the Royal Trux.

KEITH NEALY We hung out with the Royal Trux guys a bunch. They always beat us at poker and won all of our per diem.

JOHN RUBELI So word started getting around that Lollapalooza was adding this layer that was including the indie world. That gave way to getting a call out of the blue one day from Steve Shelley of Sonic Youth, who said he wanted to perform with his side project, Mosquito, with Tim Foljahn from Two Dollar Guitar and Jad Fair from Half Japanese.

STEVE SHELLEY (drummer, Sonic Youth, Mosquito) We would go to the site, play during the day and then, as the side stage started to wrap up, we would load into our minivan and we would drive off as the headliners were starting to gear up on the main stage.

TIM FOLJAHN (guitarist, Mosquito) What we were doing was really weird music, but the side stage was come-as-you-are. We'd be playing to maybe two hundred people, this little audience that was definitely more the indie-rock crew—horizontal-striped T-shirts and glasses and shit. People who were like, I don't care about that other stuff. I'm going to watch this fucking freak show because it's different.

STEVE SHELLEY Our group definitely was a bit hard to pin down, so I think we were very happy with any sort of reaction or audience.

JOHN RUBELI Ninety-three was the first year where you'd see the bands on the second stage in the advertising, and a proper stage for them to play on. And one thing I fought for, which the organizers were really great about, was there was a merch booth specific to the second stage where the bands could sell anything at any price and keep 100 percent of the sales.

TIM FOLJAHN We were actually getting paid pretty well. A lot of money for us. And the funny thing is, Lollapalooza had put all the side stage bands' names on the main tour T-shirt, so then we all got a cut of the merch money, same as anybody.

STEVE SHELLEY There was a windfall of dollars. I guess it was a mistake, but they felt like they had to take care of us because they were selling merch with our name on it. And that was really appreciated that they did that.

TIM FOLJAHN I was making more money than I'd ever made playing a show!

JOHN RUBELI Having Mosquito led to Kim Gordon [Sonic Youth bassist and singer] calling and saying, "I have a side project called Free Kitten with Julia Cafritz from Pussy Galore and Mark Ibold from Pavement. We wanna play." Then Thurston [Moore, Sonic Youth guitarist and singer] called: "My wife's on the road, I'm working on some solo stuff, can I play?" It just built on itself.

STEVE SHELLEY I think at that point in time Sonic Youth had not really felt much of an affinity with what Lollapalooza was doing—the booking was a little less adventurous than what we were interested in. But it seemed like the side stage was where the fun was happening.

KEITH NEALY I mean, on our stage there was a lewd puppet show, with marionettes who'd fuck each other and stuff. And the occasional comedian, I think. They just threw all kinds of weird shit up there.

JIM GREER (senior editor, *SPIN* magazine) It was an alternative to the alternative, or something.

THE NEW YORK TIMES (June 27, 1993) *Although Lollapalooza wasn't invented as a make-work project for obscure performers, its second stage* *is a modest gesture in the right direction, presenting independent-label bands like Sebadoh and Tsunami along with local performers.*

JOHN RUBELI That year in meetings, I also really advocated for Dinosaur Jr. on the main stage, because I felt they were a bridge to the kind of indie, alt stuff I was doing on the second stage. And so that led to me booking Sebadoh, with [former Dinosaur Jr. bassist] Lou Barlow.

LOU BARLOW (singer, multi-instrumentalist, Sebadoh) They gave us a thousand dollars in cash every day. It was great. That's all I cared about. I didn't care about the quality . . . I mean, at that point our shows were so sketchy. Some shows were good, some shows were terrible. Whether a show was going to be good or be what you thought it would be was not a question. You just did shows. But a thousand dollars a day cash, there was absolutely no question. Like, "Yeah, okay."

JOHN RUBELI Sebadoh's agent was a real supporter of a lot of what I was doing. And honestly, I just really like Sebadoh.

LOU BARLOW John was cool. Made it really easy for us. He had a little air-conditioned trailer that I'd go into every day and he'd hand me my cash. We always had a nice little exchange. The word from the top was that Perry was just really into supporting bands and was really into making the side stage a place where you could see the indie bands of the moment. And they did that.

JOHN RUBELI The big thing at the time was, "Oh, are J Mascis and Lou Barlow gonna fight?"

STEVE KNOPPER (editor at large, *Billboard* magazine) Lou was on one stage and his old band, which had essentially fired him, was on the other.

LOU BARLOW I don't remember being too bugged by it. I was not on good terms with them, but it was more that I wasn't on *any* terms with them. If anything I think I perversely got off on it. Like, "That's cool. They can play the big stage. We'll play over here."

JOHN RUBELI The only time I saw J come over to the second stage, he walks over, you know, his hair in his face, he looks up onstage and Sebadoh's playing. And he kind of just nods his head, turns around, and walks away. That was the big confrontation.

LYLE HYSEN Dinosaur Jr. were on the main stage and they were absolutely miserable. So I think all the indie bands were feeling pretty good. "I'm doing this festival, I'm getting paid pretty well. And I'm playing the cool stage, so my name won't be tracked through the mud." That whole indie-versus-major thing was still very much part of the conversation.

JOHN RUBELI By '94 the thing had grown to the point where the second stage was given its own area. And at some shows, between the Flaming Lips and the Verve and some of these bands, we'd have five to ten thousand people. So it went from a few hundred people to a few thousand people in basically one year.

STEVEN DROZD (drummer, multi-instrumentalist, Flaming Lips) We had heard that the year before, with Sebadoh and Mercury Rev, wasn't that organized. And that maybe it didn't go so well for some of the bands. But by '94 it was just really well-organized and people actually came over to watch the shows.

WAYNE COYNE (singer, guitarist, Flaming Lips) We felt like we were in the coolest spot of all. We were playing later in the day, so we had giant crowds. Some of the biggest crowds we'd ever played to.

JIMMY CHAMBERLIN (drummer, Smashing Pumpkins) When people think of Lollapalooza back then, they think of the big-picture bands—Jane's Addiction, the Chili Peppers, the Pumpkins, Soundgarden. But really, the foundation of Lolla was the second stage. That was what it seems like Perry was most into—the avant-garde part of it, or the things that are reacting to what's going on in the mainstream, but not necessarily replicating it.

JOHN RUBELI The second stage was an extension of Perry. A lot of people back then, in my experience, were sort of dismissive of his kind of grandiose, poetic imaginings. But if you leaned into what he was saying, he really was trying to be the ultimate kind of impresario. For him, having more music just made sense. The second stage became another way to grow the musical footprint that Lollapalooza was stamping across the country.

LOLLAPALOOZA 1993

DATES: JUNE 18–AUGUST 7

MAIN STAGE: Primus, Alice in Chains, Dinosaur Jr., Fishbone, Arrested Development, Front 242, Babes in Toyland (first half), Tool (second half), Rage Against the Machine

SECOND STAGE: Sebadoh, Cell, Unrest, Mercury Rev, Mosquito, Free Kitten, Royal Trux, Tsunami, Tool (first half), Mutabaruka, Thurston Moore, Sleepyhead, various

If Lollapalooza's 1991 outing was the festival's big bang moment, and '92 possibly its pinnacle, then the 1993 iteration was, well, another Lollapalooza. In retrospect, the bill doesn't elicit the same "wow" factor as its predecessors, or a similar sort of total recall (wait—*Primus* headlined?). But the fact remains that the main-stage lineup was impressively diverse.

Along with Primus, the festival presented grunge heavy hitters Alice in Chains, then at the height of their musical powers but also gripped by singer Layne Staley's worsening addictions; gnarled-guitar slacker icons Dinosaur Jr.; manic punk-funk polyglots Fishbone, the first band to play the big stage in two separate years; raised-consciousness alt hip-hop troupe Arrested Development, riding high on the wave of critical and commercial success generated by their debut album, *3 Years, 5 Months and 2 Days in the Life Of...*; long-running Belgian "electronic body music" crew Front 242, an act with only the most tenuous ties to anything remotely

American or alternative; and Babes in Toyland, a female grunge-punk trio who perpetually sounded on the brink of combustion, but, like most Lolla main stagers, benefited from the steady hand of major-label backing.

In a turn of events that mirrored Pearl Jam the previous year, the lowest-billed bands on the '93 main stage, Rage Against the Machine and Tool (who moved up from the second stage half-way through the summer to take the place of the departing Babes in Toyland), proved to be the twin breakout stars of the fest. "We put the hammer down every day," Rage Against the Machine guitarist Tom Morello recalls. "Rage and Tool were just coming in headhunting."

Much of the musical action was also taking place away from the main event, at the newly emergent second stage, which had developed from the fragmented, ad hoc attraction it was in '92 to a genuine showcase spot for left-of-center acts. "I think that what Lollapalooza was doing at the time was reflecting the frontline alternative rock and alternative rap music worlds," says John Rubeli, who began a three-year run as second-stage booker that year. "I tried to augment that with the second-stage supplement, so if somebody was there to see Alice in Chains or Primus because that's what they understand from the radio and MTV, they might wander over to the second stage, where it's like, 'Who's Mosquito?' 'What's Tsunami?'"

"If we could transport back to Houston, two thirty in the afternoon, and look out from that stage, you'd go, 'Oh, okay. It's a bunch of sweaty kids. And there's not a lot of them. And they're kind of like, What the fuck?'" says Lou Barlow, the former bassist of Dinosaur Jr., now on the tour fronting his band, Sebadoh. "But it was about all of us being part of this kind of ramshackle community that had formed in the wake of Nirvana."

Indeed, by the time Lolla '93 pushed off from Vancouver's Thunderbird Stadium on June 18, that ramshackle community had become a dominant cultural and commercial force. "Nirvana reset the bar," Tool front man Maynard James Keenan says. "And now balding record-label dudes with ponytails in jean jackets were desperate to grab any band they didn't 'get' right away, thinking, Well, maybe this is the next thing?"

He continues, "So there was a lot of scrambling. And people that were living on the edge, writing on the edge, performing on the edge, benefited because it was a chance to put them in the spotlight that they probably never would've had if something like the hair-band phenomenon had continued."

The landscape where Lollapalooza was situated had definitively transformed since 1991. So much so that the annual success of the tour was now a fait accompli. "Lollapalooza is becoming a habit: spring break for the alienated," *The New York Times* declared in a July 21, 1993, review. This was hardly conjecture. The *Times* reported that the previous summer's fest had grossed $19 million playing to 800,000 fans, and that the '93 outing was expected to draw an estimated 850,000. According to tour director Stuart Ross, '93 also marked the first time Lollapalooza announced an on-sale prior to revealing a single act on the bill. The date, in Chicago, quickly sold out. "It was proof of the value of the brand," Ross says. Additionally, prior to that year's tour, Triad Artists, the agency home of Lollapalooza cofounders Marc Geiger and Don Muller, was purchased by and absorbed into industry powerhouse William Morris, which would add another layer of muscle to the Lolla enterprise going forward.

The festival was now a major force in the mainstream music ecosystem. "When Lollapalooza became a phenomenon, it wasn't just, 'Perry Farrell is curating a nice day for the children of America to be exposed to cool new acts,'" Morello notes. "Now it was, 'We can break our new act that we've signed that sounds kind of like Nine Inch Nails or Soundgarden by jamming them onto this bill.'"

"Being on Lollapalooza at that time was an acknowledgment that you were a rare bird, or at least you were anointed to be a rare bird," says promoter Andy Cirzan. "By 1993, there was just so much competition to get on this thing."

1 "ARE WE SELLING OUT BY DOING THIS THING?"

LES CLAYPOOL (bassist, singer, Primus) The first time I ever heard of Lollapalooza, I remember we were on tour at the end of 1990, it was Jane's Addiction, the Pixies, and Primus in the States. And then we went to Europe with Jane's, and I was hanging out with Perry and Stephen and . . . for some reason the Soundgarden guys are popping into my brain, too. But we were in Nottingham, it was late night after a show, and we were in front of the oldest pub in the world or something, smoking hash under a statue of Robin Hood. And Perry kept talking about, "Yeah, we're doing this thing, Lollapalooza . . . We're gonna do this Lollapalooza . . . You gotta do it . . . You gotta do it with us . . . You gotta do Lollapalooza!" I'm like, "What the fuck is *Lollapalooza*?" I had no idea what the hell he was even talking about.

Then Lollapalooza happened, and we ended up on the third one.

STEVE KNOPPER (editor at large, *Billboard* magazine) Nineteen ninety-three was an interesting year. In '92, in addition to having massive bands with huge commercial followings, it was super memorable. You had Eddie Vedder climbing on top of speaker cabinets and jumping into the audience, Ministry playing one of the loudest and most macabre and bizarre shows I've ever seen at an outdoor festival—everything was loud and crazy and insane. After that, '93 maybe also felt like a drop-off in terms of the commercial profile of the bands.

STUART ROSS (tour director, Lollapalooza) It was very alternative. I mean, Dinosaur Jr., Front 242, Primus . . . these were very alternative acts. Looking at it now, it looks like, "Yeah, this was not the blockbuster bill . . ."

MARC GEIGER (agent; cofounder, Lollapalooza) I was not involved that year because I had changed jobs, and I couldn't tell you [how the bill came together]. Ninety-three was the only year I was preoccupied. Don Muller's the one who would remember.

DON MULLER (agent; cofounder, Lollapalooza) Look, hindsight being twenty-twenty, nobody could compete with '92. And so how do you repeat it? You can't. So we did the best that we could with what we had. And, I mean, Alice in Chains was starting to go, but they didn't go nearly as big as Pearl Jam. But I was proud of that bill and proud of that year.

HEIDI ELLEN ROBINSON-FITZGERALD (publicist, Lollapalooza) My recollection of the third one is that it was even bigger than the second one. Every year just got bigger and bigger and bigger, especially in terms of name recognition. By '93 the integrity of Lollapalooza was really solid.

STUART ROSS Nineteen ninety-three was a year where an artist representative came to us and demanded a percentage of profit because they said to us the Lollapalooza name didn't mean anything. That without their band on the bill, Lollapalooza is gonna mean nothing. It was a big demand and we considered it insulting. So I went to the promoter in Chicago, Andy Cirzan from Jam Productions, where they had the World Music Theatre, which was and probably still is the biggest amphitheater in the country, and where we had always played. I would say it holds thirty thousand. And I said, "Andy, what do you think about advertising Lollapalooza without any bands attached? Just the three-stick-men logo and the dates?"

ANDY CIRZAN (promoter, Jam Productions) I go, "Um . . . really?" Like, "Thanks, guys, and by the way, I have a huge guarantee in place as well. Can I have five minutes to think about this?" But I should preface this by saying that I was close to Don Muller and Marc Geiger and that they were two of the hottest agents in the business. They were major-league players—still are—and I trusted them. And by '93, Lollapalooza had become a juggernaut. So I said, "Okay . . . but this is *your* idea."

STUART ROSS So we went up with a full-page ad in, I think it was the *Chicago Reader.* And we sold out all the tickets in something like two hours. Then we added a second show. It was really proof of the value of the brand. And that artist representative? I'm not gonna say who it was, because it would be embarrassing. Needless to say, they were very upset with me.

DON MULLER The crazy thing about Lollapalooza after '92 was that inevitably I'd get a phone call from a high-up president, chairman, whatever the fuck, at a record label: "You need to put my band on!" "No." "You need to! Don't you know who you're fucking with?" "Yes." It was like, "Your band sucks. We're not putting it on. Sorry." I went toe-to-toe with a lot of these people. Some L.A., some New York, some out of their mind. I was like, "Oh fuck, I'm gonna go out, my car's gonna blow up." But we had to stand our ground.

STEVE KNOPPER At that point Lollapalooza was probably already too big to fail. And alternative rock itself was huge, too. This is now the heyday of Nirvana, Pearl Jam, *Alternative Nation* on MTV.

PAUL D'AMOUR (bassist, Tool) The whole thing was peaking right then. It really hit the mainstream in a big way.

JOHN RUBELI (second-stage manager, Lollapalooza 1993–95) I feel like there is a parallel way of looking at Lollapalooza and Nirvana. With Nirvana, if you're a true fan, you go from *Bleach* to *Nevermind* to *In Utero,* and it's like, where do they sell out? Even when they did *MTV Unplugged,* they bring on the Meat Puppets and Pat Smear; that's not selling out. That's selling *in,* right? So, there's a lot of people who would say, "If you're really, truly a fan, it's not their fault they got that big." In many of the same ways it wasn't Lollapalooza's fault the festival got that big. It's just that there was an audience there and they were being served. And you could argue that Nirvana and Lollapalooza were serving the same gigantic audience at the same time.

MURPH (drummer, Dinosaur Jr.) We had started doing a lot more stuff and we were on MTV and we were on a major label, but we were still coming from an alternative mindset. And so there was a bit of, Oh, this is a really big corporate machine. Are we selling out by doing this thing?

NORWOOD FISHER (bassist, Fishbone) By '93, Lollapalooza had grown for sure. But I'm gonna just say this: When we did the first one, the Butthole Surfers, Henry Rollins, Ice-T, Jane's Addiction . . . those are all kind of artistically dangerous acts, right? The Lollapalooza in '93, the bands were not notorious in the same way. In some way it was more family-friendly. Fishbone, you get a sense of danger, for sure. But it's different, you know? And Alice in Chains, there's a sense of danger there, too. But it's also very different.

MICHAEL AZERRAD (journalist, author) I saw the 1993 edition somewhere way the hell out in New Jersey and was underwhelmed. Either I didn't care for the bands, or they were past their prime, or they just didn't translate well to a big stage.

STEVE KNOPPER As the story goes, the headliner was originally going to be Alice in Chains. But supposedly Perry found them too mainstream, so he went with Primus. More "left-of-the-dial."

LES CLAYPOOL I don't even think we were *on* the dial. That may have been a big part of it. It all sounds very "Perry," you know?

JOHN RUBELI Did that happen? When in doubt, ask Stuart Ross.

STUART ROSS I don't remember that conversation. But it could very well be true.

LES CLAYPOOL What I do remember is that Don Muller was our agent and he said, "Hey, Alice in Chains doesn't want to headline. Do you guys want to headline?" And we're like, "Sure!"

JERRY CANTRELL (guitarist, singer, Alice in Chains) I think they came at us initially with us headlining and Primus right before us. And we were like, "We don't know if we want to play last . . ." We were maybe a little nervous about headlining, or maybe we just didn't want to be that band where, it doesn't matter who you are, there's a portion of the audience that's heading for the parking lot halfway through your set. So I think we strategically chose the second spot.

DON MULLER The good news for everybody is that people stayed and gave Primus the respect that they deserved.

LES CLAYPOOL The second-to-end slot is always the coveted slot, but we were like, "Screw it. We're gonna run with it!" And we're idiots, too, because Don Muller's like, "Look, you gotta put together some crazy production." So I go, "I have this idea: We're gonna do this giant screen . . ." We rented, like, the camera they shot *Lawrence of Arabia* on, this big seventy-millimeter thing, and we strapped it to the front of my boat and filmed all this crazy anamorphic stuff to project behind us. And Ler [Primus guitarist Larry LaLonde] had gone to high school with this friend who had been to two-hundred-and-some-odd Grateful Dead concerts. So, we said, "You know what? He would be a good lighting guy!" The guy had never done lights in his life. And his very first lighting gig was Lollapalooza '93. It was pretty nutty.

JERRY CANTRELL Primus played last and they were fucking great.

MIKE INEZ (bassist, Alice in Chains) The bands on the main stage were just really diverse. There was us, and we were probably the most metal of anybody. Then there was Primus, there was Tool. There was Rage Against the Machine. Dinosaur Jr.

LYNN HAZAN (front-of-house tour accountant, Lollapalooza) I remember that Dinosaur Jr. were so loud that it was an issue. They were loud compared to *everything*.

J MASCIS (singer, guitarist, Dinosaur Jr.) I must have had, like, ten amps at that point. And every day two or four of them would blow up from the heat.

MIKE INEZ You'd see Fishbone hanging out with Babes in Toyland hanging out with Front 242, these industrial guys from Belgium . . .

LORI BARBERO (drummer, Babes in Toyland) *"Front two-four-two, coming down for yooouuu!"* That's what they'd say. It was pretty badass.

RICHARD 23 (percussionist, vocalist, Front 242) We really were the bad sheep of the tour, but that was a great challenge. We were the only EU band with no guitars, no real drums, a tape recorder, and traveling in small vans instead of big rock 'n' roll Nightliners. Some people were looking at us like aliens.

LORI BARBERO They'd come down in a helicopter. Did you know that?

RICHARD 23 Not at all. That's complete delirium.

LORI BARBERO And then there was Arrested Development, which is like one of the most beautiful, loving, peaceful bands . . .

SPEECH (MC, producer, Arrested Development) People at that time were throwing us under the tag of "alternative hip-hop," with other groups like De La Soul, P.M. Dawn, Disposable Heroes of Hiphoprisy, a band called Basehead. I never liked that term—I just wanted be known as hip-hop. But I do know that Lollapalooza was a great stepping stone and opportunity to reach way more fans, because we were on our first album and we were starting to get a really serious buzz. To play in venues to fifteen, twenty thousand people takes you to a whole 'nother level. And then to be associated with the likes of Primus, Alice in Chains, Fishbone, Tool, Babes in Toyland, and so on and so forth, it was great.

MONTSHO ESHE (dancer, background vocalist, Arrested Development) Most of the tours that we had done at that time were either R&B, soul, folk, or hip-hop. I had never even *heard* of Lollapalooza.

SPEECH We were representing Black consciousness and Afrocentric philosophies and thoughts. So it was eye-opening for a lot of the audience. But they were very in tune. It's decades removed now, and I still meet fans who came to the Lollapalooza '93 that say, "That was my first exposure to you guys." Or, "That was my first exposure to rap."

MONTSHO ESHE I remember us having to get a huge set. We got these big, beautiful backdrops, and we had a house built, like this Southern-style house, and we came out of it while we were onstage. It was a big deal!

LORI BARBERO Babes in Toyland paid a hundred thousand dollars for a backdrop for Lollapalooza. The artwork was done by Cindy Sherman. I think we only got to use it once, because you could never put it up if the wind was higher than five miles per hour, something like that. Of course, when you're in the middle of nowhere—and these shows were *always* out in the middle of nowhere—there's always wind. It's flat and it's open and it's really windy. But it was Cindy Sherman's art. It was pretty great, you know?

PAUL D'AMOUR Tool, I think we might have had some blow-up sex dolls or something that kind of floated around. Other than that, we didn't have shit. We would just go out there and bring the rock.

LES CLAYPOOL It's interesting to look at that tour and see that the two lowest-billed bands became two of the biggest bands in the world.

MARC GEIGER Tool and Rage Against the Machine were Don's clients, and he believed they were going to blow up. And he was right.

DON MULLER Back in the day, when you saw either of those bands you just knew. Tool was signed for management by Ted Gardner and his wife, Nikki. And Ted and I were longtime friends. And so in the waning hours of those guys just getting ready to explode, he said to me, "I have to have somebody on point." And I knew I had to get involved. And Rage—I mean, Rage is Rage. You go to a show and you fucking strap in, 'cause it's gonna be one of those things.

TOM MORELLO (guitarist, Rage Against the Machine) It was a challenge, but it was a challenge we were ready to meet. Listen, Rage did not have a long, fruitful touring career before playing Lollapalooza. We had opened up for House of Pain in clubs. We had played a handful of dates with Public Enemy up the West Coast. We had opened for Suicidal Tendencies in Europe and had done a few club shows and open-mic nights around town. But for Lollapalooza it was just, "We're gonna go out there and do the set that we do."

TIM COMMERFORD (bassist, Rage Against the Machine) No one knew who the fuck we were. We had these little black pins that you could put on your shirt that said, in lowercase letters, *rage against the machine: we're on first.*

TOM MORELLO People were coming in with their hot dogs and their Diet Cokes, settling in for a long day of alternative music. And we scared the living shit out of them.

MAYNARD JAMES KEENAN (singer, Tool) We were presented with an option and it was us being on the second stage and Babes in Toyland being on the main stage, and then Babes went off to do their own thing halfway through the tour and we moved up to the main stage. We went on right after Rage at that point, in the Babes in Toyland slot.

LORI BARBERO We had another tour booked. To be honest, I don't remember what tour it was right now. Or maybe they only wanted us on half of it. Who knows? But I'd go over and watch Tool when they were on the small stage. I actually introduced them once and it was inappropriate. I asked everyone who they wanted to see and they're like, *"Tool!"* And I'm like "Who?" And they said, *"Tool!"* "Who?" *"Tooooll!"* I had two Tool stickers, the one with the wrenches, stuck to my chest. And I just lifted my shirt up and . . . there was Tool!

TOM MORELLO That's my favorite era of Tool right there, with the *Undertow* album and the EP *Opiate.* We would finish our set and I'd go watch them every day. Maynard would be wearing this, like, pink onesie, and they were just great.

LORI BARBERO Every single night, there was always one guy who would be out in the audience, and you could hear him go, *"MAYYYY-NAAAARDDD!"* It was just this thing where you heard this one guy over and over again: *"MAYYYYNAAAARDDD!"* I don't know if it was the same guy on the whole tour, or what.

MAYNARD JAMES KEENAN We wouldn't have been on that tour and we wouldn't have been in front of those people had we not had the manager we had, had the entire industry not been upside down and scrambling to sign things they didn't understand.

PAUL D'AMOUR Up to that point, we were just playing clubs and this and that. Then all of a sudden, you're playing in front of twenty-five, thirty thousand people. It was pretty insane.

MAYNARD JAMES KEENAN But you know, you also have to deliver. If you don't deliver, it means nothing. But all those things set you up in a place where the number of eyes on you was a captive audience. And that solidified a wonderful trajectory.

PAUL D'AMOUR To be honest, I struggled with it a little bit, because of having grown up playing in punk bands and getting my ass kicked for being a weirdo. And now, all of a sudden, these same jock kids are the ones cheering for you. But I guess you can't choose who loves you.

2 "THE MOST NAKEDEST BAND ON LOLLAPALOOZA"

LOU BARLOW (singer, multi-instrumentalist, Sebadoh) I wasn't really a fan of any of the bands on that tour, but one of the best things for me was watching Rage Against the Machine open the shows. Rage Against the Machine absolutely destroyed. I tried to listen to their records after that, and I'm not really a fan of listening to them, like, around my house. But watching them perform was fucking great. They were kind of jaw-droppingly awesome. We played in L.A., the big show, and they basically got up onstage and went, "Fuck you, KROQ!" Walking onto a stage at Lollapalooza and telling KROQ to fuck off was a radical act. And in Philadelphia they played naked. They were protesting something. I can't remember what.

STEVE KNOPPER (editor at large, *Billboard* magazine) Rage made a big splash on that tour. Especially in Philadelphia. It's probably one of the most memorable Lollapalooza moments.

RICHARD 23 (percussionist, vocalist, Front 242) In Philly, Rage Against the Machine didn't play their show as a protest against the PMRC. Don't ask me why, I don't recall.

TOM MORELLO (guitarist, Rage Against the Machine) Okay. The PMRC was the Parents Music Resource Center, which was a group of wives of Washington senators who were interested in censoring-slash-curating the music that young people would be allowed to hear. Their targets were mostly heavy metal and rap music that had language and/or themes that they deemed objectionable. So we had an idea that when Lollapalooza came to Washington, D.C., we would, in the nation's capital, where the PMRC's nest was, do a protest onstage against them. But we could not agree on the parameters of it in time. So the discussion got pushed a few cities further, to Philadelphia. Which, as it turned out, was the nearest gig to Manhattan. So our record company had invited every one of its executives to that show for their first viewing of Rage Against the Machine. And, oh, what a viewing they had!

ELLYN SOLIS (publicist, Epic Records) We were backstage in Philadelphia and all of a sudden there was a weird vibe. If you've been backstage, the energy is palpable in these situations. So when a bad vibe comes, you know it. It was like, "What's going on? Something is going on." And then Rage's manager, Brigitte Wright, was like, "Okay, everybody has to leave now. You can't be back here anymore." And it was because they were naked with socks on their penises.

TOM MORELLO The plan was we would stand naked onstage with the letters *P, M, R, C* emblazoned on our chests, with duct tape across our mouths, while our guitars fed back for fifteen minutes. That was gonna be the show. So underneath our clothes we've got the letters on our chests, we've got the duct tape in our hands . . . and at the side of the stage that day is Layne Staley. Now, Layne Staley is in one of the headlining bands. He's not usually there at one thirty in the afternoon. He hasn't seen us before. So, he's sitting there, and I sit down next to him and he says, "I hear you guys are great. I can't wait to see you." And I said, "Oh, you're gonna see us all right!" And then the time came for us to go onstage, we disrobed and we just stood there.

TIM COMMERFORD (bassist, Rage Against the Machine) Those are the moments that I'm most proud of—the ones where you try to make some sort of a stand and create change. It feels like an obligation sometimes, but you've gotta just do what's right. And freedom of speech meant a lot to us.

JERRY CANTRELL (guitarist, singer, Alice in Chains) We were in agreement with that stance. It was just an interesting way to protest it.

TOM MORELLO There was, however, a disagreement about the parameters of the protest, with one band member deciding that they were only comfortable doing it if they could, um . . . bust a nut onstage. It was my opinion that this diluted the central theme of the protest. But bands are bands, and sometimes you gotta make compromises. And Lollapalooza was a phenomenon at the time, and people were very excited about being in a football stadium to see these alternative acts. They were maybe even more excited to see a nude Rage Against the Machine open the entire day, with one of the members, for about the first forty-five to ninety seconds, furtively going at it before he realized he could not gain enough traction to produce the intended results.

TIM COMMERFORD Come on! Being out there like that, like in front of people, it would be like going in the ocean in the morning and it's forty degrees out . . .

RICHARD 23 They came onstage naked, stood still in a row, with some black tape on their mouth, the letters *P*, *M*, *R*, *C* written in big letters on their chests and with only guitar feedback as music for fifteen *loooong* minutes.

TOM MORELLO There we were, standing militant onstage, and the crowd is going berserk. And that's for about the first five minutes. Now, after five minutes, they realize that something is amiss and that this is not just a brief stunt and then the band's gonna play "Bombtrack." So the next five minutes are a standoff, where we're looking at them, they're looking at us, the guitars are squealing feedback, and nothing's happening. And the final five minutes, they're super pissed off and throwing quarters at our dicks.

TIM COMMERFORD They were throwing whatever they had—beers, cups, shoes, bottles of urine. It was challenging from a psychological standpoint.

STUART ROSS (tour director, Lollapalooza) Someone from the Philadelphia police, I don't know if he was a high-ranking officer or not, said, "Get them off the stage or we're going to arrest them." And I said, "I can't go on the stage." He said, "I'm telling you right now, get 'em off the stage or they're gonna be arrested." And I said, "If you wanna go onstage, be my guest. Nobody's gonna stop you. Go for it."

RICHARD 23 They were arrested coming offstage. I still have pictures of that.

DON MULLER (agent; cofounder, Lollapalooza) To be honest with you, I don't remember if they were arrested or not. I'm sure they were detained. But those guys, you can't say to Zack [de la Rocha, vocalist] or Tom or Brad [Wilk, drummer] or Tim—probably Tim the most—"Hey, you can't do that." You just stay the fuck out of the way. They're gonna be who they are, and you're happy to be involved.

TOM MORELLO I don't think anybody was arrested. But there was a strong police presence backstage in the aftermath of it. Cops are on site, and we come offstage and everybody just sort of scrambles. I'm still naked, by the way. And the one place where I think that a naked Black man might find refuge backstage at Lollapalooza would be on the Fishbone tour bus. So I go to their bus, which is filled with, like, weed and *Star Wars,* and just plunk myself down. Nobody bats an eye. When the cops started going around, they're knocking door to door and it's like, "Oh, this is business as usual in here."

ELLYN SOLIS We were just like, "Get the pictures! Let's get it out now over the wire. Everybody has to see this right now. This is news!" These days everyone says, "Oh, they broke the internet." That day, Rage Against the Machine broke Lollapalooza, you know?

KEITH NEALY (drummer, Cell) Our bass player, Dave Motamed, would settle up with the accountant every day and had to go to his bus. Dave came back and he's like, "Holy shit—the Rage guys were having a big argument because the accountant's like, 'Hey, you're contracted for a performance. That wasn't a performance.'" I mean, they probably got paid, but I just remember that was pretty funny. We were thinking, Well, that's pretty good logic . . .

TOM MORELLO Later on I had to have the discussion with our representative who was like, "So you guys chose the gig where I brought everyone from the record company to see you for the first time to do this?" And I said, "You're the one that signed Rage Against the Machine, bro!"

SPEECH (MC, producer, Arrested Development) I didn't know who Rage Against the Machine was at that time, but from that day forward, yeah, I did.

MONTSHO ESHE (dancer, background vocalist, Arrested Development) When I saw Rage Against the Machine that day, my jaw dropped to the ground. But I wanna say there were other people naked on that tour, too. It might have been Fishbone.

ANGELO MOORE (singer, saxophonist, Fishbone) Probably like four shows in a row I got naked onstage. Butt naked. 'Cause I caught the holy ghost, man! I saw Zack de la Rocha getting naked onstage and I was like, "Goddammit, I feel like that, too, sometimes!" And I just did it. I'd go into my fucking spell, man.

CHRIS DOWD (keyboardist, trombonist, Fishbone) Angelo just liked to take all his fucking shit off. I don't know why. Still don't understand.

NORWOOD FISHER (bassist, Fishbone) We were *all* running around naked. We might be the most nakedest band on Lollapalooza, ever.

MIKE INEZ (bassist, Alice in Chains) All of us totally worshipped at the Fishbone altar. I was watching them one time from the side of the stage, this is probably about halfway through the tour, and Les Claypool was standing with me. And Les looks at me and says, "That's the baddest band in the land right there." I'd never seen such a high-energy, just balls-out crazy act.

LES CLAYPOOL (bassist, singer, Primus) It was this vibrant, aggressive cartoon. They're fantastic, but back in the day, they were the world's greatest live band. It gives you the chills to think about how spectacular they were.

MONTSHO ESHE I remember one performance in particular, Angelo, he jumped in the audience, right? He was stage diving. They carried him all the way to the back of the crowd, and then he gets on the lighting rig, over whatever sound booth they had out front, he climbs to the top of it . . . and then jumps back in the crowd. They carried him back to the stage and he did not miss one note. I was like, "That was *amazing.*"

ANGELO MOORE The crowd surfing on Lollapalooza was *good.* And they had the big fire hose, they got water sprayin', everybody jumpin' around in mud. I remember swinging my "Fuck Racism" flag for the first time. That's some of the shit you'd see at Lollapalooza.

SPEECH Our bass player at that time, a guy named Foley who had also played with Miles Davis, filled in a lot with Fishbone. Because Fishbone was going through this court case based on some of the members kidnapping another member.

LES CLAYPOOL They were on trial, because they had tried to get their old guitar player, Kendall Jones, who was a very good friend of ours, into some sort of treatment because they felt he had been brainwashed by a cult. I don't know the whole story, but they had to keep flying back to Marin because the Marin County DA was determined to prosecute these rock star heathens, or whatever the hell his perspective was.

NORWOOD FISHER I was facing nine to eleven years in prison for the whole thing with Kendall. So I was flying in and out, doing court dates. But I was running with Foley. I admired Foley.

CHRIS DOWD I mean, dude, come on! He played with Miles Davis, you know what I mean? He was, like, one of those dudes that you would call a multi-instrumentalist before, you know, Prince got the undisputed title.

SPEECH He would join Primus. He would join Alice in Chains. He was just that kind of extraordinary player. So he was able to play on everybody's sets and it just felt like a communal thing.

JERRY CANTRELL He'd come up and play lead bass on "Them Bones" with us. Like, "Holy shit . . ."

MIKE INEZ Different guys would come and jam with us all the time. Or Jerry would go play "Black Flowers" with Fishbone or Layne would go sing with Front 242. There was a lot of cross-pollination going on between the bands.

TOM MORELLO I remember playing with Primus. And a couple times I think Zack joined Tool, and then Maynard joined us for "Know Your Enemy." I spent a lot of time hanging out with Tool and Alice in Chains and Babes in Toyland. Those were sort of my homies on that tour.

NORWOOD FISHER What was J Mascis's band's name again? Dinosaur Jr. Which is a band I love . . .

MURPH We would hang out with the Fishbone guys, but for us there was definitely a feeling of disconnect, because we didn't really feel like we were part of the big headliner clan with Primus, with Alice in Chains.

KEITH NEALY I hung out with the Dino guys a bunch. I remember them being miserable. I feel like J Mascis just felt like they didn't belong there. I remember him sitting there with a towel on his head and his A&R guy was there and he's asking, "Can we go home tomorrow?" "No, J, you have to finish the tour." He's like, "Really?"

J MASCIS (singer, guitarist, Dinosaur Jr.) It was, like, the hottest day of the year in every town we were in. So it was a tough tour.

MURPH I felt like our playing was good, and I felt like the audience was receptive. But back then, J was so weird, because he was so secretive. He would never talk about anything. So, we didn't know half the time what was happening. And I remember one day, he managed to get up and play a song with Alice in Chains, and I didn't even know about it. He's getting ready, and he has drumsticks in his hands, and I'm like, "Hey, what are you doing?" And he goes, "I'm playing a song." Like, with *Alice in Chains*?

J MASCIS I had been hearing that "Angry Chair" song the whole tour and I liked it. So in Florida I said to them, "I wanna play drums on that." Their management was thinking they'd have two drum sets onstage, but I was like, "No, I wanna be the only drummer." The band was fine with it and they ended up letting me. Afterward their roadie guy said I played it too fast, which is on par. I usually play everything too fast when I'm playing drums.

JERRY CANTRELL We were all over each other's sets. I remember one night Angelo got up onstage with us, and somewhere he'd gotten a full chicken suit. He was dancing around during "Rooster" and playing his trumpet. Fucking amazing.

CHRIS DOWD Angelo Moore wasn't like Layne Staley. Angelo's like if somebody took Iggy Pop and Sun Ra and spliced those genetic materials together. Whereas Layne was like . . . that fucking voice, man. He just sounded so different from everyone. You could see and you could hear all the influences, but somehow it was just him. I think he put his heartache and pain and life and struggles and everything in it and it just came out in that voice. It was just one of the most honest-sounding things, you know?

RICHARD 23 The best moment for me would be having Layne singing onstage with us a couple of times. We were told he was a big fan of Front 242, and he would often come in our dressing room to sneak some vodka. I'm not sure if he asked to join or if we proposed, but it was a real honor to share the stage and one of our songs with him.

PAUL D'AMOUR (bassist, Tool) Layne came out with Tool once or twice and sang "Opiate." But he was definitely struggling on that tour. He had his own bodyguard to keep him from doing drugs, is what I understood.

And that guy was brutal. A couple of times I saw people trying to smuggle drugs and that guy would be just about breaking their arms off.

LYNN HAZAN I heard, "Oh shit, the drug dealers have gotten through. How do we keep Layne safe?" But I think what we all know about addiction is that you can't necessarily save people from themselves.

MAYNARD JAMES KEENAN (singer, Tool) I'm assuming he'd gone through a rehab right before Lollapalooza. And so he was a little un-lucid at the very beginning of the tour, but by the time he got through the tour . . . he had a sponsor out there, he had a lot of support, and he was able to do the shows. He was great, clear, lucid.

LYNN HAZAN I remember Layne and Maynard became really good friends halfway into the tour.

MAYNARD JAMES KEENAN I didn't really want anything to do with him when I first bumped into him because he just wasn't present. You're not going to have a conversation, there was nothing there to have a conversation with. But as the tour went on, the light came on and was like, "Oh, this is the guy I expected was in there somewhere."

CHRIS DOWD There was a lot of concern about what was going on with Layne. But all bullshit aside, Alice in Chains would go onstage, and he just had *presence,* man. That motherfucker could sing his ass off.

MIKE INEZ There were some shows that were the best I've ever heard Layne sound. A lot of people focus on the horrible story and the doom and the darkness of Layne, but, god, the light side, it was so much more prominent. And on Lollapalooza, he just had this light and it was, like, just beautiful to watch. We would go onstage when the sun was coming down, and I have these moments that are frozen in my brain of playing bass and looking over at Layne just killing it.

TOM MORELLO I remember one day we were somewhere, I don't know where it was, but Layne had just cut his hair, so he had that real short, kind of white hairdo, and he was wearing a beautiful white suit and sunglasses. We were in a field somewhere and the sun was setting, and it was just like, "Rock 'n' roll has found itself in an awesome place tonight . . ."

JERRY CANTRELL We were all in our early twenties and kind of at the peak of our powers and becoming known and having some real success. It's that time of life that never happens again. It's almost like losing your virginity, you know what I mean? When you actually feel the first success, like, "Holy shit! People are actually paying attention and fucking want to hear what we do."

LORI BARBERO Every single night I stood on the side of the stage when Alice in Chains played, and one time Jerry's father was there. He's the "Rooster"—he's what that song and that video are about. So I'm standing next to his dad, and he decides that he wants to go onstage while they were doing it. He runs up to the mic and he's got his thumbs under his armpits, and he's laughing and saying, "I am the rooster!" He starts going from stage left to stage right, back and forth, flapping his wings. "I am the rooster!" What a beautiful man.

3 "A PARTY ON WHEELS"

ANGELO MOORE (singer, saxophonist, Fishbone) The backstage antics? God, there was so much shit going on . . .

LORI BARBERO (drummer, Babes in Toyland) It was just a party on wheels. Carnival freaks in these caravans, going from point A to point B every day, and with the fucking crazy circus music. Just so, so fun.

SPEECH (MC, producer, Arrested Development) The Lollapalooza back-stage was filled with partying and drugs and alcohol and all of that. It wasn't like we were all political and talking progressive causes back-stage or anything, even if that was the vibe of the nation at the time. Along with that was definitely people immersed in partying in various different ways, and people doing what they do.

MONTSHO ESHE (dancer, background vocalist, Arrested Development) I remember seeing a lot of supermodels at the time, the nineties super-models. They would come to the show and it would blow my mind. Like, "Oh my god! That's so-and-so!"

JERRY CANTRELL (guitarist, singer, Alice in Chains) We made friends with everybody on the tour with the exception of Arrested Develop-ment. I don't know what the deal was with those guys, but they had their own vibe and they didn't hang with anybody. It wasn't that they were excluded. They chose to kind of exclude themselves.

SPEECH I'm not a rock 'n' roller, I'm a hip-hop artist. I don't do drugs, I don't smoke. I take a casual drink, but I've never been drunk in my life. I've never been high in my life. So being backstage with some of the groups, and I won't mention any names, and seeing cocaine and seeing heavy drugs, it was, "Wow." And the level of drunkenness was new for me. It was fascinating, that's the word I would use.

MONTSHO ESHE Our security was very protective of me, because I was a teenager. So I would always try to be very aware of what was going on around me and who I interacted with. And thank god nobody ever offered me nothing.

RASA DON (drummer, Arrested Development) We became really good friends with Fishbone. Fish [drummer Phillip "Fish" Fisher], he had this little eighteen-inch bebop drum kit, and then because he had this kit in his dressing room, now you've got Primus's guitar player coming in with his little amp, you've got Alice in Chains' bass player coming in with his little amp. You have all these people jamming before their gig. Everyone just hanging out in Fishbone's room.

NORWOOD FISHER (bassist, Fishbone) We were partying to Arrested Development long before we encountered them, you know? So, upon arrival it was like, "Yo, let's hang!"

LES CLAYPOOL (bassist, singer, Primus) I would go back and jam in Fishbone's room, 'cause Fish always had his drum kit set up. I did some recordings with him and Angelo and whatnot.

JERRY CANTRELL We were backstage, on each other's buses, hanging out, playing music. It was awesome.

MIKE INEZ (bassist, Alice in Chains) I remember Les Claypool stopping by our bus to feed my golden retriever. And then the Babes in Toyland girls would come by and say, "Hey, we wanna take Chuck for a walk!" They were selling these giant fried turkey legs out in the stands, and Chuck would eat all the turkey meat off the bones.

MAYNARD JAMES KEENAN (singer, Tool) You had everybody moving as a group, so you couldn't help but start running into people in catering or people that happen to be morning people. You're up early doing whatever, going for a walk or a run, and you run into different people. So the lines between genres start to blur there and you just start to meet everyone.

LYNN HAZAN (front-of-house tour accountant, Lollapalooza) Tool are not normal people—I wouldn't call Maynard a normal person—but they're chill. Maynard and Danny [Carey, drummer] had a workout bench.

KEITH NEALY (drummer, Cell) They were always doing bench presses and shit. Like, what is this, a prison yard?

LES CLAYPOOL I remember getting to know Maynard. He'd be back there with all his workout gear, pumping iron and whatnot, talking about his turkeys he was raising. He and our drummer, Tim [Alexander], were wrestling together quite a bit, which was a very disturbing image. That was when UFC was first starting, and they both got into all the Gracie jiu-jitsu. Maynard would come by and, next thing I know, I'd look over and these guys are on the ground grappling. It was like, "What the hell are you guys doing?" Tim, he's like a silverback gorilla. He's a big man. And there's Maynard, and he's almost reptilian, you know? He's fast, quick. It was just an odd thing to see.

MAYNARD JAMES KEENAN Tim and I hit it off really well. He ended up playing with me in A Perfect Circle and Puscifer. And he's why I'm in Jerome. Before Primus he was in a bar band in Jerome, and when I was looking to get out of L.A. he's the one who said, "I think I have the perfect spot for you in Arizona. Let me show you a place . . ."

LORI BARBERO There was one time in Arizona when we all went tubing down the Salt River. It was a day off, and I think it was Alice in Chains, Tool, Primus . . . a couple of the guys from Rage, maybe Mike Johnson, who was in Dinosaur Jr. at the time. I don't know if Murph was there or not.

MURPH (drummer, Dinosaur Jr.) I might have been. I honestly don't remember. But I totally would've been the guy in the band to do it.

LORI BARBERO It was a day of just floating. Couldn't have been more therapeutic. Everyone in the hot sun, just getting *waaasted* in their inner tubes.

LES CLAYPOOL We're out with all the different bands and, hey! There's Layne, driftin' down the river with a bottle of vodka. So Ler floats up to him in his inner tube and says, "Hey bro, lemme get a hit of that." And Layne's like, "No!" Didn't let him have any. It was his bottle.

LORI BARBERO Layne and Kat [Bjelland, Babes in Toyland singer] had their own thing, their own little side project going on, if you know what I'm saying. Birds of a feather, you know?

NORWOOD FISHER Oh yeah, there was trouble there. Alice in Chains, Babes in Toyland, I don't know who the fuck else, 'cause I didn't get down like that.

LORI BARBERO Layne and Kat got in some kind of spat, because if Kat doesn't get what she wants she throws a huge temper tantrum. And I think she wanted to go on the bus with Layne at one point, and he didn't want her to. She got so pissed when the bus was taking off, she jumped on the bus and tore the windshield wiper off. And she's a little girl. But I was standing right there—she leaped up and she fucking tore a wiper blade right off the bus.

MURPH Dinosaur Jr. had a bus, but we also had a Lincoln Town Car, because J wanted a car to get around in. It was insane.

J MASCIS (singer, guitarist, Dinosaur Jr.) I just couldn't sleep on a bus. I didn't like it.

MURPH A lot of times I was like, "I'll take the Lincoln," because it was just freedom. I remember driving through the Midwest one time, and

I'm going through the radio, and Christian rock was really big out there. I had never really been exposed to Christian rock, because we didn't have that growing up on the East Coast as much. And I was just fascinated. I was listening to all these stations, because you have your pop Christian rock, metal Christian rock, grunge Christian rock. I didn't realize they had done all these genres in Christian rock. And I remember just thinking, Wow, this is amazing . . .

LORI BARBERO Lollapalooza was the first time we had a tour bus, and it was the biggest nightmare in the whole world. It was so expensive, but you had to have one because the drives were, like, sixteen to eighteen hours, sometimes overnight, and so you needed a driver. So they basically said it was mandatory. But then Dinosaur Jr. had a car, and I was like, "What's up with that?"

PAUL D'AMOUR (bassist, Tool) Dinosaur Jr. would just roll up in this Town Car with all their shit in the back. Like total gangsters.

JO LENARDI (vice president of alternative marketing, Warner Bros. and Reprise Records) J Mascis was, you know, kind of a snobby guy. But that's his prerogative.

MURPH Lou Barlow calls that J's "cowboy phase," because J was really into being eccentric and wearing a cowboy hat and drinking high-end whiskey.

NORWOOD FISHER Dinosaur Jr., I'd go to their dressing room and drink with them. 'Cause they always had single malt, and they had Guinness stout.

MURPH I don't remember the Guinness. Why Guinness particularly? Who knows?

NORWOOD FISHER I'd go drink up their shit, and then go to Primus, because Primus had Guinness, too, right? And Alice in Chains had vodka . . . Layne, he'd drink until he passed out. He'd be on the floor in the dressing room and everybody'd be like, "Is he going to be able to do the show?" And then he'd get up and *kill* it.

MURPH Norwood was great, he was just really stoned. And then, what's his name—the singer, Angelo. He would get really whacked out. And so Norwood would come in really stoned and then Angelo would come in out of his mind and start reciting poetry. It felt like this surreal fifties beat movie where we're all just kind of sitting around, like, "Yeah, man . . ."

CHRIS DOWD (keyboardist, trombonist, Fishbone) Fishbone and Alice in Chains, our thing was that we would jack the golf carts. It would be, let's say, me and Jerry Cantrell on one golf cart and Angelo and Layne on another, and we would drive through the audience on these golf carts and just grab people. Eventually there were just so many people backstage who were nonworking, that like two-thirds of the way through the tour, the Lollapalooza people were like, "Nobody can use the golf carts anymore!"

TIM COMMERFORD (bassist, Rage Against the Machine) Our day was over really early, and after that I'd just be roaming around the venue until the end of the show. So I used to take my pass and put it in my shirt, and then I would steal a golf cart or run through catering. Security wouldn't know who I was, so they would take off after me and I would lead them on a full-on chase. Then when they got real close or they caught me, and I'm in this melee of security guards and we're super deep, I'd pull out the pass. Like, "Yo! I'm in the band!"

TOM MORELLO (guitarist, Rage Against the Machine) I remember being with Tim somewhere in some sort of godforsaken backwoods a couple miles from the venue as he was driving backward in a golf cart, down a darkened hill, into the unknown. And I'm like, "If I survive, this is the last time . . ."

MIKE INEZ There were a lot of extracurricular activities where different packs of people would do different things on days off. Because it's like, bands get in trouble if they have nothing to do on days off.

TOM MORELLO I got peer-pressured into bungee jumping over a parking lot in San Francisco. I was thinking, This is gonna be a horrible way to go. The first and last time I ever bungee jumped.

LORI BARBERO I was like, "Wow, this is kind of crazy. I'm bungee jumping . . . to concrete. If I hit, *kablooee!*"

LES CLAYPOOL Me and Jerry Cantrell would go fishing quite a bit. Primus in general became big fans of Alice in Chains on that tour, and actually very good friends.

MIKE INEZ On one of our days off, Alice in Chains filmed an episode of *Headbangers Ball* at Action Park.

JERRY CANTRELL We had developed a pretty friendly relationship with MTV, especially Riki Rachtman, and they would do whatever weird stuff we wanted to do. And of course, what we wanted to do was be a bunch of fuckin' smart-asses, and try to get away with as much as we could.

RIKI RACHTMAN (co-owner, Cathouse; host, MTV's *Headbangers Ball*) I was in L.A. and MTV told me, "Hey, we've got a break with Alice in Chains and we're going to do a show at Action Park. We need you to come to New Jersey."

JERRY CANTRELL Riki was totally down with it. He was like, "Fuck, that sounds great. Let's do it!" And they hooked it up for us.

RIKI RACHTMAN So we show up, and you know, it wasn't until decades later when that documentary came out called *Class Action Park* that everyone realized, This is the most dangerous place ever.

MIKE INEZ It was your basic C-level rides—a bunch of cement troughs and way-too-steep angles.

RIKI RACHTMAN I remember being on a chairlift, because you took chairlifts to get to some of these waterslides, and there was a waterslide that did a loop. I was on with Jerry and I looked at that waterslide and I was like, "They have a waterslide that does a loop?"

JERRY CANTRELL There was this weird corkscrew one, where somewhere in the middle you kind of left the bottom of the slide and then you hit the roof and then slammed back down to the bottom of it. I think part of my Speedo was wedged up my ass from the fucking slide.

MIKE INEZ We were at this one slide and it had a weight limit of 175 pounds or something. And Big Val, our old security chief, at that point was weighing in at, like, 365. So we're at the top of this thing and this little girl who was working there, she's probably fourteen years old, she says, "Excuse me, sir. You're way over the weight limit. We can't let you go on this ride." Big Val looks right at her and he says, "I'm going down this fucking ride." And he went so slow at first, because it was too much weight. Then about halfway down, the brother starts getting this momentum, man. It was crazy.

RIKI RACHTMAN Val, he just didn't stop. He kept on going and hit the retaining wall, and then, like, flew up in the air.

MIKE INEZ He hits the pool, goes up the safety thing, flies through the air about ten feet and then down the safety ramp the other way. It was the most remarkable, most acrobatic thing I've ever seen a four-hundred-pound dude do.

JERRY CANTRELL When you're young, you don't fucking think about danger. You don't think about anything. You're just like, "Fuck, let's do that!"

MURPH There was one time I was on the same hotel floor as Jerry Cantrell, and I remember coming up to my room after maybe having dinner, and he's there. His room happened to be right next to mine, kind of in a little corner of the hotel. And I was like, "Whoa, it's Jerry Cantrell!" He had these two really hot groupie chicks with the cowboy hats on, and he just kind of winks at me and gives me that look. And I remember feeling like a little kid, like, "Wow, real rock 'n' roll debauchery. How cool." And then my second thought was, Man, Dinosaur Jr., we're totally *not* cool. We're geeks. We're nerds. That stuff doesn't happen to me on tour.

MIKE INEZ That kind of behavior for sure was happening. I was lighting a few fires myself, you know? I mean, god, at that point, we're like, what? Twenty-three, twenty-four, twenty-five years old, all of us? There were wild moments.

PAUL D'AMOUR We had our share of torn-up hotel rooms and getting thrown out of hotels and whatnot for just being assholes. I don't know if there's anything that would be outside of the norm of a bunch of rock dudes drinking and being douchebags.

NORWOOD FISHER There was one day where all of Lollapalooza rolled up into this hotel. It was in Ohio—like, middle-of-nowhere Ohio. And all of Lollapalooza is at this Holiday Inn. I woke up and everybody was talking about a barbecue.

ANGELO MOORE A barbecue and music and a band playing, and everybody would come out and hang.

LORI BARBERO There was a pool in the center, and everyone's rooms faced the pool.

NORWOOD FISHER It was all kind of shenanigans all day around the pool. And there was a Kiss cover band that night in the bar. They could've been doing Kiss covers acoustically, but in full makeup. I could be wrong about that, but that's kinda poking in my head right now. I was prone to waking up and drinking immediately. So that day, I woke up, I drank all damn day.

CHRIS DOWD We were *always* drinking at that point.

LORI BARBERO I remember at one point a few people picked up Chris to throw him in the pool. But he was fully dressed and he was screaming,

"Not with my Fluevogs!" He had John Fluevog shoes or boots or something. And he kept screaming, "Not with my Fluevogs! Not with my Fluevogs!" And then they threw him in with his Fluevogs. I'll never forget that.

CHRIS DOWD Motherfuckers threw me in the goddamn pool and fucked my Fluevogs up! These were handmade fucking shoes. I called up John Fluevog's headquarters myself to see if they would make me another pair. And they were like, "Nope, that was it. No dice. We're sorry they got ruined." I'll never forget that shit. I was fucking *hot*.

NORWOOD FISHER The day after the barbecue, I remember waking up and Chris had these two girls in our hotel room. Gorgeous girls. And I'm like, "Where . . . how did this happen?" I think I sat up in bed, Chris grabbed an open bottle of tequila, guzzled it, handed it to me, and I just did the same. Anyway, one of those girls is still one of my dearest friends today. But I didn't know her before then.

CHRIS DOWD He met her in my bed? That's highly plausible. We got fucking *wild* that night.

LORI BARBERO It's so weird how you remember the little highlights. And there's just so many of them. But yeah, I would give an arm and a leg . . . well, then I couldn't play drums . . . but I'd give an arm and leg to do it again, to reexperience all of it. It was perfect and wonderful.

MURPH It was like being in the circus. The circus is going across the country and you're along for the ride.

MIKE INEZ It took me a while to digest what happened that summer.

LES CLAYPOOL The last show of the tour, I think, was Irvine Meadows. And a lot of times people like to prank each other at the last show. So, during the Alice in Chains set, they're playing "Rooster," and when they sang "here comes the rooster," I came out in the chicken suit. But they were waiting to be pranked, and they had eggs, and they started throwing the eggs at me. I could barely see out of the suit, I'm trying to dodge the eggs, and I'm running around doing the rooster. So that was fun.

Later on, during our set, the Alice in Chains guys pranked us. They came out with basses on and danced around like me—you know, sticking the leg up. Then Norwood Fisher came out onstage with his girlfriend, and somehow she "pantsed" him. And he had, like, a full erection. He's walking around the stage during our set with this metal detector of a penis bouncing around. I was like, "Holy shit!"

NORWOOD FISHER I was running around naked, no pants on, a lot. It was just a part of rockin' and rollin' at that time. I'm looking back, like, How the fuck did that happen? But it was beautiful.

LES CLAYPOOL A spectacular way to end a tour.

TOM MORELLO It was a heady time, that Lollapalooza in '93.

4 A BRIEF HISTORY OF THE VILLAGE

HEIDI ELLEN ROBINSON-FITZGERALD (publicist, Lollapalooza) I always felt, from the very beginning of Lollapalooza, that the part that was more important to Perry was what we called the village, or the midway. Basically, the front-of-house. Always, always, always. He was trying to create a very arty environment and a very wonderful experience for people. Because that's what he does—he's an entertainer. He wants everybody to have a great time and he wants to blow their minds.

GARY GRAFF (music writer, *Detroit Free Press*) We didn't have the culture of the midway, with all the booths of merchants and social causes and whatever else, back then. It was an unusual thing.

HEIDI ELLEN ROBINSON-FITZGERALD Other than something like maybe a Renaissance fair, it had never really been done before. Not at a concert. And so people did their best to live up to Perry's vision.

T. C. CONROY (front-of-house coordinator, Lollapalooza 1991) It was not an easy get because nobody knew what we were talking about. People had a hard time conceptualizing it. "What? You're going to tour art and opinions, all in the front-of-house? Like, why?" If I recall, the first-ever date, in Arizona, I think we set up a giant tent just for the sun and the heat and everything. And we put all of our organizations and our non-profits, even the artists, into the one tent. It was just a handful of booths.

JIM GREER (senior editor, *SPIN* magazine) Perry's whole idea of the art and the politics, the counterculture stuff, the booths, was pretty lame in the first iteration. I remember showing up to the San Diego show in '91, which I think was the second date, and there wasn't much at all. It was one little tent, and the art was bad, sort of Day-Glo-ish. There was a pro-choice booth, definitely. But there was also a pro-life booth. It was weird. I wandered in and wandered out. And kids weren't really engaging with it. They were much more interested in Ultimate Frisbee and drinking. Was drinking allowed? I don't even remember. I mean, I was drinking . . .

STUART ROSS (tour director, Lollapalooza) Perry wanted art, politics, and crazy food. He wanted to shake up the paradigm. But in year one, we were not in a position yet to carry everything with us. So we trusted the local promoters to help find us find art, find political tabling, find alternative food and beverage. Asked them to find army recruiters to set up next to PETA. Things that were outside their wheelhouse. And most promoters are lazy. Like, "How little do we have to do to make this right?" For example, we asked them to provide as many alternative types of food as they could so that we could make this a unique experience. And, really, they went from hot dogs to chicken sandwiches. That was as far as they went.

So, we ended up having to re-create the wheel every day: Go out into the field and figure out who the political booths are, where we're gonna set them up. What type of interesting food can we find? Is there anybody selling trinkets or blankets or books or anything? The amount of work we had to do on any one particular day didn't give us the opportunity to take a thirty-thousand-foot view of, "Hey, what the hell is this gonna be?"

CHRIS HASKETT (guitarist, Rollins Band) It was aspirational. On the one hand you get people complaining about the price of a T-shirt, but on the other, this is also their first exposure to ACT UP, to PETA, to Rock the Vote. Lollapalooza consciously provided a podium for people to learn about alternatives. So part and parcel to the idea of, "We're going to do this thing, it's gonna make a shitload of money and put all these rock bands in front of people," was, "Hey, let's provide a forum so they can get some really cool information as well."

RICHARD PATRICK (guitarist, Nine Inch Nails) The first year, I was walking around at one of the shows and I found the Amok bookstore, and they had all these crazy books and videos. They gave me a copy of this videotape that had a ton of rare footage of weird things. At the very end, it showed the raw footage of [politician] R. Budd Dwyer's public suicide. It was scary as hell. When I formed Filter a few years later, that footage is what inspired the song "Hey Man Nice Shot."

HEIDI ELLEN ROBINSON-FITZGERALD When we played San Francisco in 1991, Bill Graham was the promoter, and I think that because of the way that Bill Graham dressed up his events and tuned in to Perry's vision of Lollapalooza, that was really the one stop on the first tour that was the closest to what Lollapalooza would become.

PERRY FARRELL Bill Graham helped. I learned so much from him at the San Francisco Lollapalooza.

HEIDI ELLEN ROBINSON-FITZGERALD The way he set up the booths, the different kinds of food . . . Bill Graham is the one who really got it right.

STUART ROSS That's accurate. Bill Graham always made sure that there was a unique and fun experience for the patron, and he had a team of people that really thought outside of the box.

JON KLEIN (guitarist, Siouxsie and the Banshees) It was like another level of production up from everywhere else that we saw. He basically put a community arts festival on around the perimeter of his shows. And this is the guy that stiffed the Sex Pistols and paid them, what, sixty-six dollars for their Winterland gig in San Francisco? He got Santana on Woodstock. He's this legendary character.

DON MULLER (agent; cofounder, Lollapalooza) In a way, Lollapalooza was an alternative version of the hippie world that the Bill Graham guys knew.

STUART ROSS On year number two, we hired BGP, Bill Graham Presents, to produce our front-of-house activities. Which basically encompassed everything except the concert. And that kicked everything up a notch.

ADAM SCHNEIDER (producer, Bill Graham Presents, 1991–92) I was working for Bill Graham Presents at that time, and we met with the Lollapalooza people and modeled out how to do a show like we had done in San Francisco the prior year, but with a consistent-quality production in every city. And that became the model for all these touring festivals. It was the touring vendors, which was the Grateful Dead thing, but also a vendor village, a second stage, performance art, static art. Social-political action groups. Smart drinks, which was a trendy thing.

LOLLAPALOOZA PRESS RELEASE, 1992 *While this year's tour brings together seven of the hottest acts in alternative music—Lush, Pearl Jam, the Jesus and Mary Chain, Soundgarden, Ice Cube, Ministry and the Red Hot Chili Peppers—music is only the beginning. There's a midway featuring crafts, multicultural food booths and charity gambling. The Second Stage or "Stage 2000" presents local bands performing during set changes of the main stage, the Jim Rose Circus Sideshow, and Archie Bell Dancers. Political booths of every dimension include Rock for Choice, Amnesty International, American Civil Liberties Union, the NRA, PETA, Libertarian Party, Coalition for the Homeless and the National Abortion Rights Action League.*

JOHN RUBELI (second-stage manager, Lollapalooza 1993–95) The combination of the second stage and the village became Lollapalooza's way of introducing another layer of the subculture to the subculture.

MIKE McCREADY (guitarist, Pearl Jam) There was a feeling you were part of something that was special and different. A progressive, cool tour.

ADAM SCHNEIDER There was Rock the Vote voter registration happening, which was a link to youth culture and its relationship to political activism.

PERRY FARRELL I believe we helped get lots of people elected. Rock the Vote, it happened during Clinton's candidacy. He played to the youth, he was very open-minded, and he wanted to speak with that generation. And I know for a fact that we got him so many votes.

ADAM SCHNEIDER That year, Perry said, "I want gambling at Lollapalooza." So we created two carnival attractions that basically had raffles—the Safe Sex Wheel of Fortune and Wake Up Mr. President. So it was gambling, but with a political and social slant. That's Perry's mind at work, taking esoteric ideas and manifesting them in really cool ways.

ROLLING STONE **(September 17, 1992)** *There are stalls hawking everything from books to temporary tattoos, virtual-reality displays and amino-acid smart drinks for the cyberpunk set, bungee-jumping at seventy-nine dollars a pop for the thrill seekers. For the charity-minded, there is the Safe Sex Wheel of Fortune, the proceeds from which go to local AIDS research organizations; fans take a spin to win CDs, backstage passes, condoms and turns in the Crush Cage, a structure set up next to the second stage that is filled with sledgehammers and smashable old televisions and appliances. "Wake Up Mr. President, What About the Homeless" is a test-of-strength meter, the proceeds from which are earmarked for the Coalition for the Homeless in each city.*

DAN CHOI (front-of-house coordinator, Lollapalooza 1994–97, 2003) In '93, Lollapalooza had a guy named Mud who was doing some kind of a poetry-slam, spoken-word thing.

MUD BARON (organizer, MC, Rev. Samuel Mudd's Revival Tent, Lollapalooza 1994) The spoken-word tent was actually the next year. The opportunity to work for Lollapalooza came up in '93, when I found out that they were doing what was called the Forum Tent, which was a horrible idea—it was basically to get pro-gun and pro-gun-control folks to argue with each other. But I took the job. I was an abused kid, and the upside of being an abused kid is I'm funny as fuck and I can improv. So I impressed the powers that be with my ability as an MC.

And I'm gonna tell you right now, it was one angry kid with his fucking journal in Florida in 1993 that made the tent happen the next year. I let him have the stage and he read his fucking heart out and it fucking just dropped everybody. I don't remember what he said, I just remember the epiphany I had. So for the planning meeting for '94, they're like, "Mud, what do you wanna do?" And I'm like, "Spoken word."

TRACIE MORRIS (poet, Lollapalooza 1994) Spoken word was a kind of an emergent phenomenon at that time on college campuses, because of things like Def Comedy Jam, the Nuyorican Poets Café in New York, the whole poetry slam scene. So we had some significant crowds in our tent in '94.

MUD BARON The scene was really happening. I reached out to Bob Holman, who's out of the Nuyorican Poets Café and was absolutely instrumental in pulling it together, and we relied on the poetry slam scene to organize slams in individual cities. I called it "Rev. Samuel Mudd's Revival Tent."

TRACIE MORRIS The thing that was funny is that we were on a tour bus with the Rock the Vote people, the pro-choice progressives, all these people, right? But then there would be people who weren't invited on the tour, but would follow the tour bus so that they could show up and read in the Revival Tent. I was like, "Really?" But that's how much they wanted to be connected with Lollapalooza as poets.

MUD BARON We had twelve people on the road, plus everything to make that happen. We had locals compete for what was called a "Road Poet" slot, where if you won we'd take you on the road with us for two weeks and you'd get paid to be a fucking poet at a music festival. We also did these different contests and events, things like human drag races, which was my pushback against homophobia by getting frat boys to dress up for stupid validation prizes. The tent had this visceral connection and it was empowering.

TRACIE MORRIS They would just set us up in random places—in the field, by the outhouses, wherever they could fit the tent. Sometimes not far from the speakers of the main stage. One time I came on at the same time as A Tribe Called Quest, and all you could hear was the performers. So I just synced my poem in time with the music.

MUD BARON In Minneapolis, we had the local alternative station set up its base right next to our tent. I imagine it's probably called 91X, maybe it's 97X, maybe it's 102X, you know the guys, right? They all look like they want to be the guitar tech for Sublime, with their glasses on the back of their head and their hair gel and their obligatory piercings. I walked over nicely and I said, "Hey guys, I love that you're here. You're the best. But we're having a spoken-word thing, and your PA is crossing." They didn't care. So, me and the Tibetan monks, who were on the tour that year, proceeded to put dry ice bombs underneath their trailer all day. Do you know what a dry ice bomb is? It sounds worse than it is. You put dry ice in a water bottle, close the lid, it makes a boom. At one point we got one of the Sublime-looking guys so good he fell off his lawn chair on the top of his RV. I had to hide in the bathroom so the local police couldn't find me.

STEVE KNOPPER (editor at large, *Billboard* magazine) Around that time Lollapalooza also started getting heavily into computer technology and the early web.

THE NEW YORK TIMES (June 27, 1993) *Part of the Lollapalooza '93 setup is a circle of Macintosh computers called Cyber Pit, which were supposed to transmit messages from audience members that would appear on a signboard above the main stage.*

MUD BARON In '93 my roommate was the guy who ran the Cyber Pit, which was basically these computer kiosks.

PETER STONE (Cyber Pit organizer, Lollapalooza 1993) It was eight or ten of these kiosks. The Lollapalooza people wanted it to have full information on everything about the village, about the bands for the day, just this kiosk of information. And they wanted it all to look really cool. I was like, "Well, we're going to make it look like something out of *Blade Runner* and have this futuristic display, kind of gritty." In the end, they looked more like *Partridge Family* coffins.

MUD BARON People would go up to it and they'd have to squint to see the screen, because you're outside . . . at a festival.

PETER STONE A friend of mine drove the AppleTalk network within the Flash program, so he figured out a way to get all the computers talking. So people could just sit there and chat with each other. And there was also this thing where you could donate money to a charity and then put in a one-liner of text that would appear over the main stage. I would collect those, and it was sneakernetted all the way over to the stage. I basically threw the text on my laptop, unedited, and I would look for the ones that were like, "Hey, Misty, come find us. We're at the blah, blah, blah." I would just put everything up, and you could hear the crowd laughing, and the kids had a fun time and they thought it was neat.

DAN CHOI The next year we had the Chameleon, a virtual reality ride. I'm not sure how successful that was. And also the Electric Carnival, which was sponsored by Interval Research Corporation, a company owned by Paul Allen, the Microsoft guy. It was a big tent that was filled with all this tech—SimCity, some MIDI stuff. They were trying to get the internet there, but at that time it was not easy. It was not one of those simple things to do in '94.

T. C. CONROY It was a thread of Perry trying to create a melded culture. I think he was really just riffing on unity.

LOLLAPALOOZA 1994 TOUR PROGRAM *Tired of being a fly in the net? Blast past the blue suit on the infobahn, and into the system of your imagination! Step inside and check out the Internet, a sprawling, anarchic spider web of computers connecting people with each other and sharing information. You can play games, hang out in virtual coffeehouses, and visit* *entire cybercities. Let a 'net barker lead you into the labyrinth, and guide you to some of its most intriguing places.*

DAN CHOI There was a lot of dial-up modem noise that year, everywhere.

JOHN RUBELI I was at every single show in in '93 and '94 and half of '95. You'd see that kids were starting to dress different, you'd see a lot more piercings, a lot more tattoos. Lollapalooza started to create permission for people to lean into sides of themselves that they wouldn't have had the strength to otherwise. By '94, there was a collective leaning that just crescendoed.

DAN CHOI I'd say that when it came to the second stage, the village, all of it, '94 was probably the pinnacle. Although in '96 we had an actual amusement park company come out, with a Ferris wheel and every-thing. Not one of our finer moments. It kind of ground to a halt. But anyway . . .

T. C. CONROY It was all "alt." It wasn't commercial, like, "Hey, get this brand . . ." It was really what Perry wanted. He wanted opinions. He wanted to create a juxtaposition. And then kids could walk around and make their own choices, their own decisions.

LOLLAPALOOZA 1994

DATES: JULY 7–SEPTEMBER 5

MAIN STAGE: Smashing Pumpkins, Beastie Boys, George Clinton and the P-Funk Allstars, the Breeders, A Tribe Called Quest, Nick Cave and the Bad Seeds, L7, Boredoms (first half), Green Day (second half)

SECOND STAGE: Flaming Lips, the Verve, Guided by Voices, the Frogs, Shudder to Think, Luscious Jackson, the Boo Radleys, Lambchop, Girls Against Boys, Stereolab, various

Although the 1994 festival would prove to be Lollapalooza's most successful, playing at more venues and outgrossing its immediate predecessor by almost 30 percent, the planning stages were anything but smooth. Accounts differ as to whether the ink was dry on the contract page, but it was widely assumed that Nirvana, the undisputed heavyweight champions of the grunge era, would top the '94 bill. "We had been in talks with Nirvana in 1993, but it just didn't happen," says festival cofounder Don Muller. "But as far as I was concerned, in 1994, we were way down the line, at the offer stage." Lollapalooza principal Marc Geiger remembers the negotiation process as even more advanced. "It was Nirvana, the Beasties, Pumpkins. Boom. That was it. We had a famous meeting with Dave Grohl, Billy Corgan, and the Beastie Boys to discuss how it was going to work." According to people familiar with Nirvana's touring operation, production planning had actually already begun for the tour, but Nirvana front man Kurt Cobain's March 1994 hospitalization in Rome put all future plans on hold even before his death on April 8.

With the top of the bill suddenly vacant, it was decided that Smashing Pumpkins would take over the final slot, with Beastie Boys playing right before them. And while neither band had the deific stature of Nirvana, both were at or near the peaks of their respective careers. "The Pumpkins were on the tail end of the touring cycle for their *Siamese Dream* album, which had come out a year before, and Beastie Boys were just about to launch *Ill Communication*, which would be their first album to go number one since *Licensed to Ill*. So they were on their way to becoming the biggest thing around again," says publicist Steve Martin, who represented both bands at the time. The remainder of the main-stage lineup was characteristically diverse. George Clinton and the P-Funk Allstars teed up the Beastie Boys daily with their timeless party grooves, and positioned squarely in the middle of the bill were the Breeders, fronted by indie rock superstar and former Pixies bassist Kim Deal and her twin sister, Kelley, who were still riding the success of their fuzzed-out 1993 hit single "Cannonball."

The early part of the bill was similarly eclectic. On the first leg of the tour, Japanese noise rockers the Boredoms, a favorite of both Perry Farrell and Kurt Cobain, were the opening band on the main stage, while on the second leg, a Bay Area trio named Green Day kicked things off with a manic, crowd-pleasing blast of pop punk. "We had just put out our first major-label album, *Dookie,*" recalls Green Day front man Billie Joe Armstrong. "So we really wanted to be on the tour. I think every quote-unquote 'alternative band' wanted to be on Lollapalooza." The chugging grunge-punk of the all-female L7, whose highest-charting album, *Hungry for Stink,* would be released a week after the beginning of the tour, followed Green Day's upbeat power pop, succeeded by the gloomy, vampiric art-goth of Nick Cave and the Bad Seeds, who, performing in the blazing sunlight, struggled to connect with an American festival audience. Cave often cites his stint on Lollapalooza as one of the worst experiences of his career, and *Variety* concurred. "Cave's slogging style, usually at home in the gothic clubs, was a total mismatch for his midday spot," the magazine reported at the time. Following Cave, jazz-inflected alternative hip-hop pioneers A Tribe Called Quest would generally manage to put the day back on track with their loping beats and righteous rhymes.

Kicking off the day's events was a group of Tibetan monks who had been invited on tour by the Beastie Boys' Adam "MCA" Yauch, and who would bless the main stage to start the proceedings. Yauch had learned about Tibetan Buddhism on a trip to neighboring Nepal in the early nineties and subsequently adopted the religion and took up the cause of freeing Tibet from Chinese occupation. "For Adam Yauch in particular, I think his experience on Lollapalooza planted the seed for him to do the Tibetan Freedom Concerts that started in 1996 in Golden Gate Park," Martin says. "I bet if you checked from '94 to '96, the proliferation of 'Free Tibet' stickers and patches on backpacks on college campuses, it's traced directly to Lollapalooza '94."

Even those for whom the Tibetan cause was not of primary concern enjoyed their calming presence. "I'll always be grateful to the Beastie Boys for the monks," Kelley Deal says. "You'd be emerging from the bus at a different location every day on the tour and you'd have to figure out where everything was: Where are the bathrooms? Where is the food? Where's coffee? But then you'd hear the monks chanting off in the distance. It was so wonderful and surreal, and really comforting at the same time."

The side stage continued to showcase alternative and indie talent to which festivalgoers might not otherwise be exposed. The groovy, hip-hop-laced Luscious Jackson—a recent signing to the Beastie Boys' own Grand Royal label, featuring original Beasties drummer Kate Schellenbach—were an upbeat favorite, along with arty, melodic math-rockers Shudder to Think, Oklahoma psych-rock weirdos the Flaming Lips, and rising Britpop unit the Verve. Also on the side stage for a portion of the tour were Dayton, Ohio's, Guided by Voices, led by Robert Pollard, a thirty-seven-year-old schoolteacher and former star pitcher who had been releasing albums since 1986, and whose short, often surrealist power-pop anthems had finally caught the ear of the music press and uber-hip labels like Matador Records, home of Yo La Tengo, Pavement, Cat Power, and many others. Guided by Voices' legendarily kinetic live shows were both celebratory and bacchanalian, with Pollard frequently executing airborne scissor kicks and other Who-inspired acrobatics. "Guided by Voices were the greatest of all time at that time," recalls second-stage manager John Rubeli. "Having Bob Pollard be Bob Pollard in those days? Dude, oh my god."

With an already-stacked lineup, it's impossible to know what a 1994 Lollapalooza with Nirvana as the headliner would have looked like. In retrospect, some involved with the tour believe it might have courted disaster. "As a festival, I don't think we were prepared enough to deal with what it would've been like with Nirvana," says production director Steve "Chopper" Borges. "Even with them off the bill, three or four dates drew over forty thousand people, another five were over thirty-five thousand, and the shows were selling out in advance with no tickets at the door. We had a couple of dates early on where people actually rushed the gates or jumped the fences, creating a real threat of injury."

In the end, Rubeli believes that despite the tragic events preceding it, things could not have worked out better for the festival—nor would they again. "To me, 1994 encapsulates everything that could have gone right," he says. "It was like a juggernaut—in my opinion the most fantastic year of the entire thing."

1 "OH SHIT—NOW WE HAVE TO DO IT!"

JOHN RUBELI (second-stage manager, Lollapalooza 1993–95) In my recollection, it was the wish of everyone involved that Nirvana do the tour. I don't know that they ever got the confirmation, but I think it was a given that it was eventually gonna happen, because everyone in that camp was deeply connected to the Lollapalooza camp. Everyone was rallying for it to happen. But to the best of my knowledge, there was never anything on paper. And if anyone says differently, I don't think that's the case.

BRIAN GROSS (intern, William Morris Agency) I remember very distinctly someone in the office had a fax on their wall of the original lineup with Nirvana. I would look at it and be like, "Oh my god, this is what this almost was."

DON MULLER (agent; cofounder, Lollapalooza) Everybody kicks around this idea that we gave Nirvana an offer for ten million. I don't remember that. I *do* remember that we knew the economics of the Lollapalooza entity well enough that we knew what a headliner could be paid without really fucking up the ticket prices. This tour was all about, "Take the day off, discover new things, cheap tickets, blah, blah, blah."

JOHN RUBELI I talked to Kurt Cobain before the '94 Lollapalooza. I think I was sent because at that point, I had met him a bunch of times and he knew I was a music fan. And I was just like, "Look, man, I know it all sucks. And I know that it's getting too big for its own good. But if we don't grab ahold of it and we don't try to wrest it from the corporateness of it all, then we've lost it. So what I'm trying to do with this side stage is have your favorite bands play here." He wanted to book the Frogs.

JIMMY FLEMION (singer, guitarist, the Frogs) We didn't have any management or anything and we didn't lobby to get in. Kurt, who we had met in October '93 in Milwaukee, and Billy Corgan both wanted us on the bill. And I knew Kelley Deal as well. She wore a Frogs "It's Only Right and Natural" T-shirt when we played in Milwaukee, which was our hometown.

KELLEY DEAL (guitarist, singer, the Breeders) The Breeders had toured a lot with Nirvana and they were really nice. Their atmosphere and the touring environment was super respectful. "Come here, eat this. Here is where you go." They were really accommodating and welcoming, and you were never just treated like the support band. They were happy to have you; you were like their guests. And they were really good at curating an evening. They would have really interesting bands play and expose their more mainstream audience to bands that they would not normally see, like the Melvins and the Boredoms. They were really good at doing that, and with Lollapalooza, one of the great things was that the headlining band had a say in the lineup.

BILLY CORGAN (singer, guitarist, Smashing Pumpkins) Lollapalooza was supposed to be Nirvana, Smashing Pumpkins, Beastie Boys, and then Nirvana dropped out and we slotted down and became the headliner. And look, it's easy to play Monday-morning quarterback, and it was the most successful Lollapalooza of the traveling version that year without them, so imagine what it would have been with them. And I would have welcomed the challenge every night to try to blow them off the stage, and I know that [Kurt] would have tried to blow me off the stage every night. We were friendly enough that it wouldn't have been dickish, but that's what you should do.

JULIE PANEBIANCO (A&R representative, Capitol Records) I was flying with Mike D from Miami to New York the day after Kurt died and we were just in shock.

BILLY CORGAN When Kurt died, I cried because I lost my greatest opponent. I wanna beat the best.

KELLEY DEAL We had been asked to do the tour before Kurt's suicide and we just didn't know whether it would be a cool thing anymore. We didn't really know whether we were going to continue on. But I think that when we figured out what the lineup was going to be, it was like, "Sweet! That sounds really fun!"

DON MULLER The Beasties had the same manager, John Silva, as Nirvana, and their business was solid. Putting Smashing Pumpkins together with them made total sense and we made it happen very quickly. And then out of the gate we went.

BILLY CORGAN We just looked at each other and said, "Fuck it, let's do it." But it was also, "Let's not be afraid, let's not be pussies."

JIM DeROGATIS (pop music critic, _Chicago Sun-Times_) Unlike everyone else in the alternative era, Corgan never even pretended to not want to be a rock star. I mean, he wanted to be Journey or REO Speedwagon, but ten times bigger.

JIMMY CHAMBERLIN (drummer, Smashing Pumpkins) We were just finishing up twelve months of touring supporting _Siamese Dream_ when we got the offer to do Lolla. It got tacked onto the end and made a solid fourteen months of touring for us. We were pretty beat up just from being on the road for so long, but obviously, when the opportunity came along, we certainly didn't want to not do it. So we just kind of rolled up our sleeves. There were rumors about Nirvana breaking up at that time and then, you know, subsequently, we lost Kurt. So those pieces, as unfortunate as they were, created the opportunity for us to play.

BILLY CORGAN You talk about going into Middle America at the height of MTV, 1994, and I was twenty-six or twenty-seven. I was not prepared for that at all.

JOHN RUBELI I mean, one stop in Detroit was three nights to 50,000 people a night. So when you're doing a festival to 150,000 people in the Detroit metro area, you're doing something right.

STEVE KNOPPER (editor at large, *Billboard* magazine) The bill was stacked that year. So much so that the first band on, in the worst slot, was Green Day.

JOHN RUBELI I can't think of a single time that Perry pushed back or vetoed a band—except Green Day.

DON MULLER Perry definitely dug his heels in on a lot of shit. But that's kind of why Lolla was as good as it was.

BILLIE JOE ARMSTRONG (singer, guitarist, Green Day) Perry was a fucking asshole, straight up. He wasn't a part of that conversation, because he'd checked out, but they asked us to play it and we said yes. And it was going to be the Boredoms on the first half, and us on the second half as the opening band. And then all of a sudden, he comes back in and he's like, "I don't want them on the bill." Apparently, he thought that we were a band that was put together by Mo Ostin at Warner Bros.

JOHN RUBELI He was like, "They're a boy band. I don't want to book a boy band." I was getting a lot of pressure from the label and management, like, "You gotta convince Perry."

JO LENARDI (vice president of alternative marketing, Warner Bros. and Reprise Records) Green Day had two records out before they signed to Warner Bros. And they already had such a strong base; they were so huge in California already. So they weren't considered a baby band by the label.

JOHN RUBELI To Perry's credit, I was able to go through the band's history in the Bay Area and how they had released indie records and eventually he said, "Okay, they can do half the tour, but I want the Boredoms on the other half." They were almost the polar opposite, so they sort of canceled each other out.

BILLIE JOE ARMSTRONG For us it was really disappointing, because Perry was someone that we really respected. I think that made us want to play it even more, actually, because we wanted to prove that he had his head very far up his own ass.

DONITA SPARKS (singer, guitarist, L7) We got on the tour thanks to our perseverance, humor, and actually being a little bit confrontational. From what I understand, Nirvana wanted us on Lollapalooza, but then when Kurt died we lost that advocate, so we had to fight for it a little bit.

JENNIFER FINCH (bassist, singer, L7) I think that Nirvana had pulled out a few weeks before they said they did, because Kurt was hospitalized in Los Angeles and the whole thing got pretty shaky at that point. And we weren't sure what was going on.

DONITA SPARKS We didn't wanna be left out, you know? So we had to push. We kept asking our manager, "Hey, what's going on? Are we on this tour or not?" And one time he said, "There's a meeting about it going on right now." We were like, "Really? Can you get a fax number for that meeting?" And he did. We sent a fax that said, "Who does L7 have to blow to serve Coors at Lollapalooza?" And we signed it: "Love L—always the bridesmaids, never the brides—7." And then we were on the tour. I think that was a determining factor!

JENNIFER FINCH The Beastie Boys stepped up for us as well. We had done some extensive touring with them. Although secretly, I think that they wanted Luscious Jackson to be on the main stage. It had that feeling of, like, "Wow, can there really only be one?" At that time, there could only be one woman, there could only be one Black person. So it was just additionally frustrating.

KELLEY DEAL There were so many more females in 1994 than the previous year or the year after. L7 and us and the Boredoms and D'arcy from Smashing Pumpkins. And then you had the whole side stage with Luscious Jackson. There was a bunch of females over there, too!

MICK HARVEY (guitarist, Nick Cave and the Bad Seeds) The whole background to us actually agreeing to do the tour was that our record company would keep asking whether we had plans to go to America. And basically, we were pretty exhausted with America by then and not really making much progress there. So we said, "Look, if we get a really good offer for a great opening spot on some big tour, or they offer us something like Lollapalooza, we'll go, we'll do it." Of course thinking that we just wouldn't be offered that. So, when they offered us Lollapalooza, we couldn't say no. We were like, "Oh shit—now we have to do it!"

NICK CAVE (singer, Nick Cave and the Bad Seeds) We went into it not wanting to be there, and it just got worse.

JIMMY CHAMBERLIN There were times where Nick didn't even show up and the band would just go on and play instrumental for forty-five minutes.

MICK HARVEY We always felt that we were a bit out of step with what was expected in America from bands. We felt that we weren't there necessarily to entertain, and Americans—and I'm generalizing here—very often find that difficult to understand. It's almost like "You are privileged enough to be able to get up there on the stage and then you don't want to entertain us? What's the matter with you?" But we weren't very much in the business of being entertaining. In a way we just wanted to present the music and be as difficult as possible.

JIMMY CHAMBERLIN But it was still so compelling, because those guys are so talented. Nick Cave is a fully developed character, I would say. Really his own brand of his own brand. In a way it exposed the kind of neophyte-ness in us all to have somebody with that gravity on the tour. And being kind of a jazzer myself, it was really in my sweet spot, watching those guys articulate that stuff behind Nick. It was pretty magical every day.

GARY GRAFF (music writer, *Detroit Free Press*) Nineteen ninety-four definitely felt like a real return to form.

JOHN RUBELI I attribute a lot of that to Mike D, who sat in on most of the planning meetings leading up to it. He really tried not to let go of the indie reins.

MIKE D (MC, drummer, Beastie Boys) It's all compromise. Our only concern was to get as far away from doing a "rock" festival as we could. We did that somewhat with the lineup.

JULIE PANEBIANCO I have to say that there was tension between the Pumpkins and the Beasties. I can't think of a person who's more diametrically opposite to Billy Corgan than fucking Adam Horovitz, Mike D, or Adam Yauch. They just didn't mesh as people.

MIKE D I guess I thought, Okay, you put all these cool bands together, you put out your message, and all of a sudden you're gonna change the face of what's going on. But you're not.

GREG KOT This is when the Beastie Boys transitioned into that series of albums where they were playing instruments again. They were sort of a hybrid band at that point. Maybe they couldn't play that well per se, but they filled out their lineup with great musicians. And they delivered.

GARY GRAFF Smashing Pumpkins all were pissy on stage.

BILLY CORGAN So we're headlining what became historically the biggest Lollapalooza ever. And there they are. There are the same football players that used to bully us in the hallways. I looked at it as, like, "No. You're the enemy and we are here to take you on." And to this day, I still have people walk up to me at airports going, "Man, I don't know what that was about." There are people to this day, and again I usually meet them at airports, who refuse to ever see the band or listen to the band after that show. You're talking about forty-three shows, one was canceled due to rain. So forty-two times, I took the mic and went after that audience.

JIMMY CHAMBERLIN You know, just because he was the mouthpiece didn't mean that the band as a whole wasn't feeling those same emotions. We were pretty congruent when it came to the emotional status of the band. For the most part, those crowds really weren't our crowd.

GARY GRAFF In Detroit they went off on Ted Nugent, which would seem like a dangerous thing to do in Detroit. They definitely were taking the piss out of him.

JULIE PANEBIANCO By the time the Pumpkins went on, everybody was, like, wilted from the heat.

JIMMY CHAMBERLIN Some of those shows were great. Some were okay. Some of 'em were a disaster. I don't know. That's usually the way it was back then.

STEVE "CHOPPER" BORGES (production manager, Lollapalooza 1993–97) They actually went over quite well. But Billy was just one of those people who believed his own press and thought he was a lot more than he really was.

WAYNE COYNE (singer, guitarist, Flaming Lips) Billy Corgan was such a raging asshole, especially back then, that you didn't want to stick around and watch them. We liked a few of their songs, but we would just despise him after a while. So we'd leave right after the Beastie Boys played to avoid the traffic, because the audience was also starting to clear out.

GARY GRAFF My impression was that during Lollapalooza, at least the shows I saw, Billy was not unlike Eddie Vedder in '92, coming to grips with this alternative rock stardom and what it meant. And there were enough shots being taken at him in the press that I'm sure he had his defenses up.

JIM DeROGATIS I never saw Corgan change. I thought he was a dick from day one.

MICK HARVEY I think I was one of the few people on the tour who actually got on okay with Billy. He and I had quite a few chats, because he couldn't connect either with what was going on. He felt sort of separate from the whole thing in a way. I think a lot of people just treated that like he was arrogant and up himself or something, but it wasn't really about that. He just didn't necessarily feel comfortable with the situation all the time.

GREG KOT Corgan was pretty incorrigible back then. He was a very demanding person of himself, of his band, of his audience, of booking agents. He wore out managers, wore out record companies. He was just brutal, all in the belief that it was making his music better and that it gave him an edge he needed in order to be who he was.

KEVIN LYMAN (stage manager, Lollapalooza 1991–92; artist liaison, main stage, Lollapalooza 1994) By 1994, I was hired in as kind of the artist liaison, believe it or not. By that point, I think the administrative team almost wanted someone to deal with the artists. But I tried to avoid Billy as much as possible back then. I thought he was a complete prick. Billy Howerdel, who later formed A Perfect Circle with Maynard from Tool, was a friend of mine, and he was such a sweet guy and he was the guitar tech for the Pumpkins. And Billy Corgan was treating him like such shit, throwing guitars at him, just being horrible.

BILLY HOWERDEL (guitar tech, Fishbone, 1991, 1993; guitar tech, Smashing Pumpkins, 1994; guitarist, A Perfect Circle) I got fired off that tour working for Billy and D'arcy—the first and only time I've been fired from a job. I don't remember guitars being thrown at me, but there were a lot of behaviors that just didn't seem healthy, that you definitely didn't want to be around anyway.

STEVE "CHOPPER" BORGES Billy was a bit of a problem. He would say, "I need a sound check." And at that point, they were the headline band, so I'd go, "I will try to get you a little time in the morning, but it's going to be while we're setting up bands in front of you. I can't just stop everything because you need a sound check." I told this to his production manager and Billy comes barging into the production office, ranting and raving and screaming. I said, "Billy, you work for the festival. We are the festival and you are one of the acts. Time is of the essence here. We can't stop everything because you need to prance around on the stage." And when he sound checked, he would just goof around. More than once, he literally flung himself on the floor, like in a cartoon, and kicked and pounded his fists on the ground when he was unhappy about something.

WAYNE COYNE We're still avoiding him to this day. We've played shows in the past couple of years where he's hanging around and you can tell he wants to come into our dressing room. And we're like, "No, we're not here!"

2 "BOXING THE SNOWMAN"

CARRIE BRADLEY (violinist, the Breeders) I remember when the Boredoms ended their run and Green Day came on, everybody was like, "Oh, these kids. These phonies from Berkeley." And they showed up and they were so nice and so fun. I had great chats with them just hanging out on the steps of the food truck or whatever.

BILLIE JOE ARMSTRONG (singer, guitarist, Green Day) Our lives were just going crazy. I was like twenty-two years old, and we had this huge record, this huge tour, huge singles, married, wife is pregnant, our drummer Tré [Cool]'s girlfriend was pregnant. It was just fucking nuts. We were still having fun, but it was just this weight on our shoulders that was constantly there. We didn't really know what stress was; it was just happening to us.

JOHN RUBELI (second-stage manager, Lollapalooza 1993–95) The first day that Green Day was scheduled to play, all of the tour buses were lined up backstage and Green Day shows up in this bookmobile that they're touring in.

BILLIE JOE ARMSTRONG We had some money left over from our recording budget, and so Tré and his dad, who was our driver at the time, bought it. And then we put a bunch of mattresses in it and set up a little coffee table, and we had a fucking Nintendo or some shit like that in there. And we just played video games and listened to music. It was still basically touring in a van, so there was no place to piss. But I remember being in the bookmobile one time while A Tribe Called Quest was playing, and we were sitting there with Tré's dad, who is a Vietnam vet. And then all of a sudden, A Tribe Called Quest hit this one song that had this fucking 808 kick drum that was like, *boooom!,* and it just shook the entire bookmobile. And Tré's dad goes, "I don't like that noise. That reminds me of napalm when I was in Vietnam." I was really stoned and was like, "Oh fuck. He went fucking 'Nam!"

JOHN RUBELI *Dookie* was just starting to take off, so all the kids who were in the know had shown up early. But they were all way up far back in the field and the seats down front were empty. The band gets up onstage and Billie Joe is like, "All you motherfuckers up there on the lawn, everybody come on down!" And so everybody's parading down, and my walkie-talkie is just going off. And Billie Joe fucking announces, "This song goes out to Perry Farrell. It's called 'Chump'!"

BILLIE JOE ARMSTRONG I'm like, "I'm not going to take any fucking shit from anybody. I'm not going to take any shit from anybody as much as Perry Farrell's not going to take any shit from anybody." He had minions that would come up and say, "Perry Farrell's really angry that you dedicated 'Chump' to him." And I'm like, "Tell him to stop acting like one." But I never met the guy until we played Woodstock '94. He was there and we shook hands.

JOHN RUBELI I had to go talk to Perry and I was like, "Look, man, that was pretty punk rock if you ask me." And somehow, they patched things up. But Green Day was just on fire for that whole tour.

KEVIN LYMAN (stage manager, Lollapalooza 1991–92; artist liaison, main stage, Lollapalooza 1994) Green Day was young, and I don't think they'd ever been in that setting. They didn't understand the dynamics of an audience when you have seats. And the first thing they did was pretty much walk out onstage and tell the crowd to rush the stage.

BILLIE JOE ARMSTRONG For us it was really odd, because we'd really only been playing clubs where we were used to these crazy mosh pits full of kids, everybody crammed into a room. So we used to call the kids down every day because we felt like our fans couldn't see us. And the tour people were saying, "If you keep doing it, you're going to get kicked off the tour," or whatever. So I remember coming out onstage the next day, and I put duct tape on my mouth, and I got up on the microphone and I was just making sounds and not saying anything. But people already knew what I was saying anyway, so kids started jumping over into the stands. We were just obnoxious fucking brats. We would do fun stuff like playing "Rock You Like a Hurricane" by the Scorpions and people would just go crazy.

DONITA SPARKS (singer, guitarist, L7) It made for a very exciting show, but it was also pretty dangerous. It got a little out of control with people actually, like, pole vaulting over the seats to get close to Green Day.

KEVIN LYMAN A lot of people got hurt and I wanted them to understand that the power of their voices now had ramifications. So I told the band, "When you tell the crowd to come forward, you're responsible if anyone gets hurt." If the venue loses control of the crowd, then it falls on the venue. But when the artists incite the crowd, then they're responsible.

DONITA SPARKS After Green Day they would clear the kids from seats and then we'd have to go on. And it was like, Fuck . . . now we've got the empty seats again! We were playing to crickets, you know? And on top of that, we're like this dirgier fuckin' trip. It was challenging, I have to say.

BILLIE JOE ARMSTRONG Donita and I would talk every day, and one day she came up and said, "Hey, how are you doing?" And she started rubbing my shoulders. And I was like, "What is going on? Why, Donita?" And she walked off and I go, "What was all that about?" And they were like, "Oh, she's on ecstasy." I was like, "Oh, okay." I had forgotten that that's what people act like on ecstasy.

DONITA SPARKS We had a really good time on that tour. We had friends that knew how to use screwdrivers as our crew and it was kind of ridiculous.

JENNIFER FINCH (bassist, singer, L7) In Los Angeles, there's always been a movie-industry tradition, but there's also always been an industrial-fabrication tradition. And through the eighties and early nineties, there were a lot of sort of graveyards for all of this fabricated environmental stuff. You'd drive down Lincoln Boulevard and it'd just be one junkyard after the next with these, like, weird environmental installations. We used to drive by this snowman every day going out to a rehearsal studio on Lincoln in the sweltering heat and we'd be thinking, Oh, we should re-create this experience for people who are literally overheating but visually seeing cold. So we bought the snowman for the tour.

DONITA SPARKS We knew it would probably be sweltering out in the audience and we thought it would be funny to have a winter wonderland thing going on onstage.

JENNIFER FINCH It was just youthful innocence and not really knowing what it means to make that kind of decision.

DONITA SPARKS What we should have had was our fucking logo behind us onstage. You know what I mean? Like, in hindsight, what the fuck were we thinking?

JENNIFER FINCH And the snowman didn't travel well. We were constantly repatching things.

DONITA SPARKS Sometimes one of our friends-slash-roadies who was sloughing on the job would just shake the snowman and make it dance instead of getting our guitars ready for the next changeover. But that's how we roll.

BILLIE JOE ARMSTRONG I remember a good friend of mine gave us boxing gloves and boxing trunks that had our names on them. And then we ran out while L7 was playing and we started boxing the snowman. There's got to be photos around of it somewhere.

DONITA SPARKS There was actually a Lollapalooza crew guy who tried to damage the snowman. That was a big scandal. We had to have road cases for everything, right? So we had this massive road case for the snowman and it had to be carted onto the gear truck by the Lollapalooza production crew, not our crew of friends. It didn't weigh a ton, but it was just huge and each side of it was a different color, so it looked very clownish. And there was some Lollapalooza crew guy who really resented that fucking case and really resented the snowman. He damaged the case a couple times, and it was a thing. We had to complain. We kept saying, "Don't fuck with the snow . . . man!" And "No snow, no show!" We would just laugh amongst ourselves that we weren't being harassed . . . our snowman was! He was the hardest-working snowman in show business.

BILLIE JOE ARMSTRONG L7 were down to clown all the time. They were funny, funny people. We had poured ketchup in each other's dressing rooms. And it wasn't even that bad . . . I don't think.

STUART ROSS (tour director, Lollapalooza) I think that was in St. Louis. I don't remember Green Day being involved, but I do remember L7. After the show, the promoter asked me to come in and said, "Check this out." I don't remember exactly what they did outside of throwing food, and I don't know if there were holes in the wall, but they trashed their dressing room. And it was like, "You trash your dressing room, you're not getting a dressing room. Stay on your bus. We'll bring your green-room supplies to you, but you're not getting the dressing room because we just had to pay a bunch of money because you guys trashed it."

BILLIE JOE ARMSTRONG Kevin Lyman was like, "L7 and Green Day do not get dressing rooms!"

KEVIN LYMAN Someone has to come and clean these dressing rooms! Some poor kid's getting paid six dollars an hour, maybe eight dollars an hour, to do that.

MICK HARVEY (guitarist, Nick Cave and the Bad Seeds) Being on these tours, there's a lot of downtime and you can get a bit bored sometimes. So you just find things to entertain yourself. And L7 weren't backward in coming forward with ideas of new things to do on the tour just to have fun.

DONITA SPARKS I just want to do something weird sometimes, you know? When L7 first started, I was doing a little performance art, which had some comedy and absurdity in it. So for Lollapalooza I had brought my roller skates along on the tour, and when the Bad Seeds were onstage, I just skated out there—in a sombrero. Then I fell, and Nick picked me up and I almost brought him down, too. I think it was a welcome thing for them, honestly. They were playing in the daytime and hardly anyone was sitting in the seats. Listen, if they were killing it and it was a packed crowd watching 'em and stuff, I probably wouldn't have done that, but because it was so absurd in the first place that they're playing to empty seats, I was just like, "Fuck it."

NICK CAVE (singer, Nick Cave and the Bad Seeds) We had to play fifty-three dates in a row, at three in the afternoon, at a time where our kind of music was really of no interest to anyone at all.

MICK HARVEY We were very often just shooting ourselves in the foot in the way we'd conduct ourselves. Both being from Australia and the time we came from—the late seventies and the punk thing—we just had a kind of "You can all fuck off" attitude. We didn't really care whether people liked us or not. Each day, we just went out and did what we could do and presented our music as powerfully as we could. And if you didn't like it, you could just go away. We were just gonna be what we were.

CARRIE BRADLEY The Breeders played to a lot of empty seats, but not nearly as many as Nick Cave. And man, that guy brought it every fucking day. But it's just the nature of the beast. People are hungry, they're going to the bathroom, they're wandering, they're checking everything out.

BILLIE JOE ARMSTRONG Nick Cave would basically walk offstage almost every day. If someone threw a shoe onstage, he'd be like, "I'm out."

NICK CAVE Lollapalooza was the most destructive thing I've ever done in my career. It really damaged our band.

BILLIE JOE ARMSTRONG Never underestimate how dumb an audience can be.

MICK HARVEY We were going on right after L7, and when we played Dallas they did a JFK assassination reenactment. There were a couple of Bad Seeds members who were up there with them.

JENNIFER FINCH When you're working with groups of people, you often try to find a common narrative. And it helped to have a craft and performance project that we all got to do together. There were, like, two days of running around to craft supply places to get paint and other stuff.

MICK HARVEY There were props and everything. It was pretty hilarious.

JENNIFER FINCH We did it between sets. Paul Bearer, who was one of the MCs, introduced us: "The Bad Seed–L7 players are going to reenact the Kennedy assassination!" We had a big cardboard car, and we were all Jackie Os and the Bad Seeds were Kennedys. And I think Mick played Lee Harvey Oswald?

MICK HARVEY I don't think I was involved.

JENNIFER FINCH He just ran onstage and started screaming and we all fell down.

MICK HARVEY It was not appreciated by the local Dallas audience. It kind of went down like a lead balloon and hasn't been talked about since.

JENNIFER FINCH When it comes to this kind of stuff, I'm the stick in the mud where L7 is concerned. I was the one that was like, "I'll photograph this, but I don't back it." I think that would have been extremely hilarious if it was a local play, but doing it in Dallas . . . You know, I had parents who were older and the Kennedy assassination was traumatic to them. So I didn't really see a purpose in reenacting it. But I do have great photographs!

3 "WHERE ARE YOU GOING TO FIND TOFU IN THE MIDDLE OF A FIELD?"

JOSEPHINE WIGGS (bassist, the Breeders) Our slot was four thirty in the afternoon, and we went into it knowing that we were going to be playing in broad daylight to people who were not necessarily our fans. Kim [Deal, Breeders singer and guitarist] was cognizant of the fact that without the benefit of lights, we had to do something else to put on a show and make it special and cohesive. That's why all of our equipment was spray-painted gold sparkle. Kim still uses one of those amps and it's still gold.

KELLEY DEAL (guitarist, singer, the Breeders) It was automotive paint, not just spray paint. And we made a backdrop, a curtain drape of this gold glitter fabric, because we'd be playing at five o'clock and the sun would be angled just right and there would be all this gold glitter just sparkling. And we also designed these risers so that each person on the stage stood on a different-height riser. The poor crew had to assemble these risers every day, but it looked good. So we really took this seriously!

JIMMY CHAMBERLIN (drummer, Smashing Pumpkins) The Deal sisters were such amazing musicians, and their ability to sing in a live setting was just mystifying.

CARRIE BRADLEY (violinist, the Breeders) Kim's voice is so unique. It's not like a breathy folksinger, and it's not like a rock screamer, although she does all those things so beautifully. It's both controlled and like a god-given gift.

KELLEY DEAL We had worked like two years straight prior to this, and we knew it was going to be a long two-plus months in the United States, in the Midwest, in the summer. It seemed so easy; there were no border crossings or different kinds of money to deal with like when you're touring Europe. You could sleep on the bus or there was often a crew hotel. I usually slept on the bus because getting on and off the grounds was like a hike and a hassle with cars. There weren't Ubers back then.

KATE SCHELLENBACH (drummer, Luscious Jackson) We had already toured with the Breeders in Europe, and they were one of our favorite bands. So that was awesome. And I was dating Josephine at the time, so that was convenient for us to go continue to tour with them. And they of course were main stage and they had a tour bus. And so most of the time I was traveling with them, which was great for me. And then also it freed up a seat and some room in the Luscious Jackson van. Oftentimes I had to be delivered to the venue maybe before the Breeders actually wanted to be there. But whatever, we figured it out every day.

KELLEY DEAL Everybody loved Kate. She was a delight to have around and Josephine was happy and contented and busy with her. So we loved her for that. And we had had Luscious Jackson open up for us on a ton of shows, so we were really familiar with those guys and great fans of theirs.

JOSEPHINE WIGGS Even though there was the fun aspect of the camaraderie, the downside of it was that many of the places where the shows were taking place were in a field outside of the nearest civilization. So, literally, you would have driven overnight in the bus and arrived at, I don't know, eight in the morning or something and have to go to these portable shower modules in order to shower. And then you were just stuck in a field in the middle of nowhere for the next eighteen hours. There's nothing to do. There's no bookshop to go to, no museum to visit if you're that way inclined, or shops to go shopping, or anything like that. You literally were stuck in the middle of a field, and that did become a bit oppressive. And the first band would start at noon or one, so there would just be constant noise all day, every day. Even if you were inside your bus, you couldn't get away from it. Carrie Bradley and I learned to do two-person juggling. That was one of the things. We were like, "Okay, we're stuck in this field with nothing to do and nowhere to go. Let's learn how to do two-person juggling with, like, six balls." We would do that just to pass the time.

KELLEY DEAL Josephine is not a touring animal. She will be the first to admit that. She's like a cat. She wants her space. I can go a week, two weeks, three weeks without a shower. No problem. It's not an issue. But Josephine cannot. She needs routine and structure and she's a fricking vegan since birth, so food is really difficult for her to organize and stuff, and she can only eat beans. And where are you going to find tofu in the middle of a field?

JOSEPHINE WIGGS Some shows were a slog. In San Diego, there had been some kind of rainstorm or something the day before, so the whole field was just a sea of mud.

KELLEY DEAL The crowds were really great, but there was a noticeable change in the vibe toward the end of the tour, and it culminated there.

JOSEPHINE WIGGS Right from the get-go, at one o'clock, the audience was just throwing mud at the performers. It was really, really awful. We got halfway through one song and Kim was hit by somebody throwing mud, and she was just like, "Yeah, I'm not here for this."

CARRIE BRADLEY Kim was wearing one of her favorite shirts. A white, kind of sporty shirt somewhere between a tennis shirt and, like, a football fan shirt.

KELLEY DEAL I mean, they were mud clods, which was basically rocks. We had tried to keep playing, but I think specifically it was when Kim opened her mouth to sing "Divine Hammer," which is like a pop song kind of thing, that mud just hit her right in the face. And it was just too gross to go on. She called it.

CARRIE BRADLEY It was very violent.

JOSEPHINE WIGGS We walked off and didn't play the rest of the set.

CARRIE BRADLEY You know, it's hard work to be a performer and give up your life. You live on a bus, you give your all onstage. You constantly have to stay focused, stay confident, not let haters get you down. It's a lot of work. So when someone comes to a show, makes their way up to the front row, pays money—a substantial amount of money—and then wreaks violence, it's a breaking of the social contract.

JOSEPHINE WIGGS L7 apparently announced before they came onstage that if anybody threw anything onto the stage, that they would leave and play a Phil Collins CD instead as a punishment for the transgression of the audience member.

KELLEY DEAL I think the specific threat was that they'd play forty minutes of "Sussudio."

JOSEPHINE WIGGS George Clinton went on right after us.

JIMMY CHAMBERLIN I always tried to make it to see their set because I was such a huge fan.

JOSEPH "AMP" FIDDLER (keyboardist, George Clinton and the P-Funk All-stars) It was cool that they had so many different types of bands together. Because I feel like it also educates people because there were a lot of brothers and sisters that came out to see us on Lollapalooza. A lot of Black people came out and they got exposed to some music that they had never heard before. A lot of white people came out and they got exposed to music that they hadn't heard before.

JIMMY CHAMBERLIN At the beginning of the tour, you would kind of walk around backstage and see the P-Funk guys, and you would see a guy in a wedding dress and another guy in a diaper, right? And you'd be like, What the fuck is going on? By the end of the tour, you'd just be having lunch with the guy with the diaper and the guy with the wedding dress and it wouldn't be a big deal. The shock and awe kinda wear off.

JOSEPH "AMP" FIDDLER I remember it was a big band up there. We had three horns, two or three guitar players, two keyboard players, bass guitar, three or four background singers, roadies. Probably about eighteen people, in two buses.

WAYNE COYNE (singer, guitarist, Flaming Lips) We were playing on the second stage at the same time as George Clinton. And so, for whatever the reason, a lot of people would come over to our stage and be like, "Yeah, we watched a bit of Funkadelic, but it was kind of long." And so we had huge crowds.

KELLEY DEAL George Clinton was my mom's favorite. My parents saw several shows because in the Midwest, they could just go wherever we were, to Chicago or Cincinnati or wherever. And he was her favorite act. She loved P-Funk. And I think at the last show, she went up to him and she said, "I have one thing to say to you: *Shit, god damn, get off your ass and jam!*" And George just threw his head back and gave her a big hug. He was really sweet. The memory of how lovely he was to her brings tears to my eyes, actually.

4 "A SCENE WHERE A LOT OF THE PEOPLE USE REALLY PURE HEROIN IS PROBABLY NOT A SCENE MEANT TO LAST"

KATE SCHELLENBACH (drummer, Luscious Jackson) I want to say that Luscious Jackson did the first month of Lollapalooza, and then it continued on for at least another month, if not a month and a half. By the end of that, I think things were pretty estranged in the Breeders. I remember that there were different factions on that tour, sort of like summer camp or high school or whatever. Certain people in certain bands, like, hang out together doing certain things. So there were the potheads, and then there were people who were doing heavier shit, maybe heroin, I don't even know. And then there was just, like, the all-day-long drinkers and that kind of thing. That seemed to be how it all broke down.

CARRIE BRADLEY (violinist, the Breeders) It was no secret that that Lollapalooza in general was very druggy. It was, like, a peak of black tar heroin everywhere.

CRAIG MARKS (editor in chief, *SPIN* magazine; author) A scene where a lot of the people use really pure heroin is probably not a scene meant to last.

CRAIG WEDREN (singer, guitarist, Shudder to Think) It was this extraordinary moment of some of the best bands and some of our favorite bands beginning to rot. I mean, it's tough. You get a bunch of people like that with nothing to do on a big summer festival tour and of course, people are gonna do bad things to themselves.

STEVEN DROZD (drummer, multi-instrumentalist, Flaming Lips) Maybe I wasn't as sensitive to that as the guys from Shudder to Think, because I was trying to get involved in it myself.

WAYNE COYNE (singer, guitarist, Flaming Lips) Lollapalooza is when Steven probably got introduced to heroin and then got it, you know, regularly. I think that's when he became a drug addict.

MICK HARVEY (guitarist, Nick Cave and the Bad Seeds) Lollapalooza happened in that ten-year period between the first time Nick went into a clinic and the last time he went into a clinic. Through that period, he'd sometimes be on the straight and narrow a bit and then he'd relapse, and he'd be doing stuff again. I think that Lollapalooza was probably a difficult environment for Nick, and for everybody in that regard. There was a lot of stuff around like that. It's a big rock 'n' roll tour; the kind of environment that brings forth behavior where you do a lot of drinking and then there's other kind of things around.

KATE SCHELLENBACH I feel like there was a date in Detroit and then a date in Toronto, and everybody who was a pothead had to bury their pot and hide it because you couldn't bring pot into Canada. The border patrol would rip buses apart and stuff for that kind of thing. And then we came back to Detroit two days later and it was all still there. I heard this from the Beastie Boys' people.

CARRIE BRADLEY There were constant rumors going around about who was doing what. That there was tons of pills and massive amounts of marijuana in the Beasties' contingent. People just started isolating more and more, I think out of desperation for privacy or because of substance use. They gave us a vacation day at this nice resort in Phoenix, and I remember bobbing in the pool on a sunny day under a grapefruit tree and feeling really sad and anxious. I was pretty lonely sometimes.

KATE SCHELLENBACH Things were getting a little hairy.

JOSEPHINE WIGGS (bassist, the Breeders) When Luscious Jackson left the tour, my tour crush became Jennifer Finch of L7. I would look up where she was and take an interest in what she was doing. It's like having a hobby.

JENNIFER FINCH I think Josephine and I were on the same wavelength about how things were going. It was a weird summer for me, and it was really the start of where I just wanted to exit music altogether. Like, the level of commercialization, the level of drug addiction after just losing a friend basically to opiate addiction. And the idea of what role the record companies and the system were playing into that.

WAYNE COYNE You could just see people deteriorating as the tour went on, you know? Everybody's having fun, but ten days in they're just zombies.

JOSEPHINE WIGGS As the weeks wore on there was a feeling like we really were only seeing Kim and Kelley when it was time to play. Everybody would coalesce in the dressing room right before the show, and then they would disappear after we'd played. Often, Kelley was traveling with the Bad Seeds, and there would be this worry as to whether she was going to arrive in time for the set.

MICK HARVEY It was just a party on the bus with all the things that were on our backstage rider that we took with us. There were, like, eight bottles of champagne or something.

KELLEY DEAL I did a lot of partying with the Bad Seeds, yeah. I'm not really sure that if I was looking for a refuge from drugs and alcohol, that the Bad Seeds' bus is where I would fucking end up. Just to underline a point.

STEVEN DROZD I remember one time I was hanging out with Nick Cave, and I think he'd been dope sick because he hadn't been able to score for a couple of days. He was like, "I haven't eaten in three days. I gotta eat something before this next show."

MICK HARVEY Nick did miss one show. He wanted to have a bit of extra time in New York with his partner. She'd turned up there, so he didn't travel with the band, and he had to travel down to West Virginia for the next show. The flight was delayed and he hadn't made it to the venue by set time, so we just had to start playing or we wouldn't have been paid for the gig. And Paul Bearer, who's an old fan of the Birthday Party and who was on tour with L7 in some capacity, just came on and did "Nick the Stripper" and something else. And then we started doing "I Wanna Be Your Dog." Nick finally got there about halfway through the show.

JOSEPHINE WIGGS If you didn't play, you wouldn't get paid. That was the thing. So you had to try and play.

KATE SCHELLENBACH Especially when you're on side stage, because every penny goes to something. You can't afford to skip a show, which almost happened to us in Providence. I was traveling on the Breeders' bus, and I had to get there earlier than them for the Luscious Jackson set. But there was a pileup on the road, so the tour bus literally got stuck. I feel like we were like close enough to see the venue.

JOSEPHINE WIGGS For four hours, we sat there in a traffic jam looking at the clock, going, "Oh my god, oh my god. Luscious Jackson are due to go on now!"

KATE SCHELLENBACH This was also before cell phones. I don't even know how we were able to communicate, but somehow my band knew that we weren't going to make it. So they borrowed the drummer from the Boredoms.

JOSEPHINE WIGGS Not only did the drummer from the Boredoms not know any of Luscious Jackson's songs, he also spoke no English. So they were doubly up against it.

KATE SCHELLENBACH I think that everything was played at double speed, and there was a lot of communication through sign language.

JOSEPHINE WIGGS I remember asking Vivian Trimble, Luscious Jackson's keyboard player, "What was it like?" She said, "You know when you accidentally put a 33 rpm record on 78? That's what it was like."

GABBY GLASER (guitarist, vocalist, Luscious Jackson) It might have bummed out some audience members.

KATE SCHELLENBACH This was our first tour of a good portion of America, so it was also the first time for us kind of seeing that we had a following, which was cool. There was actually a curtain on the side stage, and I remember the first time the curtain opened, we didn't know if anyone was going to show up. But the curtain opened and there was a shit ton of people who knew our songs and were excited to see us! Part of that had to do with the popularity the Beastie Boys brought us, because we were on their label and the Beastie Boys were huge at the time. People were just really interested in anything that they were interested in. So it was exciting.

GABBY GLASER I vividly remember very young kids. I mean, to see twelve-year-olds, thirteen-year-olds . . . I was just like, "You little cuties! How did you find us?"

STEVE MARTIN (owner, Nasty Little Man publicity) I remember being worried for Luscious Jackson, based on some of the reactions I'd seen to other clients. The first night that they were playing the second stage, I was like, "Goddamn, I hope they don't get harassed, and pelted, and booed," and whatever. But they fucking killed it. People went nuts for them, bought tons of their merchandise.

KATE SCHELLENBACH We would do autograph signings after the show, and meet fans and stuff. Lollapalooza was sort of our first exposure to our fan base, which was great.

GABBY GLASER We were signing stuff during the Verve, which was kind of mellow music, so it wasn't distracting. I don't know why, but the Verve's singer, Richard Ashcroft, would always tell me, "You're old. You're old." I think at the time I was twenty-seven and he was twenty-three. I'm like, "You're an asshole."

5 "HAVE YOU GUYS SEEN A TITLEIST?"

BILLIE JOE ARMSTRONG (singer, guitarist, Green Day) The first time I ever got turned on to Guided by Voices was at Lollapalooza. They were connected to the Breeders because they were also from Dayton, Ohio. Robert Pollard, their singer, came up and sang a song with the Breeders. Kim really fucking hyped him up, like, "This is a song by Guided by Voices, my favorite band." And he came out and I was like, "Oh fuck. This song is great!"

GREG DEMOS (bassist, Guided by Voices) I was born in '66, so we were already old. Bob was probably thirty-five or thirty-six. And I think [guitarist] Mitch Mitchell and Toby [Tobin Sprout] and Bob are similar in age. So I was the youngest by almost a decade. This tour was just what we had been waiting for and dreaming about. We didn't make any money, we were sleeping in a van, didn't shower for four days, wearing the same clothes. It didn't matter. It was just awesome.

CARRIE BRADLEY (violinist, the Breeders) I loved them. Bob's a beautiful poet, and Tobin's guitar style was really compelling. And Bob did high kicks on stage.

NATE FARLEY (roadie, Guided by Voices) I got involved with the band because I was friends with Mitch. And honestly, I was selling a bunch of weed back then, so I didn't really have to go to work every day and I could just peel off and go hang out with those guys. Then during the

Lolla thing I was like, "Hey, I'll tune your guitars and I'll drive the van." And I got paid for it.

GREG DEMOS We used Mitch's van for the tour, and it was a shit show. There was a hole in the floorboard in the front passenger area. If you pulled up the mat, you could see the road underneath. And it had a gas leak. I don't ever remember it breaking down, which is a miracle.

TOBIN SPROUT (guitarist, singer, Guided by Voices) It had radiator problems, and at one point it overheated. So we all had to take a leak in the radiator.

CARRIE BRADLEY They'd come over to the Breeders' dressing room and drink all our beer. It was kinda hilarious. I was like, "They're drinking everything!" Not that there was any shortage of stuff to drink, but it was pretty funny. You know, the Dayton clan. I remember them being very nice guys who got so drunk when they played. I don't know how they didn't get sick, but they were great.

WAYNE COYNE (singer, guitarist, Flaming Lips) We were very excited and loved them, but they would just get too drunk, you know? I mean, that's the underlying thing with them. It's like, "This is gonna be good. It's gonna be good." Then, "Oh my gosh, they are just too drunk to play." It's kind of embarrassing because you think, Man, these songs are so fucking amazing . . .

NATE FARLEY We were drunk that entire tour. Lollapalooza was a big machine, so it had a lot of rules. A lot of things were in place for a reason to keep things from fucking up. We kept getting warnings from the stage manager and we were at strike three, our last warning. I don't even remember what the first two strikes were.

ROBERT POLLARD (singer, Guided by Voices) We got two strikes on the first day. The first was for the smoke billowing from our piece-of-shit tour van that had a huge marijuana leaf painted on the side and a big sticker that said, "Inhale to the Chief."

GREG DEMOS The main-stage bands had buses and Greyhounds. We parked the van and somebody came running up to us and yelled, "You gotta get that van out of here! It's leaking gas! It's a hazard!" We were like, "Well, that's all we got."

ROBERT POLLARD The second warning was when Greg and Mitch somehow got ahold of one of the crew's golf carts and were recklessly driving it around the backstage area.

STEVE "CHOPPER" BORGES (production manager, Lollapalooza 1993–97) We had a lot of golf-cart incidents. Artists getting golf carts and driving them into lakes or rivers and stuff like that. Because these guys would just get drunk and go racing around in them, almost running people over. It happened more than once where it was totally illegal. If you were caught without a production pass driving a golf cart, I think the first time they fined you a hundred dollars. If you did it again, it was like five hundred or a thousand dollars. And if it happened a third time, they'd kick you off the tour. They didn't care who you were. Because it was a huge liability insurance-wise and festival-wise.

GREG DEMOS Mitch and I borrowed a golf cart. It must have been after we played. So we were just cruising all over the grounds. We'd come firing up on someone and slam the brakes and go, "Have you guys seen a Titleist?" and they didn't even know what we were talking about. We probably drove around for a half hour or so before someone flagged us.

STEVE "CHOPPER" BORGES Artists think it's funny. It's not funny. Bad things happened, but fortunately, no one ever really got in a wreck involving people. But they got in golf cart wrecks. They wrecked golf carts. They just didn't wreck people.

NATE FARLEY Guided by Voices went on at three every day, which meant that we had to be there at noon. But one day we saw a liquor store, so we stop and it's open and we just get . . . I know there was a fifth of Jack and I know there was beer and I think there was a bottle of Crown Royal. We got *way* too much liquor, and just started drinking it right in the van. It's horrible to think of now, you know? Like, fucking don't drink and drive. And I had no sense of, "I work for this band and I'm the one that's supposed to keep my shit together." I was just like, "Fuck it. I'm drinking, too." I'm driving at the same time and we show up just shit-faced. We're probably two hours late. Like, we were *super-duper* late. So late that it was time to get onstage and play. The stage manager goes, "I don't have time to even talk about this now."

ROBERT POLLARD He's like, "Lectures later, just get on the stage." We figured it was going to be strike three and our final performance. So they had a curtain in front of the stage that would open to present each act, and as the curtain was opening I downed practically the entire bottle of Jack, and the crowd went nuts. I was instantly wasted and ready to go. The crowd loved the show and so did the stage crew, and there were no lectures later. We stayed on the tour and made a lot of friends.

STEVEN DROZD (drummer, multi-instrumentalist, Flaming Lips) Robert Pollard and his brother Jim were really good athletes. I watched them smoke the Beastie Boys in basketball one day. That was pretty fun.

AD-ROCK (MC, guitarist, Beastie Boys) You kinda get more hyper if you play ball. It gets your blood going. On Lollapalooza, we played a lot more, all day, in the heat for hours, and it was crazy hot out there.

JIMMY CHAMBERLIN (drummer, Smashing Pumpkins) Mike D was instrumental in teaching the Tibetan monks how to play basketball. It was so out of their wheelhouse and something that they could kind of latch onto. They were all pretty athletic guys and they actually got pretty good at it. By the end they had a pretty good scrimmage team!

STEVE MARTIN (owner, Nasty Little Man publicity) I remember there were monks in saffron robes backstage, playing basketball with the band members and the guys from the Knicks.

KELLEY DEAL I love the Beastie Boys and they're really nice guys and everything, but they wore the uniforms and were really into the whole, like, fashion side of it. They really liked that pickup, street basketball, b-ball kind of thing.

STEVEN DROZD The Beastie Boys carried their own basketball goal with them, and at every show, they'd pull it off their equipment trucks so they'd have something to do.

ROBERT POLLARD We played one game against the Beastie Boys, with Billy Corgan.

KELLEY DEAL Everybody was shocked that Billy Corgan could really play.

NATE FARLEY The Beastie Boys were super all about basketball, and they're not horrible. But Jimmy Pollard is a sports god in Dayton. I've seen Bob and Jim just fucking demolish people. Jimmy would step back and drain three-pointers on you all day.

ROBERT POLLARD Let me set the record straight: The Beastie Boys sucked. The Breeders could've beat 'em. We won eleven baskets—not points—to two. I think my brother probably scored all eleven baskets. It wasn't fair. He averaged thirty-seven points a game his senior year in high school and played for Arizona State.

KELLEY DEAL There was a sense of pride because they were Ohio boys. But it was an aggressive game of basketball. Not a friendly game.

NATE FARLEY I do remember Mike D looking a little salty about it.

TOBIN SPROUT They had one of those nets that rolled up. And one of them got kind of a little upset and had had enough. They just took their net . . . and went home.

LOLLAPALOOZA 1995

DATES: JULY 4–AUGUST 18

MAIN STAGE: Sonic Youth, Hole, Cypress Hill, Pavement, Sinéad O'Connor (first eight shows), Elastica (as a replacement for O'Connor), Beck, the Jesus Lizard, the Mighty Mighty Bosstones

SECOND STAGE: Coolio, Moby, Yo La Tengo, Mike Watt and the Crew of the Flying Saucer, Superchunk, Poster Children, Helium, Patti Smith (New York date only), the Dambuilders, Blowhole, Pork Queen, Dirty Three, The Roots, various

LAB STAGE: Shallow, Lucifer Wong, Clod Hopper

Although Lollapalooza's organizers and audiences were satisfied with 1994's pair of multiplatinum-selling headliners, critics of the festival accused it of having committed alternative rock's cardinal sin: that of selling out, and perhaps rendering itself meaningless in the process. "The magic is definitely gone from the Lollapalooza tour, leaving just another rock concert in its wake," said *Variety*'s Bruce Haring, reviewing the July 7, 1994, launch at the Sam Boyd Silver Bowl in Las Vegas. "The show's safe, mainstream vibe will leave little reason for Perry Farrell to keep it alive for future editions."

When it came time to book 1995, Farrell and his co-organizers were eager to change the narrative. While some of the biggest-selling records at the time were from radio-friendly alternative rockers like

Bush, Live, and Stone Temple Pilots, Farrell would have none of it. In fact, he reportedly rejected the latter two bands out of hand as potential headliners, believing they lacked credibility. Who to choose, however, was something of a conundrum. "The festival had already been going for four years and they had done everybody," says Sonic Youth agent Bob Lawton. Even harder was finding a suitable headliner *willing* to do the tour. Farrell was at his wits' end. "I actually called the whole tour off," he admitted to the *Los Angeles Times*. "We'd gone through Neil Young and Snoop Doggy Dogg and the Clash . . . It was looking like [Lollapalooza] was out of gas, and I couldn't do anything about it."

When it became clear that the 1995 tour was not shaping up to be a box-office blockbuster, or the "wow" moment that a historic reunion would create, festival organizers realized that an opportunity still remained to make the statement that Lollapalooza, despite its detractors, continued to identify primarily with the fringe elements of the rock world. "We knew that alternative had gone mainstream," says festival cofounder Marc Geiger. "So we booked Sonic Youth, Hole, Pavement, and the Jesus Lizard to plant a flag." Although Sonic Youth's arty, neo-no-wave sound hadn't yielded the record sales generally requisite for a Lollapalooza headliner, their influence on the alternative rock scenes of the eighties and nineties was unparalleled. "They'd been one of the main architects of the community that made Lollapalooza possible," says music journalist Michael Azerrad, pointing to the fact that the members of Sonic Youth were also astute talent scouts who had helped guide the careers of bands like Dinosaur Jr., Cat Power, and Nirvana. As hoped, a Lollapalooza with Sonic Youth headlining—and helping to curate the bill—was one that the press could get behind. "Lollapalooza is topped by one of the prime shapers of today's noise-guitar aesthetic," declared the *Los Angeles Times*. "A genuine alternative-heritage band."

Preceding Sonic Youth on the main stage was Hole, fronted by Courtney Love. As the still grieving and aggrieved widow of Nirvana front man Kurt Cobain, Love was more than just a rock star—she was a full-blown celebrity whose mercurial personality and tragic story made her a magnet for media coverage that often glossed over the fact that Hole's 1994 album, *Live Through This,* was a beautifully ragged document of grunge-punk fury. Hip-hop weed evangelists Cypress Hill and Pavement, whose uniquely arch, sprawling take on guitar pop was not particularly well suited to an easily distracted festival crowd, played sixth and seventh, respectively.

Perhaps the most unexpected performer on the roster was the controversial Irish singer Sinéad O'Connor, whose standing in America had not completely recovered from her 1992 tearing up of a photograph of Pope John Paul II on *Saturday Night Live.* O'Connor would drop off the tour after eight performances and be replaced by Elastica, a punky Britpop quartet whose debut album was ascendant in both the UK and US. Beck, who had yet to release his 1996 sample-rich masterpiece, *Odelay,* and still labored in the shadow of the surprise novelty hit "Loser," and Chicago noise-rock darlings the Jesus Lizard preceded. Opening the main stage—and outliers on the otherwise largely cerebral bill—were Boston's the Mighty Mighty Bosstones, plaid-suited Boston ska-punks whose visibility was greatly increased due to their appearance in the Amy Heckerling film *Clueless,* as well as inclusion on its platinum-selling soundtrack.

In a departure from previous years, the second stage was headlined by an artist whose sales and notoriety far exceeded that of many of the main-stage acts. Coolio, a rapper who employed both humor and melody to great effect, had seen his 1994 debut album, *It Takes a Thief,* go platinum on the strength of the single "Fantastic Voyage." And he was about to get much, much bigger. "Our timing was impeccable," second-stage manager John Rubeli recalls, "because the song 'Gangsta's Paradise' came out the week before Lollapalooza and was huge."

Rotating in and out on the second stage throughout the tour were more than a dozen groups, including Hoboken lo-fi groovers Yo La Tengo; screechy North Carolina power-poppers Superchunk; a guitar-wielding, stage-diving Moby, still a few years away from perfecting the blues-sampling electronic sound that would drive his

1999 album, *Play*, to sales of more than ten million copies world-wide; the Boston trio Helium, fronted by guitar wiz Mary Timony; Poster Children, a frenetic Illinois art band enjoying a run on major label Sire Records; and the Dambuilders, a left-of-center Boston outfit riding out a rocky tenure on Elektra Records. In a historic second-stage guest appearance that would turn the July 28 New York stop at Randall's Island on its ear, punk icon Patti Smith performed one of her first shows in more than a decade. Indie bass legend Mike Watt, formerly of the Minutemen and fresh off a major-label album featuring contributions from Dave Grohl, Eddie Vedder, J Mascis, and many others, would join the second-stage roster for its final leg. Along with Love, Beck, the Jesus Lizard's David Yow, and members of Sonic Youth, Watt would also chronicle his tour experiences in nearly real time via an online diary; sponsored by *SPIN* magazine in association with America Online, the text-only chronicle might seem quaint in the era of social media, but was cutting edge at a time when laptops and internet connectivity were still in their nascency.

Despite it all, as anticipated, the 1995 iteration of the festival failed to draw the crowds of Lollapalooza '94, played in fewer venues, and grossed a reported $12.8 million in ticket sales—less than half that of the previous year. Geiger, for one, claims that the downturn was not a surprise to the Lollapalooza brass. "If you're on the outside, you go, 'Oh, it was lower than '94.' But when you book that lineup, you expect to not have the same commercial result. Actually, we were, I'd say, shocked on the high side." Sonic Youth guitarist Lee Ranaldo is less sanguine about the tour's performance. "I think 1995 failed abysmally on Lollapalooza's part," he says.

The direction the festival would take in 1996, at least, adds weight to Ranaldo's assessment.

1 "YOU CAN'T BE COOL IF NOBODY CARES"

STEVE "CHOPPER" BORGES (production manager, Lollapalooza 1993–97) Lollapalooza was sort of Perry's brainchild, but several times, for lack of a better term, he stepped on his dick. He wanted things to be counter-culture to the detriment of the tour.

PERRY FARRELL It's my fucking party and I'll have who I want.

DON MULLER (agent; cofounder, Lollapalooza) Stone Temple Pilots were begging to get on and Perry would not put them on. I think he was right.

STEVE STEWART (manager, Stone Temple Pilots) One of our agents was Don Muller, right? The guy who was running Lollapalooza. And our record had blown up by then, so it's like, "How are we not on this tour?" So we lobbied to be on it, and there were talks about us headlining. I don't know what the internal discussions were on the agency side or between Perry and Muller, but at some point it was my understanding that we weren't picked. My guess is Perry just did not like the band. And I don't think he ever really respected Scott Weiland. Certainly not to the extent that Scott respected *him*. But it wasn't like we needed to be on the tour. It was just a nice tour to be on and very easy to do, because the production was there.

STEVE "CHOPPER" BORGES Perry just went, "Too mainstream. I don't want it." And see, he'd gotten away with it the year before, because Nirvana had dropped off and we still had our biggest year. So he said,

"I can do this." So now Sonic Youth is at the head of the bill and Hole behind them.

THURSTON MOORE (singer, guitarist, Sonic Youth) We probably would have done '94. We would have been the "Nick Caves," I guess.

JOHN RUBELI (second-stage manager, Lollapalooza 1993–95) In '95, you had people who weren't on the front line making decisions *thinking* that they were speaking to the front line. When you have people that have an understanding of what it was and don't understand that that's no longer what it is, it creates a problem. I was arguing for Stone Temple Pilots, for Live, for Bush, for the Goo Goo Dolls—acts that were selling. Acts that appealed to the audience and that would get them to come. Because every day, some kid turns fourteen and turns on the radio, right? So you had the fourteen-year-old kid in '91, who's now eighteen, nineteen, and is into something else or maybe a different iteration of what that was. Every year, you have a whole new set of ears. You have a whole new grouping of impressionable people that are shopping at a Hot Topic, buying the thing that's commercial.

MARC GEIGER (agent; cofounder, Lollapalooza) It was a reaction to the overwhelming commercial success of alternative. We knew music on that front was stale.

LEE RANALDO (guitarist, Sonic Youth) What was going on in that greater world was pretty discouraging. The record companies were all looking for the next Nirvana and chewing up these bands and spitting them out when they didn't turn out to be that after one record. Spend one million making one record, doesn't do any good, you're off the label. We were just pretty disillusioned with it.

THURSTON MOORE I begged John Rubeli to let me book bands.

JOHN RUBELI The pushback against that which is commercial mattered to a lot of people who were involved with Lollapalooza. It certainly mattered to Thurston Moore.

DENNIS DENNEHY (publicist, Geffen Records) When we got the list and realized that we had three artists on our label—Sonic Youth, Hole, and Beck—on there, the buzz about it in the company was definitely exponentially bigger than a Grammy nomination or anything like that.

STUART ROSS (tour director, Lollapalooza) In 1994, we had had the Beastie Boys and Smashing Pumpkins, both of which had enormous success by the time they played Lollapalooza. And there was press who were writing about us, saying, "Lollapalooza is a rip-off. It was never designed for platinum-selling 'X,' it was designed for bands like Sonic Youth and Hole. And this is bullshit." And the next year, oddly, we have Sonic Youth and Hole. And the same press wrote, "Lollapalooza is a rip-off, there's no headliner." So literally, no matter what we did, they wanted to find a reason that we did it wrong.

NIKKI GARDNER (assistant to Ted Gardner; special groups coordinator, Lollapalooza) Nineteen ninety-five was a tricky year. I think it was due to the fact that we had already had so many great bands perform. It was just that middle hump year, I guess. Like a Wednesday.

KELLY WEISS (box office manager, Lollapalooza) I was definitely a little bit more apprehensive about the lineup than in previous years.

STEVE "CHOPPER" BORGES Lollapalooza had such momentum that they sold shows out in advance, without even announcing an act. But once the lineup was announced, it was horrible. I mean, I think the advance sale in Sacramento was only like fifty-five hundred. And I think we only did about seven thousand total. It was the least-attended Lollapalooza, I believe, in the whole time I did it.

STEVE SHELLEY (drummer, Sonic Youth) I recall that Sonic Youth was in Memphis recording what would become *Washing Machine*, and that we got a phone call, most likely from Mark Kates, who was our A&R guy at that point in time, asking us if we would consider doing the tour. And I think, as a group, we felt that it was a long shot that this would be something for us to do.

DENNIS DENNEHY There was never a discussion, like, was this the right thing for the band to do at the time? Sonic Youth moved the culture with them.

MARK KATES (A&R representative, Geffen Records) Did I believe Sonic Youth was the most important band in the world? Yes, and I think they actually were. I don't really think there's much question about that.

MARY TIMONY (singer, guitarist, Helium) I feel like they're the last band that really were creating their own genre. People just don't do that anymore.

STEVE SHELLEY There was word that, "Oh, well, Beck and Pavement and Jesus Lizard might be a part of this." And we felt very strongly that they really needed to be there for us to consider doing it. If you're committed to being on a summer tour, you want to enjoy yourself, you know? We knew Pavement and Jesus Lizard, and we were getting to know Beck, and we just knew we could have a fun time with these people.

MARK KATES Let's just say that Beck was resistant.

LEE RANALDO Did they just decide they wanted to do an indie year, or was it that indie was big enough that between Hole and what we were up to, there might be some attendance action to be had from booking a tour like that with all these bands? Because it wasn't just us; it was kind of like a dream lineup with all those bands.

DENNIS DENNEHY It felt like Sonic Youth had a heavy hand in what was happening there. As did Geiger and Muller. There were a lot of cooks in the kitchen.

JOHN RUBELI Thurston was so dismissive of anything that had any semblance of commerciality. And I was like, "Why? Because there's melody? Bands that have songs aren't any less relevant or any less important because it's not your version of cool." He raked me over the coals so much that year, saying, "Oh, you and your CMJ rock. Why don't you book Blowhole? Why don't you book Thomas Jefferson Slave Apartments? Why don't you book Pork Queen?" All of which I did. But let's be frank: It's all unlistenable music. It makes him cool. But it makes a kid in the audience indifferent. And the death of cool is indifference. The Flaming Lips had a guitar player, Ronald Jones, who was the guy who gave them that guitar sound before they went orchestral and did all the other stuff. He would always say, "You can't be cool if nobody cares."

MARK KATES Some of this stuff may have happened because of Sonic Youth, but a lot of it probably would've happened anyway based on music at that time.

LEE RANALDO I think we did it because at the time we had designs on making some money so that we could do some other stuff, like setting up a studio for ourselves. We took a whole bunch of the money we made on Lollapalooza and just sunk it back into our work, basically. We found a place in Lower Manhattan, on Murray Street, where we could set up shop, and we bought really professional studio gear. That kind of fueled our next ten years. We made our next four or five records on that gear. Actually, all the way to the end of our career.

MAC McNEILLY (drummer, the Jesus Lizard) I don't know that we completely knew what we were getting into, but the money was really good and we were gonna be on the main stage, which was pretty flattering to us, I guess. Although in retrospect, I'm not sure that that helped us so much because we went on second and very early in the day, and most people were just getting there.

DAVID YOW (singer, the Jesus Lizard) That whole tour was so stupid.

SCOTT KANNBERG (guitarist, Pavement) We had actually been considered for Lollapalooza in 1994. But they didn't ask us in the end.

BOB NASTANOVICH (percussionist, background singer, Pavement) It didn't work out mostly because of Smashing Pumpkins being on that year's bill. They pretty much hated us because of the song "Range Life," that was kind of sarcastically derogatory toward them. And I think that Billy Corgan really doesn't have that kind of sense of humor? So it became sort of an "us or them"–type situation with Smashing Pumpkins. And obviously, we were more than happy to bow out of that conversation.

SCOTT KANNBERG I'm not sure if that's completely true. But it's a good myth!

DAVID "BOCHE" VIECELLI (agent, Pavement, the Jesus Lizard) That was always just a story to me. If I'd had an offer on the table, and then it got canceled because Billy Corgan said so, I'd remember that.

BILLY CORGAN (singer, guitarist, Smashing Pumpkins) The whole idea that I kept bands off the bill is absolutely, completely 100 percent false. I recommended bands that I thought would be better.

BOB NASTANOVICH Then '95 came around, and Lollapalooza was sort of presenting themselves for the first time as being a show that really wanted to embrace indie rock.

SCOTT KANNBERG We ended up getting the most money we ever got, like twenty grand a show. It was unheard-of money at the time. So we were like, "Yeah, let's do Lollapalooza!"

SEN DOG (MC, Cypress Hill) We had played the side stage in '92, so when they came back around in '95 and asked us to be a bigger part of it, we were like, "Hell, yeah!" This is everything that I had ever imagined touring life would be like, that we'd be up there with the hottest bands in the world. And then just the multicultural racial thing that was happening in the audience—the whole mix of colors that you saw from the stage kind of blew my mind.

PATTY SCHEMEL (drummer, Hole) We all wanted to do it because . . . well, first of all, it was Lollapalooza. And then secondly, I just felt that we were going to be with a lot of other bands, it would be a little more so-cial, and it wouldn't be like the darkness of the European tour we had just done where it rained every day. And then also, I got to play with Sonic Youth and Sinéad. All the bands that were listed were personal favorites—Mighty Mighty Bosstones, Jesus Lizard. It was going to be the best summer tour of all time.

DENNIS DENNEHY Courtney had something to prove on that tour. She had to prove that Hole could play. She had to prove that she could con-form. She had to prove that she wasn't just "The Widow Cobain," as she said back then.

JOHN RUBELI I got pressured into booking Moby. Perry was a big Moby fan and I'm not, but I was asked to do it and it happened.

MOBY (artist) It was sort of a strange offer. Perry Farrell wanted me to perform at Enit, which was an electronic music festival that he was put-ting together, so I was initially contacted about that. And my managers convinced them that I should also do the Lollapalooza second stage. For me, it was a world that I never imagined I would have access to. This was the era of the grunge-rock stars—Pearl Jam, Soundgarden. These were people who were on the cover of *SPIN* magazine when I was lucky to get a small write-up in the back, next to an ad for pillows.

KRISTEN WORDEN-HARRIS (artist liaison, second stage, Lollapalooza 1995–97) The crowd loved Moby. He crushed at Lolla. He wore the same dirty T-shirt every day. So he was a little ripe.

PATTY SCHEMEL The side stage also had Yo La Tengo and Geraldine Fibbers and the Dambuilders, which was so amazing. It was perfect.

DAVE DERBY (bassist, singer, the Dambuilders) We were on our second record for East/West, but East/West had been taken over by Elektra. I mean, my take on it is that we didn't have the most imaginative mar-keting people at the label. After our first record they were just like, "The Dambuilders have to get out on the road with bigger bands and that'll help." So that year we did a lot of touring with Better than Ezra, who were very nice people, but it just wasn't a fit at all. That's the most diplomatic thing I can say.

JOAN WASSER (violinist, singer, the Dambuilders) I feel like if we went out with En Vogue or Metallica, those bands would've made as much sense. Because we were playing for, like, really normie college kids who were not in any way interested in listening to music that was different. So we rarely connected with anyone and we were basically really upset all the time.

DAVE DERBY But it was very clear that if we hadn't done that, there was not going to be any promotion for our record. We were considering touring with some really vile groups, one of which was Live, which almost broke up our band. There were people who were willing to do it and I was like, "No, I'd rather just shoot myself." So getting Lollapalooza was a lifeline for us because it was like, "Hey, Elektra, we're gonna play the Lollapalooza second stage. Have some of that!"

JAMES WILBUR (guitarist, Superchunk) I don't remember being super excited or super scared. At that time, we were touring so much that it was like, we would be on tour anyway, but if everyone's going to Lollapalooza, we might as well do that!

JON WURSTER (drummer, Superchunk) It just seemed like a cool thing that these bands who weren't really part of this big major-label world were gonna be part of this big traveling tour. There were enough bands like us who were also on, like, Helium and Built to Spill.

JAMES WILBUR It was much more like our—I don't want to say scene—but it was much more of who we would *want* to be our peers. Even though we were not as popular as them, at least we came from the same sort of aesthetic.

NATE ALBERT (guitarist, the Mighty Mighty Bosstones) Lollapalooza for us was an aspirational goal. We grew up with college radio in Boston, and all of a sudden there's a tour that now represents all of these things. And it became very much like, who was being chosen that year, only these bands were going to get the shine that year. So, it's something that we and Allison Hamamura, who was our booking agent and became our A&R person later on, really wanted the band to do.

JOE GITTLEMAN (bassist, the Mighty Mighty Bosstones) Not that long before we headed out on that tour, all of a sudden it was like, "You're not going to be a main-stage band anymore. You're going to be on the second stage." And we chased that back to Courtney Love, who didn't want Bosstones on the main stage. But through some working with the agent, we were able to assert that we had a deal that needed to be honored.

NATE ALBERT We did bounce a couple times and do the side stages, just so we could have the intensity of the crowd right in front of us. And we ended up really having this amazing, kind of summer camp experience. It was bizarre, but it was so awesome. The playing was almost secondary.

2 "I DON'T THINK ANYONE EXPECTS THAT KIND OF VIOLENCE"

STUART ROSS (tour director, Lollapalooza) The first show ever at the Gorge was Lollapalooza in '92. At that time, it was nothing more than a winery, and we played in the parking lot. We would play there every year because it was so beautiful, and Seattle was one of our main markets. They took the money they made from Lollapalooza and put it into infrastructure. They put in a stage and they put in trailers for dressing rooms one year, and then decking for the trailers.

STEVE "CHOPPER" BORGES (production manager, Lollapalooza 1993–97) We opened '95 at the Gorge, on the Fourth of July. It's a beautiful venue. The stage is at the end of a little area, and then the gorge is in the background. And then offstage left and down below is where all the catering, the dressing room trailers, and all that kind of stuff was.

BECK (artist) The Gorge is remote canyon country, three hours from Seattle. The stage is perched on the edge of a steep rock drop. Beside the stage and grounds, there is nothing in sight but wide sky, rock, sage, and green.

STEVE "CHOPPER" BORGES We had these things called Lulls, which were big, all-terrain forklifts with a telescopic fork that would go out so you could pick stuff up far away. Well, it was lunchtime on the production day before the first show of the tour and the Lull driver was heading down the hill to the catering tent. All of a sudden, I could see him getting a little panicky, and the Lull was picking up speed and starting to bounce and it was heading right for catering, which was full of people. To his credit, this guy wrenched the wheel to the left and started skidding sideways, and I thought for a minute he was going to flip. I thought, If that guy flips and that Lull goes into catering flipping sideways the wide way, it's going to kill dozens. He got it off to the left, but he ran into three porta-potties and blew them up into the air and off into the sagebrush. One of them had somebody in it, and it was one of the cooks. But it had just hit it and clipped it and threw it up in the air, and it disintegrated and this guy flew out.

By this time, I'm running down there and I'm on the radio going, "Get the medical staff! Get everybody down here!" And we got down there and the guy had only broken his wrist. He was dressed all in white, and it had been dyed blue by the porta-potty water. I was so relieved that I just started laughing. I said, "Man, I'm really sorry, but dude, we are all so lucky." And then I said, "And your blue outfit is just *stunning.*" That could have been one of the worst disasters in rock history.

STUART ROSS What I remember is that the porta-potty flew over into the gorge itself and that the guy was very seriously hurt. They had to airlift him out.

DENNIS DENNEHY (publicist, Geffen Records) Sonic Youth's first show of the tour was such a big moment. They're basically the parents of all these . . . children, figuratively. This is their fucking moment.

JIM MERLIS (publicist, Geffen Records) Sonic Youth music with the gorge as the backdrop was stunning. Just absolutely stunning.

THURSTON MOORE (guitarist, vocalist, Sonic Youth) We were heading back to our trailer after our show and I was informed that on the side of the stage while we were playing, the singer of Hole flicked her cigarette at [Bikini Kill singer] Kathleen Hanna and then sucker punched her in the face.

JOHN RUBELI I feel like Courtney was the person who felt like the rules did not apply to her. The person that shows up uninvited to the party over and over again and you just get tired of throwing them out. I think that's who she was at that time because of being vilified over Kurt.

MICHAEL "CURLY" JOBSON (stage manager, Lollapalooza 1991–92; tour manager, Hole, 1995) The Nancy Spungen of 1995.

THURSTON MOORE Kathleen Hanna and Kurt Cobain had been friends before Courtney entered Kurt's world.

MICHAEL AZERRAD (journalist, author) When Kurt moved to college-town Olympia, Washington, from provincial Aberdeen, Kathleen Hanna became one of his closest friends; she was also the singer in Bikini Kill, whose drummer was Kurt's girlfriend, Tobi Vail. As a founder of riot grrrl, Hanna schooled Kurt about third-wave feminism, which was a hugely formative experience for him. And then, of course, she and Kurt went out one night, sprayed graffiti on a teen pregnancy center that counseled young women not to get abortions, went out and got drunk, and wound up at Kurt's apartment, where Hanna took out a Sharpie and wrote "Kurt smells like Teen Spirit" on the wall before passing out.

JOHN RUBELI When you have someone like Kathleen Hanna who is affiliated with Kurt, I think the intentionality is, "This is my turf."

JIM MERLIS I think Kathleen was there that day as a guest of Sonic Youth.

ERIC ERLANDSON (guitarist, Hole) We had bulk candy backstage. I go, "Courtney, there's Kathleen Hanna. You should offer her some candy."

THURSTON MOORE Erlandson had handed her a bag of candy, telling her she should give it Kathleen as a peace offering—or possibly as a joke? Kathleen had evidently responded with something that made her see red.

ERIC ERLANDSON She grabbed the candy and just threw it at her. Everybody was like, "Oh my god, she punched her in the face," but from what I saw, she threw the candy, and kind of slapped her in the direction of her face. I don't know if she actually hit her, or what. It doesn't matter, it was not cool. The whole tour started on that note.

JIM MERLIS Courtney was kind of staring at Kathleen with this crazy look in her eye. She was so deranged looking, you kind of couldn't keep your eyes off her because it was like, "What the fuck is going on here?"

MELISSA AUF DER MAUR (bassist, Hole) Courtney did a fake cat hiss, like a joke. Like, "We're at war" kind of a thing, like "Sss!" . . . making a weird joke in passing. Next thing you know, there's this explosion of arguing. Maybe a shove, I can't remember.

JIM MERLIS I was sitting somewhere backstage and Kim Gordon came in with Kathleen. And she's like, "Kathleen, this is Jim, Courtney's publicist. Tell him what just happened." And Kathleen's like freaking out, so Kim says, "No. No. Jim's cool. Jim's cool. Tell him what happened." I think Kim probably didn't realize how bad it was because it seemed like Kathleen was almost trembling when she heard I worked with Courtney. You know what I mean? I think she hit her really hard. I don't think anyone expects that kind of violence.

KATHLEEN HANNA (singer, Bikini Kill) That's the whole thing that pissed me off, that later people were like, "They fought. There was this rivalry and they fought." It's like, dude, I was standing there watching a band and Courtney walked up and attacked me.

PATTY SCHEMEL (drummer, Hole) I remember we had to do some MTV press stuff. Me and Eric and Melissa were talking about who we wanted to see on the tour—Sinéad, blah, blah. And then I heard that it happened. I think somebody in our crew was like, "Oh my god. Courtney just tried to punch Kathleen." I was just mostly embarrassed and felt really shitty that it happened. Because I like Bikini Kill, I like Kathleen, I like that band. I like that scene, you know?

STEVE SHELLEY (drummer, Sonic Youth) It really was a big fucking bummer.

JOHN RUBELI When you're a crazy person acting entitled without permission, anything's possible. Was I expecting physical violence? No. But something absurd? Yes.

PATTY SCHEMEL Courtney ended up having to get her arm bandaged and couldn't play guitar in Vancouver the following day. She spent a lot of the set yelling at Eric to start the songs. Courtney's tempos were always different, but that day Eric played her guitar parts and every song was perfect. In footage, I can see I'm wearing a Misfits T-shirt, who I remembered was one of Kathleen's favorite bands. It was my little silent protest in support of her.

KATHLEEN HANNA It's a real bummer to be assaulted. It sucks. It's a real bummer if you're a feminist and you're assaulted by another woman, because it's just kind of heartbreaking. Especially a woman where you were hoping that you could be some kind of allies.

STUART ROSS Courtney Love's whole persona was built around the fact that you couldn't predict anything she was gonna do.

PATTY SCHEMEL It was another one of those moments where I was like, "Shit." It sucks. You were physical, and you were violent. And so that's just another part of Courtney at the time, when she's not clean and sober. It was all just craziness in a giant craziness nutshell.

STEVE SHELLEY That action just put a damper on the entire tour.

LEE RANALDO (guitarist, Sonic Youth) It didn't really put a pall over anything. There was so much weird stuff going on on that tour. It was the year after Kurt died. So in a way, it was Courtney's big coming out. And she was maybe not in the greatest shape all the time.

ERIC ERLANDSON That was only fourteen months after Kurt's death, and a year after [Hole bassist Kristen Pfaff's] death. We were still in recovery mode. Courtney was obviously stirring up a lot of stuff and going through a lot of stuff emotionally and mourning publicly in everybody's face. They say that after a suicide, it doesn't really hit you till one to two years after, so there was still a lot of craziness coming out. I think that we weren't in the best shape to be running around the country playing festivals.

JULIE PANEBIANCO (A&R representative, Capitol Records) She probably shouldn't have been there. You wanna work, but it's hard to work, you know?

MICHAEL "CURLY" JOBSON In '95 I was back at Lollapalooza because I took a job tour managing Courtney and Hole. I absolutely loved the lady, but she was somebody dealing with a particular period in her life where she was numbing the pain, and that obscured her ability to do some things in a respectful manner. People felt immense sympathy, and I think total concern, for Courtney. Part of my own therapy later on was understanding my codependency issues. I was more invested in my part in fixing the problem with her. If you knew where I was getting the deliveries of the things that she needed to keep her going from . . . I mean, it was burning a hole in my heart, keeping her going with all of this stuff. If I was asked to behave like that these days, no thanks. And today, it wouldn't be allowed. Nobody would tolerate it, because we're too tuned in to personal culpability, let's put it that way. I didn't have any perception of that. In my mind, my job was to make sure I propped her up, and that she stayed as healthy as she could be.

DANNY GOLDBERG (chairman, Warner Bros. Records; former manager, Nirvana, Hole) The level of intensity that she was dealing with, I can't imagine what it was like for her. I don't know how she did it. It was a very, very tough time. And she's grieving. She has a baby.

JULIE PANEBIANCO It's really fucking hard to even begin to explain the dynamics of that.

KIM GORDON (bassist, guitarist, singer, Sonic Youth) And that was the beginning of our tour.

3 "NERDS ON LOLLAPALOOZA"

AARON NAPARSTEK (editor, SPINonline) My buddy Ben Cooley, who was the road manager for Beck, introduced me to a woman named Liz Mitchell, who was an editor at *SPIN*. She heard I was graduating journalism school and I was interested in internet stuff. And she said, "The business schmucks on the eighth floor just made a deal with this thing called AOL. No one on eleven wants to deal with it." I was like, "Wow, I would love to do a music site on AOL." At the same time, their assistant fact checker had just died of a heroin overdose and they needed a new fact checker and a new online person. And I said, "I'm perfect for that." So I ended up getting this great job at *SPIN*. Well, it was terrible. It was the lowest job there was. But I got to start building this AOL thing on the side.

LEE RANALDO (guitarist, Sonic Youth) At the time, the internet was just this vague, theoretical thing. It wasn't what we have in our lives these days at all. And I guess in terms of online stuff, I was a pretty early adopter. I had bought one of these little tiny computers, the model 102, that was made by the Tandy Corporation that owned Radio Shack. It looked like the size and shape of a PowerBook, but maybe a little bit thicker. It had an eight-line screen and the total memory onboard was thirty-two K, like really nothing. And when the memory filled up you had to offload it onto cassettes through this really bizarre process, and then load it back in when you wanted to see the stuff again. I had one, and a guy named Paul Smith, who we worked with in England a lot, did, too. We were actually able to communicate with him in England when we were on tour in the States, through the internet, with this strange little computer. Like, you put these suction cups on the ends of the phone to connect. And I also started keeping a tour diary on the computer as we were driving places and stuff.

MIKE WATT (bassist, singer, Mike Watt and the Crew of the Flying Saucer) There's actually an art to writing diaries. There really is. Do you know about this guy Samuel Pepys? This guy ended up like a fucking admiral for England in the seventeenth century. This cat was the big granddaddy of diaries. I mean, he doctored them up and shit and self-aggrandized, but just the idea of keeping track of what's going on during the day, for ten years, he kept a diary and was writing about, you know, how many kernels of corn he found in his turds.

AARON NAPARSTEK Lee Ranaldo was the one who contacted me with the idea of doing online tour diaries on the site. He was like, "Hey, we're kind of nerds on Lollapalooza this year. I'm gonna be bringing a laptop with me. Why don't we do this tour diary idea?"

LEE RANALDO By the time Lollapalooza came around in '95, I just thought it would be a cool idea to do it. There was a way to post this stuff online, and while it didn't seem like very many people were seeing this stuff because it was still kind of new, there was definitely a community of punk rockers that were tuning in and reading it day by day. Since they were our friends, I encouraged all these other people on the tour, from Beck and Pavement to Jesus Lizard and Mike Watt, to do it, too.

MIKE WATT I'd tried to do one diary when the Minutemen went with Black Flag to Europe in 1983, but man, that was so fucked up. I got lost many times; I didn't know how to write 'em yet. So this was actually my second attempt.

AARON NAPARSTEK Pretty instantaneously I started getting the emails from the Lollapalooza artists and they were just great. Beck would send me a post at 2:00 a.m. and it would just be, "Moby in the lobby."

MIKE WATT It seemed like a lot of dudes flaked. Like, they did one fucking entry or some shit.

DAVID YOW (singer, the Jesus Lizard) They asked us to do it, and I think we did it for about four days or something like that. We just lost interest.

AARON NAPARSTEK I was really into the idea that you suddenly had this tool, and everyone with their own laptops and digital cameras could cover Lollapalooza from multiple perspectives at once. Then all of a sudden, on the first day of the tour, we get to see this crazy event between Courtney and Kathleen, two really interesting musicians who have big personal history, happen from all of these different perspectives. By the next day, the real people involved had all read each other's diaries, and now they're all talking about each other's tour diary postings. So what was happening in the tour diary was then having an impact on the tour itself.

MICHAEL "CURLY" JOBSON (stage manager, Lollapalooza 1991–92; tour manager, Hole, 1995) Courtney was absolutely obsessed with the AOL thing. It was chat rooms—and millions of them. Part of my hotel rider for Hole was to have twenty-four dinner plates. Then I would put them all around the room, for when she stubbed out cigarettes while she was sitting on AOL fighting with Trent Reznor and the rest of the world, and creating bedlam everywhere. Being the very first influencer, which I think she was, really.

AARON NAPARSTEK I was getting AOL instant messages from Courtney Love at 3:00 a.m., regularly. We would be up late chatting and she would go on and on. Sometimes you could tell she was fucked up, and things would be all crazy and misspelled and it was very personal and defensive, especially if she was being sort of attacked in the press. And it was just like, "How in the world am I, a twenty-four-year-old junior staffer at *SPIN*, suddenly in this back-and-forth with Courtney Love?" It was super weird.

4 "COURTNEY WAS THE SPECTACLE"

THURSTON MOORE (singer, guitarist, Sonic Youth) In *USA Today* there was an item about how Kathleen Hanna, singer from Bikini Kill, was filing assault charges on Courtney Love. The reality was stark. I walked into the dressing room and Lee, Kim, and others were sitting there and they said that Courtney had just come in to appeal for us to call Kathleen off, that Kathleen wanted to put her in an insane asylum.

NATE ALBERT (guitarist, the Mighty Mighty Bosstones) You knew it was a chaotic situation, but you also knew exactly why. I mean, the ability to tour after having gone through what Courtney had gone through in such a public way, and being such a public person, was very powerful. So there was this "Okay, just kind of be cool" thing going on. I think there was just so much empathy.

BOB NASTANOVICH (percussionist, background singer, Pavement) She was in a very, very tough space; it was a lot for her to handle at that point. And that kind of added a whole really intense level of freakiness to the however long the Lollapalooza lasted.

TERRY PEARSON (front-of-house sound engineer, Sonic Youth) Courtney in general could be very chaotic as far as the overall vibe, depending on her balance at the time of what chemicals, and that kind of stuff. It could be a good day, or it could be a chaotic day.

MOBY (artist) The first time I saw Courtney, she pulled up in a black stretch limousine, got out wearing couture clothes, and had two security guards around her the whole time. I had never seen anything like that. But at this point, I mean, Hole were huge, and she was Kurt Cobain's wife and muse. We never spoke during Lollapalooza. She was too protected and surrounded by security. Later on she asked me to produce a record for her, and Peter Mensch, her manager, was very polite about it. He said I wasn't even fit to tune her guitar, let alone produce a record for her.

MARY TIMONY (singer, guitarist, Helium) I remember Courtney being super fucked up, basically, and hardly being able to walk to the stage. She had to have somebody help her. And then after the show in D.C., a bunch of people went to go hang out at the Black Cat, which is a club in D.C. I just remember her acting totally nuts. Like, borrowing a dollar bill from the doorman and then going to do coke in the bathroom. And then getting all this ice from the bar, going around to all these random people, and dumping ice on their heads. She was just really acting crazy.

MICHAEL "CURLY" JOBSON (stage manager, Lollapalooza 1991–92; tour manager, Hole, 1995) I only ever had cross words with her one time. We were in this place in Arizona, and she was there doing the same stuff, the AOL, the chat rooms, the whole at-war-with-the-world thing. I needed to get her up, and I needed to get her out. I needed to get going to the show. And I just couldn't get it to happen. I went into the room, and I was so anxious over what was going on that I was like, "Fuck it, I'm quitting. I've had enough. I'm going home. I've got people at home who love me and want me to be around. This is thankless." It was the first time I had expressed the stress and anxiety that I felt in the job, and she went absolutely nuts at me. She started screaming, jumped out of bed, butt naked, and chased me outside. It was like something out of *Benny Hill*—Courtney, naked, out in some golf resort hotel, chasing me down, screaming, "Jobson, you motherfucker!" Anyway, I didn't quit.

JIM DeROGATIS (pop music critic, *Chicago Sun-Times*) Courtney was one of the smartest women I've ever met . . . and also one of the most fucked up.

STUART ROSS (tour director, Lollapalooza) Courtney and I were very friendly over the course of the tour. We shared a love of Leonard Cohen. We would sometimes eat together, and I had a good working relationship with her. But there was one thing about Courtney Love that I remember. Hole was second from closing, right before Sonic Youth. Now, the universal truth about Lollapalooza is that it didn't have to start on time, but it had to end on time. There was no leeway in terms of going past eleven o'clock. That show had to be over. And it wasn't as much about noise restrictions as the fact that we had to pack up all of these trucks, all of these buses, the food craft, political booth vendors, move on to the next city, and open those trucks up and start the process all over again and be able to let people in at noon. It was a ridiculously tough schedule. And Courtney started to go onstage later and later.

Eventually, the stage managers came up to me and said, "Look, you gotta do something. She's playing long. We can't make up time in the set change. You gotta fix this." So I sat down with her and I said, "Listen, out of respect for every other band playing, we really need you to come offstage when you're supposed to. If you start late, you start late. But you have to end on time." And she said, "I understand. I'm gonna do my best." I said, "Look, I just gotta tell you, if you go long, we're cutting the power. I don't wanna do that, but I have no choice." And she said, "Stuart, I completely understand. Just leave it with me." And from that point forward, she went long, we cut the power, she jumped into the audience, crowd-surfed, and came back onstage. I was always at the downstage edge and I pulled her out of the crowd, and she was laughing her ass off, but they were doing a set change behind her as she was being passed around. Because, literally, we didn't have time to waste.

PATTY SCHEMEL (drummer, Hole) Courtney would say, "I want to be able to stage dive, like guys in bands do." A part of her had to know she's going to let herself be abused and have her clothes taken off her and all that. I think in a way, it was her sort of allowing it. But also, it just was so disturbing and out of control. It was just so fucking shitty.

JIM MERLIS (publicist, Geffen Records) I wouldn't say most of the people that were holding her up when she was crowd surfing were doing anything to her. But there were definitely a few. I think people felt her up. I think people punched her. I think it was very intense when she did that. She would never talk to me about it afterward. I mean, god, why would she constantly do that to herself? And it was such an interesting thing, because the post-punk alternative world is like, "Oh, we're not like that." But some of those fans are.

MICHAEL "CURLY" JOBSON It was pretty heinous, man. Dreadful. I would be on guys with my fists, with my teeth, with my forehead, guys that were doing that kind of stuff to her, to get her back in. That's why I struck that deal with her. If you see videos, there came a point in the tour where she didn't go in the crowd anymore—because she was on my shoulders. I would run up and down the crowd with her. And she was no waif.

JIM DeROGATIS Sometimes you got the sense that it was out of anger or out of "fuck you," and other times it was a sense of "We're all in this together." But we sexualized these things, right? I mean, I can't tell you the number of times I've seen Iggy Pop come out onstage, tear off his shirt, hock a loogie in somebody's face, and throw the twenty-five-pound, lead-base microphone stand without caring where it was going, just to land on somebody's head. Courtney's doing the same thing, and she's getting felt up and she's also getting embraced and hugged.

STUART ROSS There was a time in Pittsburgh where she was singing, and somebody threw a shotgun shell onstage and she saw it. I just happened to be at stage left at the time. And she stopped the performance and came up to me and said, "Fuck this crowd. I'm not doing it." I had to make the announcement: "I'm sorry, the show's gonna be a little bit delayed." That wasn't cool.

LEE RANALDO (guitarist, Sonic Youth) Courtney was the spectacle. People were curious about Hole just because they wanted to see if Courtney would do something weird or say something weird from the stage. And because everybody read about her, she was kind of notorious in a way.

PATTY SCHEMEL People would come for the music, but I think an equal amount came for the hysterical . . . the performance art was part of it. There was always some kind of situation going on in between songs if she was in a mood. I tried to make the best of it. I'd started asking for the local paper, and I would read the paper while she was doing that. She never knew the whole time. I make a joke that I almost had enough time to go off and make a bologna sandwich and come back.

JAMES McNEW (bassist, Yo La Tengo) I watched them from the side of the stage a few times and the thing that I noticed was that Courtney Love would do this sort of performative trashing of the gear at the end of the set, but she never touched the drums. I mentioned that to Patty and she was like, "Yeah . . . we have an understanding." What a power-house Patty is. It was really great to watch her go.

PATTY SCHEMEL I played as hard as ever, but as our shows had turned into spectacles, I found I didn't care to be sober anymore. Five months clean on the road was good enough. We were in Chicago when I used for the first time since New Year's. It was as easy as calling up Blackie Onassis, the drummer from Urge Overkill, who had a regular hookup in town.

JIM DeROGATIS So much shit gets talked about Hole, but Hole was a great band. Erlandson was great, Patty Schemel was great, and Court-ney, you could not take your eyes off her.

STUART ROSS Courtney was sort of a really valued person in my world because I considered what she was doing more of a character perfor-mance than a musician coming onstage. And I never considered Court-ney a celebrity except kind of in her own head. Like, there was one time I was sitting with her on a break or getting a coffee, and she said, "I can't do the show on Wednesday." I'm like, "What do you mean you can't do the show on Wednesday?" She said, "I got invited to this really cool Hollywood premiere and I wanna go to it. Jack Nicholson will be there!" I was like, "No, no, Courtney. That's not how it works."

PATTY SCHEMEL She'd get obsessed with one CD and would listen to it over and over, or a movie and watch it over and over and over again. I remember on Lollapalooza it was PJ Harvey's newest record, which had "Down by the Water" on it. I think from those days I've learned to sleep anywhere, with any sound. I can sleep through PJ Harvey being blasted at 3:00 a.m., even to this day.

SCOTT KANNBERG (guitarist, Pavement) She'd always follow Malkmus around because she thought she was better at Scrabble than him.

DAVE DERBY (bassist, singer, the Dambuilders) I feel like I saw Stephen Malkmus doing a crossword puzzle *with a pen* backstage. He was just aloof and brilliant and doing his own thing.

BOB NASTANOVICH Malkmus had this reputation of being, you know, very intelligent? And obviously, Courtney is a very smart person and she was constantly wanting to challenge Malkmus to crossword puzzle competitions.

SCOTT KANNBERG I mean, from the first show, with the fight and stuff, Lollapalooza basically became the Courtney Love show. And it was just pure entertainment. She was great, you know?

BOB NASTANOVICH I've never been a fan.

5 "SPIÑAL TAP PLAYING AT THE THEME PARK"

THURSTON MOORE (singer, guitarist, Sonic Youth) We set up our stage thing in a way where it would sort of engage everybody no matter how far away they were. We did a lighting thing that was just really interesting, and our sound man was really good.

SUSANNE SASIC (production designer, Sonic Youth) It was the first time Sonic Youth had any kind of custom stuff made for them. We had a painted backdrop and made three six-foot-diameter globes that were covered with a sort of a gray mesh material and they had little star strobes studded all over them. Those hung from a truss in the middle of the stage above the band's heads. And then, the real main piece of it was a curtain made out of these little capsule strobes, made into twenty vertical hanging strings that hung from a bar, from the ceiling to the floor. That was the big effect. It was a big step up for them.

LEE RANALDO (guitarist, Sonic Youth) Susanne had been our lighting person almost since we started. She went from someone who basically had to be shown how to turn on a slide projector in the early days to becoming this consummate professional lighting engineer. We liked her because she had a really good design sense and we knew we had to come up with something for this tour. And we also knew we had the budget to do so. I thought it came off really well. I was really pleased with the stuff she designed and how it actually got fabricated. And pretty much from that point into the future, we did have some stage production for every subsequent tour. So it was also kind of the beginning of that for us.

STEVE SHELLEY (drummer, Sonic Youth) The backdrop was a painted depiction of someone's idea of what a juke joint would look like, as we had just recorded in Memphis. It was sort of wood floors and it was down-home kind of looking. I don't think a lot of that translated to the audience very well at all, but the strobe curtain was beautiful.

LEE RANALDO We were playing this song called "The Diamond Sea" that was on *Washing Machine*, our new album that hadn't been released yet. It's like twenty minutes long—noise, distortion, and stuff. To me and to fans of Sonic Youth, one of our very best periods. But still, it's a little cruel to be playing music that nobody knows.

DENNIS DENNEHY (publicist, Geffen Records) It's a beautiful song. And it's arguably one of their masterpieces.

DEB PASTOR (roadie, the Jesus Lizard) Getting to see Sonic Youth be on a stage that big with that light show, especially when they played "The Diamond Sea," was a glorious thing. That song just pulls everything out of every emotion you have. One of the most magical moments ever because it was so grand.

THURSTON MOORE The way Lollapalooza is set up, the second-to-last band is really the heavy celebrity band. It sort of worked that way with Alice in Chains. That was the band that all the kids wanted to punk out to, and then Primus was the more serious muso thing.

MICHAEL AZERRAD (journalist, author) Mainly what I remember about the 1995 Lollapalooza was people leaving in droves as the ostensible headliner Sonic Youth played. Already there was a new alternative rock audience that neither knew nor cared who Sonic Youth were. That was a bummer.

KIM GORDON (bassist, guitarist, singer, Sonic Youth) It was really kind of crazy. No record out, playing four or five new songs and even old songs that maybe people weren't that familiar with.

STEVE "CHOPPER" BORGES (production manager, Lollapalooza 1993–97) In Sacramento, by the end of Sonic Youth, there was probably fourteen hundred people. I mean, it looked like a club.

LEE RANALDO We experienced this thing where on many, many nights, halfway through our sets, we could see people streaming to the exits. It was late. They were like, "We've been drunk and sober, and drunk and sober, and stoned five times today. We're leaving." It doesn't matter who's onstage. They'd heard enough Sonic Youth. They weren't really our fans and they got whatever they needed out of Courtney.

JIM DeROGATIS (pop music critic, *Chicago Sun-Times*) They weren't good enough to command an audience of thirty thousand people, not with that many distractions—a second stage, all those art booths and food, beer, ogling the opposite sex. I mean, it was a party. But then, I'm a Sonic Youth skeptic.

THURSTON MOORE It definitely teetered on Spiñal Tap playing at the theme park.

GREG KOT (music critic, *Chicago Tribune*) Sonic Youth totally held true to their vision. They weren't in any way pandering to that audience. "If you want to leave, leave, but we're going to play our set." And it fucking rocked. I thought they were really, really good. But a lot of people didn't; there was no MTV hit that Sonic Youth had. And at that point, the audience was basically there to see bands because they had a hit on alternative-rock radio. Or they had a hit on MTV, which was now taking these videos from once alternative bands and playing them. Sonic Youth was still not playing that game. And for that reason, as a headliner, they were a bold choice. And it bombed.

STEVE SHELLEY We would have these long discussions with Mike Watt, who played the side stage on some of the shows that year, about that kind of thing. He would get into these long debates with us about how we were fucking up by not going on before Hole and then just leaving and not having to deal with it. But our argument was, "We're headlining." And we thought it was important to headline. Mike just thought that that was no good, that we should be playing to those people.

MIKE WATT (bassist, singer, Mike Watt and the Crew of the Flying Saucer) I had a whole fucking perspective on that. Especially with the way that lady set up the situation with her running her mouth and shit. I said, "You should let her choke on your smoke." As far as a strategy and doing your Machiavelli thing, it's a bad place. You're doing the wrong move. You're letting people leave on you. What, for the honor of your name being bigger or going on last? I call playing in that slot cleanup, you know, with the broom. If they would've gone on before her, they would've made her look so weak.

6 "SINÉAD ENDED UP JUST WALKING OFF THE TOUR"

JON KLEIN (guitarist, Siouxsie and the Banshees; touring guitarist, Sinéad O'Connor) Sinéad's manager, Steve Fargnoli, was actually very nervous because he'd heard the set that we were doing and it wasn't the *Lion and the Cobra* album, with rock-anthem stuff. It was generally a lot of very esoteric stuff based on almost Irish folk music or dub remixes of tracks. But it was a supertight band and it actually worked quite nicely.

BOB NASTANOVICH (percussionist, background singer, Pavement) For the first six, eight, ten gigs, we were playing after Sinéad O'Connor, who of course is . . . very famous. She had her following of six, eight, ten thousand people at every show, and they were probably wondering what in god's name she was doing playing before us. And to be quite frank, I was wondering the same thing—not only before we got there, but because she was playing this very choreographed set in which they did the same songs in the same order with the same shtick. The drummer would come out and salute the crowd at the same time every show; everything was choreographed. It was theatrical. And I'm not criticizing that in any way, shape, or form, because I think that that probably is a very good approach to something like big-league outdoor concert tours. And I think her crowd really appreciated it.

ABBY TRAVIS (bassist, Beck, Elastica) Sinéad was my favorite act on that whole tour. Her band was fantastic and her voice was just transcendent. I was like, "This is real. This is from this woman's heart. This is true."

STUART ROSS (tour director, Lollapalooza) I'll tell you that I was more excited about Sinéad O'Connor being on the tour than probably any of the acts, because of what a beautiful, angelic voice this woman had. But there was one thing . . . we were going from somewhere in Chicago to somewhere in Indiana, not a long drive, but there was a time change. And somebody in her camp did not factor in the time change, and she showed up late. Her set was at a particular time, she's not there. So where is she? Well, we don't really have cell phones to say, "Dude, where are you?" She shows up, I don't know, fifteen minutes after her set was supposed to start. And Chopper says to her, "Okay. If you go on right now, you can do thirty minutes." She says, "I do my own set or nothing." And he goes, "Well, that's completely up to you."

STEVE "CHOPPER" BORGES (production manager, Lollapalooza 1993–97) I said, "This is your job. My job is to make sure this all works. If you're late, a minute or two or something like that, or five even, that's kind of your business. My business is you're done at this time. That's inviolate." And she couldn't deal with it. So I said, "And here's the thing. If you don't go out there and do"—I don't know what the contract was, twenty-five minutes, thirty minutes, whatever it was—"you don't get paid. It's that simple. You need to be here and do your job in a timely fashion. It's part of being on a festival."

JON KLEIN Our musical director at the time, John Reynolds, was Sinéad's ex-husband and the father of her first child, Jake, who was actually out on that tour with us. Maybe he was eight or nine. The poor guy, John, had ended up in a life that was orbiting the chaos that was Sinéad O'Connor, you know? Anyway, Sinéad was definitely kind of getting friendly with Courtney and I remember John Reynolds saying, "Oh my god, I'm really worried about this. You know what this will lead to—they'll get friendly and the next stage is, they'll fall out."

ERIC ERLANDSON (guitarist, Hole) The day before she left the tour, Sinéad hopped on our bus.

PATTY SCHEMEL (drummer, Hole) Sinéad was in the bunk across from me. I flipped out, of course. And then she goes in the back.

ERIC ERLANDSON The back lounge area was reserved for Queen Courtney.

PATTY SCHEMEL There was not so much hanging out back there. It was sort of a private-ish area. They watched *Ryan's Daughter* and they talked all night. It's an overnight drive and the next morning we get to Chicago. And then the bus is parked, and everyone slowly gets up and checks into their rooms.

STUART ROSS Courtney came up to me the day after Sinéad disappeared and said, "Stuart, I gotta tell you something about Sinéad: She's nuts." And I swear this is true. I said, "Courtney, coming from you, I consider that expert testimony."

STEVE "CHOPPER" BORGES Sinéad ended up just walking off the tour. Didn't tell her tour manager. Got on a bus, left. We were afraid she'd been kidnapped.

STUART ROSS We had the day off in Chicago. And Ted Gardner called me and said, "Hey, somebody just told me that Sinéad O'Connor was in *Melody Maker* today, getting off a plane in Dublin." He said, "Check it out." So I called the tour manager. I said, "Hey, is everything okay?" He said, "Yeah, she didn't feel very well. She's got kind of a digestive thing, but she's fine."

JON KLEIN Sinéad had gotten pregnant and she found out while she was on the tour. And it was a heat wave in America. So she wasn't physically able to continue.

STUART ROSS Ted called me back and said, "I don't think she's here." I called again, and of course it was, "No, no, she's fine." Well, what ended up happening is she got to Chicago, she left the hotel, took only her passport, didn't even take her luggage, went to the airport without telling anybody, and got on the next flight to Dublin. And it's like, "Okay, she's gone, now what do we do?"

MARK KATES (A&R representative, Geffen Records) I got a call from Lee Ranaldo and he was like, "Everybody's talking about this and everybody wants Elastica."

JUSTINE FRISCHMANN (singer, guitarist, Elastica) We just got a phone call saying, "Sinéad's pulled out. Do you want to join the party?" And we thought, We can't resist it, really.

JUSTIN WELCH (drummer, Elastica) We had only just arrived home from a run of dates in Japan a couple of days earlier when the call came in for us, asking if we'd be up for joining. Our album was doing well in the States, so I guess we were a strong contender for her slot. Also, we had all our crew in place and valid American visas from a US tour we'd just previously done, so it was just a case of booking flights and heading out.

JUSTINE FRISCHMANN When we came to the States for a second time, it was really amazing because our video for "Connection" was on MTV and people were coming up and saying, "Do that face!"

JUSTIN WELCH Our bass player, Annie, played a number of the shows, although she was burnt out from our rigorous schedule. We were contracted to play two festivals in the UK, so we had to leave Lollapalooza for just one weekend in August. We had just gotten home from Japan, flew to the US for Lollapalooza, flew back to the UK for the festivals, and then flew back out to the US to join the Lollapalooza tour once again. It's insane, but that puts into perspective how hard we were working. After the Irish date, we got a message the morning that we were flying back to the US and that Annie had decided to go home and wouldn't be rejoining the tour with us.

JIM MERLIS (publicist, Geffen Records) Annie was the only musician to ever ask me to help them get drugs, which I unfortunately had no idea how to do.

JUSTIN WELCH I didn't even see Annie to say goodbye the morning we left. She was our friend, she was one of our gang, everything we'd achieved with Elastica was with her. I remember sitting on the plane, looking out of the window, thinking, What are we fucking doing? We should have stopped then, supported Annie, and taken a break. But no, we pushed on without her. Instead, management just said, "Don't worry, she'll be fine and we'll get you a replacement bass player." News travels fast, and while we were flying back to the US, word had got 'round about Annie and that Elastica were now looking for a bass player for the rest of the tour. Melissa from Hole and Abby from Beck were both really up for playing.

ABBY TRAVIS I think we were in Texas or somewhere in the South. I get some phone call, but I might have been a tiny bit hungover and I was like, "Can you call me later?" It may have been Mark Kates, I don't remember. Then I walked down into the lobby, and Beck's tour manager, Ben Cooley, says to me, "So are you gonna do it?" And I go, "Do what? What are you talking about?" He goes, "Are you gonna play with Elastica?" And I'm like, "I don't know what you're talking about, but I would love to do that." And he says, "Call Mark Kates right now." I called Mark Kates and he was like, "I couldn't get in touch with you." So they had asked Melissa Auf der Maur instead.

MELISSA AUF DER MAUR (bassist, Hole) Courtney decided the public perception would be too confusing because I had just joined Hole. I was kind of bummed. Luckily for Elastica, there were two female bass players on the tour.

JUSTIN WELCH Melissa had her show later in the day, so it seemed a wiser choice for us to ask Abby, who was performing with Beck in the slot before us. When we landed back in the States, I think we went straight to some shitty rehearsal room somewhere in Austin, Texas, and started rehearsing our set with Abby. We were ready for our show the very next day.

ABBY TRAVIS The sets were back-to-back, so all they had to do was push my amp to the other side of the stage.

JUSTIN WELCH Abby was a different bass player than Annie; she played with her fingers and Annie played with a pick. Abby jumped around on stage in hot pants and no shoes, while Annie stood by her Ampeg bass rig and wore Doc Martens.

ABBY TRAVIS I think I did a good job, and I have to say that being on-stage with a bunch of other women was nice, because sometimes it gets kind of old being the only girl on the bus with all guys.

JUSTIN WELCH Once we arrived we were instantly made to feel welcome by everyone on the tour. Arriving at the first show I particularly remember the Sonic Youth family coming to our dressing room to meet us. Kim Gordon, Thurston Moore, and all their kids and nannies—there were *a lot* of kids and nannies on that tour.

JON KLEIN After Sinéad left the tour, I actually flew out to Dallas to go to one of the first shows where we'd been replaced by Elastica. And that was interesting, because the gang that I knew in Dallas, they were all super fit, going to the gym, getting full-body waxes and all that stuff. That wasn't fashionable in England in 1995. But they were all massive Elastica fans, and during the show they were like, "Oh, Justine! Justine! We *love* you!"

Then halfway through the set Justine goes, "Hello, Dallas!" And lifts up her arms. And I see, like, a lot-thousand people going, "*Ahhhh!* Armpit hair!" It was like that Patti Smith *Easter* cover. There were literally people covering their faces, totally scared. Oh, it was hilarious. It reminded me of the shower scene in *Psycho,* the reaction of the audience.

7 "IT WAS PROBABLY A VERY BRIEF BIT OF NUDITY"

LEE RANALDO (guitarist, Sonic Youth) We had toured a lot with Pavement and Jesus Lizard and Beck, so we had bonds with them already. But this was a chance to spend the entire summer with all these people. It's like being in a traveling circus or something like that. I have to say, I think that was part of Perry's inspiration for doing it.

STEVE SHELLEY (drummer, Sonic Youth) Beck, Jesus Lizard, and Pavement, they all had a really difficult time.

LEE RANALDO Beck was a young artist at that point. He had had this massive hit with "Loser," but he was playing to an empty house because it was so early. Also, he was still finding his footing as a live performer, trying to figure out how to present his live show. He had put together a band, and I don't know if that band stayed together very long.

JOAN WASSER (violinist, singer, the Dambuilders) Beck did not have his band together at all.

MARK KATES (A&R representative, Geffen Records) He was not where he wanted to be musically yet. And in particular, I think he didn't feel the confidence level that he wanted to, to play shows at that scale.

ROSE MARSHACK (bassist, Poster Children) I would walk over by where the fans were, behind the gate, and I remember some girl was screaming,

"Come here! Come here!" I went over and she's like, "Do you know Beck? I love Beck!" And I said, "Well, I'll tell him." So I went over and I found Beck and I was like, "Beck, there's some girl out there who really wants to meet you." And he goes, "Oh, that's nice." And he was holding a flower and he says, "Well, tell her I just sniffed this flower for her." And I was like, "Okay, I'll do that," and went back.

DENNIS DENNEHY (publicist, Geffen Records) I think Beck enjoyed being around the Pavement guys and Sonic Youth. But he played so early in the day on the main stage, like one o'clock. I remember that, after the tour, he did an interview for *SPIN*, and we were in Silverlake by the dog park. The quote never got used, but the writer asked him, "You just got off the road with Lollapalooza. What are your memories of that?" And he just looked at him and said, "Empty seats. Lots and lots of empty seats . . . And then maybe far away in the amphitheater up the hill, ten or twenty kids getting into it and security quickly descending on them."

THURSTON MOORE (singer, guitarist, Sonic Youth) Beck referred to it as a reverse mosh pit. All the moshers are up on the hill and all the "buddy" guys are in the seats.

JON WURSTER (drummer, Superchunk) My main memory of those amphitheater shows was Pavement, Jesus Lizard, and Beck playing to like 60 to 70 percent empty seats.

LEE RANALDO I would go out every day and watch Pavement play because I was just in love with them. And you would sit in the best seat in the house because there was nobody in them. You would walk out there with your laminate and sit anywhere you wanted. And you were just in a sea of empty chairs. It was a real bummer, actually.

DAVID "BOCHE" VIECELLI (agent, Pavement, the Jesus Lizard) They were used to their own environment and people who would specifically come to see them. It's a little bit different to deal with a crowd that isn't necessarily there for you.

MARY TIMONY (singer, guitarist, Helium) I remember playing through our set and being really distracted, because people were tossing all these beach balls around the audience and then onstage. And there was a kid standing at the edge of the stage giving us the finger the entire set. It was really intense. Now, as a fiftysomething-year-old person who's been doing shows, I would probably deal with it in a much different way. But at the time I wasn't comfortable performing. I was kind of trying to ignore it, but I just couldn't, and it stayed with me. So fucked up. He spent so much energy giving us the finger.

DAVID YOW (singer, the Jesus Lizard) Lollapalooza was just clumsy, and it wasn't that good. I wasn't a fan of playing at three in the afternoon to half-full sheds of people who couldn't give a fuck about us.

MAC McNEILLY (drummer, the Jesus Lizard) David would do a lot of stuff where he would climb down around the security guys and mess around with them a little bit. Take their hats off or try to lift up their shirts. Or he would go down and sit in the seats, and sing parts of songs from sitting down.

DAVID YOW It was just a pathetic plea for somebody to show some excitement and passion and, like, enjoy themselves. Our soundman had a hundred-foot cord for my microphone, so I could go way out there, either fuck with people or sit in their laps or lay down or whatever.

JOAN WASSER I remember seeing Yow at 11:00 a.m. just downing Jack Daniel's. Because part of his thing was being wasted onstage. So the fact that they were first or second, they played at, like, 2:00 p.m., was a disaster for them. Jesus Lizard is not 2:00 p.m. music.

ABBY TRAVIS (bassist, Beck, Elastica) I spent a fair amount of time drinking with the Jesus Lizard on that tour. The bands that got done early would then be like, "All right, well, we've got another zillion hours to go." So there was a lot of drinking.

STEVE SHELLEY Daytime was tough for that tour. I think that's partly what led to the incident with David Yow. He was just like, "I don't give a fuck. There's nobody here. Who cares?"

MAC McNEILLY David's a guy that likes to see what he can get away with, you know? He's a mischievous type of a soul. That kind of translates pretty well to being a front man. These gigs were probably harder for him than us, because we're rooted to our instruments, but he's got this huge wide stage to try to fill up with activity.

DEB PASTOR (roadie, the Jesus Lizard) There was one show in Canada where it had been raining and it was so muddy that they had put plywood down. And somebody lifted the plywood up and somehow David got himself on it and was surfing it like a surfboard around the crowd. It was fricking fantastic.

MAC McNEILLY In Cincinnati David exposed himself temporarily, partially . . . I don't even remember what exactly he did. But yeah, he got in trouble for that.

DAVID YOW Sometimes, somehow, by some act of God, my pants would end up off. And when we were playing that Cincinnati show, I said something about the Mapplethorpe thing [In 1990, Cincinnati's Contemporary Arts Center and its director, Dennis Barrie, were brought up on obscenity charges for displaying work by photographer Robert Mapplethorpe], and that happened. Then when the song was over, I pulled my pants back up.

DUANE DENISON (guitarist, the Jesus Lizard) I think it was probably a very brief bit of nudity. Like, maybe him changing an outfit really quick by the side of the drum riser. I don't think it was some big, nude interpretive dance or something.

DEB PASTOR David has been known to pull out the jewels and do dick tricks. So it didn't look like anything different than the usual. But in our world, censorship didn't really exist because when you're in small clubs, who cares? But now he was on a stage with thousands of people around and doing something similar. And I guess he went a little farther than usual.

DAVID YOW Deb Pastor came onstage and she said, "Hey, apparently the DA is in the audience. And he said that if you do that again, you're gonna be arrested." And I said, "Okay, well, that's easy enough. I won't do it again." Then we finished the set, and these two cops came back-stage, arrested me, and took me to the jail.

DEB PASTOR All of a sudden he was gone, and he didn't come back. And as the day went on there was an underlying tension that we might have lost him for days, and that we would be putting Lollapalooza in a bad position or lose the slot.

MAC McNEILLY He ended up making friends with some of the cops at the station.

DAVID YOW These idiot cops were saying, "Oh, this is great! We haven't had a rock star in here since Ted Nugent!" It was just humiliating and stupid. They were so disrespectful. I was married at the time. They made me take off my earrings and my wedding ring and they detained me for three or four hours, and then I had to pay a fee. A couple of 'em said they wanted my autograph before I left. I said, "Oh, okay." And then somebody came to pick me up from the production team, and one of the cops said, "What about our autographs?" And so I just wrote, "Fuck you!" And put my name on there.

When I got back to the venue Hole had finished, and Sonic Youth was playing. I was in the production office talking to our manager on the phone, and Courtney Love came in and plopped herself down on the desk in front of me. And she goes, "I showed my cooch, and they didn't do anything!" And I said, "Um, Ms. Love, I'm on the phone."

ABBY TRAVIS The next day after he got arrested, he did the exact same thing: dropped his pants and mooned the camera operator for the big jumbotrons on the sides of the stage. I was watching from the side and

I remember looking at the camera operator and David had a shit-eating grin on his face. He was just laughing.

DAVID YOW A few months later I had to go to my hearing, and because my name is Yow I was near the end of their little procession. And case after case after case after case was domestic abuse and wife beating. When they finally called me and they said, "David Yow . . . recklessly and knowingly exposing his private parts," everybody looked at me like I was Satan. Like, "Okay, people saw my dick, but you beat your wife. Fuck off!" They fined me, like, $370 and I wasn't allowed to go to Hamilton County for a year. Can you imagine not going to Cincinnati for a year?

8 "FUCK YOU, FRAT BOY!"

BOB NASTANOVICH (percussionist, background singer, Pavement) The strangest thing about how we approached Lollapalooza is that everybody else toured on a bus. But we'd never had a tour bus at that point and I used get these unbelievable deals on rental cars. So, when we got to Seattle, I rented a couple of Ford Windstars, unlimited mileage, and we just traveled around in those, which allowed us tremendous flexibility to get to the venues when we wanted and leave when we wanted. We kind of turned that whole Lollapalooza into a really fantastic tour of America's bowling alleys. I think we probably bowled in about thirty or forty different bowling alleys.

That said, it was this huge pain in the ass getting into a lot of the shows because they wouldn't believe that we were a band, and we had a real hard time proving that. Even though we had the fancy laminate with the holograms all over it, there's at least ten instances where we'd sit there for anywhere from fifteen to thirty minutes while some guy on a walkie-talkie was not convinced that we were playing on the main stage.

MAC McNEILLY (drummer, the Jesus Lizard) We didn't take a bus. We were traveling in two vans. David Yow and I would usually drive together, and we were referred to as the kids' van, and the other van, with Duane and David, we referred to them as the adults' van. Because they were a little more serious about things. Whereas I think we were a little more . . . I don't know . . . not serious about things.

DAVID YOW (singer, the Jesus Lizard) A good example of the difference between the adults' van and the kids' van? I don't remember where it was, but Mac was driving and I was in the passenger seat and I had a bag of chili-cheese Fritos. And for the hell of it, I don't have a good explanation why, I was just licking the little powdery coating off all of them, and then putting the coating-free Fritos into this sort of dashboard thing in between the seats. I did that with the whole bag.

The next morning at the hotel, we got up and the van wasn't there. We were going, "Where's the van?" Somebody said, "Oh, Duane took it for an oil change." When Duane gets back from getting an oil change with the van, all those Fritos are gone. And I said, "Oh, you cleaned up all those Fritos—thanks a lot." He said, "No, I ate 'em." And I had to tell him that I had licked every one of 'em. He wasn't too happy about that, but I just felt like, why would you eat Fritos that are sort of sitting there in the little separator between the seats, not in a bag?

BOB NASTANOVICH Another great thing about Lollapalooza for us was when you first get there, they show you that you have access to a certain amount of space in a tractor-trailer truck to put all your gear and your stage props. Most of the bands would pretty much fill their space, but ours was like one-eighth full, so we bought a Ping-Pong table. And Lollapalooza would do a fantastic job every day of finding a place for our Ping-Pong table. We would just play all day long.

SCOTT KANNBERG (guitarist, Pavement) That Ping-Pong table survived up until this summer, when it got destroyed in a forest fire at my dad's house in Montana.

MAURICE MENARES (touring staff, Sonic Youth) My knees have never recovered from diving for the balls.

DEB PASTOR (roadie, the Jesus Lizard) Pavement, they are competitive when it comes to sports.

TERRY PEARSON (front-of-house sound engineer, Sonic Youth) All the guys in Pavement, to a man, were really good Ping-Pong players.

Malkmus and Scott Kannberg were excellent, but I could beat them. But Bob Nastanovich, I don't think I could ever beat Bob. Bob just seemed unbeatable.

MICHAEL "CURLY" JOBSON (stage manager, Lollapalooza 1991–92; tour manager, Hole, 1995) I was better than anybody on the tour at table tennis. Nobody beat me. Absolutely undefeated through my entire time at Lollapalooza. I played down low, from under the table.

BOB NASTANOVICH A lot of places would also have basketball hoops set up. And I remember shooting baskets one day and Courtney came rushing through the parking lot and said to me, "Let me take a shot. Let me take a shot." So I handed her the ball and . . . the ball didn't end up anywhere near the basket. She missed badly. So I went and collected the ball, and I gave her another shot . . . and she missed badly again. And then—and I didn't smile or laugh—I said, "You wanna take another shot?" And she said, very angrily, "Don't you fucking laugh at me, frat boy!" And I said, "I'm not laughing at you at all." And she said, "Don't you ever fucking laugh at me, frat boy!" And I said, "All right." And after that, basically whenever I saw her, what she said to me was, "Fuck you, frat boy!"

MICHAEL "CURLY" JOBSON For me, Pavement was the musical highlight of the tour.

JOAN WASSER (violinist, singer, the Dambuilders) I fucking love Pavement. But it felt like they were maybe a little bit dorky for the tour.

MARY TIMONY (singer, guitarist, Helium) It was different back then. I feel like people are just so accepting of all kinds of genres now, because they're exposed to so much because of the internet. But in the nineties, people were still shocked by things or didn't like things. Now, everyone's just like, "Oh, it's music, it's fun." But at the time . . .

SCOTT KANNBERG I think we were a little, um, maybe intimidated, because it just didn't seem like people really cared.

BOB NASTANOVICH Pavement had reached this level of sort of, like, malaise. If Lollapalooza sold fifteen thousand tickets in some places, maybe a few hundred people were Pavement fans. Everyone else was just like, "Who in the hell is Pavement? And why are they so far up on this bill?" You realized really fast that you didn't really even matter to these festivalgoers, and that you weren't really gonna change their minds or convert that many people into being Pavement fans. So it quickly developed into a situation where we were just getting up there and really doing everything unusually loosely—even, like, making up songs. It was fun . . . in a way. But it was also a bummer.

DUANE DENISON (guitarist, the Jesus Lizard) I do remember watching their set and seeing Stephen Malkmus thanking people in the audience, seat by seat. "I'd like to thank the person in seventeen A. I'd like to thank the person up there in thirty-four B." They kind of tried to be funny about it, but it's hard.

SCOTT KANNBERG We played in Ranson, West Virginia, and it was kind of a really bad vibe. People were throwing mud. I'm pretty sure that it had been going on before us, when Mighty Mighty Bosstones and Jesus Lizard played. But it just started to get worse and worse. It was kind of weird, because the security guards were hosing people down and it was just creating this huge mud pile.

BOB NASTANOVICH They started spraying the crowd with fire hoses as a safety precaution because the heat level was dangerous, and of course we were playing at the hottest time of the day. And the crowd was like, "I don't know who these assholes are who are playing, but I've never heard their music before." They'd rather see Cypress Hill or Courtney or anybody else that's on the bill.

SCOTT KANNBERG All of a sudden people were just like, "All right, we're just gonna throw mud." It started hitting us, and we were dealing with it. But then I saw a big clod hit Malkmus in the face and I was like, "Man, all right, fuck this shit." I put down my guitar and bared my ass to the world and yelled out, "Try to hit this!" I don't think they hit my ass, but they definitely hit my amp. I actually still have that amp with mud on it, which is pretty funny.

BOB NASTANOVICH Malkmus actually got hit by a rock. And Scott lost his temper and mooned the crowd and that caused some insanity. Then David Berman from Silver Jews was there, and he came out and insulted the crowd, which riled them up even further. Also, my father was there—that was particularly embarrassing. I just kind of felt bad for whoever had to clean up the mess so Cypress Hill could come on, you know? I think Cypress Hill thought it was funny.

SEN DOG (MC, Cypress Hill) We went on right between Pavement and Hole. The Pavement guys I had never met. But I did see people throwing the shit.

SCOTT KANNBERG Sometimes we'd be playing our set, and all of a sudden people would start filing into their seats and there'd be this roar from the crowd. And you'd be like, "What's going on?" Then you'd see that somebody in the backstage area was blowing up the inflatable Buddha for the Cypress Hill show.

SEN DOG When I first saw the inflatable Buddha, I hated it. I couldn't stand it. I tried to sabotage it. I tried to burn it with cigarettes or whatever the fuck I could do so it wouldn't work that day. But as soon as it went up, the fans started cheering like crazy. I was like, "Wow, man, they really fucking like this fucking blow-up!"

DEB PASTOR (roadie, the Jesus Lizard) Inflating the fucking Buddha was the best. I'd go to see the Buddha deflate and inflate, and watch Cypress's crew move the torches and spears. Which shows you how much time I had on my hands every day!

JOAN WASSER I was a daily smoker and I didn't have any weed on the road. So I was like, "Well, those guys perform with a giant bong onstage; they've got weed." I'm not particularly shy, but I was a little bit hesitant to ask them. I just said to [DJ] Muggs, "Hey, would you mind, like, smoking me out? I don't have any weed." He took me into their dressing room and there was a posse of twenty-five dudes and a giant pyramid of buds on the coffee table in the middle of the room. I had never seen anything like that before. And their weed was unlike anything I had ever had, or ever had since. So I was sort of in this other frame of mind, shall we say, for most of the days.

SCOTT KANNBERG Bob tried to go in the Cypress Hill dressing room once, because they were all getting stoned. And I think they all looked at him like, "What are you doing in here, white boy?"

DEB PASTOR I was talking to [Cypress Hill MC] B-Real and he goes, "Yeah, these other bands really don't like us that much and never hang out with us." And I'm like, "What? You're kidding." So Joan and I went and tried to get some guys to go over to their dressing room, and we got Bob and Mark Ibold from Pavement, and maybe somebody else. And it was so uncomfortable. They were just like, "Oh god, look at these nerdy white dudes." Afterward, Bob's like, "Pastor, that was the most excruciating thing I've ever done. Those guys just like hanging out with you and telling you a sob story because you're cute girls."

DAVID YOW We didn't really cavort with Cypress Hill or anything, but after I got arrested, they thought I was really cool and they wanted to hang out with me. You know, "Hey, man, you wanna get high?" They had sort of a personal gym with them, like a bench press and all that kind of stuff. So one day I went over and I said, "Man, get outta the way. Let me show you guys how to do this."

SEN DOG I do remember that guy coming up and saying, "Hey man, I could lift that." Sure, whatever.

DAVID YOW I laid on the bench with whatever barbell they had on there and I couldn't even budge it. I was like, "Get it off me! Get it off me!"

9 "FANTASTIC VOYAGE"

RICK VALENTIN (guitarist, singer, Poster Children) Lollapalooza wanted to have a higher-profile second stage with a headliner-type act, and that was how they sold it to Coolio. Like it was going to be a parallel to the main stage.

JOHN RUBELI (second-stage manager, Lollapalooza 1993–95) I was actually really pushing for Coolio to play on the main stage. And I remember there was this big push to have the Jesus Lizard on the main stage. I'm like, "You guys are out of your minds. I've seen Jesus Lizard so many times that I can quote David Yow lyrics to the best of them. But you have to understand that if you're in a gigantic amphitheater and the Jesus Lizard is the first act on, no one will be there." Whereas if Jesus Lizard was playing at the end of the day on the second stage, which is usually when the sun went down, 'cause we didn't have any lights, that was doing everyone a service—the fans that came to see them, the band itself, and Lollapalooza as a brand. You build in moments in a festival like that. That to me was the moment I wanted to book Coolio on the second stage. I love that "Fantastic Voyage" song, and he was a charismatic guy. Long story short, I didn't have enough money to book Coolio. I needed an extra five hundred dollars per show. And I went to Ted Gardner and I said, "Look, I really want to book Coolio, and I don't have enough money." He goes, "Whatever it takes, just go do it."

DAVID YOW (singer, the Jesus Lizard) I met Coolio at a festival we did in Belgium. My wife at the time really loved him. And so I went over to his trailer and he was surrounded by these huge bodyguards. And I just said, "Hey, my wife is a huge fan. Can I get your autograph for her?" And he wrote, "To Susie, be sweet." I told him, "If you want any beer or whiskey, we've got a lot over here in our trailer." He said, "Yeah, man, maybe I'll come by." But he didn't.

KRISTEN WORDEN-HARRIS (artist liaison, second stage, Lollapalooza 1995–97) Coolio wasn't a rock star. He was so down-to-earth and great. But I mean, you can imagine the weed that would travel with that crew. It was pretty freaking unreal.

JOHN RUBELI I had this Polaroid camera that I'd take people's photos with to make their laminates. I said to Coolio, "Hey, do me a favor. You've got an entourage and I don't know who's with you. Here's this camera. Take a bunch of pictures, give me their names, and I'll make you some laminates." So an hour goes by and I'm like, "Where's my camera?" I find Coolio. "Hey man, where are the pictures?" He's like, "Oh, I need more film." So I give him more film. And then the next time I see him, he asks for even more film. I'm like, "What's going on?" So I go by the merch booth and he's selling signed Polaroids for twenty-five dollars apiece.

JAMES McNEW (bassist, Yo La Tengo) Coolio had the triumphant head-lining slot on the second stage. They were pretty much as obnoxious as you would've wanted them to be, I guess. There were lots of Super Soakers and lots of video cameras.

ROSE MARSHACK (bassist, Poster Children) In Denver, the pre-Coolio second-stage extravaganza consisted of a hickey contest, an impromptu woman rapper who had jumped on the stage from the crowd who was pretty good, and a spanking contest. These are things that never happen at our shows. The second-stage crowd was applauding now, not because the woman rapper had finished, but because two nubile young bikini-clad women had jumped on the stage, wanting to be spanked by "Trigger," a member of one of the rap bands. Howie, our drummer, had the pleasure of standing backstage, watching members of Cypress Hill videotaping the women and screaming, "Show us your tits! Show us your fucking tits!" And watching the drunken girls eagerly comply.

KRISTEN WORDEN-HARRIS Every day when he would go on, we'd have to be ready. It was extra security, all hands on deck. People were flipping out. He'd hype the crowd up and the energy level would go up tenfold. More stage diving, more crowd surfing.

JOHN RUBELI You had about eighteen thousand people watching Coolio. While in the big amphitheater, you had five hundred people watching the Jesus Lizard. I remember Marc Geiger walked up to me and said, "You fucked me! You did this to fuck me!" And I was like, "No, I actually did this because this is what the fans wanna see."

MOBY (artist) Coolio was a star. He was way too big to be on the second stage. You could tell the audience for his shows was twice as big as the audience for mine, and it was a phenomenal show. He would ride a BMX onstage. I remember being very glad that I was not going on after him.

JOHN RUBELI I remember watching Coolio's set in Chicago or something with Ira Kaplan from Yo La Tengo. And he leans over to me and says, "We'll never be as big as that."

10 "IT WAS A BEAUTIFUL AFTERNOON"

STUART ROSS (tour director, Lollapalooza) I had managed this Australian band, the Church, for a while, and their drummer at the time—he was sort of a hired hand and the only not-Australian in the band—was Jay Dee Daugherty of the Patti Smith Group. He called me about a week before the two New York shows at Randall's Island and said, "Hey, me and Patti would love to come." At that point Patti had not performed in a really long time; I guess she was raising her family. And I said, somewhat flippantly, "Great, would you be interested in playing?" So Jay Dee says, "Let me find out, I'll call you back."

LENNY KAYE (guitarist, Patti Smith Group) We were in the studio at Electric Lady, working on Patti's *Gone Again* album, which was the first time we had been together as a band for quite some time.

JAY DEE DAUGHERTY (drummer, Patti Smith Group) Patti and I had a discussion and she saw that it would be a cool thing to do off the cuff. Like a trial balloon of performing live with a band.

PATTI SMITH (singer, Patti Smith Group) It was one of the most difficult times of my whole life. Well, hopefully, *the* most difficult. Hopefully, I'll never have a more difficult time. My husband had died in November. My brother died a month later in December. Both of them were under forty-five. I had two young children and had to almost immediately start life over. I hadn't performed hardly at all for sixteen years and didn't really expect to be back in the public arena, but it was a way of gathering with friends and also to make a living, because I was obliged to do that. I was also still living in Michigan and going back and forth to New York trying to work again and making *Gone Again*.

LENNY KAYE Patti's husband, Fred [MC5 guitarist Fred "Sonic" Smith], had died the previous fall and she had decided to return to being Patti, being a performer. But again, we hadn't really figured out how to present a live thing. There was no sense that we could play out, but when we received the offer, and I can't say who I received the offer from or how, we went up to Randall's Island.

STUART ROSS Jay Dee called me back a little while later: "She said yes." And in my head, I'm going, Are you kidding me? Are you fucking *kidding me*? I don't remember how far in front of the show this was. It couldn't have been more than a couple of days. And we rearranged the schedules for the second stage and Patti showed up.

PATTI SMITH I'm sure it was the first festival I had done in sixteen, seventeen years. Starting to perform again was challenging. It wasn't challenging because I was afraid, because I have always been comfortable in front of people. It was challenging because every time I performed, a part of me knew I was there only because of the really tragic events in my life.

LENNY KAYE You have to realize that Patti lived a very private life with Fred in Detroit for all those years. She was not used to being out in the universe, and so there was a lot of acculturation of how to be. I mean, this was one of the first legitimate shows we'd ever played in the nineties because with her partnership with Fred, they didn't play out.

PATTI SMITH I wouldn't have been playing Lollapalooza had my husband lived. I would have been in Michigan taking care of our family. Everything I was doing was at a great cost.

TONY SHANAHAN (bassist, Patti Smith Group) The whole idea was that it was to be unannounced and we would play on a small stage. There was no way she was walking out on the main stage.

STUART ROSS Moby was very upset because I think we put him after Patti Smith. We just kind of pushed a slot in and pushed him later. I recall he was just yelling at me about this, but there was literally nothing I could do. The decision had been made.

MOBY (artist) I don't think I was annoyed. I was confused. I was like, "Wow, I can't believe Patti Smith is playing on the second stage." But I was the one right after and I was like, "Oh, how do I follow Patti Smith?" It seemed wrong that technically she was going on before me. I was like, "Shouldn't she be the headliner?"

KRISTEN WORDEN-HARRIS (artist liaison, second stage, Lollapalooza 1995–97) Moby was pissed.

MOBY Years later, and I almost shouldn't say this because I don't need the headache, but years later I reached out to her through her manager to see if she'd ever want to collaborate. I said, "Even if she just wants to do some spoken-word poetry over of some of my more melodic, ambient music." And the manager in no uncertain terms said, "Patti said that she fucking hates electronic music and she would never work with a techno guy." It was weird because usually when you ask people to work together and they're not interested, they politely say no. But this was like saying to someone, "Hey, you want to go get a cup of coffee?" and they stab you in the throat.

TONY SHANAHAN We had a friend of ours who had some kind of big old convertible, and we all got into it and drove up to Randall's Island.

LENNY KAYE We just left the studio, went up there. There was some equipment there that might have been ours, I don't remember. And we played a short set. I remember Sonic Youth being there, Courtney Love. I'd met these people over the years, so I knew them, but there was a sense of, we're suddenly out in the sunshine and we're a little bit dazzled by the sudden light after being in the underground of Electric Lady for a couple weeks.

TONY SHANAHAN I was not feeling well. I had some kind of summer stomach bug. I felt like hell, and Patti was being very motherly and everybody was trying to make sure I was okay. Patti was saying, "Why are we doing this if he doesn't feel well?"

PATTI SMITH Tony, are you kidding? I remember looking over at him and he was so pale and sort of bent over his bass. Once, I think it was in Australia, he banged his head so bad he had a concussion, and he tried to stumble back onto the stage and I wouldn't let him. He was seeing double and he still wanted to get back there.

STUART ROSS It was the only show where literally every performer on the tour who wasn't performing on the main stage at the time was watching her. It was incredible. It was truly one of the greatest things that ever happened on Lollapalooza. I mean, a lot of fun things happened. There were a lot of great performances, but Patti Smith at Randall's Island, dude, it changed everything.

PATTI SMITH It was a sea of people. I don't know how many people were there at Lollapalooza that year, but for a person who hadn't performed in quite some time, in my memory, it was like a sea of people. I don't normally suffer things like stage fright. I had my people with me. Everyone was rallying. They were all doing their best to be strong for me. I can't tell you what happened. I just know that we got to a certain point in the set, the song "Pissing in a River," which is probably the most emotional song that we have, and, for me, one of my most personal songs because it has a line in it: "Should I pursue a path so twisted? Should I fall defeated and gifted?" I had written it when I was really thinking about what I should be doing in my life, in 1976, and here I was again with the same question. "What am I doing? What am I doing here? What am

I doing with myself? My life?" I don't know where in the song it happened, I don't know if it was in the beginning or after the guitar solo, I couldn't tell you anymore, but I completely froze. Totally froze.

JOAN WASSER (violinist, singer, the Dambuilders) Jeff Buckley, who was my boyfriend at the time, was there, and we had both been listening to Patti for a long time. She played shortly after the Dambuilders and it was really exciting. She seemed so thrilled and kind of freaked out to be on the stage. There was a little bit of shyness, but still all of that incredible power. And then, of course, it was also really fun to see a woman that wasn't, like, twenty-five, onstage and killing it. It was really inspiring.

TONY SHANAHAN Jeff Buckley was either sitting on the floor or in a chair on my side of the stage. We had befriended him that summer. He used to come and hang out every night down at Electric Lady and smoke pot and just kind of listen to what we were doing. He ended up singing and playing on our record.

PATTI SMITH I'm very sensitive to energy, especially when I'm performing, because I channel a lot of people's energy. So I was standing there, and, to my left, I felt an enormous . . . some kind of empathetic or enormous energy force. I looked over and there was this boy. I couldn't see him clearly, but he was a dark-haired kid, and I could see his face and he was suffering with me. I didn't recognize him, but he kept drawing closer to me, sending me everything that he had, without words. He'd get me back on track. I know it's an abstract thing, but these things are real. It was like unconditional love. Whatever it was this boy was sending filled me with strength. I was so desperate that I just accepted what he was sending, and I was able finally to leap over this hurdle and to deliver the song with its full intensity, and then finish the set.

LENNY KAYE It was just great to feel the energy of playing live because, of course, one misses it. One misses it terribly. And to take the journey with Patti, it was a beautiful afternoon. Beautiful to see the ripples of influence flow out from Patti.

JAY DEE DAUGHERTY We were a generation or two past most of those fans, and it was cool and validating to see that we'd been part of their musical development.

PATTI SMITH When we went backstage, Jeff was practically in tears. I didn't know him. I met his father once or twice when I was younger, and I loved his father. Robert Mapplethorpe and I used to listen to Tim Buckley records all the time, and I saw him play at the Fillmore East. I thanked Jeff and I said, "It's incredible because I felt you before I saw you. I was standing onstage and felt you." He said, "Every fiber." He was sending me everything that he had, from every cell, every fiber of his self to help me get through that moment. After that experience, I was okay. I was okay for all of the other things that we had to do, which included going on tour with Bob Dylan and finishing recording *Gone Again*, which was pretty much done in memory of my husband.

LEE RANALDO (guitarist, Sonic Youth) For us, seeing Patti play was major. It was monumental. We were just getting to know her a little bit at that point in time, and it was definitely one of the most significant events that happened on that tour.

PATTI SMITH I felt very welcomed by these people. I had been out of the public eye for quite a long time, the whole eighties really, and it was the first time I heard things that I felt that I identified with since being part of whatever movement the Patti Smith Group were part of. I started getting a sense of this movement in everything. All of a sudden, I would see things in fashion magazines that I loved. It would be like fashion's version of grunge. I saw it in everything. I wore combat boots and old dresses. It's just the way I dress, the way I saw things. It's a mix of all this passion and anger and energy and love that came out of that anger. I greatly identified with them.

LEE RANALDO I think Allen Ginsberg was there that day as well. We had the great poet backstage, and then our other great rock poet returning to the stage for the first time. It was massively important to us.

STUART ROSS I got a call from this very well-known music producer, Hal Willner, who said he wanted to come to the show, and he said, "I'd like to bring Allen Ginsberg." Allen wanted to meet Beck, because apparently Beck's father was a contemporary of Ginsberg. Anyway, it was probably nine at night and we're winding down, and Hal Willner comes up to me and says, "Allen Ginsberg would like to thank you." And I'm thinking, Allen Ginsberg wants to talk to me? How is this possible? In my head I'm freaking out, because what can I possibly talk to the father of beat poetry about? It turned out to be a nonissue, because Allen was like everybody's favorite Jewish grandfather. He just talked incessantly, and I couldn't even get a word in edgewise. He said, "You know what you need?" He said, "You need to have the Fugs play Lollapalooza. I can help you make it happen." This was the greatest thing anybody had ever said to me at that point in time. Blew my mind. So he wrote down his address and phone number and says, "I want you to call me when you're in New York." I still have it framed in my office. It's like, "Oh my god, Allen Ginsberg is talking to me and giving me his phone number. And Patti Smith just played the second stage!"

11 "IT FELT LIKE WE WERE WINNING FOR A FEW YEARS"

LEE RANALDO (guitarist, Sonic Youth) We were the tour that was all the obscure, indie, underground music. There was a contingent of people that were super excited about that Lollapalooza, but it wasn't the big contingent that was excited to see Eddie Vedder swinging from the yardarms and all that kind of stuff. It was just a smaller audience. I don't think they realized that at the time.

CRAIG MARKS (editor in chief, *SPIN* magazine; author) In some ways, it just became a numbers game. The sound of those bands in '95 wasn't mass enough to fill the same space that Nirvana, Soundgarden, and Pearl Jam occupied.

LEE RANALDO I don't think they had the ticket sales or attendance or anything that they'd had the years before.

SCOTT KANNBERG (guitarist, Pavement) We used to always joke that we killed off Lollapalooza. But I don't think it was us.

DENNIS DENNEHY (publicist, Geffen Records) So many stories written about Sonic Youth in the post-*Nevermind* world were like, "Is this finally Sonic Youth's moment?" It was frustrating for me. It was constantly frustrating for the band. Nobody wants to hear, "Is this finally your moment?" for fucking five years, when you've been doing it for eleven or twelve years and when you're the most influential band in that scene, maybe besides R.E.M., of all time.

LEE RANALDO We signed to Geffen in '90 or so, when we made *Goo* and then *Dirty*.

GARY GRAFF (music writer, *Detroit Free Press*) Listen, if *Goo* didn't do it and *Dirty* didn't do it and *Jet Set* [1994's *Experimental Jet Set, Trash and No Star*] didn't do it . . . this was as commercial as these guys were going to get. This was as far as Sonic Youth were going to lean into that world, and it wasn't going to do it, which is fine. You don't fault 'em for it. In fact, I credit them for being honest.

STEVE SHELLEY (drummer, Sonic Youth) I don't think we were disillusioned by the way that the music business was turning in the mid-nineties. Because I don't think we really felt like anything was promised to us. We felt pretty lucky to be putting out these records and to be creating this music together. And that, actually, Geffen treated us okay. I know they always wanted more for us, and that things would follow Nirvana's lead. And that obviously didn't happen.

BOB NASTANOVICH (percussionist, background singer, Pavement) Really, we were in that position because of the way the industry changed because of Nirvana.

DAVID "BOCHE" VIECELLI (agent, Pavement, the Jesus Lizard) I don't view Nirvana as being as transformative as a lot of people do. On some level, in commercial music, yes, they were, I suppose. But they were peers, right? They were listening to Sonic Youth and the same bands that we all were, and they were part of that world—what began as a relatively youthful, independent-labeled world. So to me, it felt like it was just this crazy fluke that they became this big thing.

Well, not so much a fluke. The simple fact of the matter is that Nirvana wrote great pop songs. If they happened to be clothed in what came to be called grunge or whatever, with loud guitars and stuff like that, so be it. But those songs were catchy as pop songs, which is why they gained purchase at radio and MTV. I suppose there was something revolutionary about that.

SCOTT KANNBERG Pavement, we felt like we were succeeding a little bit. It was pretty cool to be on MTV or to be on [*The Tonight Show with*] *Jay Leno* or something. All those kind of things were icing, you know?

DUANE DENISON (guitarist, the Jesus Lizard) By '95 we had been courted by different major labels, and even though we hadn't signed to anyone yet, there were offers on the table. So playing Lollapalooza was kind of a strategic move. You're definitely a higher profile from there because it's a big national thing.

DAVID "BOCHE" VIECELLI I mean, the Jesus Lizard never would've been signed to Capitol if it weren't for Nirvana. But major labels came calling. In fact, in a more direct way than some people may even know. The champion for getting the Jesus Lizard signed at Capitol was an A&R guy there named Dave Ayers. And he partnered up with a more senior A&R person in Julie Panebianco.

JULIE PANEBIANCO (A&R representative, Capitol Records) I love the Jesus Lizard. I love David Yow so much.

DAVID YOW (singer, the Jesus Lizard) There were a handful of labels that were sniffing our butts. Dave Ayers, who ended up being our A&R guy at Capitol, and also a guy from Warner Bros., I think. He was swell and stuff, but I told him, "Man, you're barking up the wrong tree. Nothing's gonna happen with us. We're not gonna sell a bunch of records. We're not gonna have a huge fan base. It's just the way we are."

DAVID "BOCHE" VIECELLI The reason the offer came is because the head of Capitol at that time was Gary Gersh. And Gary Gersh had made his bones because he signed Nirvana to Geffen. Not that he thought the Jesus Lizard were going to have Nirvana-sized hits, but Gersh saw in the Jesus Lizard a band who could potentially be that kind of a landmark, signpost artist. They're an influential, respected band beyond what their commercial numbers would suggest. And Gersh recognized that and said, "This will look very credible, and this might get us a leg up on signing something that will become the next Nirvana, even though this band won't be it."

DUANE DENISON We worked out a good deal with Capitol and we came out ahead of the situation. And that was that. I don't think any of us had any illusions about being pop stars or about having hits. We just didn't write that way. We didn't perform that way. We didn't think that way. So we just took it for what it was worth, and that was it. I don't regret it.

SCOTT KANNBERG Jesus Lizard did it for their reasons. At the time there were really cool A&R guys. I remember there was a guy that signed Royal Trux to a four-record deal!

DAVID WM. SIMS (bassist, the Jesus Lizard) There was a kind of gold-rush feeding frenzy.

JIM DeROGATIS (pop music critic, *Chicago Sun-Times*) Who wouldn't welcome the dump truck full of cash that would arrive at your doorstep in those heady, nutty nineties alternative days?

WAYNE COYNE (singer, guitarist, Flaming Lips) The way I always describe it, it's like a good party. It's fun, everybody's doing something cool, but the party just attracts too big of a party, you know? And then at some point, the party is just about people who like to party. It doesn't really have anything to do with the reason everybody's there. You see that over and over and over. And we saw it even when we were in it. There would be people who, a year earlier, were like, "We think you guys are horrible. This sucks. It's never gonna go anywhere." You run into them a year later, it's like, "You guys are so great. I can't believe how great you are!"

STEVEN DROZD (drummer, multi-instrumentalist, Flaming Lips) In 1995 we did [*Beverly Hills,*] *90210*. And it was just fun as hell. One of those pop-culture things. I actually watched the show, like, sarcastically, quotations there, you know? I watched the show 'cause it was just so dumb. And then we did it and I knew some of the characters or whatever.

WAYNE COYNE Steven knew all the characters and all their real names. A couple of 'em came up to us on the set and were like, "Man, I can't believe you guys are doing the show!"

STEVEN DROZD I was disappointed because Jennie Garth, she played the blonde, wasn't there. But Tori Spelling was there. And I asked her, "Hey, where's Jennie Garth?" And Tori Spelling looked at me and goes, "What, am I not good enough for you?" I was like, "Oh, wow. She really is a weirdo."

DAVID YOW We signed a three-record contract with Capitol. After the second record, they said, "Okay, well, you can go." And so we broke up.

SCOTT KANNBERG The were some majors that were trying to sign Pavement, but we never really wanted to do that. When we did Lollapalooza we did have a meeting with Danny Goldberg at Atlantic, because that's who did Matador's distribution for our album *Wowie Zowie*. And I remember at the meeting he just like kinda looked at us like, "What are you guys doing here? Obviously you don't want to be big." We're like, "Yeah, you're probably right."

BOB NASTANOVICH I think that we stayed enough in our own cocoon and experienced enough success everywhere that we went that it made us very comfortable. I think Lollapalooza would be one of the only experiences—and that might be why it sticks out—where we felt like we were completely failing.

WAYNE COYNE We were on a major label, but the people at Warner Bros. that loved us, I mean, they absolutely loved us. And that meant a lot to us. We were kinda left alone to do cool stuff. That moment after Lollapalooza, after *90210*, after we had a sort-of hit with "She Don't Use Jelly," the singles we put out and the videos we made, clearly we were satisfied doing our own weirdo thing. We made the *Clouds Taste Metallic* album, which was not a commercial record that was going to get played on the big alternative stations or whatever. Which was fine with us.

DAVID WM. SIMS Here's another thing you have to remember. It's 1995, and it's a little difficult to conceive of this now—it just seems quaint and weird—but this was a time when there was a ferocious amount of vitriol around the concept of someone "selling out." That still had a lot of credence, and we sort of got caught in the middle of that as much as anybody I know.

DAVID YOW I think we might have sold fewer records on Capitol because there was a lot of animosity with fans that we had left Touch and Go [Records]. I guess they had some sort of integrity that we didn't have.

STEVEN DROZD Doing *90210,* you could say we were selling out, or you could say we were being subversive. I'd say we were kind of doing both.

GINA ARNOLD (journalist, author) At that time, making money of any kind, at least in the non-mainstream world, was considered a crime. "How dare you sign to a major label." "How dare you make money." We don't live in those times now, where young people worship, like, Elon Musk.

DUANE DENISON Nowadays artists routinely put music in commercials and films, and do all these tie-ins and this and that, and no one bats an eye. And you know, we played some reunion shows starting back in 2009 and played some of the songs from *Shot,* the first album on Capitol, and they went over ridiculously well. So there you go.

LEE RANALDO With Sonic Youth, by the time we got to 1995 and *Washing Machine,* that was the point where we were already fed up and done with the major-label record company thing. We stopped communicating. We stopped turning in demos. We were slowly reverting back to being in the real, true underground, and the bands that were not being signed to major labels or trying to be the next Nirvana or whatever it was. Pretty much from *Washing Machine* on forward, we reverted to playing more and more obscure music and just following our course back into our own home turf.

STEVE SHELLEY There were other avenues to pursue. So there was no huge disappointment at all.

STEVEN DROZD By '96, '97, it felt like the whole thing was starting to die out. And we were kind of like, "Thank god. This has just gotten so stale and old and we're glad to see it pass." But that said, there was this brief period of time where this music coexisted with the mainstream. And it was pretty exciting.

WAYNE COYNE The weirdos have their moment. And that's inspiring. It's like, "If these freaks can do it, so can I!"

SCOTT KANNBERG It felt like we were winning for a few years. It ran its course, obviously, but it lasted longer than most marriages. So it was a fleeting moment. And then they all figured out—Lollapalooza, too—that the classic-rock stuff was just gonna sell more in the end.

LOLLAPALOOZA 1996

DATES: JUNE 27–AUGUST 4

MAIN STAGE: Metallica, Soundgarden, Ramones, Rancid, Shaolin Monks, Screaming Trees, Psychotica

ON SELECT DATES: Cocteau Twins, Rage Against the Machine, Waylon Jennings, Cheap Trick, Wu-Tang Clan, Steve Earle, Devo, 311, Violent Femmes, the Tea Party, various

SECOND STAGE: Sponge, Melvins, Beth Hart Band, Girls Against Boys, Ben Folds Five, Ruby, Cornershop, You Am I, Soul Coughing, Satchel, Jonny Polonsky, Fireside, various

THIRD STAGE: Cows, Moonshake, Long Fin Killie, Chune, Varnaline, Crumb, Lutefisk, Capsize 7, Thirty Ought Six, various

Like any enterprise of its stature, Lollapalooza had come in for plenty of criticism almost since day one, and for sure by year two, when its success had already raised questions about whether its alternative heart and commercial mind were acting at cross purposes.

Following the 1995 tour, the festival stood at a crossroads, grappling with its own legacy but also a larger question: What, exactly, constituted commercially viable alternative rock in the latter half of the 1990s? Clearly, Sonic Youth and their ilk were not built to fill the Nirvana-size hole in the mainstream music world. And the bands that did, despite embracing often angsty subject matter, feedback-drenched sonics, and other stylistic signifiers, lacked the innate edginess or the boundary-pushing spirit that would make them congruent with the Lollapalooza brand. And so, the festival went another way, seeking out an alternative to alternative.

The band they landed on? Metallica.

"I felt that Metallica was credible," festival cofounder Marc Geiger asserts, also pointing out that the stadium-dwelling thrash metal pioneers, now with shorn hair and a more rock-focused sound, "were about to put out a record that was probably going to get on alternative radio." Even so, he acknowledges, "Perry and I had different views at that time." So different that Farrell, in protest, would remove himself from the Lollapalooza picture that year, with the *Los Angeles Times* reporting in March that the singer and festival cofounder was "negotiating a financial settlement to buy out his Lollapalooza share."

Farrell's wasn't the only dissenting voice. "Metallica was an incredibly controversial headliner," *Detroit Free Press* music writer Gary Graff, who had been covering Lollapalooza since its inception, recalls. "And in choosing them I think they confused the audience. If you're saying Metallica's alternative, what does the word even mean?"

The remainder of the main-stage bill only helped to further an argument that Lollapalooza had lost the alternative plot. While perhaps under different circumstances festival vets Soundgarden, along with the Ramones, Screaming Trees, and Rancid, each made sense on the Lollapalooza stage, in tandem with Metallica they combined to form an all-male, predominantly white, overwhelmingly aggro bill that some derogatively referred to as "Monsters of Rock," in reference to the eighties-era heavy-metal fest, and that *The New York Times* posited "might as well be called the Guys with Guitars Tour."

"I was way into the whole concept of Lollapalooza and loved it," Metallica's Kirk Hammett says. "I had gone to every single one up to that point. So it was really disappointing to hear the reaction when we got announced."

Which is not to say that Lollapalooza's organizers didn't attempt to balance out the perceived uniformity of the bill. The Shaolin Monks, a sword-strapped Buddhist martial arts ensemble, performed between Screaming Trees and Rancid, and the festival also introduced rotating main-stage "mystery guests," ranging from Rage Against the Machine, Wu-Tang Clan, and Cheap Trick to British dream-pop trio Cocteau Twins, outlaw-country legend Waylon Jennings, and new-wave pioneers Devo, at various stops. Unsurprisingly, some of these acts received a less-than-warm welcome from the metal-craving crowds. "My fleeting memory of our performance is looking out at rows of people who seemed quite hostile," says Cocteau Twins guitarist Robin Guthrie. "Although I'm sure just by the law of averages *somebody* must have liked it."

As always, the second stage offered greater variety, with blues belter Beth Hart next to grunge legends the Melvins; piano-pop combo Ben Folds Five alongside Scottish electronic project Ruby; sitar-wielding British indie act Cornershop sharing space with grand-gesture hard rockers Sponge. The third stage, highlighted by cult noise-rock surrealists Cows, showcased all manner of experimental, post-everything weirdness.

But Lollapalooza 1996 was built around—and, in some significant ways, in service to—its headliner. This was reflected in changes to the festival's very operation. To manage Metallica's massiveness and subsequent requirements, Lollapalooza played in venues that were sometimes two to three times larger than in previous years, and often in open fields with minimal traditional concert infrastructure. As a result, the festival took on additional six-figure production costs per date and raised ticket prices for the first time in its six-year run. "The tail was now wagging the dog, to some extent," says production manager Steve "Chopper" Borges.

Call it a deal with the metal devil or merely, as Geiger puts it, "a repositioning." The fact remains that even as the tour took its share of lumps throughout the summer ("One could tell immediately that Lollapalooza had lost its vision," began the *New York Times*' review of the June 27 opening date at Kansas City's Longview Lake), it also drew larger crowds and, depending on who you ask, sold more tickets than the year prior. And how could it not? "Forget about anything else," says Graff. "At the very least, Metallica playing *anywhere* was going to do great."

1 "IT LOOKED LIKE A SCENE FROM *ISLAND OF LOST SOULS*"

STEVE "CHOPPER" BORGES (production manager, Lollapalooza 1993–97) Ninety-five did the worst business we ever did. And so I imagine the Lollapalooza people said, "We've gotta do something else." Then somebody came up with this idea of, "Let's do Metallica."

MARC GEIGER (agent; cofounder, Lollapalooza) By '95 and into '96, "commercial-alternative" became a term. And bands like Third Eye Blind, Better than Ezra, Candlebox, I mean, you can come up with a whole bunch, were on the scene. And they were in the same name category as what we were presenting to the world. So in '95, we went super indie. Sonic Youth headlining, Beck, Hole, Jesus Lizard . . . it was more "college radio." And so Lollapalooza was trying to not be a mainstream follower, but to lead and expose culturally.

KORY GROW (senior writer, *Rolling Stone* magazine) You could see a big shift in what was considered alternative music between 1992 and 1995. I've read interviews with Marc Geiger where he calls a lot of bands that came out in that period "imitative" bands. And I think that's a pretty astute observation about bands that saw this alternative and grunge explosion, and were inspired to form a band from that. And maybe they had always had these interests, but a lot of them sounded pretty similar.

CRAIG MARKS (editor in chief, *SPIN* magazine; author) It felt like there was a new band selling two million albums every other month. But then that dried up and there was no movement. Grunge, for instance, was not just like a band here and a band there; it felt like it was a cohesive-ish movement. And that's always great as a magazine editor. Because there's a scene involved and it's not just like, "Here's a band and there's a band." But that kind of ceased by '96 or so.

JOHN RUBELI (second-stage manager, Lollapalooza 1993–95) Also, when people really started hopping on the internet in '95-ish, '96, it just became a different thing. How can you have a subculture if you can web-search everything? And at the same time, you have major labels now signing a lot of these acts they weren't necessarily signing in '91, '92, or '93. Maybe partly because of Lollapalooza.

STUART ROSS (tour director, Lollapalooza) When Lollapalooza started out, Perry's idea was to get bands that were incredible but that were not getting enough attention, put them all together, and show everybody that alternative music was worth listening to. And he was absolutely right. But the more he was right, the more alternative music became mainstream. We were a victim of our own success.

MARC GEIGER And so the market, in my humble opinion, and in Perry's, and in everybody's, became polluted with sort of the follower-imitators, let's just call them. And it didn't feel good. So we wanted to point to credibility. Perry at that point had very much started to immerse himself in dance music, in the early days of dance culture and raves. He wanted to do an electronic show, or incorporate DJs. We thought it was early and not significant enough. I thought we should go for great, credible bands who have integrity. At the same time, Metallica was trying to get onto KROQ. They had made a record I knew about through their management [*Load*, released just prior to Lollapalooza, on June 4, 1996] that they felt very strongly about, and they were hoping that there could be a catalyst and a story there.

LARS ULRICH (drummer, Metallica) After the initial shock of being approached by Lollapalooza had sunk in, I realized that although we may not have been appropriate in '91, Metallica in '96 was more appropriate.

KORY GROW When Metallica broke into the mainstream a few years earlier with the Black Album [1991's *Metallica*]—and that's the album that had songs like "Sad but True" and "Enter Sandman" and "Nothing Else Matters"—they completely overhauled who they were trying to be, image-wise. They were simplifying their sound and getting rid of some of the jagged elements that had defined thrash metal and their early albums.

And with that, as legend has it, they all took a big vacation after the Black Album, and when they saw each other again, let's say '94, '95, somewhere in there, they surprised each other that they'd all cut their hair. And in that time, Lars and Kirk specifically had gotten really into visual art and conceptual art, and they decided that they wanted to do something a little bit different with the band's image. That's when they started wearing eyeliner in photo shoots. And it also explains why they had the Andres Serrano artwork, "Semen and Blood III," on the cover of the *Load* album. It was like they were turning Metallica in some ways into an art project. Which in hindsight should have made them very popular with fans of alternative music, because Nirvana and Kurt Cobain and a lot of these artists were very art-forward. But it wasn't perceived that way, because Metallica were coming off the success of this major, big-box, Walmart-ready metal album.

KIRK HAMMETT (guitarist, Metallica) That whole period was fantastic because it was all a bunch of stuff no one ever expected from us. Everyone wanted the first four albums on repeat, but then we took them for a wild ride.

KIM THAYIL (guitarist, Soundgarden) I remember the offer that came to Soundgarden in 1996 was that Metallica's name had come up about doing Lollapalooza. They were interested in doing it, and they said they would do it if we did it. That's what we were told, at least.

MARC GEIGER We were very close to Soundgarden, who loved Metallica, and also the Ramones, who we wanted to feature on Lollapalooza, and they loved Metallica. And so I made a big case that after the indie rock that we should go in that direction—go loud and cred. You take Soundgarden and the Ramones, it's loud and cred. Metallica, loud and cred. So that was sort of a theme. And Perry was alienated by that. He didn't want it.

PERRY FARRELL Metallica, in my estimation at that time, wasn't my thing. I was into alternative and punk and underground. My friends were Henry Rollins and Gibby Haynes and Ice-T . . . So I was not sure about Metallica back in those days.

MARC GEIGER Perry felt like we didn't get it, and he sort of said, "I want to start my own festival called Enit." Which was basically an early rave. Now, in fairness to Perry, in some ways he was very right, just early. But Perry felt a little alienated and he tuned out. I don't remember how un-involved he was, but he was definitely tuned out of it. Now, remember that with Perry, you have a lot of things. You have projects he's working on at the time. You have drugs. But he was definitely not psyched about Metallica.

KIRK HAMMETT I saw that more as him trying to protect the brand name. Nothing really personal against us or the music, you know?

PERRY FARRELL It was a strange time, because they were transforming, we were transforming. Their music was aggressive, but what I was fight-ing for with Jane's Addiction was to bring a sound to the world that was aggressive but also somewhat androgynous. I was not afraid of the fem-inine side of sound, shall we say. But Metallica proved themselves, and they are great, great people. I've become friends with them.

NIKKI GARDNER (assistant to Ted Gardner; special groups coordinator, Lollapalooza) I think both Perry and Ted were not happy with the head-liner that year. Ted felt it was the beginning of the end, really. It was kind of at the point where we were looking at recycling bands. So Me-tallica, I think from the agents' perspective, was the best option. But it was difficult. Everybody was trying to do their best.

JIM DeROGATIS (pop music critic, *Chicago Sun-Times*) Metallica on their own have had high points and some very, very low points. But they never belonged on a Lollapalooza bill.

KIRK HAMMETT There were so many detractors and so many protesters and people saying that Lollapalooza is ruined now that Metallica's become a part of it. It's lost its alternative-slash-grunge spirit or whatever. It was unfortunate to hear, but I wasn't surprised. In fact, I was expecting it. We've been the unwanted guests to the party ever since *Kill 'Em All* came out. We've been well conditioned to expect stuff like this.

KIM THAYIL We figured, "Okay, this is a different demographic for them. And since Soundgarden has done Lollapalooza, maybe that would be a nice little bridge." And the Lollapalooza guys came to us and said, "You can pick other bands to be on the bill. Is there anyone you'd like?" We said, "Let's get the Ramones." Because we had toured with the Ramones in Australia in '94 on the Big Day Out, which is sort of the Australian version of Lollapalooza. We got to be great friends with those guys and we said, "We can't believe they haven't done a Lollapalooza, because they're founding fathers for many of the acts."

MONTE A. MELNICK (tour manager, Ramones) We had done a lot of festivals in Europe. But not in the United States. No one had ever asked!

C. J. RAMONE (bassist, Ramones) The fact that groups like Soundgarden and Rancid and Nirvana and Pearl Jam and Green Day all listed the Ramones as an influence, it definitely helped to bring attention back on the band in the nineties. Was Metallica directly influenced by the Ramones? I don't know if they're directly influenced. I'm sure they were fans, but the Ramones definitely influenced the Misfits, who definitely influenced Metallica, you know what I mean? And I was a huge Metallica fan. When Cliff Burton died, I tried to get an audition. That's how much I love Metallica.

KIRK HAMMETT I announced the Ramones onstage a few times on that tour, and that's where Johnny Ramone and I forged our friendship. Then we became freaking best friends after that.

MONTE A. MELNICK All the bands became friends with the Ramones, and they all told them that if it wasn't for the Ramones they may not have formed these groups.

KIM THAYIL So Metallica asked for us, we asked for the Ramones, and we suggested the Screaming Trees, who were also on the bill.

GARY LEE CONNER (guitarist, Screaming Trees) We had the same managers as Metallica, and that's probably one of the reasons we got on there. But we were really excited, because we had a lot of success with our previous album, [1992's] *Sweet Oblivion,* and then for a lot of our own reasons, like our singer, Mark Lanegan, taking a deep dive into heroin during '93, '94, '95, we had a long downtime when the alternative stuff got really big. We were like, "Man, we gotta get this thing going or the whole chance to make some cash is gonna pass us by." So in '96 we had a new record and we got on the tour . . . and that seemed to be the year the bottom fell out of the whole alternative/grunge thing. Like, "Well, this stuff is old hat now. We want something new." And I guess for Lollapalooza that was Metallica.

KIM THAYIL And then there was a rotating slot on the main stage. And that rotating slot was where you get Rage Against the Machine on a few dates or a Wu-Tang Clan on a few dates or a Devo in the Southwest on three or four shows.

GERALD CASALE (bassist, singer, Devo) I certainly have vivid memories of that tour, because it was a head-scratcher. It was Metallica and Soundgarden at the height of grunge and metal, and, you know, "Here's Devo!" But Perry Farrell asked us, and [Devo vocalist and keyboardist] Mark Mothersbaugh, who usually was saying no to everything all the time, for some arbitrary reason said yes. So there we were.

VAN CONNER (bassist, Screaming Trees) Fucking Devo blew every single band on that fucking tour off the fucking stage. It was un-fucking-believable. They ruled.

KIM THAYIL I watched Devo every set they did in that guest slot. I think they helped give some balance to the bill.

GERALD CASALE We knew what the lineup was, obviously, but I guess I didn't know what I was about to see and experience in reality. When I saw that crowd and when I watched how they interacted, I thought, "You know what? De-evolution really is real!" It looked like a scene from *Island of Lost Souls*. Everybody kind of looked like ex-cons and the sort of guys that used to run the rides at carnivals. It just looked like a mob of criminals. And then they're staring at us, like, "What in the fuck are you doing?"

DON MULLER (agent; cofounder, Lollapalooza) Booking Metallica changed Lollapalooza immensely. All of a sudden they came in, they were the headliners. It just killed the vibe. It fucking killed everything.

STUART ROSS Metallica made a lot of demands that year. We were not used to people telling us what to do, but Metallica took positions that they were not going to veer off of. For example, one of the things about Metallica is they did not want to play amphitheaters, and pretty much all we played were amphitheaters. They said, "We'll do outside fields or we're not doing the show." And it became a serious point of contention. Now, full disclosure, I ended up going to work for Metallica in 2003 and worked for them for a number of years. I consider them good, smart businesspeople and family. But they took the position that it's their show and they're gonna do things the way they want to.

C. J. RAMONE What was going on was that Metallica had their own tour booked for later that year. So, instead of playing the A and B markets, we were playing the C and D markets in the middle of nowhere, especially in the Northeast. That's how it was explained to me, anyway. And of course Metallica is a headliner, so they can do that.

***THE NEW YORK TIMES* (June 6, 1996)** *Putting together Lollapalooza this summer may be one of the hardest jobs any concert booker or promoter* *has had to face. The festival is operating with many new handicaps. Chief among them is its desire to travel only to outdoor fields that can hold 35,000 to 40,000 people (as opposed to last year's amphitheaters, which held about 18,000). Along with the fact that Metallica and other bands want to tour major cities on their own after the festival ends in August, this has situated most of Lollapalooza's shows in rural areas. For many of these smaller towns, which are not used to big rock shows, especially not in traditional venues like stadiums or arenas, Lollapalooza's lineup is a scary freak show.*

STEVE "CHOPPER" BORGES All the pressures that Metallica put on the festival—where you can play, where you can't play, "We're not gonna play at the major venue in major cities 'cause we're gonna go out and do a headline tour afterward so we've gotta play thirty miles out of town"— they had a bunch of stuff. And since we were in fields, we needed to build stages, and I needed to have several roofs, several sets of scaffolding, leapfrogging ahead of me to the next shows. Also, that was the year of the Atlanta Olympics, so the bigger companies, the Mountain Productions and those kind of people, they had a lot of gear already being used in and around Atlanta. So there was a bit of a dearth of infrastructure— roofs, stages, scaffold, that sort of stuff. I'm trying to rent stuff and it's just not out there. And I'm just patchworking it together. "Can I get this from here?" "Can you bring that out of Atlanta for this one show?" It was a quite a task.

STUART ROSS Then there's the difficulty in obtaining a piece of land to do a show, which is not like it is today. People in those days remembered Woodstock, and towns being overrun by people they didn't want in there. Dynamically, there were a ton of issues.

ANDY CIRZAN (promoter, Jam Productions) I'll give you an example: The World Music Theatre, or whatever the hell Live Nation's calling it now that they've bought it, was always the Chicago play back then. That was my venue. But the 1996 location was moved to a small town in central

Illinois called Pecatonica. And I literally had to go out there and meet with the . . . I don't know if it was the mayor or whoever . . . and basically tell them, "Um, so we'd like to bring this gigantic rock show to your state fairgrounds." And they're like, "Huh?" I had to assure them, "Our company has been doing this since the seventies, we're Chicago-based, here's our backstory . . ." I actually ended up having to go on local TV. And then we made some deal with them where we gave them money per head for their civic causes and things like that. But we played the Winnebago County Fairgrounds, and the audience size was probably two or three times the population of the entire town. It was like the invading Mongol hordes.

THE NEW YORK TIMES (June 6, 1996) *Metallica has presented tour organizers with an additional problem: ticket sales. Though record executives expect the band's new album, which was released on Tuesday, to sell close to a million copies in its first week (a nearly unprecedented coup), tickets to this year's Lollapalooza have been selling much more slowly than last year's, when the more obscure Sonic Youth was a headliner. And this summer success is more critical than ever, because of the extra $250,000 to $300,000 it costs to produce the show in such large fields.*

STUART ROSS We had to bring in porta-johns, generators, gates, fencing, outside catering, parking attendants . . . stuff that we wouldn't normally need in an amphitheater.

DAN CHOI (front-of-house coordinator, Lollapalooza 1994–97, 2003) We had mist tents, but you couldn't get a hose out to the middle of a field. So then you had to think about water tanks. One of the tour positions was "plumber."

STUART ROSS Our expenses were considerably higher. And I don't remember exactly what we paid Metallica, but it was way more than our usual budget would allow. So our ticket prices went up for the first time ever, from $27.50 to $35.

ANDY CIRZAN I don't think the ticket price had a dramatic impact on things. But there had been remarkable consistency, and this was a percentage increase, so . . .

MARC GEIGER When you produce a show in a field, expenses go up. Stages are bigger. Crowds are bigger. That's real. But tickets, the pricing was still embarrassingly cheap. I mean, compared to today's festivals, or even ten years ago, it was nuts. We were dramatically underpriced when you look back in history.

STUART ROSS Today, thirty-five dollars is the price of a beer in a stadium. You can't even get parking for thirty-five dollars. But it was significant. Elliott Lefko, who's now at Goldenvoice, was one of the talent buyers at that time in Canada. He said, "It's too much. You're gonna get pushback." I thought he was crazy, but he was right.

ELLIOTT LEFKO (promoter, MCA Concerts Canada) Raising the ticket price was not a good thing. But it just seemed like it was doomed from the beginning. The results were not good.

STEVE "CHOPPER" BORGES To my recollection, the thing went on sale and it didn't set the world on fire.

STUART ROSS It was not a stellar year.

DON MULLER You either experiment and grow, or you don't.

2 "WELCOME TO THE LOLLAPALOOZA THAT HAS A BIG COCK!"

STEVE "CHOPPER" BORGES (production manager, Lollapalooza 1993–97) It was called the "Summer of Noise '96." That's what it said on the T-shirt. Metallica, Soundgarden, Ramones, Rancid, Screaming Trees, Psychotica on the main stage. Oh—and the Shaolin Monks. They were very interesting. They had a seventy-year-old guy who would sit in the lotus position and, from there, stand up never touching his hands to the ground. And everyone would go, "Oh, what's the big deal?" I said, "Yeah, sit down and try it. Don't care how old you are. Try it."

ROBERT "NITE BOB" CZAYKOWSKI (front-of-house sound engineer, Psychotica) The Shaolin Monks were spectacular. They'd do all kinds of martial art-y, wacky things.

VAN CONNER (bassist, Screaming Trees) They used to pick me up and throw me. And I was six-four and weighed 275. They were fucking crazy.

C. J. RAMONE (bassist, Ramones) One show in the Northeast I invited the Hells Angels. They come in, line their bikes in front of the Ramones' dressing room, and I get my guys to set them up with a cooler and chairs on the side of the stage. We play the set and we're all walking back to the trailer, shooting the breeze, blah, blah. And as we get to the trailer, I look over and here's the monks . . . sitting on the Hells Angels' motorcycles, taking pictures.

ROBERT "NITE BOB" CZAYKOWSKI I think over the period of the tour, some of them started to get the curiosity of the Western world, right? I walked into catering once and there were two monks sitting there in their full monk outfits, staring at bacon. Just staring at strips of bacon. I was like, "Okay, maybe they've never seen bacon before."

VAN CONNER I'd open the door to our bus and three of 'em would be standing there with their whole decked-out thing, their orange shawls or whatever. They'd say, "Do you have *cigarette*?" "Yeah, dude, come on in." And we'd sit there and drink beer and smoke cigarettes. They would never rip the four-foot bong, though. I did offer it to them once.

C. J. RAMONE So I'm standing there with the president of the Hells Angels, we're looking at the monks on their bikes, and I turn to him to start explaining the whole thing. And he goes, "It's okay. They're warriors. We don't mind that." And the Hells Angels walk over and start taking pictures with the monks around their motorcycles. Only the Ramones could get together the Shaolin Monks and the Hells Angels. I don't know if that has ever happened in the history of the world, but it happened right there in front of the Ramones' dressing room on Lollapalooza 1996.

VAN CONNER The Ramones . . . One time I'm sitting on the bus smoking the four-foot bong, and I look out and I see Joey and Johnny, and they're wearing those leather coats . . . in hundred-degree weather. They never changed clothes. And they have these Super Soakers, and Joey's laughing, Johnny's laughing, like, *huh huh huh*. And then Johnny just fucking *nails* him. Squirts him in the face, in his eye, in his jacket. Joey's like, "I can't believe you did that to me!" And Johnny goes "Fuck *yoo!*" And Joey kind of runs toward him and they get in a huge fight, in their leather jackets. I'm thinking, Should I go break this up?

ROBERT "NITE BOB" CZAYKOWSKI I'm going to give you a quick Ramones vignette. Since Psychotica were from New York, people decided they would put the New York bands' dressing rooms near to each other, right? Every day, we'd be in the dressing room and I would hear Johnny rehearse the show with the band. Drillmaster Johnny Ramone. And this is the farewell tour, right? The last show was going to be the last show of the Ramones ever, and it pretty much was. So they would run through everything, not once but twice, in the dressing room. They would play the whole set and there would be some yelling about things.

GARY LEE CONNER (guitarist, Screaming Trees) The dressing rooms just had curtains between them, and we'd hear the Ramones practicing without being plugged in. *Duh duh duh duh duh duh.* And then Johnny talking. I was like, They still need to practice after twenty years?

GERALD CASALE (bassist, singer, Devo) They'd be eating pizza before they went on. So. Much. Pizza. It was crazy. I don't think it was part of catering. I think they just had 'em, you know? It was part of their rider.

MONTE A. MELNICK (tour manager, Ramones) They always liked to have that backup pizza, just in case they didn't get a decent meal on the road. That's why we had it on the rider. And we would order the Domino's, because you never knew what pizza was like in different cities. So they said, "Give us Domino's." Because they knew that would be fairly consistent.

C. J. RAMONE The setup to that tour, and the thing that was really beautiful about it, was that at least Johnny and Joey really got to understand what a huge impact they had. Joey had been diagnosed with lymphoma in '94. So Johnny had been holding the whole organization together, and Johnny was tired. And one thing he used to say is, "We want to retire while we're still playing fast, while we still sound good." So we announced our retirement in '95, and we were still doing our usual crappy little club tour through the States. Five-hundred-, fifteen-hundred-, three-thousand-seaters. I thought, These guys deserve a better ending to their career than just hashing it out in these little clubs. They deserve to be in front of bigger crowds and be celebrated a little bit more.

MONTE A. MELNICK Metallica, Soundgarden, they're huge groups, you know? Selling a hell of a lot more albums than the Ramones. But when I put the Ramones onstage, all these other groups are all of a sudden on the side of the stage watching the band, and they're all big fans and they're all influenced by the Ramones.

VAN CONNER We would all stand on the side of the stage and watch the Ramones play every night. Because they were the gods. Not fucking Metallica.

MARC GEIGER (agent; cofounder, Lollapalooza) How do you not love the Ramones? Perry Farrell loves the Ramones. So we got the Ramones and Rancid, okay? Screaming Trees. Soundgarden. Psychotica, who were new and were Ted's client. And we created a special main-stage guest slot, and these were picked by Metallica, Soundgarden, me, Ted. And we had Rage Against the Machine, Cocteau Twins, Waylon Jennings, Cheap Trick, Violent Femmes, Wu-Tang Clan, Devo.

ANDY CIRZAN (promoter, Jam Productions) Cheap Trick came on the show in Pecatonica. Because they're from nearby, in Rockford, right? They just got in their big car and drove over. So that was really a treat. And of course, all the other bands loved Cheap Trick. I don't know any bands that don't love them. I think the Metallica guys in general were totally stoked about that.

GARY LEE CONNER Seeing Rick Nielsen talking to Joey Ramone? That was fun.

MARC GEIGER Then on the side stage: Beth Hart, Girls Against Boys, Ben Folds, Ruby, Cornershop, You Am I, Soul Coughing—who I love—Sponge—who I don't like—the Melvins, Satchel, Jonny Polonsky, Fireside. We had a third stage, the indie stage, with Moonshake, Capsize 7, the Cows, Long Fin Killie. But all people say is, "It was the Metallica year."

BUZZ OSBORNE (singer, guitarist, Melvins) There had been lots of talk in previous years about us doing Lollapalooza, and I can give you the exact reason why we didn't: Perry Farrell didn't like our band. That was told to me, a hundred percent, directly from our agent. "He does not like your band." Now, the year Metallica does it, Perry Farrell steps down because he doesn't like all their macho energy. And we get asked immediately. So guess what I think about Perry Farrell? Perry Farrell can blow me.

C. J. RAMONE I watched the Melvins every day. They went on just before us, so I'd go see their set, and then I'd have to run from one stage to the other to make it on time to our set.

BUZZ OSBORNE We played to a lot of people every single night, as opposed to some of the bands that were on our stage.

VINNIE DOMBROSKI (singer, Sponge) When I think about the history of the Melvins, the influence they've had on so many killer bands, I'd sit there and be like, "Well, now we gotta follow *that*." But the thing about Buzz was he was just such a cool fucking guy. There was none of this shit like, "Here comes this band on a major label, blah, blah, blah." And we've gotten our fair share of that over the years, or we did in the early days. But Buzz was never like that.

BUZZ OSBORNE We became very friendly with the Sponge guys. And that was not the kind of band that we would've, you know, palled around with. I mean, I don't really pal around with anybody. But they were super nice. At the time they had a hit record and were doing pretty well. They were the biggest band on that side stage.

JOEY MAZZOLA (guitarist, Sponge) The Melvins went on right before us, and to our amazement, the crowd would double when we went on. Because Sponge was hot right then. Those hits were being pumped on the radio and people knew them. They were singing along.

BUZZ OSBORNE Sponge had more of a teen-girl kind of thing. So a lot of our shows would be teen girls right in the front who were just like looking at us, and I would make sure to be as gross with my guitar feedback as possible. These people, they need to be schooled, you know? So that was fun.

VAN CONNER The Melvins are one of my favorite bands that ever existed. And I've known Buzz since I was in high school—we're all small-town people from Washington. So me and Barrett [Martin, Screaming Trees drummer] and my brother Lee—I call him Lee, his real name's Lee Gary, and Gary Lee is his stage name—would all be at the side stage when they played, headbanging in the front row.

BUZZ OSBORNE The Screaming Trees, it looked like their singer was kicking dope the whole tour. When it's July, August, and you're somewhere in Florida and you're freezing, something's not right.

GARY LEE CONNER The band itself, we were going through a lot of problems with Mark [Lanegan]. Drug problems. We would hit a town and he'd head straight to the ghetto and almost get killed. But at the time, that was just kind of the way things worked.

VAN CONNER So on Lollapalooza we had a gofer. He was with us all the time, and every morning we'd get to where we needed to be and then he'd have to "go for." He would go and scope out the shit part of town to find where to buy heroin. Or crack. Or meth. Or whatever they had. Now, if Mark was lucky, the guy would just come back with the goods. But sometimes Mark would get pissed 'cause it wasn't enough or it wasn't good enough. Then he'd just go himself. And sometimes he wouldn't come back, and we'd be like, "Is he dead?" This is before cell phones were readily available, right? We're like, "Are we gonna play tonight?" That happened a lot.

GARY LEE CONNER We managed to not have to cancel any shows during Lollapalooza. At least that was good. I'm sure we came pretty close sometimes.

BUZZ OSBORNE God rest his soul, you know? He was obviously a tortured person for a long time. And he didn't look happy on that tour. None of 'em looked happy.

GARY LEE CONNER We were having our issues, but personally I had a really good time. It's like, you're going to a festival every day . . . and then you're playing, too. And you're backstage, hanging with the other bands. It was kinda neat.

VAN CONNER One day I see Buzz and I go, "Hey, you wanna go backstage and watch Metallica?" And he's like, "*Fuuuuckkk . . .*" Because Buzz is playing the second stage, so he has no backstage pass. And if you didn't have the proper pass, basically you'd be murdered. So I walk backstage with Buzz. I show my pass. Buzz has no pass. His hair is about eight feet tall. And he just walks straight in. Then we get to the backstage Metallica area, where you could sit and watch them while they played. And you *definitely* can't get up there without a pass. But Buzz just walks right in. Buzz doesn't need a backstage pass, okay?

GINA ARNOLD (journalist, author) Metallica, one of their amps, or maybe several, had what I considered politically incorrect stickers on it. Like NRA stickers. And I was like, Oh, that's unfortunate.

STEVE "CHOPPER" BORGES We had some issues with the Metallica staff. There were some guys—not all of them, but one or two—who were sort of white supremacist kind of guys, with funky slogans on their gear. So there was some friction there. I had to say, "You know what? You need to just cover that stuff up. When you're not here, you do whatever you want. But here you need to cover it up." And they did.

STUART ROSS (tour director, Lollapalooza) There were also social-dynamic issues with having a Metallica fan base, or a partially Metallica fan base, at these shows.

KRISTEN WORDEN-HARRIS (artist liaison, second stage, Lollapalooza 1995–97) The audience was different. It was very heavily male. A lot of aggression. It definitely had a different feel than the previous year.

VAN CONNER The crowd was *very* Metallica. I'm not gonna say the word "metal," because I love what metal is. I just know that there was a bunch of buttheads going to the show, who wanted to have a fight 'cause they drank alcohol three times.

TIM COMMERFORD (bassist, Rage Against the Machine) They had their fans there, man. It was their show. There was no question about it. It was solid and it was dope. Whereas we got added to the bill as a guest; it was like we were put into, like, the other team's stadium.

GARY GRAFF (music writer, *Detroit Free Press*) It was quite a collision of sensibilities. As opposed to '94, when the Smashing Pumpkins fans existed okay with the George Clinton fans and the Beastie Boys fans. That wasn't as much the case in '96 when the alternative world met the Metallica crowd.

MAYNARD JAMES KEENAN (singer, Tool) There's a particular crowd that's going to go see Metallica. And they don't give a shit about anything else but Metallica.

KIRK HAMMETT (guitarist, Metallica) There was a question with having certain guest bands on the bill, like Cocteau Twins.

MARC GEIGER The Cocteau Twins were my clients and one of my favorites. And Kirk Hammett was a massive fan. So he had asked me, he said, "Do you think we can get them?"

ROBIN GUTHRIE (guitarist, Cocteau Twins) We did the first show, somewhere in a big field outside Kansas City. And Metallica, the guys in the band made such a big fuss over us in the dressing room. They were so encouraging, and they were showing me how they knew how to play our songs and stuff. Kirk especially was so lovely. He was so nerdy about guitar pedals and so knowledgeable about what we'd done. Whereas I couldn't even sing you anything that they'd ever done. I was like, "I did not expect this." I really didn't know what to expect, but I didn't expect *that*.

KIRK HAMMETT We were a little nervous about how our fans would kind of coexist with the more alternative-type bands. But we would endorse certain bands by going out and announcing them. I announced the Cocteau Twins when they played.

ROBIN GUTHRIE The band were at the side of the stage watching, and the audience, the first three rows of people, had baseball caps on backward and they were just flipping us off all the time. Then they started to throw mud and shit like that. Liz [Cocteau Twins singer Elizabeth Fraser] got hit by a big a load of mud. And the guys in Metallica were getting really involved, arguing with the audience and trying to get them to, you know, not be dicks, basically. It was kind of a "does not compute" sort of thing.

GARY LEE CONNER There was a horrible experience where Steve Earle opened one of the shows in Dallas and people were . . . I don't think they booed him, but they didn't like him. And then also Waylon Jennings was on one of 'em, and people were just not into it.

STUART ROSS I mean, Waylon Jennings playing Lollapalooza! It was incredible. And I remember that [Metallica singer and guitarist] James Hetfield came out to introduce Waylon, and he walks out onstage and the crowd goes crazy. He says, "I wanna introduce you to my hero. I want you to give it up for Waylon Jennings." Then Hetfield goes off to the side of the stage and Waylon starts playing . . . and they start throwing shit at him. It was, I don't want to say discouraging . . . It was disgraceful.

ROBERT "NITE BOB" CZAYKOWSKI The audience wasn't having it. They were like, "We don't want no fucking country!" And Hetfield came out and said, "Hey, this is super important and you need to respect Waylon Jennings." Shut the whole crowd down. I gave him points for that. Redneck that he is or wannabe redneck that he is. I don't know. Who knows?

KIM THAYIL (guitarist, Soundgarden) What we didn't see when Sound-garden did Lollapalooza in '92, and that we did see in '96, were girls flashing. They were on their boyfriends' shoulders, or who knows, maybe their stepdads' shoulders, and they'd flash the band. Not so much with us, but we noticed it more with Metallica. Surprisingly, we noticed it a lot with Rage Against the Machine. It's probably the repet-itive, hypnotic rhythm of Rage. I mean, they're more danceable than Soundgarden, probably more danceable than Metallica. But you'd see a little bit of that, and that was kind of strange. And we knew that was probably because that '96 tour was a little bit more hard-rock-y and metal than '92.

STUART ROSS I saw the documentary about Woodstock in '99, right? Where they got some very aggro, Limp Bizkit/Kid Rock–type acts and it just went totally sideways. Lollapalooza did not ever have that issue. But, you know, some of the crowd did not really love some of the choices that year.

BUZZ OSBORNE I don't blame the crowd. The crowds are mostly kids who want an opportunity to go crazy and be away from their parents for a long period of time. I get it. I don't think that's a problem at all. The devil is in the details, as they say.

KIM THAYIL I remember Chris [Cornell] addressing the audience at one point and saying, "Hey, welcome to the Lollapalooza that has a big cock!"

GERALD CASALE (bassist, singer, Devo) Devo's first show on the tour was in Arizona, in, like, searing heat. And we're facing this crowd of people that are just wasted from being there all day, and weathered by the wind and the sun and having ingested every imaginable combina-tion of booze and drugs.

KRISTEN WORDEN-HARRIS I'll never forget—that was the show where a giant sandstorm rolled in.

C. J. RAMONE It was maybe 115 degrees that day. And the Ramones would always go onstage in our leather jackets. First five or six songs, at least. I said to Johnny, "We going to go all the way to . . . ?" I think it was "Rock 'n' Roll High School," "Rock 'n' Roll Radio," one of the rock 'n' roll songs. Between the song before it and that one we'd let the chord ring out, we'd pull off our jackets and go into the next one. So we're playing the set, we're just roasting in the sun, and all of a sudden a huge storm blows in. There was this matting on the stage, and the matting lifts up, and literally the monitors and everything spill backward. We got out of having to do the full set that day.

GERALD CASALE It was amazing because one of the trusses, I don't remember how or why, but one of the trusses caught on fire. And they're trying to put the fire out, and the wind is so gusty and so powerful that all the backline trusses start to tilt. The roadies and all these guys have got these cables and they're trying to batten down the hatches, like sailors in a storm on the ocean.

KRISTEN WORDEN-HARRIS The singer from Sponge had on a scarf and goggles, and he got up on, they must have been road cases, and he stood there in kind of a lunge stance as the storm hit. The sand and the wind is blowing his scarf and he's got his goggles on and he's just standing there and we're all like, "What is going on?" I don't even know what he was doing.

VINNIE DOMBROSKI I wanted to play in the sandstorm, man. I was suiting up. I'm good to go. But they just kept telling me, the technicians, the production guys, that if we run our generators in the sandstorm it's going to ruin them. I was like, "Can we find some AC plug somewhere here in the desert so we could plug in and do our set? Because people are going to want to hang out and see this shit." But it just didn't happen.

STEVE "CHOPPER" BORGES We stopped the show. And we had mud in our gear for the next week and a half. We'd try to wipe it off, but it blew into everything.

334 | RICHARD BIENSTOCK AND TOM BEAUJOUR

DANNY ZELISKO (promoter, Evening Star Productions) The good thing about those storms there is they come and they go pretty quick. But that was definitely a downer for everybody.

VINNIE DOMBROSKI I just hopped in a car and went to [Tucson music venue] Club Congress for three days.

STEVE "CHOPPER" BORGES We did a lot of shows in nontraditional sites. Just out in the boondocks. Park-type things. Fairgrounds.

DAN CHOI (front-of-house coordinator, Lollapalooza 1994–97, 2003) A field is really good in many ways. The only thing you need is power, and we had a whole flatbed full of generators. After that, you can design anything. So we started at Longview Lake in Kansas City, which is where we rehearsed, and then we did the Iowa State Fairgrounds in Des Moines. And then we went to Pecatonica in Illinois. But after that we ended up moving a few of the shows to amphitheaters. If you look at the planned dates versus the actual dates, there are differences. And I think that was a combination of not being able to get staging, and the fact that initially the shows weren't drawing well.

STEVE "CHOPPER" BORGES We played a date in Indiana, and we were supposed to play in a field next to a shed, but we ended up actually doing the shed, which was Deer Creek.

DAN CHOI In Indiana I know we were not supposed to play the Deer Creek Music Center. We were supposed to build a stage out on a lawn there or something. It was supposed to be a much bigger show.

STUART ROSS Nobody remembers this, but we also carried a Ferris wheel that year. Because we wanted to fill in a very large space, which were these big fields, with as many fun attractions as we could think of. And we thought that sitting way up above the crowd watching the bands, that was gonna be awesome.

ANDY CIRZAN I haven't thought about the Ferris wheel in a long time. That was completely unnecessary.

STUART ROSS We carried it from city to city. I think it may have been my idea. And, you know, Coachella right now has a huge hundred-foot Ferris wheel. We didn't have one quite that big, but it was a real Ferris wheel. We just thought, If we're gonna restuff this envelope, let's see how much we can fit into it.

DAN CHOI We hired real carnies to run it, and they were supposed to be making money, I believe, by selling tickets. Which, in retrospect, is a terrible idea, because you've already paid to come to the festival. Why should you have to pay to get on a Ferris wheel?

STUART ROSS I remember calling Dan Choi, and I said, "What's wrong with the Ferris wheel?" And he said, "Nothing's wrong with the Ferris wheel." I said, "Then why isn't it moving?" He goes, "Because nobody wants to ride on it." And it was like, "Oh man, am I getting stuff wrong or what?"

DAN CHOI That year was funny because it was supposed to be, "Okay, Metallica is a big deal." But I think it also became clear, early on, that we weren't selling that well. Yeah, Metallica's a pretty big draw. But while people like to see Metallica, they might rather see *just* Metallica.

STEVE "CHOPPER" BORGES The thought may have been, Metallica's good for twenty thousand people, Soundgarden and the others are good for ten thousand, we'll be doing thirty thousand a night. The reality is—and this is all my opinion, and opinions are like assholes, everybody's got one— the Metallica fans were saying, "We don't wanna go sit through five hours of watching bands with pins in their faces to see Metallica do ninety minutes instead of two and a half hours. We'll see them on their own."

DANNY ZELISKO As far as the Metallica thing goes, I don't have any recollection of anybody being unhappy. I remember thinking it was pretty weird, but it's like, if you wanna look at it that way, what was Ice-T doing on the first one?

ANDY CIRZAN All I know is we did that show out in Pecatonica, basically a field in the middle of Illinois, and we sold thirty-five thousand tickets.

So for all the talk about having Metallica on Lollapalooza or whatever, it did terrific business for us.

STUART ROSS I don't remember it being as financially successful as previous years. But a lot of that, you know, you look at ticket sales as one metric. If you were in an amphitheater, and the biggest amphitheater in the country at the time was the World Music Theatre in Chicago, that was thirty thousand, maybe a couple more. I don't know. But you did thirty thousand in an amphitheater, you made a lot of money. If you did thirty thousand in a field, you might lose money because your expenses are significantly higher.

MARC GEIGER The Metallica year exceeded expectations the most since year one. It was our biggest year ever—gross *and* tickets.

GARY GRAFF I'm not surprised to hear that at least claimed. But listen, it was a Metallica tour, okay? Put everything else aside, including the cool brand of Lollapalooza. The great secret—or, I should say, not-so-great secret—of any successful package tour is that you have a headliner who could do it on their own. The rest is value-plus. So you were going to do big numbers for Metallica in '96. They'd been away for a while, they've certainly gotten jaws flapping about their new look and their new sound . . . that wasn't really that new a sound. But this is one of the most wisely marketed bands in the world. And the confluence of them as part of Lollapalooza is going to be more notorious, which made it that much greater.

ROBIN GUTHRIE To this day, it's one of those great things I like to occasionally drop into conversation with young people. "I remember that time with Cocteau Twins where I was playing with Metallica . . ."

STEVE "CHOPPER" BORGES We wrapped up at Irvine Meadows, and that's a place we had played a lot. I think we played there almost every year. So that was a super-easy one, because I already knew how to solve 90 percent of the problems. By that point, I was just relieved that nobody had died and that we had all gotten through it. The promoters had all gotten through it. It was more a feeling of relief. Because it was a tough year. It was tough juggling the gear. It was tough juggling the personalities. It was by far the hardest year, that's for sure.

DON MULLER That tour was a beast. But if we were going to be successful, we knew we had to cross that line. We knew we had to cross the line of bands that weren't alternative bands, that weren't punk rock bands.

MARC GEIGER We wanted to fuck people up and make them go, "Oh, no." That's how you stay in the discussion zone. You've got to take some risk. You're supposed to be ahead of the market, not behind it. That's what Lollapalooza was known for. And Metallica, in fairness, is one of the best live bands ever. And we wanted to show people what a great live band is.

KIRK HAMMETT We were just like, Okay, yeah, whatever. Go out there and play our shows, fucking kick ass. We knew that if we just went out there and we could just be ourselves, it would be just fine. And you know what? It was just fine.

MARC GEIGER Metallica, of course, has now played Lollapalooza many times. The whole world has changed. And Perry and Metallica are friendly, good, great, and love each other.

KIRK HAMMETT We played Lollapalooza a few summers ago and when we saw Perry, it was like seeing an old friend. We have such a different relationship now. We can acknowledge that we're all in this together, and to a certain extent we're kind of survivors. All those weird trips and issues, grievances and competition that we had when we were younger, all that stuff just isn't as prominent or important anymore.

PERRY FARRELL I kind of look at them as brothers, and I'm happy to share the ride through life with them.

MARC GEIGER By the way, I also know thousands of people I've run across who have said, "I didn't ever see Metallica until I saw them on Lollapalooza in '96. They were fucking amazing." And I go, "See?"

LOLLAPALOOZA 1997

DATES: JUNE 25–AUGUST 16

MAIN STAGE: Orbital (select dates), the Orb (select dates), the Prodigy (select dates), Devo (select dates), Tool, Snoop Doggy Dogg, Tricky, Korn (exited in July due to illness), James, Julian & Damian Marley and the Uprising Band, Failure (as a replacement for Korn)

SECOND STAGE: Failure, Eels, Radish, Old 97's, Pugs, Lost Boyz, Demolition Doll Rods, Molly McGuire, Skeleton Key, Jeremy Toback, Porno for Pyros, Orbit, various

If its 1995 "artypalooza" and 1996 "dude-apalooza" iterations saw the festival swerving wildly across multiple stylistic lanes, the return of Perry Farrell to the Lollapalooza brain trust in 1997 indicated that even if the tour could not fully recapture its past glory, it would at least be reinvigorated by its cocreator's eclectic vision. "Lolla has a lot to prove this year—including whether it's even worth staging anymore," wrote *Variety* in an article published July 1. "Does the original all-day Gen-X music event started by Perry Farrell in 1991 still have its own identity?"

By 1997, Farrell seemed focused on anything but the guitar-driven rock that had been Lollapalooza's bread and butter. In fact, during his 1996 sabbatical, Farrell had spent part of the summer touring the country with Enit, an electronic-music-leaning festival of his conception that featured the Orb, Meat Beat Manifesto, Black

Grape, and his own Porno for Pyros, and attractions such as tree-planting ceremonies and a communal meal included with the price of admission.

Enit, advertised as "an inter-planetary festival celebrating cosmic peace and sexuality," drew its name from the obscure 1970 Ludwig Pallmann book *Cancer Planet Mission*. "The book theorizes that Earth was not mature enough in the constellation of intergalactic civilizations," explains then Farrell manager and Lollapalooza '97 concourse creative director Adam Schneider. "It was considered too warlike, not together. So the Enit Festival is like an intergalactic festival that was a way to signal to the cosmos that we were evolving to the point of being ready to join the league of worlds."

He continues, "I do not think Perry took this literally, by the way. It was just a cool idea."

Although Enit was not profitable (Farrell admitted that he might personally lose almost five hundred thousand dollars on the tour), the acts chosen for Lollapalooza '97 seemed to reflect a similar sensibility. The almost dizzyingly variegated main stage opened with the reggae sounds of Julian and Damian Marley, followed by the placid Britpop of James. Third on the bill, and wildly more aggressive than the two acts preceding them, were dreadlocked outliers Korn, whose funky, hip-hop-infused brand of nu metal was establishing itself as the dominant sound of hard rock for the decade to come. Notoriously mercurial producer and rapper Tricky came next, and struggled from the get-go to communicate the dark moodiness of his music in the still-blazing sunlight. Whatever tension Tricky managed to build was quickly dissipated by the crowd-pleasing stoner rhymes of Snoop Doggy Dogg (soon to rebrand as Snoop Dogg), who behind the scenes was on high alert for fear of becoming another victim of the East Coast/West Coast hip-hop wars that had recently claimed the lives of Tupac Shakur and The Notorious B.I.G. Although billed as headliners, Tool, triumphant returning alumni of the '93 tour, chose to play second to last, followed by a rotating seventh slot that featured '96 Lollapalooza vets Devo, electronic acts the Orb and Orbital, and, on select dates, British electro-punks the Prodigy, whose album *The Fat of the Land* would hit number one on the *Billboard* chart during the tour.

Although populated almost exclusively by bands whose major-label status gave them the leverage to secure a spot, the second stage's more-than-solid lineup still exhibited impressive quality and diversity. Alt-country pioneers Old 97's, indie-rock depressives Eels, emo-prog virtuosos Failure (who would eventually pull double duty on the main stage), and a still-teenaged Ben Kweller, fronting his Texas grunge trio Radish, insured that anyone who ventured to the second stage would not be disappointed—assuming they had any affinity at all for the genre of music being performed at that particular moment.

Faced with competition from more targeted festivals like the nascent metal juggernaut Ozzfest (conceived by Sharon Osbourne after her husband, Ozzy, was rejected as a Lolla headliner), the jam-band–packed H.O.R.D.E. outing, former Lollapalooza stage manager Kevin Lyman's punk-oriented Warped Tour, and singer Sarah McLachlan's exclusively female-artist-driven Lilith Fair, the eclectic mash-up of Lollapalooza's '97 lineup was a hard sell. "I don't want to be critical of those who booked it, but it was pretty underwhelming," says front-of-house coordinator Dan Choi. "There wasn't anything that people really wanted to see." According to promoter Andy Cirzan, who had been booking Lollapalooza in the Chicago area since its first year, box office performance was nothing short of dismal. "The real drop-off, the crazy scary one, was '97," he says. "That's when the bottom totally fell out."

When the dust settled, it was Lilith Fair, which filled venues to an average 93 percent capacity and grossed more than twelve million dollars, that was the top tour of the summer, while Ozzfest, tallying almost a hundred thousand fewer attendees, won the silver medal. Lollapalooza, with little more than half the receipts of Lilith and an average attendance of 67 percent of venue capacity, could barely even claim to be in the same race, limping to the conclusion that what it had to offer was no longer particularly compelling to a new generation of concertgoers. "Lolla had its run, and we knew the model was breaking," festival cofounder Marc Geiger concludes. "It became too generic, it burned too bright . . . and it needed a break."

1 "I BEGGED PERRY TO SHUT THE FUCKING THING DOWN"

STEVE "CHOPPER" BORGES (production manager, Lollapalooza 1993–97) We all were concerned because it wasn't a super-strong year.

KRISTEN WORDEN-HARRIS (artist liaison, second stage, Lollapalooza 1995–97) I remember a lot of talk about, "What's left to do, and who do we get? Is this gonna be it?"

GARY GRAFF (music writer, *Detroit Free Press*) To me, '97 felt like, We're trying to find the new alternative. What's that going to be? And the new alternative was in the electronic realm. That's why we were getting the Orb, Orbital, Prodigy—even Devo as a heritage kind of act. And even though you could say, "There's nothing electronic about Tool," the ambience of a Tool set actually made sense within the context of these other acts.

STUART ROSS (tour director, Lollapalooza) You know, if Lollapalooza is going to be an alternative-music festival, then techno music, or whatever name that genre took back in the late nineties, was alternative. I would think that the path made sense.

GREG KOT (music critic, *Chicago Tribune*) Perry was a DJ, and he actually called me that winter to tell me he was going to be at [Chicago venue] the Metro. And he said, "Listen, I want to talk to you. I think I'm going to come back to Lollapalooza and really going to put my heart and soul into this one." Because he had checked out in '96. And I go, "Okay. I'm not sure that's a great idea." But we had a very thoughtful discussion about it. He knew the festival was kind of nearing the end, but he wanted to reinvigorate it and see if he could give it some juice. If he was going to end it, he wanted to end it on his terms. So he brought in the DJ stuff, which wasn't a bad idea at the time. He was coming from a pure place on that one, because he genuinely loved house music. I talked to him enough to know, Okay, you know your shit. You're invested in this in a way that's serious, you're not just in it to jump on a bandwagon.

DAN CHOI (front-of-house coordinator, Lollapalooza 1994–97, 2003) I don't think the electronic acts really meant anything to the audience.

MARC GEIGER (agent; cofounder, Lollapalooza) You could argue, "Oh yeah, they came back, they were ahead on electronic music. Look at all the stuff they had." It's true to an extent, but I think the public tired of it. Tool was on it and some others, but it wasn't groundbreaking.

ANDY CIRZAN (promotor, Jam Productions) And Tool weren't nearly as big as they are now.

MAYNARD JAMES KEENAN (singer, Tool) I think when you started pushing up to '97, like anything when there's an opportunity to make money, quite a bit of the behind the scenes was definitely . . . I don't know if I would go so far as say "cutthroat," but they were definitely trying to shove things into the mix that would make money for the festival because early on, they probably promised too many people too many percentages and now they were scrambling to make up for it.

DAN CHOI They were just trying to get more out of it.

ANDY CIRZAN See, it's about the available inventory in any given year and who wants to get paid what. Major bands were looking at Lollapalooza going, "You guys are cranking out giant money and have been for forever. So if we're gonna be the motor for your tour, we need to get paid."

LIAM HOWLETT (producer, keyboardist, programmer, the Prodigy) We just wanted to play America. It was like, "Lollapalooza? Us? Wicked."

SAUL DAVIES (guitarist, violinist, James) We were also offered a very big European tour from the north of Sweden right down to Portugal. And the debate was, "We could do this big tour in Europe, but this is our chance really to go back into America." We'd had the beginnings of some real success in the States, and it was appealing to us, some of us anyway, to explore the country. Being brought up as a working-class lad in the north of England, I never thought that I would go to America.

DON MULLER (agent; cofounder, Lollapalooza) Marc and I were both gone at ARTISTdirect at that time. We were gonna change the world of technology or something.

MARC GEIGER I was building a big internet company. Don and I were employees of Triad when we started Lollapalooza. And when the employees at a company do something and start an asset, who owns the asset? The company or the employees? The company. So Lollapalooza wasn't ours. After William Morris bought Triad, it was William Morris's money and Perry's money. So not a lot of incentive. I didn't get paid. I was doing it as a side hustle anyway, and I wasn't making money.

DON MULLER I just wish, in hindsight, that they would've shut it down with the '96 one. I begged Perry to shut the fucking thing down because we tarnished an amazing . . . I don't know what you would call it. I guess "art" would be the best way to describe it. It was an amazing piece of art, and they ran it into the ground. The people who were involved in it and in charge of '97 didn't fucking have a clue about what they were doing. And I would tell them that to their faces when they would walk in my office. Like, "You don't live it. So get the fuck out of it and let it go down and just be done."

ANDY CIRZAN I think everybody knew before it even went up for sale that this was gonna be tough. But I don't think anybody knew that that was gonna be the swan song.

GREG KOT The fact that Korn was on that bill, that was tough to stomach. That was a rough one. But they did diversify the festival. The lack of people of color, the genre diversity that was completely absent in recent years, it was there again. They had Julian and Damian Marley on that bill. Snoop Dogg. Tricky. Tool kind of representing the heavier end of the spectrum. There was an attempt there to revive the spirit, but people just weren't having it. They were done with it. And that was it for quite a number of years.

MAYNARD JAMES KEENAN I think quite a few mistakes were made. But it was still an enjoyable tour.

2 "TO SOME ALTERNATIVE KIDS, 'NU METAL' WAS A DIRTY WORD"

DON MULLER (agent; cofounder, Lollapalooza) I remember Korn being on the bill, and I was like, What the fuck are we doing? I was just . . . embarrassed. Not that they're a bad band. I don't believe one way or the other—good, bad, or indifferent—about Jonathan [Davis, singer] and that whole crew. But I was just like, "That was a mistake." Metallica was a mistake, but this was *really* a mistake. It was just grasping at straws.

DAVID "BOCHE" VIECELLI (agent, the Jesus Lizard, Pavement, Jon Spencer Blues Explosion) Jon Spencer Blues Explosion got an offer and we had confirmed the third slot on the main stage. But they were trying to book Korn, and Korn refused to play if they had to play before the Blues Explosion. And so, Lollapalooza came to us and said, "Will you play second so Korn could play third?" And I talked to the band about it and it was a "no." It was like, "You made us an offer, we accepted it, we negotiated all the terms and conditions. And we had a finalized agreement. Why would we change that?" In the end, it was so important to Lollapalooza that they be tweaking things for maximum attendance that I said, "If you'd like us not to play so we get out of Korn's way, let's just decide what kind of a check you need to write to make us go away." And that's what happened.

PETER KATSIS (manager, Korn) I vaguely remember that that came up, but there was no way Jon Spencer Blues Explosion were popular enough to compete with Korn at that point.

JAMES "MUNKY" SHAFFER (guitarist, Korn) We had toured for about eight or nine months and had just come back from Europe, and our manager called us and told us, "We're doing Lollapalooza." It was such a good opportunity, especially at that point in our career, that I don't think there was any asking us whether we wanted to. It was the first big festival that we got to be on.

JONATHAN DAVIS (singer, Korn) We were really excited, because this was definitely more of an alternative-type festival. At that time, we were try- ing to move away from being pigeonholed into just doing metal tours like opening for Megadeth. The metal scene is the one that took us in and embraced us and I love it, but I was really trying to venture out and play for different crowds. So we were really stoked. I couldn't even be- lieve it. I remember being like, "We're going to play Lollapalooza! We're playing with Tricky, and Tool . . . and the Orb!"

PETER KATSIS To some alternative kids, "nu metal" was a dirty word. But we were watching music change at that point and recognizing that alternative kids were listening to harder music. And I think Korn always considered themselves to be an alternative-rock band. A very heavy one, but indeed an alternative-rock band.

BRAD TOLINSKI (editor-in-chief, *Guitar World* magazine; author) Critics often grappled with how to categorize Korn. With their use of dissonant seven-string guitars, bagpipes, and funk-inspired bass lines there was very little to connect them to traditional metal. And Jonathan Davis's damaged-antihero lyrics were certainly closer to Perry Farrell's than say, Ozzy Osbourne's or James Hetfield's. Furthermore, they didn't look like metal kids. They had braided hair, dreadlocks, tracksuits, and white sneakers, and they appeared more like disenfranchised white B-boys than members of Megadeth or Judas Priest.

JAMES "MUNKY" SHAFFER Our bass player, Fieldy, and Jonathan were liv- ing in Long Beach at the time, and Fieldy was getting into this low-rider culture. He got a low-rider bike, and then Jonathan got one, too. Once they found out that we were going to be on the tour, they were like, "We should get a couple more and all ride out onto the stage on them." I was the only one who said, "I'm not doing that. Fuck that. That's not Korn." I always wanted to keep the aesthetic dark. But I see the pictures of it now, and it's cool. We were just a conglomerate of everything that we loved. When people first saw us, white dudes with the Adidas and the dreads, they were like, They look like a hip-hop act, but they're playing this crazy heavy metal that nobody's ever heard before. What the fuck is happening?

JONATHAN DAVIS I still have that bike. It's in my studio.

JAMES "MUNKY SHAFFER Because we went on so early, I was thinking that no one was going to be there and that we would be playing in front of half the audience if we were lucky. In some cases that was true, but for most of the shows, we had at least three-quarters of the crowd in the building, which was great for us. Word got out that, "You guys have got to get there early to see this band."

I think that happened on a lot of the Lollapalooza shows, because I remember going to the '91, '92 shows and I was like, "Oh, you want to maximize your dollar when you spend that much money on a concert ticket. I'm going to make sure I see every band." I remember going to the first one at Irvine Meadows in 1991. Nine Inch Nails, I had never heard of them, and we were there early because I was going to see every band. I was just like, "Holy shit. What just happened? What did I just see?" It was incredible. I was a fan ever since. Didn't know anything about them, saw that show.

PETER KATSIS Korn had a Jägermeister sponsorship. So it got pretty out of control. Never so much violent as it was just a lot of fun, actually. But you also had to get up and deal with some pretty intense hangovers.

JONATHAN DAVIS A lot of Lollapalooza is fuzzy to me because back then, I was a fucking raging alcoholic. I wouldn't say an alcoholic, but I was partying a lot. But from what I remember of those shows, they were just some of the best.

JAMES "MUNKY" SHAFFER The kids would go crazy. Maybe not every night, but every three or four nights someone would set a fire out in the grass or the kids in front would start tearing out the seats. They would stand on the seats, and then at some point it had a confined feeling, and they'd look at the kids back on the lawn and think, I paid more money for this seat that's closer, but they're having all the fun back there.

PETER KATSIS There were a couple of discussions with the Lollapalooza people where they were like, "Help us. Can you guys talk to the audience?" And we were like, "No, that's what we do. That's who we are. That's what you booked." Obviously, they would have been better off if there was a pit in front of the stage, but if there wasn't, then kids got rowdy.

JONATHAN DAVIS Korn was this new thing that was going on, and at that time, nobody knew what the fuck to do with us. We would go on and then shit would just go apeshit. But that was normalcy for us. When we played our shows, it was just what would happen.

PETER KATSIS Before Lollapalooza, there were some alternative-rock stations playing Korn, but active rock was really who played us. Alternative-rock stations, like KROQ, kind of jumped on board more on the third record, which came after Lollapalooza. Lollapalooza was the stamp of approval for alternative-rock stations. And the audience doubles when you've got all the hard-rock kids and all the alternative-rock kids coming to see your band. When the band could cross over both genres, it meant the world was totally open at that point.

JONATHAN DAVIS I remember Mark Mothersbaugh from Devo standing there and when we came offstage, he was just clapping. He didn't say a fucking word. He was just clapping his hands and following us, clapping his hands. You know how he's just this fucking odd dude and I love Devo. I had every album as a kid. But that was the biggest compliment. I'm like, "Oh my god, Mark Mothersbaugh is loving Korn." That was rad.

TIM BOOTH (singer, James) We had just done our own tour with Third Eye Blind, and I had ruptured two discs in my neck. After the fourth gig, I was in a hospital in San Francisco and we had to cancel the whole tour. Which meant that we couldn't cancel Lollapalooza, because then our insurance would take a really big hit and we might not be able to tour again. I was in no state to travel at all, and I was in agony the whole summer. I had a nurse with me, and I was in a neck brace. You blew on me and I was in the hospital again. It was a rough, rough time.

SAUL DAVIES (guitarist, violinist, James) A period of time where men still needed to be men.

TIM BOOTH We played before Korn, and the first gig, we come out and all these people are screaming abuse at us within a few songs. "Faggots" was the particular slur that we were hearing. And it was like, "Oh, this is interesting. We haven't been heckled for years." But we were just being heckled and shouted at and screamed at by Korn audiences who had never heard melodies and thought that the music we played came from another planet—Planet Gay.

SAUL DAVIES I mean, welcome to America. Today, that would be stopped 'cause it would be regarded as being abused. But then, that wasn't quite the case.

JAMES "MUNKY" SHAFFER I couldn't even sit and watch their set. A few times I went out to watch from the side of the stage, but if someone in the crowd saw me they'd start chanting "Korn!" And you're like, "Dude, okay. We're going to go on in five minutes, just chill." But they would just be chanting in the middle of James's set, and it's like, "Fuck, dude. Save your energy. Show some respect."

TIM BOOTH By the third gig, I went out in the auditorium after we played, and I found this stall that sold mirror-ball shirts and miniskirts. They were pastel-colored—pink, mauve. And I went back to the band and said, "Look, if we're gonna be 'faggots,' let's dress the part and really stir 'em up. 'Cause we've got six weeks of this."

SAUL DAVIES So we're standing up there with our dresses on and they're shouting, "Faggots! Faggots! Faggots! Faggots!" "English faggots!" "English fucking faggots!" And throwing shit at us. And I would've been wearing a dress with little white socks on, with "fuck" written on one leg and "me" on the other. And lipstick. So this is kind of a piece of theater. Fuck me? Actually, fuck *you*. You're gonna stand there and scream at me? You know, where's the limit? Like, we are on the stage, you're in the audience, but you seem to think that you're in control of us. Probably, you are.

TIM BOOTH Saul would just point at whoever was screaming "Faggots!" and he'd go, "I want you to suck my cock!" So we were winding them up. But you know, we'd just worn dresses for the cover of the *Laid* album. We were very much into "gender is irrelevant." We were totally happy to be called gay.

MISCHA TEMPLE (lighting director, the Prodigy) James would all come offstage wearing these different-colored skirts and go out into the audience and wander around in these clothes and pick up chicks. It worked for them every day. They would always be back at the tour bus by about 1:00 p.m. with a bunch of girls there. That was their thing. They'd done their job and now they're just gonna shag chicks and party on while the rest of us were working.

SAUL DAVIES I remember early on going, "I've still got seven weeks of this to deal with." And then you get to the last week and you're like, "Wow, we're going home soon." In fact, we were going home to the Reading Festival, to play with Suede. It was like, "Thank god."

TIM BOOTH At the end of the Lollapalooza, Korn came up and said, "We watched James every day and you are our favorite band. Would you come on tour with us as our support band across the States?" And we went, "Thanks . . . but I think we've done our time."

3 "I HAVE TITS, PUT ME ON YOUR SHOULDERS"

JAMES "MUNKY" SHAFFER (guitarist, Korn) Tool were so much fun to watch every night. They blew me away. It inspired me as a musician, just the way they kept this ominous surging tempo that [Tool drummer] Danny Carey carried through a show. It's always just this growing tension. There's something about it that's just its own thing. It's special.

JONATHAN DAVIS (singer, Korn) I have nothing but fond memories of watching those guys every night. It was awesome. I loved Maynard's whole vibe. He had titties and this crazy fucking ponytail, and I'd never seen anything like that.

MAYNARD JAMES KEENAN (singer, Tool) Danny Carey had this bodybuilder friend, Killer Kirk, who was standing there and I was like, "I have tits, put me on your shoulders."

JONATHAN DAVIS They were really cool to us. We had a good time. I remember we all went on this crazy canoe trip in Ohio somewhere and that was fun. It was like a bunch of the tour went canoeing down this river. It was me and Munky, and Adam and Justin [Tool guitarist Adam Jones and bassist Justin Chancellor] and maybe Danny. I think everybody dropped a bunch of acid or some shit and they went down. I didn't fuck with that shit, but it was definitely interesting.

MAYNARD JAMES KEENAN We had a great time on '97.

STEVE "CHOPPER" BORGES (production manager, Lollapalooza 1993–97) The eighth position, or last slot, on the bill was one of the least desirable positions. Because by that time, people were tired. They'd seen seven acts, they'd been outside all day. It was hot. And usually, by the end of the eighth act, whoever it was played to half a house.

KEN ANDREWS (singer, guitarist, Failure) Tool had a lot of control and decided, "Yeah, we're not going on at the end."

MAYNARD JAMES KEENAN We played second to last and there were a bunch of bands like Devo that were rotating in the final slot.

KEN ANDREWS Adam and Maynard are big Devo fans.

MAYNARD JAMES KEENAN I'm from Akron, and Devo is from Akron. So it was inspirational. And those guys are crazy. You don't come out of Ohio without some kind of baggage. I mean, Chrissie Hynde of the Pretenders, I love what she does, but she's a handful. I'm a handful. Mark Mothersbaugh's a handful. Gerry Casale's a handful. But it creates beautiful results for the art.

GERALD CASALE (bassist, singer, Devo) I could relate to what Maynard was doing, because Devo always used masks and theatrical ploys. And then Devo itself became a meta-mask, something bigger than individuals, that allowed us to operate inside it where the whole was more than the sum of its parts. What Maynard was doing onstage was very similar and really cool. And also kind of frightening, in a surreal, theatrical way.

KEN ANDREWS It was sad to me because after Tool finished, the whole audience left. I mean I have to imagine that a huge swath of Tool fans at that moment in time had never even heard of Devo and had no idea what they were about. And I think when they heard them, the disparity between Devo and Tool was just too much. So, by the time Devo were finishing their set, there were less than a thousand people in the amphitheater.

GERALD CASALE We would never have wanted to play after Tool. That's too heavy of an experience and they were huge at that point. And they had bigger production that we couldn't match. Once you see a show like that, you can't come on with less of a show.

KEN ANDREWS I didn't particularly dig that. I always thought it was a weird thing to have the big band go on before the end of the show. But that's just the way it ended up.

GIZZ BUTT (guitarist, the Prodigy) Some people were saying that the Prodigy were being put on the bill as a "walkout act." Meaning, once you've watched Tool, you pick up your shit and get ready to go, and you've got some music whilst you're leaving. But I couldn't see anyone walking out. The reaction to the Prodigy was massive.

STEVE KNOPPER (editor at large, *Billboard* magazine) This was a moment where America was really getting into electronic dance music, and the Prodigy were able to reap the benefits. *The Fat of the Land* hit number one on the *Billboard* chart that July, which was pretty amazing.

MISCHA TEMPLE (lighting director, the Prodigy) That was an interesting run. When you're the number-one band in the world, you're in a bubble, and the buzz from the media and everybody else is very different. So that was kind of fascinating, to be in the middle of all of that. The buzz just grew and grew and grew as that tour went on. We actually got off Lollapalooza for a couple of shows and went to Japan to play the Fuji Rock Festival, but the day we were supposed to play was canceled because there was a typhoon. So we flew all the way to Japan to not do a show, and then flew back to America to pick up on Lollapalooza again.

GIZZ BUTT The craziest thing that happened was that this guy from our management company flew over to the US for one of the dates, it might have been in Dallas. We'd done a good gig, and then he mentioned something to Keith [Flint, Prodigy singer] about a piece in the *Daily Mail*, which is a big paper in the UK. And in this piece, it sort of claimed that Keith is just a big softie, that he's a pussycat who enjoys cooking and bird-watching and interior design, and that he failed academically. And there was a school photo of Keith from around eleven years old. To top it off, there was also a photo of his house where he lived at that time. And this guy from management was telling this story to Keith, and he was laughing. He just kept saying, "Oh, man, it was *fucking wicked*."

MISCHA TEMPLE Generally speaking, the Prodigy were kind of anti-rock stars. But Keith was on the cover of *Rolling Stone* magazine and everybody wanted to talk to him, so that can't *not* affect you.

GIZZ BUTT I was overhearing this, and Keith was just kind of taking it in. But you could see this volcano about to erupt, because what had happened was an invasion of his privacy and they'd tried to make him look foolish. And Keith just fucking exploded, you know? When he was back at the hotel, there was screaming and, like, smashing. It was bloody awful. The next time we saw Keith, he looked like he was ready to murder everyone. That guy was fired from management straight away.

4 "ALLEGEDLY, THEY DREW GUNS ON HIM"

JAMES "MUNKY" SHAFFER (guitarist, Korn) Snoop's security detail and a few of our security guys grew up together in the same neighborhood. So those guys would start hanging out, we would start hanging out, and then it was just two camps that effortlessly merged together because of mutual friends.

JONATHAN DAVIS (singer, Korn) I hung out with those fools all the time. I befriended them all. They thought I was the craziest white boy they'd ever seen. I'd just come hang out and I'd fuck with Snoop. Not disrespectful or anything. But that first time I met him, he was cool as fuck.

KEN ANDREWS (singer, guitarist, Failure) The Nation of Islam was doing his security. They were all wearing suits. They were all like, not bright colors, but they weren't black suits; they were like gold and green. They had a look. And they were strapped.

STEVE "CHOPPER" BORGES (production manager, Lollapalooza 1993–97) He had the guys in the suits with the guns, and they just lined from his dressing room to the stage. They were on both sides. And they never hardly said a word. It was a little bit uncomfortable for us.

GARY GRAFF (music writer, *Detroit Free Press*) Hip-hop by that time had become dangerous. The murders of Tupac and Biggie had both happened within the last year, and most anybody of prominence in the rap world at that time wondered if they didn't have a target on them. It wasn't just Snoop.

JONATHAN DAVIS Snoop had his armored van he was pulling behind his bus.

GERALD CASALE (bassist, singer, Devo) It was a modified panel van, without windows except where, you know, you want windows, like the front window. And it had been plated on the inside and upholstered, and there were these little viewing holes you could peek out of, or presumably put a gun barrel out of. It was impressive.

MISCHA TEMPLE (lighting director, the Prodigy) I remember one day he turned up and there was this kind of ruckus around the armored van. Some sort of security thing had gone off in it and they couldn't open the door, so Snoop was stuck inside it. They had to call the manufacturer of this fucking thing and work out how to open it. It was like a full-on *Spinal Tap* thing. He was in there for a little while and finally, they got it open.

GERALD CASALE These guys were taking their daily reality on the Lollapalooza tour.

STEVE "CHOPPER" BORGES I forget where we were, but Snoop's main personal guy flew back to L.A. on a day off, and he got capped and killed. So it was real.

TIM BOOTH (singer, James) We now understood what the armored car was about.

JAMES "MUNKY" SHAFFER A couple of times, it was like, "Ooh, get ready, shit's gonna happen." And they'd rush him back to his bus or something. But nothing ever did.

MISCHA TEMPLE When Snoop was on, all the techs setting up other bands' gear behind the backdrop would disappear from the stage. Because they said, "We don't want to be upstage when the bullets come through the fucking backdrop."

JAMES "MUNKY" SHAFFER We never felt threatened by anything or anybody for having him there. Having him there was exciting, because it was so different. And seeing everybody rock out to Snoop Dogg every night was so much fun.

BEN KWELLER (singer, guitarist, Radish) We would watch Snoop every night. His setup was the best—a bodyguard on each side, just kind of standing there, a DJ, and I think one hype man. And it was the same show every fucking night, but it never got old. He'd go, "It's time for a motherfucking smoke break," and the crowd would go wild. He'd pull a big-ass blunt out of his pocket, and then he'd be searching his other pocket and be like, "Shit—anybody got a lighter?" And thousands of lighters would get thrown at him. Then he'd be like, "Goddamn, hold up!" He'd light his blunt and he'd say, "It's time for a motherfucking moment of silence." And he'd just stand there. It was just the funniest shit. People loved it.

GERALD CASALE I just couldn't believe the way he moved these crowds to saying stuff. Like, *"Do the ladies run this muthafucka?"* Over and over, you know? And of course, these girls with all their tattoos are screaming, *"Yeah! We run this muthafucka!"*

BEN KWELLER On the last show that we played, one of the women who worked on the second stage came up to us and said, "Hey, boys, we've got something special for you. We've arranged a meeting with Snoop." So we fucking roll to the backstage area, past the armed guards with machine guns, and into the dressing room. You can't even see anything—it's just a cloud of smoke. We're walking toward the back of the room, and Snoop emerges and is like, "What up?" I don't even know what we talked about. We were just these young Texans. And we got our photo with him and we fucking threw the West Coast shit. So we're hanging, and then all of a sudden this other dude pops through the cloud and he's like, "What's up? I'm Snoop Dad!" And it was Snoop's daddy, bro. So now we're hanging with Snoop and his father, and my dad's there, too. And my dad's a doctor, so Snoop's dad is talking to him about his ailments and shit, and my dad's diagnosing him in a cloud of pot smoke.

STEVE "CHOPPER" BORGES My stage manager, RT, Randy Townsend, was kind of a biker dude and an ex-marine who had done two tours in Vietnam. A very bright guy who has since passed. His girlfriend was the head of catering and did all the catering stuff in the dressing rooms. She was kind of a groover and a free spirit, and she got in with all the bands. She really liked rap, and one day something went wrong—she was a little too spontaneous about something and one of the guys in Snoop's crew gave her a backhand, like, "You're shooting your mouth in the wrong spot there." That didn't go over well. The next day, Randy knocked on the door of Snoop's bus and walked on with a claw hammer. And those guys had guns and shit. I heard about it and went, "Randy, come on, man. You've gotta get out of here."

TIM BOOTH Allegedly, they drew guns on him. And then the next day he was fired.

STEVE "CHOPPER" BORGES Snoop lived in a fog of weed and he smoked almost nonstop, but he was really smart. And I had a long sit-down with him. I said, "Look, we need to get through this." And he goes, "I know what happened. I know it's the guy's girlfriend. I get it, but that's never a solution." And I said, "You're absolutely right. My guy was wrong." Randy actually had to go home for a couple of days. We just said, "You need to go home. Pull out for a couple days." That was hard, because he was my main guy. He ran all those risers on and off, and this and that and the other thing. And so, between me and my site coordinator, we had to step into that breach.

5 "WE WERE STILL ALWAYS GOING TO BE THESE OUTCASTS"

KRISTEN WORDEN-HARRIS (artist liaison, second stage, Lollapalooza 1995–97) In '97, I feel like the side stage was so much better than the main stage. Like, we crushed it.

RHETT MILLER (singer, guitarist, Old 97's) I think that the folks working at Lollapalooza probably felt a lot more kinship with the second-stage artists. In a lot of ways, we were the kind of artists that typified what Lollapalooza was about to them. Kind of up-and-coming, more sort of the hardworking indie-rocker types rather than the Korns and maybe Tools, and certainly the Snoops of the world, who were more entitled rock stars.

KRISTEN WORDEN-HARRIS It very much felt like we were in our own world. At least from my perspective, it felt like so much more of a community than the main stage.

RHETT MILLER God, man, we were so excited. We'd gone to all the Lollapaloozas in the years prior. I remember seeing Beck in Dallas and he was so young and nervous and awkward and great. It felt like something that was supposed to be happening; as we were becoming a major-label band, we go on Lollapalooza.

KEN BETHEA (guitarist, Old 97's) By the time we got on Lollapalooza, everybody had been telling us for a couple of years while we were being courted by all the major labels that we were going to be huge, so of course, we believed it a little.

RHETT MILLER I think we all envisioned something much grander than what the side stage on Lollapalooza wound up being. But it really was a great vibe. It gave me a sense that despite the fact that we were entering the major-label world, we were still always going to be these outcasts or outsiders. There wasn't some silk smoking jacket presentation and now we're on the inside and everybody treats us like rock stars. No, we were just these nobodies that were lucky to be there.

KEN BETHEA It's a different world to be on the second stage than the first stage. I promise you that all the second-stagers we were with, we always felt like we were the Not Ready for Prime Time Players. We thought, Well, we don't deserve to be over there. But it was nice.

KRISTEN WORDEN-HARRIS Our crowds were great.

E (singer, guitarist, keyboardist, Eels) We were the headliners of the second stage for the first half of the tour, so we always had a good crowd. And it was really fun, because we were on at the same time that Snoop Dogg was on the main stage, and he was really loud and he was overpowering us at times. On that tour I had a telephone sitting on my electric piano that I would use as a microphone for some songs, and I used to pick it up and act like I was calling Snoop on the main stage. And I would say, "Snoop, could you turn it down just a notch? How about you let me be the Doggfather this year?"

BEN KWELLER (singer, guitarist, Radish) E was a guy who'd be leaning against the van reading *The New Yorker*. He rarely spoke to anyone, but he was very kind to me on Lollapalooza, because I was just this young, eager, hungry rocker kid that should have been out on the lawn watching the music. But I was playing the side stage, you know what I mean? I was a fan *and* an artist.

JEFF LILLES (performer, Cottonmouth, Texas) I remember walking into the production office one day and Rhett was yelling at his agent, saying,

"Get us off this thing! Every time we start playing, Korn starts playing and we lose our audience!"

RHETT MILLER We did feel lucky to be there, despite the fact that most days we were playing to pretty much nobody. And then if anybody did wander over, it would be these kind of white-boy, dreadlock, gross, whatever-kind-of-looking dudes. They hated us and they would flip us off and they'd make fun of us and they'd call us the F slur for gay and it was just like, "Man, okay, you can make it to the top, but they're still going to throw things at you."

BEN KWELLER We definitely got really good at performing. We knew what songs really worked for us; because when you're an opener, which is essentially what we were on the side stage, your job is to just sort of engage people and have them give a shit about what you're doing. We knew what worked if you didn't know who the fuck we were.

MARC GEIGER (agent; cofounder, Lollapalooza) Perry came back in '97 and he begrudgingly played with Porno for Pyros, because Lollapalooza was a vehicle and he'd gotten electronic and hip-hop on the tour.

JEFF LILLES Porno for Pyros played in this tent called the BrainForest that I was also performing in three times a day. The tent held about two hundred fifty, three hundred people, so it was really stripped down, and they didn't have a full back line. The way that room was configured, the stage space was in the middle of the tent, and people would walk in a circle around the stage while you were performing. And there was probably a half dozen or so other kind of performance artists and dance people and trapeze artists, that kind of thing. They were dressed in really elaborate costumes and shit.

SPIN (September, 1997) *Not even a bare-chested Farrell could take the poorly ventilated sauna for long: Porno for Pyros' unannounced acoustic set lasted only four songs, after which everyone stumbled out into the 95-degree sunlight to cool off. Somehow, a multimillion-dollar extravaganza couldn't manage to pull off an attraction that any two-bit rave impresario could have planned in her sleep.*

KEN BETHEA Tricky's show was him facing the drummer with his arms out and vibrating, and it was at three o'clock in the afternoon. There was no light show. I never met him, but I understand why he wasn't having any fun. It was the wrong bill. It just didn't really translate.

E I knew Tricky because we had done some shows with him in Europe and he was an Eels fan. We were always trying to record together on his bus during Lollapalooza. Tricky was also quite flaky, I guess you'd say. To the point where one day, he just disappeared off the tour. We got promoted from the headliner slot on the second stage to Tricky's slot on the main stage, and we probably only did three or four shows, but it went really well. Then Korn, who was also a main-stage act and who were playing before us, got pissed off and gave Lollapalooza an ultimatum. They said, "If the Eels get to play on the main stage we're quitting." It was ridiculous.

KEN BETHEA They acted like total little bitches and folded their arms and said they shan't perform. "We're not performing before a second-stage band." This kind of drama would leak down to us on the second stage, and we'd be like, "Oh, man, did you hear? Korn has said, 'We shan't perform in front of a stupid second-stage band.'"

STUART ROSS (tour director, Lollapalooza) Korn came in and said, "No, we want somebody else." And they caused a fucking stink. Management got involved and agents got involved, and it was just nasty. And at the end of the day, here's the punch line: When Eels figured out that they weren't getting that slot after all, they went to Korn and said, "Dude, what the fuck?" And Korn blamed me, even though it was their decision. So I'm in the bus and E and his tour manager want to talk to me, and they come in and they're really fucking worked up. And I said, "This was Korn's decision, not mine. We were great with this." And they said, "Nope. Korn said they had nothing to do with it, and it was your decision."

E I thought it was petty, but whatever. We got booted back to the second stage because of Korn.

KEN BETHEA This was back in the day when those SST Records stickers that said "Corporate Rock Sucks" were everywhere. So someone found the font that Korn used—that crooked-letter stuff—and they made a backward *K* and printed up all these flyers that said "Korporate rock sucks" in the Korn font, and stuck them all over the backstage areas. Which was really funny, since every band on the tour, including us, was a corporate-rock band.

6 "I WAS NEVER ONE OF THESE COOL DRUG ADDICTS"

KEN ANDREWS (singer, guitarist, Failure) I don't know if I ever got the official word, but it was pretty freaking obvious that Tool put us on the tour.

KRISTEN WORDEN-HARRIS (artist liaison, second stage, Lollapalooza 1995–97) Failure were supertight with Tool. Danny Carey would have these parties in his loft, and they were always there.

GREG EDWARDS (guitarist, bassist, Failure) We had done a lot of touring with Tool. A theater-size tour of the US with the Flaming Lips and Tool, and a relatively small tour through France and Spain a year and a half before or something. So being on Lollapalooza just seemed like an extension of the touring we had already done. Anyway, that's how I remember it.

MAYNARD JAMES KEENAN (singer, Tool) We were trying to get people to go see Failure.

KEN ANDREWS Tool gave us the best slot. Not only because we were closing the second stage, but because there was no music really happening on the main stage when we played and that was a huge advantage for us. We were between whoever was before Tool and Tool. And since Tool had the longest set change, because they had more lights and production and stuff, our set basically fit inside of that entire set change. And the people who were there watching us were only there because we were playing. After the band who was before us finished, all the people piled in.

GREG EDWARDS We had this crazy bus driver who brought his wife on the bus. All of a sudden, there was this woman on the bus when I got up in the middle of the night. It was his wife, and she was just gonna travel. Our management said no to him, so he took off with the bus and all of our equipment and drove like one hundred fifty miles away from whatever venue we were at for one of these very early shows.

Then he finally came back, and we got our equipment back, but he took off and we had to find a bus to continue on the tour. The only bus we could find that was available had been Aerosmith's bus in the late seventies through the early eighties. It was all blue crushed velvet and was about two-thirds the size of a modern Prevost bus. And it still said "Aerosmith" on the little marquee above the driver's cab of the bus. It just felt like you could feel the things that had happened in that bus. The ghosts of those things were still there.

KRISTEN WORDEN-HARRIS The main-stage bands were always coming over to see our bands. I was super proud of that.

KEN ANDREWS Actually it's a bit nerve-racking, because it's a lot when all your peers are watching you. I mean, especially if you're the low band on the totem pole and you haven't really proven yourself with a lot of success or notoriety. This has always been something about our band—we always have a lot of bands watching us. But Lollapalooza '97 was insane. I mean, there were times where on the second stage I would look out and it would just be like big band, big band, big band watching us play. If you're a little insecure or if you lack some confidence and you do have a drug issue already in effect, it can push you over.

GREG EDWARDS I was flying through that period. I was heavily self-medicated, and Lollapalooza was the beginning of the steep slope to the bottom.

KEN ANDREWS Greg was strung out on heroin. And so, having said everything I've already said about being excited about the tour, the reality was that during the tour, I became convinced that the band was over because he was barely functioning by the time Lollapalooza ended. Barely getting to the stage, barely getting through the sets.

GREG EDWARDS I just wasn't even there. I was a ghost.

MONICA SEIDE-EVENSON (publicist, Warner Bros. Records) As far as I know, those of us working with the band weren't privy to the depth of their internal problems.

KEN ANDREWS Steven Baker, who was the president of Warner Bros. at the time, came backstage when we had just finished our set and he's like, "Hey, can we talk for a minute?" I go, "Yeah, of course." He was basically saying, "Look, you've toured on your album *Fantastic Planet* for six or nine months and we made some headway, but we don't want to promote this record anymore. We want to put you guys back in the studio." And as he was telling me this, I see something over his shoulder off in the distance. I look over and it's Greg, doing a drug deal over the fence. Literally handing money over for a bag of smack. And Steven's literally asking me to make another Failure record. I didn't sleep that night because I didn't know what was going to happen. It just didn't seem feasible that we'd be able to make another record.

GREG EDWARDS I've heard Ken tell that story to someone else and I just don't think that's true at all. That's just not how I was getting it; I had a whole system of procurement that was based at home here in L.A. And I didn't have a crazy-heavy habit—I was maintaining and self-medicating for anxiety and depression. So for me, the main thing was to have it and know that I was covered for a few weeks down the line. I was never one of these cool drug addicts who was very resourceful and good at networking. I always looked at that in awe. So maybe it was something else. Maybe someone was passing a sandwich over to me.

KEN ANDREWS After the tour was over I made some attempts to try to get Greg into rehab, talked with his parents. He wasn't ready. The band broke up right after Lollapalooza, in September of '97.

7 "HE WAS DOUBLED UP IN PAIN"

JAMES "MUNKY" SHAFFER (guitarist, Korn) When we played on Randall's Island in New York, there was so much dust everywhere, it was so hot, everybody was dehydrated. It was just so chaotic. I feel like I might have gotten something at that point, and then the following shows I started not feeling great. I was having these headaches and vomiting very violently. A migraine headache that was just like, I have to be in the dark. I had to wear sunglasses onstage, and I couldn't really rock out with the rest of the guys. It was frustrating.

JONATHAN DAVIS (singer, Korn) I knew it was bad when I heard Munky crying in the bus bathroom, saying, "Just kill me. Kill me, please." He was in so much pain.

STUART ROSS (tour director, Lollapalooza) Clearly, I'm not somebody who can diagnose illnesses. But when he came onto the bus he was not feeling well, and he was doubled up in pain. And I remember going to their manager and their tour manager and saying, "Get him to the hospital right now. This is not right. He can't perform." And we had to go through a bunch of shit, but he got taken to the hospital, and diagnosed appropriately.

JAMES "MUNKY" SHAFFER Peter Katsis came out on the road and he was like, "We've got to get this guy to the hospital." I'm just laid up in the bed in the bus very sick, and nobody really knows. We thought I just had a flu or something. After the Cleveland show at the Blossom Music Center, they took me to the hospital and did a spinal tap, and realized that I had meningitis.

JONATHAN DAVIS We got the word that he was gravely ill. He had viral meningitis and his brain was swelling and it was not good. Of course, we were all super worried, and that's when we hopped off the tour.

JAMES "MUNKY" SHAFFER I felt so bad, not only for being sick, but there was a lot of guilt because this was such a big tour for us to be on. I wanted the guys to continue on the tour, but they didn't feel right doing it without me, so it was worrying me. I remember the doctor was like, "The anxiousness is not helping, all your symptoms are worse."

JONATHAN DAVIS I think at the time, Tool's guitar player offered to fill in, but we were like, "No, that's not going to work. We should just go home."

PETER KATSIS (manager, Korn) Everybody was saying that no matter who they picked, guitar-player-wise, that even if they could play the parts and the detuned seven-string madness, that the energy was not likely to be the same. So it seemed like we just couldn't do it.

JAMES "MUNKY" SHAFFER This is before anyone in our camp had cell phones. The guys in the band would call my hospital room and be like, "Hey, how're you feeling? We miss you." They mentioned that for a few shows, Maynard stopped in the middle of Tool's set and had a prayer moment for me. Which was very cool to hear, because it's a serious illness and you never know how it's going to turn out.

KEN ANDREWS (singer, guitarist, Failure) I just remember our manager calling and saying, "You guys go to bed early tonight. You have to be up because the bus is going to be driving you into the grounds early because you have to play first on the main stage—and you're still head-lining the second stage." I don't completely understand why they just didn't bring in a different, bigger act to fill Korn's slot. But I'm guessing it was just money. Like, Korn was getting a certain amount of money and they were probably like, "Hey, now we don't have to pay that for the rest of the tour. Failure's already here, we'll just give them half or something and we'll save some money." I'm pretty sure Tool also probably said, "Give it to Failure, they're already here." But I have to say, just in hindsight, that that was a cool moment for us. It was one of the few times I felt the band had been recognized by the touring industry as somewhat important.

MONICA SEIDE-EVENSON (publicist, Warner Bros. Records) When Failure were moved from headlining the second stage to playing the main stage as well, everyone working with them thought this was *the* moment for the band. It was coming on the heels of the "Stuck on You" video and a fair amount of radio play, so it seemed like a natural progression, and recognition that Failure was moving into more mainstream, for lack of a better word, awareness.

KEN ANDREWS The Lollapalooza production team would commandeer four flatbed golf carts for us every day. And they gave us two or three stagehands to help our crew ferry our equipment, because our equipment never actually rode with us once they asked us to do the main stage—it rode on the main-stage trucks. By the fourth or fifth show, our crew were over it. They were just like, "This sucks for us." I mean, it was a lot more work because not only did they have to do the whole show twice, but at the end of the second show, when we finished the second stage, instead of just loading right into our trailer where our bus was parked behind the second stage, they had to get those fricking utility golf carts again, pack all the gear up, and drive it back over to the main stage to put it all back on the main-stage trucks for the next day. I remember them just moaning about that every day.

GREG EDWARDS Because we were now doing two performances, it was, um, a bit of a challenge to work out being at the proper "level" of my intake to account for both shows.

KEN ANDREWS I don't believe there was ever an announcement or any advertising that had us playing early on the main stage. So, essentially, we were just playing to people who were fans of the main-stage acts, which was great. It was a chance to make new fans, but it was much more chill. It was so early in the day that it didn't feel super rock 'n' roll. But we were still playing to roughly double what we would play to on the second stage.

MONICA SEIDE-EVENSON They imploded not that long after that, and I remember thinking at the time what a lost opportunity it was.

8 "A TEPID SUCCESS"

DAN CHOI (front-of-house coordinator, Lollapalooza 1994–97, 2003)
When you look at ticket sales for '97, you can tell that the lineup wasn't about all that much of anything. Lollapalooza used to be a slam dunk, and now it was a struggle to just sell some tickets.

ADAM SCHNEIDER (concourse creative director, Lollapalooza 1997) I think '97 was . . . a tepid success. But it was successful. I don't think it was *un*successful. I do think the musical lineup was kind of weak compared to other years.

DAN CHOI Honestly, Lollapalooza was always cool because it was kind of new. Ninety-one to '94 it was like, "Okay, what are they gonna do next?" Then '95, I felt like there was a big let-down in terms of things just not really coming out that well. Ninety-six, they tried to revive it with the big metal deal and were vaguely successful, but not terribly. I think they lost a lot of the audience there, too, because people were like, "Well, I'm not going to a Metallica show." So we get to '97 and they're thinking, Okay, back to the roots. But the fact is, there were no roots left. There wasn't anything exciting to show people.

ADAM SCHNEIDER Ninety-seven wasn't a deal-killer. There could've been a '98.

STUART ROSS (tour director, Lollapalooza) We were absolutely talking about it. After the '97 tour, I was on another tour and I remember Peter

Grosslight said, "We've got to get you off this tour. We need to start working on '98."

MARC GEIGER (agent; cofounder, Lollapalooza) I wasn't involved, but that was nothing I ever heard of.

GARY GRAFF (music writer, *Detroit Free Press*) I felt like we'd be seeing Lollapalooza in '98 and that it would continue to go on. But certainly, the profile had changed, and it had a lot more competition, probably more with H.O.R.D.E. and Lilith Fair than anything else. Lollapalooza was the granddaddy of them all, but the daylong festival experience was not the unique thing that it was in 1991.

STEVE "CHOPPER" BORGES (production manager, Lollapalooza 1993–97) Nineteen ninety-seven didn't feel like it was the last year. We said—and Perry was even there—"Let's bring Jane's back and put them up at the top of the bill; it's time." Because they were very strong by that time.

ADAM SCHNEIDER I was the booking agent for Porno for Pyros during the *Good God's Urge* period. And that led into Dave Navarro joining the band for the Howard Stern *Private Parts* thing. [In 1997, Navarro, along with the Red Hot Chili Peppers' Flea, recorded the Porno for Pyros song "Hard Charger," which appeared on the soundtrack to Stern's 1997 film, *Private Parts*]. Then at the Howard Stern video shoot, they came up to me and said, "Adam, we're putting Jane's Addiction back together. Would you like to manage it?" And we did the Relapse tour at the end of '97. Ted was already gone by this point.

TED GARDNER (manager, Jane's Addiction; cofounder, Lollapalooza) My conversations were totally with William Morris. And they said it was a wish of Perry's to have Jane's headline Lollapalooza.

STEVE "CHOPPER" BORGES Just as we were getting started, I think something happened with Perry . . . and that was it.

DAVE NAVARRO (guitarist, Jane's Addiction) How about a Plan B? I mean, you're talking about a couple of guys with a history of drug addiction and canceling shows.

ROLLING STONE (April 3, 1998) *Once thought to be an impregnable franchise, the seven-year-old summer festival was unable to secure enough upper-echelon acts, so it won't rock out at all. This year, a handful of prominent modern rockers like Jane's Addiction, Green Day, Garbage, the Foo Fighters, Marilyn Manson and Radiohead turned down headlining slots. Jane's waffled about their decision for four months, reportedly holding up the recruitment process, before ultimately declining the offer.*

TED GARDNER We just couldn't put the key headlining act together.

GARY BONGIOVANNI (editor, *Pollstar* magazine) Obviously, they were not comfortable with the talent they had and rather than fall on their sword, they decided not to do it.

MARC GEIGER Ultimately, Lollapalooza led to such a mainstreaming of the movement that by '96, '97, you couldn't sustain the edge. That happens in every musical genre when it gets that popular. I don't care what it is. So, in some ways, that's the answer for why Lolla took a break. It didn't feel good at that time presenting what was seen as the edges that weren't the edges.

MTV.COM (April 3, 1998) *After weeks of rampant speculation and conjecture about the likelihood of the granddaddy of alternative-rock festivals getting it together in time for the highly competitive summer package-tour season, Lolla cofounder Ted Gardner said Friday simply, "There won't be a tour."*

STUART ROSS And then, Lollapalooza just kind of faded away.

EPILOGUE

In the wake of the 1997 tour's shaky performance and 1998's failure to launch, Lollapalooza was mothballed indefinitely. Cofounders Marc Geiger and Don Muller focused their efforts on keeping their sprawling online music venture ARTISTdirect afloat, while Farrell pursued a solo career and turned his attention to global activism, championing issues like debt relief for developing countries and working with organizations helping to free enslaved people in Sudan.

Jane's Addiction, meanwhile, with Red Hot Chili Peppers' Flea on bass, had embarked on a short reunion tour in 1997 that quickly fizzled out. In 2001, Farrell resurrected the band once again, this time to headline the Coachella Valley Music and Arts Festival. The destination event in Indio, California, premiered in 1999 as a two-day affair, and got off to a rocky start despite appearances by Tool, Beck, Morrissey, and Farrell himself as a solo act. "It wasn't very big, maybe twenty thousand people came each day, and it was a financial disaster. A lot of people didn't get paid, or it took a really long time to get paid," says Lollapalooza tour director Stuart Ross, who had assumed the role of festival director for the fledgling event. After taking the next year off, Coachella's organizers, Goldenvoice (who would soon be acquired by AEG), decided to try again, and Farrell helped out by offering his band as a headliner—a successful move that jump-started what would become a Coachella tradition of booking once-dormant-but-now-reunited big-name acts in the top slot. For 2001, the Jane's-led event was scaled back to a single day, and Farrell reportedly deferred his band's appearance fee in order to help Coachella's organizers navigate a financial rough patch.

Jane's Addiction continued to tour following their Coachella performance, and also began work on *Strays*, a new album helmed by Kiss and Pink Floyd producer Bob Ezrin. Discussions about how to promote the record, ultimately released in July 2003, led ineluctably to one place. "Jane's tried to come back big, and Lollapalooza was the vehicle," Geiger says of the band's 2003 headline turn on the resurrected fest. Jane's manager at the time, Adam Schneider, argues that the return of the festival was not necessarily a linchpin of the band's promotional plan. "I think the idea to do Lollapalooza in 2003 was an organic, logical thing," he says. "We made *Strays* with Bob Ezrin, we were touring all over the world, and we were funding the record through the money we were making doing gigs. We were doing it by ourselves, and we had our hands full making a great record. As much as Lollapalooza was a plan, it wasn't a sure thing, because we'd still be relying on other bands to make it happen. We would have done a record and toured it either way."

In fact, Farrell and Schneider, in tandem with the William Morris Agency, were able to secure a solid, if not particularly cutting-edge, lineup for the fest. Second on the bill behind Jane's was Audioslave, the new supergroup consisting of three-quarters of Rage Against the Machine fronted by former Soundgarden vocalist Chris Cornell. Sun-kissed SoCal nu-metalists Incubus played third from the top, preceded by desert-riff cultists Queens of the Stone Age for most of the summer before A Perfect Circle, featuring erstwhile Tool front man Maynard James Keenan, stepped in for the final week. Alternative hip-hop vets Jurassic 5 came next, followed by all-female rock revivalists the Donnas. Kicking off the proceedings were Los Angeles power-poppers Rooney and, sometimes, Australian gutter-punk crew the Distillers. On the second stage, *Jackass* star Steve-O took top billing with a set of gross-out antics, and was joined by post-hardcore musos Cave-In, garage rockers the Mooney Suzuki, actor Jared Leto's Thirty Seconds to Mars, and others.

Also making an appearance in 2003 was the sort of high-visibility corporate sponsorship that Farrell had shunned in the first incarnation of Lollapalooza, with Microsoft's gaming platform Xbox and mobile carrier Verizon underwriting the tour. "Both Lollapalooza and Xbox draw on the same key audience of 16–24 year-olds (Gen Y), making the Xbox sponsorship and strong presence at Lollapalooza venues an added value to the festival experience," read a 2003 Microsoft press release. Verizon, for its part, crowed in its own PR, "This 2003 tour is one of the most exciting young adult events of the year and provides an incredible venue where we can interact with one of our most important market segments."

Even with noticeable changes, as well as increased competition from now-established traveling-festival offspring like Warped and Ozzfest, Lollapalooza 2003 was successful enough that a 2004 tour was soon in the works, this time with a twist: Each stop on the itinerary would see two shows on separate days, one topped by former Smiths front man Morrissey and another by jam-rockers String Cheese Incident. A bold idea, but one that floundered badly at the box office. Lollapalooza 2004 was canceled in June of that year, shortly before the tour was to begin.

"We made a bet on some jam bands for the first time with String Cheese Incident, and that was a bad bet and didn't work," says Geiger, who had by then returned to William Morris and was once again working on the festival. "The year before, it was rock. This was a little hippie-ish; it wasn't rock."

There were other forces at play: Along with the aforementioned Coachella, by 2004 destination fests like Austin City Limits, Bonnaroo, and the Sasquatch! Music Festival, hosted at longtime Pacific Northwest Lollapalooza venue the Gorge, had taken hold. And by all accounts, the 2004 summer concert season was soft at the box office, with high-profile reunions from the likes of Van Halen and

Simon & Garfunkel struggling to fill venues. "The music was changing, too," Schneider suggests. "You weren't dealing with Nirvana and Soundgarden and Alice in Chains anymore. Alternative was turning into frat rock."

Whatever the cause, Lollapalooza 2004 "was puked on by the public," Geiger says. "They hated it for whatever reason. It went on sale, it didn't do well, and we canceled it. It was a very tough decision."

Farrell, for his part, told *The San Diego Union-Tribune* he was "hugely embarrassed" by the fiasco, which left many bands involved with the fest scrambling to salvage their summers. It was at this low point that Farrell and his partners were contacted by the organizers of Austin City Limits, who were expanding their live music footprint and wanted to use the Lollapalooza name for a destination festival, ultimately held in Chicago's Grant Park. Relaunched in 2005, Lollapalooza continues at this location to this day, drawing hundreds of thousands of attendees every summer. Global versions of the festival can be found in locales as far-flung as Chile, India, and France, and the brand partners with numerous environmental organizations to be a leader in furthering eco-friendly education, sustainability, and conservation initiatives. The alternative-music universe that boomed alongside Lollapalooza in the 1990s may no longer be a mainstream cultural concern, but Lollapalooza the brand, admittedly in radically different form, has survived and thrived—an outcome that likely no one involved with planning the first festival in 1991 could have envisioned.

Well, almost no one. "I'm probably the one guy who would say, 'Yes, I knew it would be this massive,'" Geiger says. "When I saw what it became in history, I remember telling Perry: 'You don't understand, we have the Super Bowl. The Super Bowl doesn't die.'"

1 "AMAZING ILLEGAL CHEESE"

DAN CHOI (front-of-house coordinator, Lollapalooza 1994–97, 2003) Lollapalooza was definitely a different animal in '03.

PERRY FARRELL We had a five-year hiatus and what we did was take a rest. It's never a bad idea to take a rest, especially when you're exhausted—think about things and re-strategize and wait for the perfect wave.

DANNY ZELISKO (promoter, Evening Star Productions) I think the break that Lollapalooza took between 1997 and 2003 actually helped create the legend that it became, because it was shelved for a little while and it was rethought. And then, when they came back with it, it was a big deal. The spirit was still there. There were some tweaks and so forth, but overall it was just a continuation of an already good idea.

DAN CHOI Teamwise, Ted Gardner wasn't there. Stuart wasn't there. Marc and Don weren't really around. The driving people were Adam Schneider, who managed Perry, Michael Abrams, who was sort of the money person, and Paul Chavarria, who was more of the actual tour director. And William Morris was always happy to run that flag up one more time and see what happened.

ADAM SCHNEIDER (former manager, Jane's Addiction, Porno for Pyros, Perry Farrell; producer, Lollapalooza 2003) I was Perry's manager, and obviously William Morris was a huge part of it. But working with Perry and bringing in the corporate partners, that was a huge thing. The linchpin to the festival was bringing in Michael Kassan, who procured sponsorships with Verizon and Xbox. We had an area called the Mind Field, and we integrated the technology, specifically with gaming.

DAN CHOI With Xbox, there was another separate tent entirely called GameRiot. A team came on the tour and we would supply them with a space and some labor and forklifts or whatever they needed. They would install this tent and put a bunch of video games in it. And they were connected to the internet, I believe.

ADAM SCHNEIDER We were leaders that year in that lean-in interactive space of using cell phones and text messaging to create a gamification overlay to the festival. We had fans voting on which song a band should play for an encore by texting.

CLAUDETTE SILVER (political-tent organizer, Lollapalooza 2003) Or we'd come up with questions, like, "Which is the first country that has committed to becoming an economy run entirely off of alternative fuels by 2015?" You could pick a multiple-choice answer—Germany, the United States, Iceland, whoever—and then text it with your little T9. And "x" number of people who got it right would get a prize.

DAN CHOI Perry was pretty resistant to sponsorship as a concept, so I think there was a lot of back-and-forth about that.

DANNY ZELISKO Sponsorships were already becoming a way of life back then. Now, everything that moves has a logo on it. But at that time those things were new to the culture, and it fit in.

ADAM SCHNEIDER It wasn't sponsorship from Coke, Pepsi, and a credit card company. It was a cell phone company and a video game company that we literally embedded into the festival experience. So we were ahead of the curve. We were the first to recognize the importance of mobile gaming and video gaming as part of the music-festival experience.

DAN CHOI At some point I think Perry felt like he just wanted to play music, basically.

ADAM SCHNEIDER Having Perry reaching out to the artists, and getting Audioslave, was also huge. In real estate, it's "location, location, location." For a festival like this, it's "talent, talent, talent."

TOM MORELLO (guitarist, Rage Against the Machine, Audioslave) Perry and I went way back, all the way to L.A. in the eighties. For guys who had peed in a lot of Hollywood alleys together and weathered the storm fairly unscathed, it was a nice sort of celebratory go-round.

BILLY HOWERDEL (guitar tech, Fishbone, 1991, 1993; guitar tech, Smashing Pumpkins, 1994; guitarist, A Perfect Circle) I had a lot of history with Lollapalooza. Fishbone took over for Nine Inch Nails for the last few shows of Lollapalooza in 1991, which I was there for, and they did the whole tour in '93 and I did that run as well. Then in 2003, I'm on the tour with my own band. Emotionally, it was a big time for A Perfect Circle. We had had a good friend of ours—our bass player Paz's little brother, who was basically my assistant—pass away, and that was kind of a nasty beginning to the rollout of our record *Thirteenth Step*. But Lollapalooza was an amazing kickoff to the whole tour, and the clouds parted from there.

STEVE KNOPPER (editor at large, *Billboard* magazine) There were a lot of repeat performers who had done the tour before. But by 2003 we're looking at a new generation of bands as well, and there were musicians on the stage who had actually grown up going to Lollapalooza as fans.

BRANDON BOYD (singer, Incubus) I saw the '92 and '93 tours when I was a teenager and it blew my mind. I grew up relatively sheltered in a very rural part of Los Angeles—I didn't hang out in the city, I wasn't in Hollywood—and it was the first time I saw people with piercings and lots of tattoos. It was the first time I saw activism about social causes. I went with Mikey [Einziger, guitarist] and José [Pasillas, drummer], and we had just started Incubus the year before. I remember losing both of them in the mosh pit at one point.

MIKE EINZIGER (guitarist, Incubus) That first Lollapalooza we went to was at Irvine Meadows, with Soundgarden, Pearl Jam, and the Red Hot Chili Peppers, and Rage Against the Machine on the side stage. To be on a bill ten years later with some of the same artists was totally surreal.

BRANDON BOYD I'd like to give Perry a big hug and say to him, "You changed my life by setting that whole thing up."

BRETT ANDERSON (singer, the Donnas) I loved Jane's Addiction so much. When I was thirteen, I watched *Gift,* the movie Perry made about the band, probably five million times. I was like, "If only I could die of a heroin overdose, it's so romantic . . ."

TOM MORELLO There was very much a sense of camaraderie that year. I remember having philosophical conversations with the guys in Jane's Addiction, or sitting with Mike from Incubus and having him try to explain to me why Phish is great, or just hanging out on the beach with everybody.

BRANDON BOYD I think we were in Florida somewhere on a day off, and we went down to the beach with the guys from Audioslave. I'm a surfer, but on the East Coast there's not many waves, so we were just swimming and dicking around. To see Chris Cornell and Tom Morello flail around with boogie boards, it earthed them to me. They're musical gods, and then looking at them with sand coming down their face and boogers coming out of their nose and having a great time, those are the memories that really stick with me.

CLAUDETTE SILVER Some of those kids who saw Audioslave didn't necessarily know who Soundgarden was. Well, they probably knew Soundgarden, but they hadn't seen them live, because they were too young.

TOM MORELLO It was a new kind of fan. Whereas there was a real sort of desperately passionate rock fan or political fan of Rage Against the Machine, now we had these kind of really massive radio hits in Audioslave. So it was more people who loved "Like a Stone" and Chris Cornell's cheekbones.

BILLY HOWERDEL I think Audioslave were great, but it was strange to me—not in a bad way—to watch them. I guess you could equate it to your parents getting divorced and now your mom's with this new guy. And you actually really like him, but you're like, "I feel weird because he's not my dad . . . but he's funny and he's good to my mom."

TOM MORELLO It was a fine array of alternative-rock radio's favorites at the time, with Jane's Addiction now in kind of the senior emeritus role. A very different animal from the nineties, but still a fun multiband tour and a great rock show.

BRETT ANDERSON I remember Perry Farrell was nice to my mom, which was awesome. She was backstage and he was just so cordial, like, "Oh, I'm so happy you could be here. It's so great when family members can come. Are you having a good time? Who are you excited to see?" Really, he was invested in whether everyone was having a good time.

BRANDON BOYD We'd see Perry backstage and he'd be like, "Brandon, Mike . . . I got this amazing illegal cheese and this great pinot and this incredible merlot from France that I really want you to try, so come back after the show and try them with us."

PERRY FARRELL In those days, I had a good something going on with this guy who was connected to the mob. I found out that he could get unpasteurized cheese imported. The reason I mention him is every Friday, I would have a Shabbos with the best imported wine, imported meats, and unpasteurized cheeses that you could only get through the mob, you know? And then I would invite everybody to come back. We had Kings of Leon and all these young single guys and all these dancing girls back there for Shabbos.

BRANDON BOYD I've been lactose intolerant my whole life, so I don't really do cheese, but I was like, "I'd love to try these wines . . . and maybe I'll have a nibble of illegal cheese and pay for it." So we would accept. And without fail, every time we would knock on the dressing room door after the show, someone would crack it open and they'd look at us like, "What do you want?" We'd say, "Perry told us to come." And whoever was at the door would open it. And then there'd be Perry and Dave and Stephen, and sometimes Chris Cornell was in there as well. And it was as if we were walking into a very private conversation, like, "What are you guys doing here? Who invited you?" By the fourth or fifth time it happened, Chris would go, "Hey, Brandon, Mikey, come in here!" And he would pull us in and normalize it.

TOM MORELLO Every show day we had a dance party in Audioslave's dressing room right before we went onstage. And it had to be like *American Bandstand,* where there's dancers on different levels. Some people had to be on the couch. Some had to be on the table. Some had to be on the floor. Some were maybe out in the hall. There might have been forty shows on that tour, and we probably did thirty-nine dance parties.

BRETT ANDERSON In some interview at the time, Perry was like, "I got a pair of silk pajamas so that I can have a slumber party with the Donnas." It was just a funny sound bite, but reading it now I think, Oh, was that weird? But we did call our record *Spend the Night,* so, you know, he wasn't saying it to be like that. And I never felt on Lollapalooza that we were a token girl band or anything. I felt like they were very intentional about having a variety of genres, a variety of different kinds of people. It wasn't just white rockers.

ADAM SCHNEIDER It was as diverse a group as possible. And all these progressive ideas—sustainability, diversity—were embedded into 2003.

CLAUDETTE SILVER The ethos was still very much the same from 1991. The world was different, but in terms of the groups that were involved, I would say that there was definitely a thread that continued through it.

ADAM SCHNEIDER We used an acronym for every year with Lollapalooza. We call them SPAGs—Social Political Action Groups. And that had to do with anything from Greenpeace to voter registration.

TOM MORELLO Every show day I would go out to the booth for Axis of Justice, the nonprofit I started with Serj Tankian from System of a Down. We'd invite local grassroots social justice organizations, and I'd sign posters that we would sell to raise money for them. It was a great part of the tour.

CLAUDETTE SILVER Perry was really into alternative energy sources that year, and we were powering the second stage on biodiesel. And also the buses when we could. For a little while we actually carried 250-gallon totes on one of the trucks. But Perry's main thing was hydrogen, which is clear and very flammable. So I found this technology research center up in Humboldt, California, that had a portable hydrogen fuel cell, and we subsidized this kid who was an expert to come on the road with us. Every day he'd be in a tent talking to people about fuel cells. And then we would power a blender with a hydrogen fuel cell and make smoothies with it. Perry used to come out once a day, the expert would talk about hydrogen fuel cells, and Perry would drink the smoothie. Sometimes we would pass it out to the audience. It was Perry's vision, and he really let me run with it.

DAN CHOI There was an attraction called "Booty Camp" that year, which was something Perry really wanted, because it wasn't corporate, and it wasn't specifically related to a band. It was a crew of people, and they would get concertgoers to do stuff.

ADAM SCHNEIDER Booty Camp was a troupe of performers—we called them agents—and they would go up to the fans and basically punk them. Like, someone would come up to you and say, "Hey, will you sign a petition to pave the rainforest?" A little tongue-in-cheek.

CLAUDETTE SILVER How it landed, whether people got the irony, I don't know. But he definitely wanted there to be a participatory element, which is where I think something like Booty Camp, which I'd completely forgotten about, came in.

ADAM SCHNEIDER It was this overarching interactivity that was present with the artists, with technology, with gaming. It's something that Perry had been all over since the nineties. And 2003 was like the apotheosis of this idea.

2 "A FULL-ON BLOODBATH"

DAN CHOI (front-of-house coordinator, Lollapalooza 1994–97, 2003) Steve-O from *Jackass* was involved that year, which was annoying as hell.

STEVE-O (performer) I was closing the second stage. I think people enjoyed it and that it was a good fit. It drew a huge crowd and the audience was quite pleased with what they saw, because it was high-impact fucking shocking shit.

THE NEW YORK TIMES (July 7, 2003) *Lollapalooza also accepted the frat-party sensibility of rock radio and MTV. Steve-O, who has his own MTV stunt show,* Jackass, *made an appearance, using a staple gun on his genitals.*

STEVE-O The whole idea of my tour back then was to express to the audience that my experience with being on television had led me to become very well acquainted with the rules of what cannot be shown on MTV. And my performance on the stage would be to systematically demonstrate what cannot be performed on MTV.

JEFF TREMAINE (cocreator, director, *Jackass*) The reason MTV got so freaked out over *Jackass* was that a kid in Connecticut who was a fan lit himself on fire and filmed it with his friends. He didn't die, he just got hurt. And Senator Joe Lieberman of Connecticut got on his high horse, talking about how MTV was irresponsible and *Jackass* was going to ruin the generation. He put all this political pressure on MTV to clean up its act.

STEVE-O The first thing on my set list at Lollapalooza was something called the Tequila Stuntman, where, just like when you do a shot of tequila, you have salt and lime, but I would have a huge cylindrical container of Morton Salt, pour a mountain of it on my hand, and just snort it up my nose like Scarface. Then I would chug the tequila out of the bottle like crazy, and I would squeeze all the juice from a lime into my eyes. Then, with my eyes burning, I would bring my *Jackass* buddies onstage, and they would deeply hock loogies—for the benefit of the microphone—directly into my eyeballs, which would inspire me to vomit all over the stage. And that was how my set began.

JIM ROSE (founder, performer, MC, Jim Rose Circus Sideshow) If you mixed the Jim Rose Circus with Tom Green, you get *Jackass*.

DAN CHOI They did "Pin the Tail on Steve-O," where people actually came and tacked lunch meat on Steve's butt with a staple gun, which is not a great idea in my opinion. His bus driver learned that that's not a good idea, either, because you have to sit down when the bus is being driven. And if you have a staple that has infected in your butt, it's really not gonna work out. Apparently, he drove Steve-O from town to town standing up a lot, because he couldn't sit down.

STEVE-O No, I wouldn't have been stapling lunch meat to my ass. Who cares about lunch meat when you can have a ton of chicks throw bras and panties onstage? I would pick up the bras and panties and staple one right on my chest. *Kapow*! [Late *Jackass* cast member] Ryan Dunn would hold the microphone next to the stapler so you could hear the clink. It wouldn't fly on Lollapalooza, but it wasn't unusual on other tour stops for me to actually staple my ball sack to my leg with the staple gun. But getting your cock out onstage on that tour wasn't going to fly.

DAN CHOI Steve did get arrested in North Carolina, when he got an underage girl onstage and somehow she managed to get down to her naked butt so they could throw lunch meat at it. They were waiting for him when he got off the stage. It was like, "See ya! Have a nice day!"

STEVE-O There was only one arrest, and it was a really underwhelming one. I think we would generally card people and have them sign release forms if they were going to come onstage, so that we could use the footage later if we wanted to.

MTV.COM (July 22, 2003) *"Jackass" co-star Steve-O has been arrested again, this time after allegedly urinating in public during a Lollapalooza stop near Pittsburgh. The stuntman was arrested Saturday and charged with disorderly conduct after allegedly urinating in front of patrons and staff members near a booth at the rock festival, according to a Burgetts-town, Pennsylvania, police citation.*

STEVE-O I was very, very temporarily taken into custody on location. And I was certainly cited for public urination, which I think I had to address at a later time. But it wasn't such a full-on arrest that I was actually handcuffed and put in the back of a squad car, driven down, and processed into a police station. It was a catch-and-release situation.

JEFF TREMAINE Steve-O was well on his way to becoming a total nightmare by this point in time.

STEVE-O The set closer would be the time to do a full-on bloodbath. I would smash a lightbulb over my head with the microphone, pick up one of the larger pieces and show it to the crowd. Then I would stick my tongue out and cut it with the broken glass. Now, the tongue is one of the fastest-healing parts of the body, but it bleeds a lot. I think it was a good five thousand people that fit in front of that second stage, all packed together shoulder to shoulder, and without fail, you would see pockets open up in the audience. Because people straight fucking fainted.

DAN CHOI You definitely wanna avoid any interaction with that guy if you can. But that said, 2003 was a successful tour. More successful than

1997, and promoters weren't taking the bath they did that year, or even that they did in '95, for that matter. And it provided Jane's the platform to do more touring after that.

ADAM SCHNEIDER (former manager, Jane's Addiction, Porno for Pyros, Perry Farrell; producer, Lollapalooza 2003) I mean, 2003 was awesome. I think it was a great tour and very successful.

CLAUDETTE SILVER (political-tent organizer, Lollapalooza 2003) Obviously, because there was a 2004 tour that was happening. But I feel like it wasn't that soon before that tour was supposed to go out that it got canceled.

3 "I DON'T KNOW HOW MUCH YOU KNOW ABOUT LOLLAPALOOZA . . ."

MARC GEIGER (agent; cofounder, Lollapalooza) I was just returning to William Morris in '03. I was going down on a dot-com; ARTISTdirect was not succeeding. So I got on board again with Lollapalooza on the way to '04, tried to give it a spin, make it two days.

DAN CHOI (front-of-house coordinator, Lollapalooza 1994–97, 2003) The concept was a two-day festival. We were gonna do two shows everywhere we went. The first day the headliner was going to be String Cheese Incident, and the second day the headliner was going to be Morrissey.

CLAUDETTE SILVER (political-tent organizer, Lollapalooza 2003) We had big ideas for '04. We were primed to power the second stage on a hydrogen fuel cell. And we had this whole thing worked out with MoveOn called the Revolution Solution. It was a program where we'd bring in various political speakers and have them be on the main stage, have them in the tent area, concertgoers would be involved . . . Shepard Fairey did the logo, and Perry and Moby even did a song together for it.

ADAM SCHNEIDER (former manager, Jane's Addiction, Porno for Pyros, Perry Farrell; producer, Lollapalooza 2003) We were leaning into the youth-vote thing, and Claudette was awesome with overseeing that. But with things like Lolla, you need critical mass. You need that act that's worth four, five, six thousand people to build on. In '03 it was Jane's Addiction. It was Audioslave. Incubus. I think '04 didn't have the acts.

MARC GEIGER It was a debacle. Which was, I think, the catalyst for everything that happened afterward.

PERRY FARRELL I didn't know what to do. And also, I must say, I was frightened.

MARC GEIGER Two thousand four was, I think, the first attempt toward a little bit of a Coachella-ish direction. And ultimately, when it failed, it pushed Lolla into the more traditional festival setup that you now know today.

ANDY LANGER (Austin, Texas–based journalist and radio host) Today's Lollapalooza was conceived in Austin by principals from a team that these days is called C3 Presents. One of the C3 founders, Charlie Jones, started as an event producer who made his name with a handful of huge events early in his career—a series of homecoming shows celebrating Lance Armstrong's Tour de France wins, and a giant New Year's Eve party in 2000 that wound up being a several-hundred-thousand-person celebration with a roster of Texas talent like Lyle Lovett, Robert Earl Keen, and Shawn Colvin.

A few years later, Jones had the idea to license the Austin City Limits name from the PBS show and put it on a music festival. I think to his surprise, the city of Austin gave him the green light, and he brought in Charles Attal, an Austin concert promoter and the co-owner of the famous venue Stubb's, to book it. It was a very successful, initially two-day music festival. Once they had two years of ACL under their belts, Attal, Jones, and their other associates at the time revived Lollapalooza in Chicago.

CHARLIE JONES (founding partner, C3 Presents) The Chicago Parks District held a meeting: "All right, we need to create a new event. It doesn't matter where it is, we just need to create a new event." The story was, we had interns in our office paying attention to all the markets we were looking at to possibly expand our model of these large, multiday, multistage events. . . . We didn't have a name. We didn't know if we were going to be the Chicago Music Festival or the Chicago Cultural Arts. We didn't know.

MARC GEIGER Charlie Jones called me and said, "Hey, can we come have a meeting about Lollapalooza? Can I talk to Perry?" I said, "Yeah, absolutely." Because we were down after the 2004 cancellation. And he came to L.A. and said, "We've been looking to launch another festival and we did a brand study. Lollapalooza is one of the most recognized brands in the world. In fact, it's top ten next to Coke and McDonald's." I said, "Wow, that's impressive."

CHARLIE JONES Perry and I met, and it was almost like someone had died. I was like, "No, Perry, this is perfect. Now we can relaunch it as a stand-alone, real cultural event." We did a deal to acquire the brand and take control of it.

MARC GEIGER Charlie said, "I believe in it. I want to change the format of the festival to a stationary one, like Austin City Limits and Coachella." We said we were game. And he said, "Let's go to the various mayors around the country and put it to bid."

PERRY FARRELL I thought, to gather our thoughts and to gather our bearings, let's pick the best destination that we can, and that turned out to be the city of Chicago.

ANDY LANGER I know that Charlie and his partner Charles Attal took their relationship with Perry very seriously, and that they were young and sort of flexible enough and impressed enough that they were sitting in rooms with Perry Farrell to do what Perry Farrell wanted and to follow his lead. I know Perry didn't look at it as, "We're just licensing the name and we'll let these guys go make some money with it." I think he was in and he was very hands-on. And he had the added benefit of working with people who were experienced enough to pull it off but also green enough to really listen to him.

***BILLBOARD* (April 22, 2005)** *The Pixies, Weezer, Widespread Panic, the Killers, the Arcade Fire, Liz Phair, the Black Keys and Death Cab for Cutie are among the acts that will play the reconfigured Lollapalooza festival, which, as previously reported, will be held July 23–24 in Chicago's Grant Park.*

Also on the bill are Cake, Dashboard Confessional, Dinosaur Jr., Kasabian, Kaiser Chiefs, Louis XIV, Tegan & Sara, M83, Los Amigos Invisibles, Blue Merle, the Redwalls, the Changes, Dandy Warhols, Digable Planets, Brian Jonestown Massacre, Billy Idol, the Bravery and Blonde Redhead.

GREG KOT (music critic, *Chicago Tribune*) I was kind of thrilled to see it, because Grant Park is a beautiful space. A beautiful, beautiful area. The festival was fairly contained and only two days long and I thought the weekend went off smashingly.

JIM DeROGATIS (pop music critic, *Chicago Sun-Times*) What Central Park is to New York, Grant Park is to Chicago. It is the city's front yard. It is unparalleled in its beauty and lakefront location. Daniel Burnham, the architect, called it "The People's Park." But Lollapalooza shuts it down for effectively the entire summer. It takes eight or ten weeks to set up Lolla, and six or eight weeks to repair the destruction.

STUART ROSS (tour director, Lollapalooza) I was there in 2005 with Weezer, who I was tour managing at the time. It was a well-run, fine festival, but very different from the Lollapaloozas I worked on. The name remained the same and some of the logo elements were there, but I thought it skewed very young and it wasn't edgy at all. But I was there with Weezer, which was not an edgy band.

ANDY LANGER Real early on, I think in 2006, there was a freakish 103-, 104-, 105-degree kind of ridiculously hot day. And I remember they made the decision to bring giant flatbed trucks filled with bottled water onto the fields and distribute them for free. The last thing they wanted on a practical business level was to have people die at the festival, and it was better to give away water and lose potentially hundreds of thousands of dollars than it was to have multiple deaths on their hands. I guess my point is it was corporate, but it was responsible.

JIM DeROGATIS In 2008, there was a several-hundred-person-strong gate crash right when Rage Against the Machine started, and they tore through the fences in the press area, ran over us—the laptops, the cords, everything is trampled. I saw somebody knocked out of their wheelchair, right? And then the next morning, Lollapalooza is saying that never happened. I'm like, "I'm here—look at the fucking black-and-blues. What are you talking about?"

TOM MORELLO (guitarist, Rage Against the Machine, Audioslave) We had to stop the show fifteen times because the crowd was just so bananas. But being in my hometown, with the Chicago skyline in the background, hanging out with Perry and friends afterward, it was really a full circle moment. Just kind of high-fiving one another and going, "What a crazy journey from peeing in those alleys or hanging out on that grubby carpet in L.A. way back in 1986."

TIM COMMERFORD (bassist, Rage Against the Machine, Audioslave) We've been on Lollapalooza a lot, man. It's a big part of my life, and there's not anything that I remember about it that I'm like, "That sucked." At the end of the day, those were some of my best experiences.

KIM THAYIL (guitarist, Soundgarden) It was always fun. Counting a South American leg in 2014 and the headlining gig in 2010 at the one that doesn't travel, Soundgarden did Lollapalooza four times.

GERALD CASALE (bassist, singer, Devo) We played Lollapalooza again in 2010. By then Devo were the grandfathers of new wave and a legacy act and iconic in a way that the crowd was just like, "Oh, yeah, Devo. All right, cool." They were very enthusiastic. We preceded Lady Gaga.

DON MULLER (agent; cofounder, Lollapalooza) It's a different beast from what it was in the nineties in the sense that it's so big. But they've done a great job in booking talent. It brings so many different people together.

PERRY FARRELL I get picks, a lot of times I get run over. It's very political in those rooms when we pick the bands. I mean, you have to imagine, there's management, and record companies, and lots of money all putting their heads down and charging at C3.

STUART ROSS I've represented Tom Waits since 1987, and I once got a call from somebody at C3, saying, "Hi, I'd like to make an offer for Tom Waits to play Lollapalooza in Chicago." And I said, "Well, that's very nice. I think the festival skews a little young, and Tom doesn't really do outdoor shows, but I'm willing to listen." She made me a financial offer which was absurdly low, and I said, "I can make much more playing one night at a theater in Chicago." She said, "I think it's a very fair offer." And I responded, "I'm sure you do, but I don't think he's going to consider it." And then she said to me, and I quote, "Well, I don't know how much you know about Lollapalooza . . ." I go, "Okay, hang on a minute. Here's what I want you to do: Go into your boss's office, either one of the Charlies, and tell them, 'I just spoke to Stuart Ross about Tom Waits, and I said to him, "I don't know how much you know about Lollapalooza . . ."' Let me know what they say."

MARC GEIGER Does the current version of Lollapalooza still reflect what the festival was in the nineties? No. And it shouldn't. Lollapalooza in 2024—when the entire music business has changed, when there's no more alternative—can't be what it was. I think that's where festivals like Warped and Ozzfest got stuck.

GREG KOT At this point the music is almost an afterthought. And the problem with booking 170 bands over four days is that your batting average is going to get below the Mendoza Line. You're just not going to hit that many home runs, and it's a long slog. So, kids do drugs and pick up girls, or girls pick up guys, or guys pick up guys, and it becomes something other than the music. It becomes this other thing altogether.

MARC GEIGER Lolla had to grow into something that's for a lot more people, like Coachella or Glastonbury. Something much broader, where they don't try to represent a narrow genre or a musical movement per se anymore. It's not relevant. Certainly not in the age of streaming. There's a lot of purists who want that, sure. But there's people who want record stores, too.

PERRY FARRELL I look at it like I'm trying to create a social gathering where people can feel like they were at the right place at the right time and they can brag about it and they can tell their kids and their grand-kids about it. They can meet the love of their life there and they can find out and discover who the hell they are there. It's a rite of passage.

CHRIS HASKETT (guitarist, Rollins Band) One of the things that's really interesting is to see how much "-apalooza" has become a suffix for things, right? Everything these days is "-apalooza."

TOM MORELLO It's still incredible to me how this idea, this crazy word that came out of Perry's brain, became this massively successful tour that crystallized a genre of music. And then when the tour faded, it reemerged as one of the global pillars of festival shows.

MAYNARD JAMES KEENAN (singer, Tool, A Perfect Circle) I think when you're playing Lollapalooza in South America or wherever, those people just really enjoy music, and they don't give a shit what label you put on the genre. They just enjoy music, so they show up. So it is inspiring in that way. Lollapalooza figured out where to go for that open-minded audience.

MARC GEIGER It still has a purpose. If you haven't been to South America, go to South America and see those kids who go to Lollapalooza. It has a purpose. It's doing something. If you see it and you see what it's doing in these different societies, you go, "Wow." That's how I look at it in terms of relevance.

PERRY FARRELL My ultimate dream for it is not there yet. I have more dreams that I'm chasing. Actively chasing. I cannot tell you what they are, but I will promise you that.

ACKNOWLEDGMENTS

The authors would like to thank all the interview subjects for being so generous with their time. We are also deeply indebted to the following individuals who went above and beyond to help us reach the finish line: Michael Azerrad, David "Beno" Beneviste, Jordan Bogdonavage, Scott Booker, Steve "Chopper" Borges, Brady Brock, Dan Choi, Lily Cronig, Jonathan Daniel, David Dunton, Perry Farrell, Maria Ferrero, Jennifer Finch, Marc Geiger, Gary Graff, Jan T. Gregor, Robert Grom, Kory Grow, Chris Haskett, Dave Hill, Robby Hoffman, Leah Horwitz, Lyle Hysen, Michael James, Michael "Curly" Jobson, Peter Katsis, Daniel Kohn, Steve Knopper, Ben Kweller, Andy Langer, Joe Letz, Anna Loynes, Kevin Lyman, Tom Morello, Don Muller, David Newgarden, Martin Quinn, Mac Randall, Marc Resnick, Heidi Ellen Robinson-Fitzgerald, Stuart Ross, John Rubeli, Kate Schellenbach, Jeff Schroeder, Monica Seide-Evenson, Tony Shanahan, Steve Shelley, Patti Smith, Nick Stern, Rob Tannenbaum, Kim Thayil, Brad Tolinski, Jeff Tremaine, David "Boche" Viecelli, Ken Weinstein, Sarah P. Weiss, Josephine Wiggs, and Shanna Zablow.

This book took the better part of four years from conception to completion and publication, and in that interim, several of our interviewees sadly passed. Our gratitude goes out to Van Conner, Ted Gardner, and Jon Zazula. We extend our deepest sympathies to their families and loved ones.

NOTES

Introduction

1 *seven raucous bands:* Jon Pareles, "Lollapalooza, a Day Full of Sound and Fury," *The New York Times,* August 11, 1992, https://www.nytimes.com/1992/08/11/arts/music/lollapalooza-a-day-full-of-sound-and-fury.html.

4 *What happened with Lollapalooza:* Jonathan Zwickel, "An Oral History of the First Lollapalooza," *SPIN,* May 17, 2011, https://spin.com/2011/05/oral-history-first-lollapalooza.

8 *I wanted to be in a great group:* Paul Elliott, "Jane's Addiction: How LA's Weirdest Band Made *Nothing's Shocking,*" *Classic Rock,* August 13, 2014, https://loudersound.com/features/jane-s-addiction-the-wild-weird-world-of-nothing-s-shocking.

12 *I got introduced to the band: The Guestroom* (podcast), Australian Broadcasting Corporation, August 19, 2011.

14 *The genesis of it all:* Ibid.

16 *I got too fucked up:* Brendan Mullen, *Whores: An Oral Biography of Perry Farrell and Jane's Addiction* (Boston: Da Capo Press, 2006), chapter: "'Alternative Nation,' Reading, the Gathering of the Tribes the Proto Lollapaloozas."

17 *That probably sounds like something stupid:* Interview with Daniel Kohn, used by permission.

19 *I told Marc:* Jonathan Zwickel, "An Oral History of the First Lollapalooza," *SPIN,* May 17, 2011.

20 *No one could pronounce it: The Guestroom* (podcast), Australian Broadcasting Corporation, August 19, 2011.

Lollapalooza 1991

33 *the worst summer concert season:* Chuck Philips, "Rock Ain't Rollin': Prices Up, Attendance Down Nationwide," *Los Angeles Times,* August 10, 1991, https://www.latimes.com/archives/la-xpm-1991-08-10-ca-300-story.html.

33 *the advantage of Lollapalooza:* Sheila Rule, "Pop Concerts Shake Off Last Summer's Malaise," *The New York Times,* June 11, 1992, https://nytimes.com/1992/06/11/news /pop-concerts-shake-off-last-summer-s-malaise.html.

40 *Our equipment was . . . duct tape and homemade cases:* Nicole Briese, "30 Years Ago, the First Lollapalooza Felt Like One Wild 'House Party,'" MTV.com, July 28, 2021, https://mtv.com/news/3luoh2/lollapalooza-30th-anniversary-perry-farrell-trent -reznor-gibby-haynes.

43 *Dave was really like the child within a divorce: The Guestroom* (podcast), Australian Broadcasting Corporation, August 19, 2011.

50 *He looked like a pro wrestler:* Daniel Kohn, "Perry Farrell's 5 Favorite Lollapalooza Moments," *SPIN,* July 31, 2021, https://spin.com/2021/07/perry-farrell-5-favorite-lollapalooza -moments/.

61 *Body Count were fucking amazing:* Jonathan Zwickel, "An Oral History of the First Lollapalooza," *SPIN,* May 17, 2011, https://spin.com/2011/05/oral-history-first-lollapalooza.

69 *They were the only group that was messing:* Andy Greene, "Lollapalooza's Greatest Moments: Perry Farrell Looks Back," *Rolling Stone,* August 2, 2017, https://rollingstone.com /music/music-lists/lollapaloozas-greatest-moments-perry-farrell-looks-back-253448/.

71 *I am not going to be pretentious enough:* "NIN—Hammering It Home," *Lime Lizard,* November 1991, http://nin-pages.de/1991_Lime_Lizard_November_english.htm.

72 *I look back at that as a real turning point:* Nicole Briese, "30 Years Ago, the First Lollapalooza Felt Like One Wild 'House Party,'" MTV.com, July 28, 2021, https://mtv.com /news/3luoh2/lollapalooza-30th-anniversary-perry-farrell-trent-reznor-gibby-haynes.

74 *The show developed as we got more angry:* Dave Henderson, "Didn't We Have a Smashing Time?," *RAW,* August 31, 1991, https://nin-pages.de/1991_RAW_August_english.htm.

80 *I'd kind of gone into it:* Jim Greer, "Nine Inches of Love," *SPIN,* March 1992, https://spin .com/2013/08/nine-inches-of-love-trent-reznor-interview-spin-cover-march-1992/.

80 *So we open up:* Ibid.

81 *The point when it actually became humorous:* Ibid.

81 *Musically, it felt like:* Nicole Briese, "30 Years Ago, The First Lollapalooza Felt Like One Wild 'House Party,'" MTV.com, July 28, 2021, https://mtv.com/news/3luoh2/lollapalooza -30th-anniversary-perry-farrell-trent-reznor-gibby-haynes.

87 *I had found out that my mother:* Jonathan Zwickel, "An Oral History of the First Lollapalooza," *SPIN,* May 17, 2011, https://spin.com/2011/05/oral-history-first-lollapalooza.

Lollapalooza 1992

101 *In this case, you're talking about creating a new scene:* Ryan Leas, "We've Got a File on You: Perry Farrell," *Stereogum,* July 2, 2019, https://stereogum.com/2049259/perry -farrell-kind-heaven-lollapalooza-janes-addiction-foo-fighters/interviews/weve-got-a -file-on-you/.

105 *I remember flames shooting up:* Lollapalooza, "Episode 3: The Early Years," https://you tube.com/watch?v=N0vTPM3Lgwc.

113 *I remember Eddie did a second-story dive:* Andy Greene, "Lollapalooza's Greatest Moments: Perry Farrell Looks Back," *Rolling Stone,* August 2, 2017, https://rollingstone .com/music/music-lists/lollapaloozas-greatest-moments-perry-farrell-looks-back -253448/.

114 *We'd get to the hotel: Pearl Jam Twenty,* Cameron Crowe, dir., Vinyl Films, 2011.

115 *Over the gigs . . . you'd notch it up:* Ibid.

119 *Lollapalooza was a ten-week tour:* Kyle Eustice, "The Jesus and Mary Chain Interview," *Thrasher,* https://thrashermagazine.com/articles/music-interviews/the-jesus-and-mary -chain-interview/.

119 *That was the worst experience:* Olga Sladeckova, "Jesus and Mary Chain—Interview with Jim Reid Part 2," *Penny Black Music,* September 26, 2002, https://pennyblackmu sic.co.uk/Home/Details?id=11123.

119 *We tried to get off the tour:* Kyle Eustice, "The Jesus and Mary Chain Interview," *Thrasher,* https://thrashermagazine.com/articles/music-interviews/the-jesus-and-mary-chain -interview/.

120 *The whole show was a lovefest:* Anthony Kiedis, *Scar Tissue* (New York: Hyperion, 2004), chapter 11, "Warped."

120 *One time they went too far:* Ibid.

133 *The Jim Rose Circus . . . :* Daniel Kohn, "Perry Farrell's 5 Favorite Lollapalooza Moments," *SPIN,* July 31, 2021, https://spin.com/2021/07/perry-farrell-5-favorite-lollapalooza -moments/.61.

141 *I had so much fun:* Ibid.

143 *And then the other cat:* Ibid.

144 *Just looking for attention:* Eric Weisbard, "Past Ten," *SPIN,* August 2001, https://spin .com/2017/08/pearl-jam-oral-history-2001.

Lollapalooza 1993

161 *Lollapalooza is becoming a habit:* Jon Pareles, "Lollapalooza, Tattoos and All," *The New York Times,* July 21, 1993, https://www.nytimes.com/1993/07/21/arts/music/lollapalooza -tattoos-and-all.html.

161 *the previous summer's fest:* Neal Karlen, "Lollapalooza Love Story," *The New York Times,* July 11, 1993, https://www.nytimes.com/1993/07/11/style/lollapalooza-love-story.html.

Lollapalooza 1994

205 *Cave's slogging style:* Bruce Haring, "Lollapalooza," *Variety,* July 11, 1994, https://variety .com/1994/music/reviews/lollapalooza-1200438031.

208 *Lollapalooza was supposed to be:* Apple Music podcast with Zane Lowe, May 12, 2023, https://youtube.com/watch?v=2rDAh56douk.

209 *When Kurt died:* Ibid.

209 *We just looked at:* Michael Azerrad, "Artist of the Year," *SPIN,* December 1994.

210 *You talk about going: Rockonteurs with Gary Kemp and Guy Pratt,* "S124: Billy Corgan," February 13, 2021, https://youtube.com/watch?v=K5EPl1nt0aU.

212 *We went into it:* Dave Thompson, "Nick Cave," *Alternative Press,* 1996, https://www .rocksbackpages.com/Library/Article/nick-cave.

213 *It's all compromise:* Keith Cameron, "It's the Looza Baby, Why Don't You Kill It?," *New Musical Express,* July 30, 1994, https://www.rocksbackpages.com/Library/Article/its-the -looza-baby-why-dont-you-kill-it.

213 *I guess I thought:* Ibid.

213 *So we're headlining what:* Apple Music podcast with Zane Lowe, May 12, 2023, https:// youtube.com/watch?v=2rDAh56douktsor.

222 *We had to play:* Dave Thompson, "Nick Cave," *Alternative Press,* 1996, https://www .rocksbackpages.com/Library/Article/nick-cave.

223 *Lollapalooza was the most destructive thing:* Ibid.

239 *You kinda get more:* Simon Price, "The Beastie Boys: Super Fly Guys," *Melody Maker,* March 4, 1994, https://www.rocksbackpages.com/Library/Article/the-beastie-boys -super-fly-guys.

Lollapalooza 1995

241 *The show's safe, mainstream:* Bruce Haring, "Lollapalooza," *Variety,* July 11, 1994, https:// variety.com/1994/music/reviews/lollapalooza-1200438031.

242 *I actually called the whole tour off:* Steve Hochman, "Lollapalooza Finally Gets Its Top Bands," *Los Angeles Times,* April 24, 1995, https://www.latimes.com/archives/la-xpm -1995-04-24-ca-58277-story.html.

242 *Lollapalooza is topped by:* Mike Bohm, "A Stage-Two Blastoff," *Los Angeles Times,* August 10, 1995, https://www.latimes.com/archives/la-xpm-1995-08-10-ol-33387-story.html.

245 *It's my fucking party:* Kory Grow, "Perry Farrell Talks New Mystery Project, Kurt Co- bain Meetings," *Rolling Stone,* May 21, 2015, https://rollingstone.com/music/music -features/perry-farrell-talks-new-mystery-project-kurt-cobain-meetings-44480/amp.

246 *We probably would have:* Unpublished 1995 interview with Mac Randall, used by permission.

246 *I begged John Rubeli:* Various, *Online Diaries: The Lollapalooza Tour Journals of Beck, Courtney Love, Stephen Malkmus, Thurston Moore, Lee Ranaldo, and Mike Watt* (New York: Soft Skull Press, 1996), July 1 entry.

250 *The whole idea that:* Michael Azerrad, "Artist of the Year: Smashing Pumpkins," *SPIN,* December 1994, https://www.rocksbackpages.com/Library/Article/artist-of-the-year -smashing-pumpkins.

254 *The Gorge is remote:* Various, *Online Diaries: The Lollapalooza Tour Journals of Beck, Courtney Love, Stephen Malkmus, Thurston Moore, Lee Ranaldo, and Mike Watt* (New York: Soft Skull Press, 1996), July 5 entry.

255 *We were heading back:* Ibid.

256 *Kathleen Hanna and Kurt:* Thurston Moore, *Sonic Life: A Memoir* (New York: Double-

day, 2023), chapter 65, "Cream Puff War," https://www.rocksbackpages.com/Library
/Article/artist-of-the-year-smashing-pumpkins.

256 *We had bulk candy:* Allison Stewart, "Alternative Nation's Last Stand: Lollapalooza
1995, an Oral History," *The Washington Post,* August 11, 2015.

256 *Erlandson had handed:* Thurston Moore, *Sonic Life: A Memoir* (New York: Doubleday,
2023), chapter 65, "Cream Puff War."

257 *She grabbed the candy:* Ibid.

257 *Courtney did a fake:* Ibid.

257 *That's the whole thing:* Sini Anderson, dir., *The Punk Singer* (film), 2013.

258 *Courtney ended up having:* Patty Schemel, *Hit So Hard: A Memoir* (Boston: Da Capo
Press, 2017), chapter 18.

258 *It's a real bummer:* Ibid.

259 *That was only fourteen:* Allison Stewart, "Alternative Nation's Last Stand: Lollapalooza
1995, an Oral History," *The Washington Post,* August 11, 2015, https://www.washing
tonpost.com/lifestyle/style/alternative-nations-last-stand-lollapalooza-1995-an-oral
-history/2015/08/10/cb6857e4-3087-11e5-8f36-18d1d501920d_story.html.

260 *And that was the beginning:* Sini Anderson, dir., *The Punk Singer* (film), 2013.

264 *In USA Today there:* Various, *Online Diaries: The Lollapalooza Tour Journals of Beck,
Courtney Love, Stephen Malkmus, Thurston Moore, Lee Ranaldo, and Mike Watt* (New
York: Soft Skull Press, 1996), July 25 entry.

268 *I played as hard:* Patty Schemel, *Hit So Hard: A Memoir* (Boston: Da Capo Press, 2017),
chapter 18.

270 *We set up our:* Unpublished 1995 interview with Mac Randall, used by permission.

271 *The way Lollapalooza is set:* Ibid.

272 *It was really kind:* Ibid.

272 *It definitely teetered on:* Ibid.

275 *The day before she left:* Allison Stewart, "Alternative Nation's Last Stand: Lollapalooza
1995, an Oral History," *The Washington Post,* August 11, 2015, https://www.washing
tonpost.com/lifestyle/style/alternative-nations-last-stand-lollapalooza-1995-an-oral
-history/2015/08/10/cb6857e4-3087-11e5-8f36-18d1d501920d_story.html.

276 *The back lounge area:* Ibid.

277 *We just got a phone call:* MuchMusic (Canada), *Lollapalooza 1991 to 1996—Short Documentary,* https://youtube.com/watch?v=2–5tfVpBF5w.

277 *When we came to the States:* Jim DeRogatis, "Best New Band: Elastica," *Rolling Stone,*
January 25, 1996, https://www.rollingstone.com/music/music-news/best-new-band
-elastica-50364/.

278 *Courtney decided the public:* Allison Stewart, "Alternative Nation's Last Stand: Lollapalooza 1995, an Oral History," *The Washington Post,* August 11, 2015, https://www
.washingtonpost.com/lifestyle/style/alternative-nations-last-stand-lollapalooza-1995-an
-oral-history/2015/08/10/cb6857e4-3087-11e5-8f36-18d1d501920d_story.html.

281 *Beck referred to it:* Unpublished 1995 interview with Mac Randall, used by permission.

293 *In Denver, the pre-Coolio:* Rose Marshack, *Play Like a Man: My Life in Poster Children.* (Champaign: University of Illinois Press, 2023), chapter 12.

Lollapalooza 1996

310 *"negotiating a financial settlement":* Steve Hochman, "Lollapalooza's Metallica Maelstrom," *Los Angeles Times,* March 12, 1996, https://www.latimes.com/archives/la-xpm-1996–03–12-ca-45895-story.html.

310 *might as well be called the Guys with Guitars Tour:* Jon Pareles, "Lollapalooza, No Longer So Ambivalent About Bigness," *The New York Times,* July 12, 1996, https://www.nytimes.com/1996/07/12/arts/rock-reviewlollapalooza-no-longer-so-ambivalent-about-bigness.html.

311 *One could tell immediately:* Neil Strauss, "Bikinis, A Sign Festival is Aging," *The New York Times,* June 29, 1996, https://www.nytimes.com/1996/06/29/arts/rock-review-bikinis-a-sign-festival-is-aging.html.

314 *After the initial shock:* Steven Daly, "Summer Festivals: Three Tribes," *Rolling Stone,* June 13, 1996, https://www.rollingstone.com/music/music-news/summer-festivals-three-tribes-177635.

316 *Metallica, in my estimation:* Kory Grow, "Perry Farrell Talks New Mystery Project, Kurt Cobain Meetings," *Rolling Stone,* May 21, 2015, https://rollingstone.com/music/music-features/perry-farrell-talks-new-mystery-project-kurt-cobain-meetings-44480.

Lollapalooza 1997

339 *Lolla has a lot to prove this year:* Troy J. Augusto, "Lollapalooza 1997," *Variety,* July 1, 1997, https://variety.com/1997/music/reviews/lollapalooza-1997–1117906356.

375. *My conversations were totally:* Gil Kaufman, "Lollapalooza's Last Ditch Effort to Tour in '98," MTV.com, April 2, 1998, https://mtv.com/news/t6ctes/lollapaloozas-last-ditch-effort-to-tour-in-98.

375 *How about a Plan B:* Ibid.

376 *Obviously, they were not:* Gil Kaufman, "Lollapalooza Called Off for Summer '98," MTV.com, April 3, 1998, https://mtv.com/news/h0jy55/lollapalooza-called-off-for-summer-98.

Epilogue

380 *hugely embarrassed:* "Farrell rebounds from losses with Satellite Party," *The San Diego Union-Tribune,* July 25, 2007, https://www.sandiegouniontribune.com/2007/07/25/farrell-rebounds-from-losses-with-satellite-party.

381 *We had a five-year:* "Lollapalooza Is Back!," NME.com, February 11, 2003, https://nme.com/news/music/queens-of-the-stone-age-274–1377745.

385. *In those days, I:* Daniel Kohn, "Perry Farrell's 5 Favorite Lollapalooza Moments," *SPIN,* July 31, 2021, https://spin.com/2021/07/perry-farrell-5-favorite-lollapalooza-moments.

394 *I didn't know what:* Alan Sculley, "Farrell Rebounds from Losses with Satellite Party," *The San Diego Union-Tribune,* July 25, 2007, https://www.austinchronicle.com/music/2020-02-28/as-charlie-jones-exits-c3-he-traces-his-journey-from-college-station-to-founding-acl-fest/.

394 *The Chicago Parks District:* Raoul Hernandez, "As Charlie Jones Exits C3, He Traces His Journey from College Station to Founding ACL Fest," *The Austin Chronicle,* February 28, 2020, https://www.austinchronicle.com/music/2020-02-28/as-charlie-jones-exits-c3-he-traces-his-journey-from-college-station-to-founding-acl-fest/.

395 *Perry and I met:* Ibid.

395 *I thought, to gather:* WGN News broadcast, July 28, 2022, https://youtube.com/watch?v=5d3cOOZPI4k.

397 *I get picks: Heavy Consequence* (podcast), March 22, 2002, https://youtube.com/watch?v=FvzbYba2pNo.

399 *I look at it:* Rhian Daly, "A Brief History of Lollapalooza, from Touring Carnival to a Global Network of Festivals," NME.com, August 2, 2023, https://nme.com/features/music-features/a-brief-history-of-lollapalooza-from-touring-carnival-to-a-global-network-of-festivals-3475763.

ABOUT THE AUTHORS

Carla Fredericks

RICHARD BIENSTOCK is a journalist whose writing has appeared in *The New York Times, The Wall Street Journal, Rolling Stone, Billboard, SPIN,* and other publications. He is a former senior editor of *Guitar World* magazine and executive editor of *Guitar Aficionado* magazine. He has authored several books, among them *Kurt Cobain: Montage of Heck,* the companion to the documentary film of the same name. He is also the *New York Times* bestselling coauthor of *Nöthin' But a Good Time: The Uncensored History of the '80s Hard Rock Explosion.*

Maria McKenna

TOM BEAUJOUR is a journalist as well as a cofounder and former editor in chief of *Guitar Aficionado* magazine and *Revolver,* America's premier hard rock and heavy metal monthly. Beaujour has produced and mixed albums by Nada Surf, Guided by Voices, the Juliana Hatfield Three, and many others. He is also the *New York Times* bestselling coauthor of *Nöthin' But a Good Time: The Uncensored History of the '80s Hard Rock Explosion.*